I0605922

Praise for

INJUSTICE TOWN

"Rick Tulsky's account of the outrageous injustice done to Lamonte McIntyre in Kansas City, Kansas delivers a harsh blow to faith in our criminal justice system. A dirty cop, utterly incompetent defense lawyers, and an unethical prosecutor literally in bed with the judge, it is a story of mind-boggling malfeasance. It also illustrates how Kansas makes it easy to lock up anyone its authorities deem a 'criminal type.' One need only glance at prison demographics to see who fits that description."

—Mark Bowden, *New York Times* bestselling author of *Black Hawk Down*

"A riveting page turner. *Injustice Town* is a must read, especially for those intrigued by public corruption in its most extreme form."

—Jim McCloskey, coauthor of *Framed: Astonishing True Stories of Wrongful Convictions*

"*Injustice Town* is a tour de force of reporting and revelation: it is the best exposé of corruption I have ever read. The place Rick Tulsky writes about is rotten to the core with a result that ranges from false incarcerations to morally perverse prosecutors to dirty cops who prey on the impoverished with demands for sexual favors and rape. Anybody who cares about what is happening in America should read it."

—Buzz Bissinger, author of *Friday Night Lights* and *The Mosquito Bowl*

"*Injustice Town* is the unforgettable chronicle of how an innocent man spent half his life in prison, doomed by a justice system contorted by corrupt cops, incompetent lawyers, a compromised judge and intimidated witnesses."

—Bill Marimow, two-time Pulitzer Prize–winner, former editor in chief of *The Philadelphia Inquirer*

"*Injustice Town* is appalling and inspiring—appalling because the criminal justice system conspired against Lamonte McIntyre, and inspiring because journalist Rick Tulsky has fought to deliver long-delayed justice to an innocent man. This is a vital and compelling book that exposes the racism baked into our justice system. A triumph of investigative reporting."

—David Zucchino, Pulitzer Prize–winning author of *Wilmington's Lie*

"In these pages, prepare for a nightmare tour of the injustices and indignities an innocent man suffered at the hands of policemen, judges, prosecutors, prison guards, even his own court-appointed lawyers. With page-turning prose, Tulsky tells this disturbing story but also introduces you to heroes and the history of how this legacy of racial injustice took root centuries ago. *Injustice Town* is required reading, and by the last page, you'll realize this book is not just about Kansas City, Kansas. It's about your town, and mine."

—Dan Biddle, Pulitzer Prize–winning author of *Tasting Freedom: Octavius Catto and the Battle for Equality in Civil War America*

"Among the most vicious and systemic civil rights train wrecks in an American city."

—Barry Scheck, cofounder of The Innocence Project

INJUSTICE TOWN

A Corrupt City, a Wrongly Convicted Man, and a Struggle for Freedom

RICK TULSKY

PEGASUS BOOKS
NEW YORK LONDON

INJUSTICE TOWN

Pegasus Books, Ltd.
148 West 37th Street, 13th Floor
New York, NY 10018

First Pegasus Books cloth edition February 2026

Interior design by Maria Fernandez

Library of Congress Cataloging-in-Publication Data is available.

ISBN: 979-8-89710-042-2

10 9 8 7 6 5 4 3 2

Printed in the United States of America
Distributed by Simon & Schuster
www.pegasusbooks.com

To Kim, Elizabeth, and Eric

Contents

	Author's Note	xi
	List of Names	xv
PART I	**FAILED JUSTICE**	1
1	A Double Murder in Broad Daylight	3
2	Empty Opportunities	9
3	The Wrong Lamonte	17
4	Why, God?	22
5	Return to Quindaro	26
6	The City Is Wide Open	32
7	"Historically Corrupt"	38
8	Being Black in KCK	44
9	"That's the Man"	48
10	Becoming Muggz	56
11	"I Don't Believe This"	61
12	"I'm Innocent. That's It."	69
PART II	**TRAPPED INSIDE**	73
13	Fresh Meat on the Block	75
14	Curb Your Anger	81

15	On Their Own	85
16	Another Door Closed	91
17	Not the Finest	99
18	Dead in the Water	104
19	No One Gets to Skate Through Life	112
PART III	**UNCOVERING INNOCENCE**	115
20	Winning the Lottery	117
21	Peeling the Onion	126
22	A Detective's Obsession	131
23	The Shunning of Max Seifert	139
24	"It Doesn't Satisfy My Heart"	148
25	A Monster Enters	151
26	"This Case Cannot Die"	156
27	"Everybody Knows Muggz Did Not Do This"	165
28	Collecting Affidavits	170
29	No Place For Honest Cops	174
30	Righting Wrongs	183
31	A "Good Trick"	186
32	"A Very Corrupt Place"	192
33	Winking at Misconduct	195
34	Building the Atom Bomb	199
35	Time for Change	203
36	Boom	209
37	A New Day	217
38	A Fresh Look	224
39	"It's Nice Outside"	229

PART IV	**SEEKING JUSTICE**	233
40	On His Own	235
41	"Sick and Tired" of Injustice	241
42	"Amazing," "Disgusting," and "Nasty," Too	252
43	A Pattern of Misconduct	264
44	The Empire Starts to Crack	267
45	Called to Account	282
46	Fundamental Change	290
47	Tying the Loop	299
48	The Defendant Fails to Appear	309
	Afterword: Half Full or Half Empty?	320
	Coda	323
	Acknowledgments	353
	Notes	355
	Index	393

Author's Note

The story of Lamonte McIntyre, in one sense, is as old as America: A young Black male wrongly accused and harshly punished. Decades of his life ripped away by a racist system of justice. It's a cancer on the promise of the country, one that started at 1619 and grew with slavery, Jim Crow, the Scottsboro Boys, the Central Park Five, and the dawn of the second Trump administration.

From the moment I first heard about Lamonte's case in 2017 and visited him in a Kansas prison, through the five years of actively researching and writing this book, these echoes of history were ever-present. I never lost sight of Lamonte, the man, who had experienced a singular and shameful horror.

I've spent a career as a lawyer-journalist, a half-century at this point, focused on the criminal justice system. I've revisited unsolved murders of Black men in the Mississippi Delta; examined how the criminal justice system worked for Los Angeles County defendants *not* named O. J. Simpson; and written extensively about cases of wrongful convictions. I've cofounded a nonprofit devoted to examining injustices. Along the way I've been lucky to win more than my share of awards, including a Pulitzer Prize.

Not much shocks me, but what happened to Lamonte did. It shocks me to this day because his one case included the many different faces of injustice that I had seen over the course of my career.

Wrongful convictions occur for a range of reasons: Bad cops, poor defense work, overzealous prosecutors, and judges who tip the scales, to name just some. Lamonte experienced all of these, in extreme measures—as well as other injustices I had never come across in any previous case.

The detective who investigated his case was a sexual predator and a pedophile who preyed on girls and women in the Black community of Kansas City, Kansas, including women who were witnesses or otherwise connected to Lamonte's case.

The court-appointed lawyer who represented Lamonte at trial failed to take many basic steps that could have proven his client's innocence. A second attorney appointed to represent him after conviction never even bothered to contact Lamonte, much less properly expose the wrongs. Both were later disbarred for their failures in a string of cases.

An eyewitness who mistakenly said she had seen Lamonte pull the trigger in a double murder almost immediately recanted, but the prosecutor ignored her and never revealed what she said to the defense. The prosecutor had secretly slept with the judge in Lamonte's case, and she too was later disbarred after a series of complaints that she was unethical.

The flaws in Lamonte's case, and deep unfairness and racism at its root, were easily discoverable. They did not occur in a backwater, but in Kansas's third-largest city, long governed by a white, insular, and deeply entrenched establishment. The simplest thing to say is that it took years until anyone took his claim seriously, leaving him locked in his prison cell from the time he was a teenager until he was a forty-one-year-old man. The truth is always more complex—but no less vital for us to hear.

I wrote this book because I want people to know Lamonte's story—to understand there are other Lamontes languishing in prison—and to be enraged at a system that dealt him such pain. The work took on urgency in recent months as Donald Trump took office and worked to, as he put it, "unleash" American law enforcement. The very checks on the system have been turned on their head; the concerns over the fraying of democratic institutions have somehow pushed aside attention to the inequities built into criminal justice.

Americans are fascinated with true crime. If they were as fascinated with true justice, we'd be a better nation.

List of Names

Ethel Abbott: Ethel Abbott, the ex-wife of Detective Roger Golubski, was the aunt of a murder victim.

Carolyn Adams: A private investigator and owner of Action Investigations, Rosie McIntyre hired Carolyn Adams after her son was convicted.

David Alvey: A member of a prominent family that had resided in Wyandotte County for generations, David Alvey was elected mayor of the consolidated Kansas City/Wyandotte County government in 2017 and served for one term, from 2018–2021.

Doug Bach: Doug Bach was a longtime Wyandotte County employee who served as administrator of Kansas City/Wyandotte County combined government from 2014–2022.

Dennis O. Barber: A twenty-five-year veteran of KCK police department, Dennis Barber retired as lieutenant in 1997. Barber led the officers who took Lamonte McIntyre into custody on the day of the murders.

Edward Bouker: Senior circuit judge Edward Bouker of Hays, Kansas, was specially appointed to oversee the 2017 motion by Lamonte McIntyre to overturn the verdict.

Barron Bowling: Cheryl Pilate represented Barron Bowling in his federal civil lawsuit contending that DEA agents had beaten him following a traffic accident, and that KCK police helped cover up the evidence of federal wrongdoing.

Edmond Brancart: Wyandotte County assistant district attorney Edmond Brancart prosecuted the murder case of Olin "Pete" Coones, who became the first person exonerated by the office's Conviction Integrity Unit established by District Attorney Mark Dupree.

Melody Brannon: Brannon was the federal public defender for the Kansas district. Brannon joined the office in 1998, became chief in 2014, and filed disciplinary complaints against prosecutor Terra Morehead.

Cecil Brooks: Convicted KCK drug trafficker Cecil Brooks is the brother of Joe Robinson, and was a cousin of Aaron Robinson. Brooks was locked in federal prisons when Jim McCloskey first met him.

Terrance Brown: A cousin of Lamonte McIntyre, Brown was arrested in the "pizza heist" case and later his picture would be included in the photos shown to eyewitnesses to the Hutchings Street murders.

Russell Bucklew: Cheryl Pilate spent years arguing all the way to the U.S. Supreme Court that for Missouri to apply lethal injection to death row inmate Russell Bucklew would amount to cruel and unusual punishment because of his rare condition. Bucklew was executed in 2019.

J. Dexter Burdette: A Wyandotte County circuit judge from 1988 until retiring in 2018, Burdette was the trial judge in the prosecution of Lamonte McIntyre on murder charges. Burdette had worked both as an attorney representing KCK and as an assistant county prosecutor before winning a seat on the bench.

Darryl Burton: Wrongly convicted of murdering a customer in a St. Louis gas station, Darryl Burton was exonerated in 2008. Burton moved to the Kansas City area, entered the seminary, and became associate pastor at the Church of the Resurrection. Burton and Lamonte cofounded Miracle of Innocence.

Tricia Rojo Bushnell: As executive director of Midwest Innocence Project, Trisha Bushnell took on supporting Cheryl Pilate in Lamonte's exoneration once Centurion had bowed out. MIP would go on to push for justice on behalf of other Golubski victims.

Mike Bussell: A private investigator, Mike Bussell played a key role in the later stages of Lamonte's post-conviction case, including a key interview with Cecil Brooks. Later, Bussell would assist Lamonte after his release.

Paul Casteliero: A New Jersey defense attorney, Paul Casteliero worked pro bono to help Jim McCloskey in exonerations from the time Jim took on his first case. Decades later, Casteliero would join Centurion as legal director.

Dan Clark: A private investigator, Dan Clark worked with Jim McCloskey and Cheryl Pilate on three different exoneration cases: Ellen Reasonover, Darryl Burton, and then Lamonte McIntyre.

Steven Clymer: Assistant U.S. attorney from the Northern District of New York, Steven Clymer was specially assigned to represent the government in connection with a scandal over the discovery that members of the U.S. attorney's office in Kansas had obtained recordings of many conversations between defense attorneys and their clients awaiting trial.

David R. Cohen: Cohen was the special master appointed by U.S. District Judge Julie Robinson to determine several factual issues concerning the taping scandal involving the U.S. attorney's office in Kansas.

Olin L. "Pete" Coones: The first exoneree by Wyandotte County Conviction Integrity Unit, Pete Coones was convicted of the murder of his grandfather's former caretaker.

Carl Cornwell: An experienced Wyandotte County defense attorney, Cornwell was hired by Rosie McIntyre to represent Lamonte after he was convicted of murder.

Maxine/David Crowder: The parents of Rosie McIntyre, and grandparents to Lamonte, Maxine and David Crowder had met and married in Memphis. They emigrated with their children to KCK when Rosie was a child.

Peggy/Johnny Crowder: Peggy and Johnny are brother and sister-in-law to Rosie McIntyre.

Steven Culp: The lieutenant in charge of the investigation into the murders of Doniel Sublette Quinn and Donald Ewing, Steven

Culp assigned Detectives W. K. Smith and Roger Golubski to the case. Years later, while a colonel, Culp had responsibility for the investigation of the car accident involving DEA agents and resident Barren Bowling.

Thomas Dailey: Dailey had been vice commander when he was indicted on federal extortion charges in 1973; after he was acquitted, Dailey was welcomed back to the force and worked his way up to be chief of police from 1989 until 1995, including the time when Lamonte McIntyre was arrested.

Lamont Drain: Drain was the young man who dated Ruby Mitchell's niece.

Mark Dupree: In 2016 Mark Dupree became the first Black elected district attorney in the state of Kansas.

Neil Edgar Jr.: Nicknamed "Monster," Neil Edgar Jr. was said to have a willingness to commit murder even as a young teenager.

Donald Ewing: Ewing was sitting in the parked Cadillac with Doniel Quinn when a man in black walked up to the car and fatally shot them both.

Lindsey Erickson: The young associate to Carl Cornwell, Erickson was a veteran defense attorney hired by Rosie McIntyre.

Kate Germond: Germond joined Jim McCloskey's efforts to free wrongly imprisoned individuals in 1987, became executive director of Centurion, the organization they created, from the time of Jim's retirement in 2015 until 2019.

Roger Golubski: Golubski joined the KCK Police Department in 1975. He served as a detective in crimes against properties when assigned to the murders of Doniel Sublett Quinn and Donald Ewing. Golubski rose to detective captain before retiring in 2010 and joining the suburban Edwardsville (KS) police department as captain until he retired from that job in 2016.

Jerome Gorman: Longtime first assistant to Wyandotte County district attorney Nicholas Tomasic. Gorman succeeded Tomasic as the DA and held the office until 2017, following his defeat in a contested election by Mark Dupree. Gorman later served as director of a special investigations unit in the state Department of Revenue, until he was dismissed following a complaint about his inappropriate comments on several occasions. Gorman returned to private practice in Wyandotte County, and on occasion served as judge pro tempore in Wyandotte County Municipal Court.

Tim Hausback: He was a retired KCK police officer who became incensed when he read of former top officials of the department testifying that they were unaware of misconduct by Roger Golubski.

Alan Jennerich: An FBI agent who transferred to a Kansas City district after working on public corruption cases in the Chicago office, Jennerich worked closely with Julie Robinson, then an assistant U.S. attorney, on corruption within the KCK Police Department.

Donald Johnson: Donald Johnson was a half brother of Rosie McIntyre.

Donald Johnson Jr.: "D. J.," as he was known, gave his younger cousin Lamonte McIntyre rocks of cocaine to sell even before Lamonte was a teenager.

Corisha Josenberger: Corisha was the young woman Lamonte first met in the visitor's room in Lansing prison when she came there to visit her brother Cortez.

James Krstolich: KCKPD detective James Krstolich first interviewed Ruby Mitchell on Hutchings Street the day of the murder, and then with Roger Golubski interviewed her at the station.

Gloria Labat: An aunt to Donald Ewing, Gloria Labat witnessed Niko Quinn's comments outside the courtroom after Niko had testified as a prosecution witness in the murder case against Lamonte.

Bobby Lane: The former KCKPD detective who interviewed Barren Bowling following his car accident, Bobby Lane then encouraged fellow officer Max Seifert not to report the wrongdoing by federal agents.

Gary Long: Lamonte's court-appointed trial attorney, Long had a long but unsuccessful legal career. He twice was disbarred by the Kansas Supreme Court, a rare distinction.

Stephen McAllister: McAllister was a University of Kansas School of Law professor chosen to be U.S. attorney for the Kansas District in 2018 by Donald J. Trump. McAllister assumed the position in the midst of a significant scandal that erupted over federal prosecutors' gathering of conversations between defense attorneys and their clients awaiting trial. He served until Joe Biden assumed office in 2021.

Jim McCloskey: Jim was still at the Princeton Theological Seminary when he developed evidence that a New Jersey prisoner named Chiefie was wrongly convicted. From there, Jim built Centurion Ministries, more recently rebranded as Centurion, and spent his career proving the innocence of prisoners wrongly convicted of serious crimes. By the time Jim retired he had played an instrumental role in freeing more than sixty wrongly convicted men and women.

Jock McFarlane: Retired physicist Jock McFarlane became a volunteer at Centurion Ministries after hearing Jim talk about the organization at church; Lamonte's case was his first assignment.

Lamonte McIntyre: The teenager wrongly identified as the murderer of Donald Ewing and Doniel Quinn, Lamonte McIntyre discovered how unjust the criminal justice system can be.

Rosie McIntyre: The mother to Lamonte McIntyre, Rosie McIntyre never gave up fighting for her son's exoneration.

James McIntyre Jr.: The ex-husband of Rosie and father to Lamonte and three other boys: James, Reggie, and Jermaine, James McIntyre walked out on the family when the boys were young.

James McIntyre III: The oldest son of Rosie, James McIntyre III helped Jim McCloskey navigate the streets of KCK. James suffered a significant traffic accident and died in 2019.

Ronald L. Miller: Miller joined the KCK police department in 1972 and worked his way through the ranks to be named chief in 2000. Miller retired from the department in 2006 and became chief in

Topeka, where he served until his appointment by Barack Obama as the U.S. marshal for the Kansas district.

Ruby Mitchell: A resident of Hutchings Street, Ruby Mitchell lived between Josephine's house and the house in which Niko lived, and provided the KCK detectives the first eyewitness identification after seeing a man murder Doniel Sublett Quinn and Donald Ewing.

Terra Morehead: Upon graduating law school, Terra Morehead worked for two years as the county attorney in rural Kiowa County, in southwestern Kansas, before being hired in 1988 to the Wyandotte County District Attorney's Office. Morehead was the main prosecutor in about eighty murder cases, including that of Lamonte McIntyre, during her time as a Wyandotte assistant district attorney. She was hired in 2002 as an assistant U.S. attorney for the district of Kansas, a position she held until she left the office and surrendered her law license in the midst of ongoing disciplinary proceedings against her in 2024.

Saundra Sublett Newsome: The mother of Doniel Sublett Quinn, Saundra Newsome held her ex-husband, John Quinn, responsible for Doniel's death.

Doug Parisi: Doug Parisi had the reputation as a by-the-book officer but was accused of violating residence requirements and forced off the force once he was assigned to investigate allegations of misconduct by a high-ranking officer.

Cheryl Pilate: A principal partner in the law firm Morgan Pilate, Cheryl Pilate has focused her practice on representing prisoners contending they were wrongly convicted and on court-appointed representation of defendants on death row. Cheryl and Jim McCloskey, founder of Centurion Ministries, successfully won exonerations in two St. Louis cases before they took on the case of Lamonte McIntyre in 2011. Cheryl developed extensive evidence of wrongdoing far beyond the single case of Lamonte.

District Judge Matthew Podrebarac: The son of Yugoslavian immigrants, Matthew Podrebarac was elected to the Wyandotte County district court in 1978 after six years on the county commission. Assigned to the juvenile court, Podrebarac was assigned to a juvenile case involving the robbery of a pizza deliveryman, and later to the early stages of the murder charges involving Lamonte McIntyre. Podrebarac died in office in 1996.

Doniel Sublett Quinn: The son of John Quinn and Saundra Sublett Newsome, Doniel was one of two victims, with Donald Ewing, of a shotgun-wielding assailant on April 15, 1994. Lamonte McIntytre was arrested and charged within hours of the crime. Doniel was known to some, including on the program from his funeral, as Doniel Sublett.

Freda Quinn: An aunt of victim Doniel Sublett Quinn and sister to John Quinn, Freda provided information to Cheryl and Jim about Golubski's relationship with her late niece Stacey.

Josephine Quinn: A resident of Hutchings Street, Josephine Quinn was the mother of Stacey and Niko, aunt of Doniel. By the time Jim McCloskey and Cheryl Pilate reinvestigated the double murders, Josephine Quinn had died.

John Quinn: Josephine Quinn's brother, John Quinn was the father of murder victim Doniel Quinn.

Niko Quinn: One of Josephine's daughters, Niko Quinn was a witness to the double murder. She lived up Hutchings Street with a boyfriend known as C. Love and her young children.

Stacey Quinn: Josephine's daughter and apparent eyewitness to the murders, Stacey had been murdered before Jim McCloskey and Cheryl Pilate reinvestigated the double murders.

Randy Rathbun: A Wichita attorney, Rathbun was appointed by Bill Clinton to serve as the U.S. attorney for Kansas district from 1993 to 1996. Rathbun, who assisted in the prosecution of the Oklahoma City bombing cases, personally tried the case against former KCK mayor Joseph Steineger.

Michael Redmon: A veteran KCK criminal defense lawyer, Redmon offered Cheryl Pilate and Jim McCloskey what help he could, including key introductions to former clients. Redmon also had previously represented members of the McIntyre family and believed in Lamonte's innocence.

Aaron Robinson: Cousin to Cecil Brooks, who ran a drug house near the murder scene, where Doniel Sublett Quinn worked on occasion as a "doorman," responsible for protecting the drugs.

Joe Robinson: A brother to Cecil Brooks and cousin to Aaron Robinson, Joe Robinson was part of the drug world in the 1990s in KCK.

Julie Robinson: After joining the Kansas district of the U.S. attorney's office in 1989, Julie Robinson teamed with FBI agent Alan Jennerich to investigate corruption in the KCK Police Department. The investigation ended when Robinson was appointed to be a federal bankruptcy judge and, later, the first Black federal district judge in Kansas. On the bench, Judge Robinson handled several cases that exposed corruption in the Kansas City justice system.

Jackie Rokusek: Criminal defense lawyer Jackie Rokusek was the person who first learned that federal prosecutors in Kansas City were gaining access to tape recordings of confidential conversations between defense attorneys and their clients who were being held pretrial in the federal detention center.

Lindsay Runnels: Runnels was the attorney at Morgan Pilate who worked with Cheryl Pilate on Lamonte McIntyre's case and assisted Lamonte after his release. Lindsay then joined her alma mater, the University of Missouri–Kansas City School of Law, where she also worked simultaneously on innocence cases with the Midwest Innocence Project. In 2019 Lindsay rejoined the Morgan Pilate firm where she continues to work on criminal defense at all stages.

Mark Sachse: He was appointed to represent Lamonte McIntyre on his post-conviction petition contending he had been victimized by poor representation at his trial. Sachse, who would soon be found to have repeatedly committed misconduct, never contacted his client during his time as Lamonte's attorney.

Derek Schmidt: In 2011 Derek Schmidt, majority leader of the Kansas State Senate, became Kansas attorney general. He was reelected twice, holding the seat until he ran unsuccessfully as the Republican candidate for Kansas governor in 2022. Schmidt was elected in 2024 as a U.S. congressman.

Max Seifert: The former KCK police detective Max Seifert joined the force in 1975, among the academy class that included Roger Golubski and Ruby Ellington, the first Black woman on the force. Seifert "crossed the blue line" once he concluded his department was covering up misconduct by federal DEA agents who beat KCK resident Barren Bowling.

Bernard Smith: A member of the KCK police department from 1976 until 1998, Bernard Smith rose to lieutenant despite a continuing drug problem that, ultimately, forced him to take a medical retirement. While on the force, Smith was indicted but acquitted of extorting a drug dealer in 1989, the first of a series of cases from a federal investigation into KCK police corruption. After he left the force Smith pleaded guilty to unrelated charges of forgery, a case put together by KCK detective Max Seifert.

W. K. Smith: A member of the Kansas City police department for thirty-two years, William K. Smith retired as a detective assigned to homicides. Smith partnered with Roger Golubski on several homicide investigations, including the murders of Doniel Quinn and Donald Ewing, though the police reports reflect that Smith took only one statement in that case.

Herbert Smulls: Convicted of the 1991 murder of a Missouri jeweler, Herbert Smulls was represented by Cheryl Pilate in his final appeals before he was executed in 2014 by lethal injection.

Joseph Steineger: A popular mayor of Kansas City, Joseph Steineger was elected to the first of two terms in 1987. Steineger was indicted while in office of federal charges of bribery and obstruction and justice; he was acquitted by a jury days before Lamonte McIntyre went on trial for murder. Residents celebrated his acquittal but rejected Steineger's effort to win the third term in office that he sought, in part, to clear his name. Months after Steineger died the city erected an honorary street sign in his name.

Melissa Testrake: Paralegal Melissa Testrake joined Morgan Pilate in 2015 and became close to Lamonte McIntyre as she assisted during his incarceration. Melissa joined investigator Mike Bussell on a key interview.

Erin Slinker Tomasic: In 2017 the U.S. attorney fired Erin Slinker Tomasic, a special assistant U.S. attorney, reporting the discovery she had listened to privileged conversations between attorneys and their clients, and misled the court about that issue. But it would turn out the scandal went far beyond Tomasic, a less experienced member of the office, and ultimately brought down senior prosecutors including Terra Morehead.

Nicholas A. Tomasic: The longtime face of Wyandotte County criminal justice, Nick Tomasic served as the district attorney from the time the office was first created in 1972 until he retired in 2005. He ran unopposed six of his eight times running for office. Tomasic retired as the longest-serving district attorney in the history of Kansas.

Dennis Ware: As a Kansas City police detective in 1994, Dennis Ware accompanied Detective Golubski on key interviews in connection with the murders of Doniel Quinn and Donald Ewing. Years later, Ware was a major in the department when the police investigated the collision of motorist Barren Bowling and federal agents.

Kenneth Michael Warner: A veteran state and federal prosecutor, Mike Warner became first assistant U.S. attorney for the Kansas district in 2010. He had extensive experience as a state and federal prosecutor who became frustrated by the overly aggressive culture of the Kansas City office.

Terry Zeigler: The KCK police chief from 2014 until he retired in 2019, Terry Zeigler first joined the force in 1990. During his time on the force, he served as Roger Golubski's partner for three years while a detective, and later headed internal affairs.

PART I

FAILED JUSTICE

1
A Double Murder in Broad Daylight

Nobody paid much notice as two men sat in the aging pale blue Cadillac DeVille parked on Hutchings Street that sunny afternoon.

Doniel Sublett Quinn, twenty-one, and Donald Ewing, thirty-four, were inside the car with a crack pipe, a common accessory in the hard-luck community of Kansas City, Kansas.

Their car was across Hutchings Street from the home of Doniel's aunt, Josephine Quinn, who was on her porch sorting through a box of clothes she had picked up that morning from her mother.

It was Tax Day, the local newspaper reminded readers—April 15, 1994. In Washington, tobacco company executives testified before Congress that their product was not addictive. A jury was being seated in the civil case brought by Rodney King against the Los Angeles police officers who brutally beat him, an incident caught on tape and witnessed by the nation.*

Not enough attention was paid back then to the fact that how much justice a person received seemed to depend on the color of their skin

* In addition to the civil suit brought by King, four officers had been indicted and tried in state court, and their acquittal prompted a major riot in South Los Angeles. The four were then later charged in federal court, and two of them were convicted at trial.

and the size of his bank account. The newspaper that morning quoted the new assistant U.S. attorney for civil rights, wondering upon being sworn in, how a nation dedicated to "equality, opportunity and fair play" could "sometimes fall so short."

The morning paper also reported that the U.S. House of Representatives voted to add the death penalty as punishment for several new crimes, while President Bill Clinton told police officers at a White House event that supporting his tough-on-crime bill was neither partisan nor driven by any racial animus. "If anything should truly make us a United States of America," he said, "it should be the passionate desire to restore real freedom to our streets."

Hutchings Street was literally a road to nowhere, worlds away from whatever took place in the nation's capital or even Rodney King's LA. It started at a gas station on Quindaro Boulevard and ended after two blocks of poorly paved asphalt, run-down houses, and empty lots. If Hutchings Street was connected to anything, it was the crack cocaine network snaking its way across the nation, injecting a new venom into communities already suffering from the poisons of racism and neglect.

Josephine Quinn had two brothers, John and Robert, and as she sorted through the box of clothes, they drove up with news. That clothes dryer that Robert was supposed to bring to her? He had sold it for some quick cash.

That set off an argument right there on the street.

Niko Quinn watched the argument unfold as she pushed a stroller up the street toward her mother's house. Niko lived two doors up the street with her two children and a boyfriend known as C. Love, whom Niko met at a skating rink just after he had been released from prison.

The quarreling caused Ruby Mitchell, the neighbor whose house was in between Niko and Josephine, to come to her screen door to see what the ruckus was all about.

The bad news imparted, Robert began to drive away as Josephine marched to her front door, loudly fussing about how her brothers treated her. Another daughter, Stacey, stood near the doorway and cut her mother off, saying she did not want to hear about it.

Just then a man in black carrying a shotgun emerged from an empty lot of weeds that ran to Hiawatha Street, one block over. The man walked right up to the passenger window of the parked Cadillac, lifted his weapon, and fired at Doniel Quinn* and Donald Ewing, who were still sitting inside, before retreating over the same path.

Ruby Mitchell went inside and called 911. Stacey Quinn began crying, "Oh my God, it's little Don," and ran toward the parked car. Hearing the gunfire, John and Robert, who had just pulled away, sped back. John looked in the car and saw the face of his son, Doniel. It had been blown apart by shotgun fire. The car was locked, so John grabbed an empty wine bottle from the sidewalk and smashed open a window.

Josephine said a prayer as Doniel took his last breaths. Donald Ewing struggled to say something, but the Quinns told him to just hang on. Help was coming.

The calls came into 911 just after 2:00 P.M. The KCKPD, as it is locally known, had about 300 sworn officers, but the combined impact of the crack cocaine epidemic and gang violence had the department stretched thin. This was the fifth shooting in the city of 150,000 in three days,

* Doniel was known to some people as Doniel Sublett, his mother's maiden name.

and this one—two unarmed men shot at close range as they sat in a car, in broad daylight on a residential street—demanded attention.

The first two officers on the scene went right to the car, where the two men were still sprawled inside—Quinn dead, Ewing still gasping for breath, the victim of several shotgun blasts to his chest and arms. Blood and pieces of glass were everywhere. One officer got whatever information he could on the victims' identities and dutifully recorded the parade of personnel that commonly descends on a murder scene: patrol officers; emergency medical technicians; crime scene techs; detectives; various department brass up to the level of captain; and a prosecutor.

The other officer secured the scene with crime tape, then learned from Ruby Mitchell that the culprit had retraced his steps after the shooting, fleeing through the empty lot to Hiawatha Street. Two officers followed that path. They searched the weeds, a nearby vacant building, and then knocked on doors on Hiawatha. A resident there reported seeing the apparent shooter climb into a dark blue sedan with a getaway driver waiting.

These were the routine crumbs that police on the scene get at the beginning of an investigation; details that, under the right circumstances, build into a comprehensive investigation.

Doniel Quinn was pronounced dead at the scene. Donald Ewing was taken by ambulance to Bethany Medical Center, where doctors performed emergency surgery in a desperate effort to save his life.

The Cadillac was dusted for prints, and three officers collected the crack pipe and other evidence from inside: a $10.00 bill and a $1.00 bill under the driver seat; a pair of eyeglasses; a cigarette lighter; plastic waddings from the shotgun blasts on the floorboard, above the dashboard, and on the front seat. In the back seat was a tan hat. A blood sample was taken from the front seat. On the ground outside, police collected more blood samples, broken glass, and four spent shell casings. An officer photographed and videotaped the scene.

Uniformed officers and detectives fanned out to talk to the neighbors on Hutchings about what they saw and heard.

Niko Quinn, stunned by witnessing her cousin's shooting, told Detective W. K. Smith that she had seen the shooter come through the lot, approach the car, and open fire. "He had on black," she told Smith. "A black shirt, black hat, black pants, and black tennis shoes." The Quinns did not trust the police, and Smith could not pry much from Niko. The brief tape-recorded interview ended with just two questions from Smith, a veteran homicide investigator. No, she had never seen the suspect before. Yes, she would be able to recognize him if she saw him again.

Smith then went to talk to Niko's mother, Josephine, who told the detective that as she heard the gunshots and looked toward the scene, the shooter turned his head away, obscuring her view. Ruby Mitchell told another detective, James Krstolich, that she had gotten a look at the shooter from her front door. Like Niko, Ruby described the shooter as wearing black, and added detail: a thin Black man, maybe 5'6" tall, with slicked-back hair. She, too, said that she could identify the shooter if she saw him again. She left to collect her children from school, and Krstolich left his business card with her.

Lt. Steven Culp assigned Smith and Roger Golubski as the detectives on the case. Years later, Smith could not explain why he did nothing more on the case after he completed his interviews. Nor could he explain why, once Niko said she could identify the shooter, he did not arrange for her to come to the station, just the way Krstolich did with Ruby Mitchell.

After she picked up her children, Ruby Mitchell contacted the detectives. Golubski collected her and drove her to the station where he and Krstolich would question her further to try to pin down the identity of the shooter. Neither he nor Krstolich were on the elite homicide team; both were assigned to the lesser "crimes against persons." Krstolich, who was obese, preferred to work from the comfort of headquarters rather than on the streets.

Golubski grew up in KCK surrounded by neighbors like his own family: descendants from Eastern Europe, almost all Catholic, and of modest means. He once had studied to become a priest but abandoned that pursuit as a young man and instead joined the force.

He had a reputation among department officials as someone with good contacts within the area of north Kansas City that was largely Black and overwhelmingly poor. Within that community, Golubski had developed a different kind of reputation: He was a cop who would use his badge to satisfy his sexual appetite. Specifically, an appetite for Black women.

Years later, Ruby Mitchell would remember Golubski's creepy behavior as he drove her to the station. He asked if she liked to date white men and told her he liked Black women. He told her that she had a nice body and nice breasts.

She responded by moving closer to the passenger door and took hold of the door handle.

2
Empty Opportunities

Lamonte McIntyre awakened the morning of April 15, 1994, at the home of his aunt and uncle, Peggy and Johnny Crowder. It was Friday, a school day for most teenagers. Lamonte had other things to do.

He was the middle of five children born to Rose McIntyre, whom everyone knew as Rosie. She had been born in Memphis, the daughter of Maxine and David Crowder.

As a child, Maxine learned to be mindful of which water fountain she drank from. Like everyone else with dark skin in Memphis, she could not ride in the front of the buses, nor could she go to the same schools, restaurants or churches as white people. Maxine had her first child, Ernest, when she was thirteen years old, and love had nothing to do with it. She had two more children, Donald Johnson and Christine Johnson, while she was still a minor. But then she met David Crowder, who was kind, and the two of them married and had two more children together, including Rosie.

When Rosie was ten, the Crowder family piled into their Winnebago and headed north to Kansas, where David's uncle had a factory job; they hoped the move would lead to a better life for their children.

It was a migration that echoed the past.

The end of the Civil War ushered in the development of the Kansas City region. The Hannibal Bridge, at a cost of $1 million, opened in 1869, the first rail bridge built to cross the Missouri River, linking the Kansas and Missouri sides and enabling train travel to the West.

One year later, Philip Armour, a wily businessman, partnered with Milwaukee industrialist John Plankinton to establish a meatpacking plant in what came to be called "The Bottoms" of Kansas City, Missouri. Kansas City was the end of the trail for cattle drives, and the newly constructed train lines could then be used to transport the beef to Eastern cities.

To the west of the Bottoms was the state line, and across the line in Kansas was Splitlog Hill. The hill once had been owned by Mathias Splitlog, a wealthy Wyandotte tribe member, who sold off parcels of the land to railroad companies, the Catholic Church, and to developers. German and Irish settlers built fine homes on the hill, but many would move farther west, away from the stench of the meatpacking plants. The neighborhood was renamed Strawberry Hill, and by the turn of the twentieth century immigrants from Croatia, especially, but also Slovakia and Poland were lured by the job opportunities. Many discovered, after arriving, that they had been misled. The new workers were given "the most difficult, unpleasant, low paid work that was available," as one historian put it. Many of the workers were paid 3½ cents per hour. Over time, they moved into homes atop the hill vacated by early settlers. The new arrivals would descend daily for work in the Bottoms, where the Armour & Company plant grew to be one of the largest in the world.

By the early 1900s meatpacking had become the largest employer by far in Kansas City. A report published in 1910 found that 86 percent of those working in the meatpacking plants were foreign-born, many from Eastern Europe. "The areas around the packinghouse were soon filled by 'joints,' pool halls, gambling dens, and every unsavory vice to take advantage of the vulnerable workers," one historian noted.

Meatpacking, like the building of the railroad, offered opportunities for Black people as well. At the end of the Reconstruction era, as Jim Crow laws took effect, thousands of formerly enslaved people who became known as Exodusters left the South in 1879. Lured by stories of how the state had been established free of slavery by heroes like John Brown, not to mention rumors of free Kansas land, they came by the thousands to Wyandotte County. A poster circulated in Louisville, Kentucky, declaring: ALL COLORED PEOPLE GO TO KANSAS. It claimed that for $5.00, payable in installments, Black people could claim "an abundance of choice lands now belonging to the government."

The poster was a lie. The Black people who arrived found that there was no government land waiting for them. "Images of the promised land were quickly replaced by the unholy scenes and stench of blood and slaughter," said a report produced in 1982 by the City of Kansas City. "The Exodusters often encountered discrimination in wages and job assignments, and there were a few companies that refused to hire them altogether."

The lure of jobs, though, continued to attract Black families; by 1890, the number of Black residents of Kansas City, Kansas, was almost 7,000; then came the Great Migration from the South, and by 1930 the number of Black residents had tripled, to more than 21,000 residents.

The Black families settled mostly in the north end of town in the ensuing decades.

On the eve of the United States entry into World War II, the federal government chose KCK as the site for a plant to manufacture B-25 bombers; a Chamber of Commerce brochure offered the enticement:

"American-born citizens make loyal, intelligent workmen." The brochure noted the "farm boys" had machinery experience that would make them "adept mechanics." During the war years, the plant produced 150 medium range bombers a month, employing more than 10,000 workers on two shifts.

General Motors leased the plant at war's end and produced millions of Pontiacs and Oldsmobiles and Buicks over the next four decades. GM's decision to build a new plant in KCK in 1985, replacing the outdated facility, was hailed as "the most anxiously awaited announcement in city history." The new plant put more than 2,000 area residents to work and was the place where Saturn Auras were assembled.

But by 1990 more people were leaving Wyandotte County than were moving in; and more than 14,000 young residents were living in poverty. A disproportionate number of them were Black residents.

Like many Black people who migrated to KCK over the decades, the Crowders did not find the gateways to prosperity they hoped for. Still determined to make a go of his situation, David started a junk business, and Maxine made and sold sweets in the neighborhood and worked as a domestic to help ends meet while she raised their children.

Their daughter Rosie had a daughter, Glasia; then fell in love with and married James McIntyre, with whom she bore four boys. But James had a heroin addiction. When Lamonte was still a child, James walked out on the family forever, leaving Rosie to raise them on her own.

Rosie had trouble just keeping a roof over the heads of her family, and the McIntyres moved around a lot. She had a series of jobs; at Bethany Hospital, then at a fruit market, and then at a neighborhood spot, Fifi's Restaurant.

Rosie's children spent much of their time with their grandparents, and David served as a father figure for the family. Maxine was strict, and the switch was there to be used anytime the young ones stepped out of line. As Maxine put it: "It was the only way I knew to keep them from trouble." Though David had never learned to read and write properly, he hoped Lamonte, or Monte as the family called him, would finish high school and even attend college. Lamonte dreamed of going to the University of Michigan, a school he favored because of their sports teams.

But Ann Arbor might as well have been another universe. As the McIntyres scrambled for housing, Lamonte was enrolled in one elementary school after another, making it difficult to make friends. His world was the extended Crowder family, and he hung around regularly with older cousins, especially the children of two of Rosie's brothers.

It was a neighborhood that had life to it, despite the poverty. People went to church together and sang in the choir or just as loudly from the pews. They supported each other in times of crisis. They came outside in the summer evenings to mingle, gossip, and share a beverage or two. It was a community of neighbors, friends, and relatives.

And yet, trouble was all around them. As the public radio station described Kansas City, Kansas, in the 1990s:

> "People are moving out as fast as they can pack up the truck, fleeing to nearby Johnson County or over the state line to Missouri. The city government is hit with scandal after scandal, plagued by rumors of patronage and corruption. There isn't a movie theater or shopping. A new grocery store hadn't opened in the urban core in decades."

KCK made up almost the entirety of Wyandotte County, among the most impoverished counties in Kansas. Wyandotte residents, known locally as Dottes, suffered near the very bottom in lowest median income and highest unemployment of anywhere in the state. In the mid-1990s, 14 percent of its population was on food stamps and more than 30 percent of residents who were twenty-five or older had never finished high school. The poverty brought with it more sorrow; the rate of major crimes was nearly double the rest of the state.

Things were so bad, a newspaper article noted, that a recent mayor sold his house in 1993 and fled to Johnson County.

From the time he was eleven, Lamonte saw his older cousin D. J. with money to buy sneakers and other things he coveted. D. J. was dealing crack cocaine, but to limit the risk he sold only to a tiny circle of people. Then D. J. found he could expand his circle but still restrict his exposure by giving his kid cousin handfuls of cocaine rocks and telling him at which corner to go stand to sell.

It was that simple. Lamonte had an entry-level job into the drug business, and money to buy sneakers for himself and his brothers. He did not use cocaine himself, though he had been smoking weed since even before he was a teenager. He joined a gang when he was eleven years old, as he put it, seeking the structure he did not get at home. But the gang was not about violence to Lamonte; it was about going to monthly meetings and discussing order in the community.

Relatives and friends knew him as a happy-go-lucky kid who enjoyed telling jokes. He aspired to grow up to be a comedian. One time, Lamonte's older sister called him from her friend's house to come join them; it turned out, his sister just wanted Lamonte to make them laugh.

Four days after Christmas in 1992, Lamonte, then fifteen, went to hang out with his older brother, James, who lived nearby with his girlfriend Angie. Their cousin Terrance was also there, and Terrance and James hatched a plan for dinner.

The two went to a neighbor's house and placed a call for two meat lover's pizzas to be delivered to a vacant nearby apartment. When the Pizza Hut delivery man arrived, they held him up, took the pizzas, and brought them back to Angie's apartment. Terrance had brought along his mother's gun.

The driver called the police and described being robbed by two men, one with a gun. The police went to Angie's apartment where they found the pizza boxes, Angie, James, Terrance, and Lamonte. The police took all three young men into custody, even though the delivery man said just two men had robbed him, and both James and Terrance said that Lamonte was not involved.

At the station, after midnight, police convinced the three to waive their rights and took statements from each of them. Lamonte told the officers that he was inside Angie's apartment and was not part of the ill-fated plan. James told police that he and Terrance had gone out and committed the robbery and that Lamonte was not involved. Terrance told the police that he had taken his mother's gun and reiterated that Lamonte was not involved.

But the police charged all three with robbery. Rosie scraped together money to hire a lawyer. The prosecutors offered a deal: If all three youths pleaded guilty, they could each be placed on probation.

The deal dismayed Lamonte, who insisted he was not a part of it.

But the lawyer, Michael Redmon, warned that if it went before the juvenile judge, Matthew Podrebarac, there was a good chance Lamonte would be judged guilty and ordered confined. Besides, since he was just a minor, if Lamonte stayed out of trouble the case would end up wiped from his record.

And so Lamonte accepted the plea bargain and falsely admitted to his guilt. His mug shot was put into police files where it would, months later, become relevant.

The incident left Lamonte disillusioned and alienated. He ended up in an alternative school, in a GED program, and bitter at how things had turned out. He started ditching school.

He spent that Friday morning with Peggy Crowder's brother, Mike Williams, at his Aunt Peggy and Uncle Johnny's house.

Like so many others in the neighborhood, they had no telephone, so when Mike was ready to go home, Lamonte ran across the alley to his other aunt and uncle's home to call a taxi for Mike. When that taxi did not show up, Lamonte ran back across the alley to call the company again.

The day was largely uneventful. Until, that is, the early evening when the trouble erupted.

3
The Wrong Lamonte

Once Roger Golubski delivered Ruby Mitchell to the detective headquarters, she was directed to sit with Detective Krstolich as he pulled out the Identi-Kit, a handy box of 37 plastic noses, 52 chins, 102 pairs of eyes, 40 lips, 130 hairlines, and an assortment of eyebrows, ears, mustaches, spectacles, wrinkles, and headgear.

The kit had been developed by Hugh C. McDonald, who had joined the Los Angeles County sheriff's department after rising to the rank of major in military intelligence during World War II. McDonald had spent years after the war studying tens of thousands of photographs of suspects' faces, which he gradually reduced to 500 different types. From that work, McDonald developed the kit with plastic strips resembling facial features that could be laid on top of each other to create a face. It was a police version of Mr. Potato Head.

In 1959, the Los Angeles sheriff's detectives used the kit successfully for the first time, helping a store owner to provide a clear description of the man who had robbed his store at gunpoint. Word of Identi-Kit spread quickly, and within two years Scotland Yard used the kit to identify a murderer in Soho.

Smith & Wesson bought and marketed the kit. McDonald went on to become chief of detectives for the Los Angeles County sheriff before retiring, after which he spent years attempting to prove that a rogue CIA agent named Saul, and not Lee Harvey Oswald, fired the gun that killed President John F. Kennedy in Dallas.

The Identi-Kit lived on, a handy device for departments across the United States and beyond that could not afford a sketch artist. The value of Identi-Kit became a matter of debate among forensic psychologists, with many experts concerned it led witnesses into misidentifications.

By the time of the murders on Hutchings Street, many police departments had abandoned it and moved to computerized systems for creating composites, a system that did little to alleviate the risks of false identifications.* In any event, Kansas City, Kansas, was hardly on the cutting edge of police technology, and Ruby was left to try to create the face of the man who had committed murder on her street that afternoon using the plastic strips of the Identi-Kit.

No one considered whether Ruby even had a view of the killer's face from her front door. That question wouldn't come up for another two decades.

Ruby dutifully completed her Mr. Potato Head composite. She also added a detail: She had nearly called out the name "Lamonte" as she saw the shooter walk up to the car, because she recognized him as the young man "who used to try to talk to my niece."

Detective Golubski gathered five photographs of Black men to show to Ruby Mitchell—a critical moment in an investigation built on eyewitness identification.

---

* If the Identi-Kit was junk forensics, the computerized systems may have been just as bad, but more modern.

The courts have long recognized the dangers of mistaken identification that often originates at the lineup—either from photos or in person. In 1967 the U.S. Supreme Court noted, "The vagaries of eyewitness identification are well known; the annals of criminal law are rife with instances of mistaken identification." Either through state law, court orders, or local regulation, many jurisdictions today have enacted a series of steps to minimize the risk. Witnesses should be shown photo arrays, for example, by an officer who does not know which photograph is of the suspect. Police are also advised to instruct the witness in advance that the person who committed the crime may not even be among the suspects they are about to view.

But no such protections were in play when Golubski handed the five photographs to Ruby. She picked out Suspect Number 3.

It was nearing 6:00 P.M., not even four hours after the murders. Detective Krstolich transcribed the following exchange with Ruby:

> Q: Ms. Mitchell, did you tell me after we took your statement that you almost called out a name when you saw the man run down the hill?
> A: Yes.
> Q: What name did you almost call out?
> A: Lamont.
> Q: Why did you almost yell Lamont?
> A: Because he used to try to talk to my niece and I know him.
> Q: When you got to headquarters did we show you a series of five pictures?
> A: Yes.
> Q: Were you able to pick out the shooter of the picture [*sic*]?
> A: Yes.

Q: Is there a number on that picture?
A: Yes.
Q: What number is that picture?
A: Number three.
Q: Are you absolutely sure this is the party who did the shooting?
A: Yes.
Q: Who is this party?
A: Lamont.
Q: Do you know his last name?
A: Yes.
Q: What is it?
A: McIntyre.
Q: How do you know this party?
A: Because he used to talk to my niece.
Q: How long have you known him?
A: For a couple months.
Q: Once again, you are absolutely sure this is the party?
A: Yes.

In fact, Ruby's niece had not been seeing Lamonte McIntyre at all. Ruby had somehow confused Lamonte McIntyre with the young man her niece was seeing, Lamont Drain.

Ruby never could explain the confusion, except to say the two young men looked alike to her. Not only do the men not closely resemble each other, but left unexplained is how the police report quoted her as providing Lamonte's last name, "McIntyre." Ruby would later insist she never said "McIntyre," regardless of what the police transcript shows.

Krstolich's report states that "pictures of different Lamontes were shown to her in a picture interview of five (5) separate Black individuals."

But that wasn't exactly the case. There was only one Lamonte in the photo array: Lamonte McIntyre. Neither Lamont Drain nor any other Lamonte was included in the group of photos. But the five photographs they showed to Ruby also included Lamonte's brother, James McIntyre; and Lamonte's cousin, Terrance Brown.

Having three relatives in a five-person lineup is highly irregular, raising questions about whether the officers had a reason to want Ruby to identify a member of that family. Years later, Lamonte's mother would voice her suspicions of why Detective Golubski would target a member of her family.

By the time Ruby chose Lamonte's picture, the shooting was a double murder. At 4:25 P.M., Donald Ewing died on the operating table at Bethany Medical Center.

Ruby's identification was all the detectives needed. Detectives Golubski and Krstolich, along with Lt. Dennis Barber and backup uniform officers, went to the address they had on file for Lamonte—2908 Parkwood, a little over a mile from the murder scene.

When they arrived, they found Maxine Crowder sitting on her porch.

4

Why, God?

Lt. Barber told Maxine that they were investigating a serious felony and needed to talk to her grandson. Maxine said she did not know where Lamonte was but would get in touch with him. The lieutenant, who left his card with Maxine, remembered later how polite she was.

Once the police left, Maxine called Lamonte, who called his mother at Fifi's Restaurant to come get him. Fifi, a woman from Africa, ran the dining spot near where the McIntyres then were living. She took regular trips back to Africa and largely left Rosie in charge. As soon as Rosie got the call she left work and hurried over to her brother's house.

As Lamonte got in the car Rosie demanded, "What do the police want to talk to you about?" Lamonte said he didn't know, but guessed it was probably about that incident that occurred a couple weeks earlier, when officers had come up to his cousins' house while a large group was out front. The police conducted searches and arrested several of those present. Among them was Lamonte, who had three rocks of cocaine in his pocket.

Rosie told Lamonte to get in her van, and they headed off to straighten out whatever the trouble was. As Rosie drove past Fifi's Restaurant, she saw the police in the parking lot and pulled in to speak with them.

She told Lamonte to stay inside as she parked, then got out and walked over to the first cop she saw. She told the officer that Lamonte was in her van, and she understood they wanted to talk to him. Rosie misunderstood the questions and thought police were asking about an incident that happened the day before. She said Lamonte had been working at Fifi's that day, thinking that would quickly erase whatever suspicions they had.

She signaled for Lamonte to come over and the police began questioning him: Was he involved in any gang activity that day? Did he know anyone in a blue lowrider? Had he fired a gun that day, or did he know anyone who did?

When Lamonte denied knowing anything about what the officers were asking, Lt. Barber asked him to come to the station. He told Rosie she could follow them, that Lamonte was not under arrest and it should not take too long.

Lamonte vividly recalls what officers told him when he asked why he was being taken into custody: "I had nothing to worry about if I didn't do anything wrong."

At about 8:00 P.M., Lamonte was put in an interview room, alone with Golubski and Krstolich. Golubski advised Lamonte of his rights, a situation that is fraught with dangers for youth who are without a lawyer or parent. Lamonte refused to sign the form acknowledging his rights but agreed to answer questions, which quickly became more pointed as the detectives pressed him about the killing. Lamonte told them he had spent the day at his aunt's house on Wood Street. He named the cousins he hung out with. The detectives sensed a conflict, since Rosie had told them that Lamonte was working at Fifi's.

Who drove a blue lowrider? they asked him. Who was Doniel Quinn? Who was Donald Ewing? Lamonte didn't know any of the answers.

In most places around the country today—and pretty much everywhere back in 1994—officers are permitted to lie in their questioning to try to obtain a confession. Because false confessions are another major source of wrongful convictions, a growing number of jurisdictions have passed laws to guard against defendants falsely confessing, measures like prohibiting officers from lying to suspects, especially teenagers, or requiring interviews to routinely be tape-recorded.

But KCK had no such restrictions; it was not until 2017 that the state enacted a law on recording interrogations of subjects in serious felonies. As long as the suspect was not coerced, pretty much anything else was permitted. And so, when Lamonte responded that he did not know Ewing or Quinn, one of the officers raised his voice and declared that it was odd he didn't know them because there had been a shooting off Quindaro Boulevard, and one of the two victims lived long enough to say that Lamonte had done the crime.

Lamonte couldn't believe it. Nothing in his life prepared him for the shock of that accusation. He never went past the gas station on Quindaro to the area where the shooting occurred, a neighborhood that Lamonte thought of as disgusting and nasty. "Crime City," was how Lamonte described it.

"I don't know who you're looking for, but it isn't me," he told the detectives. They reacted with anger. "Are you fucking kidding?" one shouted at him. "Do you think this is a fucking game?" Lamonte recalled later that one of the detectives, though he is not sure which one, used a racial slur and called Lamonte a killer.

Lamonte said he was done talking, that this had nothing to do with him. He asked to be able to talk to his mother. Instead, he was told, "You're not going anywhere."

The interrogation was over in minutes. Six hours after the shots were fired, Lamonte was under arrest. Two counts of first-degree murder.

The detectives walked Lamonte out of the interview room toward the booking area, and in the hallway he spotted his mother. He was crying as he called out to her, "Mom, they're charging me with two counts of murder."

It was beyond anything she could imagine. "No, you have the wrong kid," she called out to them. "He didn't murder anyone." She pleaded with them to test Lamonte's hands for gun residue.

Their answer: We don't do that kind of test here in Kansas.

Lamonte was taken to the juvenile detention area in the basement of the jail and was on suicide watch for the next seventy-two hours. Guards locked him in a cell with a bed, a sink, a toilet, and a window through which they could check if he was still alive.

Most everything but his shirt was taken from him. He was given the brown uniform that marked him as a juvenile awaiting trial. It was cold and dark, but he was not provided a blanket.

He asked God why he was there. He got no answer.

5
Return to Quindaro

Lamonte spent the first days in the suicide-watch cell. It was cold, always cold, and he didn't belong there. He was bewildered, both by his surroundings and the accusation that he had killed two men. Lamonte didn't know the victims and had no reason to kill them. He had never committed a violent crime. He had spent the day at his cousin's house, more than a mile from the murder on Hutchings Street. It left Lamonte feeling sure that it would all be straightened out soon enough.

Detective Golubski felt otherwise. Armed with the identification by Ruby Mitchell, the detective now set out to prove Lamonte did it.

Early the next morning, Golubski visited the neighborhood where Lamonte's cousins lived. He took photographs of a car outside that neighbors said James and Lamonte often drove. Armed with his Polaroid photographs and with the photos of Lamonte and four other men, Golubski returned with a second detective, Dennis Ware, to the neighborhood where the murders had occurred, out Quindaro Boulevard northwest of downtown Kansas City.

The Quindaro neighborhood of the 1990s was not remotely the community that Abelard Guthrie had envisioned almost a century and a half earlier. Guthrie was a former federal land clerk in Ohio who had fallen in love with the daughter of a Wyandotte tribal leader. When the Wyandottes were pushed out of their lands in the Sandusky Valley of Ohio for the unsettled areas west of the Mississippi River, Guthrie chased after them.*

The Wyandottes stood for peace and freedom. The tribal members were descendants of the Wendat tribe of the Huron Confederacy, who were forced south from Ontario in the 17th century after the tribe was decimated both by a series of wars with the Iroquois Confederacy and by outbreaks of smallpox and measles brought to the region by French settlers.

They resettled in northern Ohio and adopted many of the ways of the Europeans: They were the first tribe to have a Methodist mission; they took up farming, and fought alongside the colonists against the British. Afterward, the young American government entered a series of treaties assuring the Wyandotte tribe its lands in perpetuity, and by the 1830s tribal members had become among the wealthiest of Ohioans.

But the quest for expansion by the colonists was insatiable, and after Andrew Jackson was elected president in 1828 and signed the Indian Removal Act, tribes were pushed west, one after another, off their lands. First came the southern tribes, forced to migrate to Oklahoma on the Trail of Tears. Then came the northern tribes, pressured and cajoled to give up their lands, treaty or no treaty.

In 1842, a majority of the Wyandotte tribe agreed to sell their Ohio lands, among the last tribes to move west. A train of more than 150 wagons carrying 650 members of the tribe departed Sandusky the next year bound for Cincinnati, where they boarded steamboats for

---

* French settlers had called members of the Wendat tribe Wyandottes. The English later shortened it to Wyandot. Since the Kansas County where the murders occurred is named Wyandotte County, that spelling is adopted here.

Westport, Missouri. Just across the Mississippi River from Westport sat the new Wyandotte home: 25,000 acres of mostly barren land in the Kansas territory that the tribe had bought from another displaced tribe, the Delaware.

Among those who settled the new land was the family of Adam Brown, whose father had been a tribal chief. It was Brown's daughter, Nancy Quindaro Brown, whom Guthrie pursued from Ohio. Once in Kansas, Guthrie married her and was admitted to the tribe himself.

Despite all the efforts to accommodate, peace and security remained elusive for the Wyandotte members. The violent period known as Bleeding Kansas followed congressional passage of the Kansas-Nebraska Act in 1854, igniting skirmishes between Missourians, who sought to take up residence in Kansas and expand slavery to the new territory, against antislavery advocates, including John Brown and his sons.*

Adam Brown's son-in-law, Abelard Guthrie, retained his antislavery idealism, and in 1856, he and a dozen other Wyandotte members formed the first free port on the Missouri River, a counterpoint to Westport across the water in the slave state of Missouri. The new village, a few miles west of where the Wyandotte tribe had settled, was named Quindaro, for Guthrie's wife.

With help from the New England Emigrant Aid Company, which sent immigrants who opposed slavery, Quindaro flourished. It had two hotels, a sawmill, a grocery store, a hardware store, and a newspaper. It became a stop on the Underground Railroad, a place where enslaved Black people could escape from the shackles of neighboring Missouri by crossing the river.

---

* No relation to Adam Brown.

But the Quindaro of the late 1850s, a haven for those desperate for freedom and opportunity, vanished almost as quickly as it began. With the Civil War many residents left, and afterward the railroad and meat-packing plant pulled residents a few miles east. Quindaro was mostly deserted by 1872, when the town of Wyandotte was incorporated with two other small towns just across the river from Kansas City, Missouri. Developers knew just the name for the new community, to help it grow and prosper: Kansas City, Kansas.

By the early twentieth century, what was left of Quindaro was annexed into Kansas City, Kansas. A new freeway built in the 1970s isolated the ruins of the old settlement. Long gone is the Quindaro Freedman's School, the first school west of the Mississippi founded to educate Black children, with its offspring being Western University, one of the nation's first Historically Black Colleges and Universities. Western closed its doors in 1943, and about all that remains is a statue of John Brown, dedicated in 1911 in honor of his fight for freedom.

By the late twentieth century, drugs and sex were the commercial enterprises along Quindaro Boulevard. At the corner of Quindaro and Hutchings Street stood McCall's Gas Station, owned in the 1990s by a drug dealer named Cecil Brooks. Not only were gasoline, soda pop, and snacks available, customers could also easily find crack cocaine nearby.

A detective since 1986, Roger Golubski was very familiar with the neighborhood up Quindaro Boulevard. He headed up Hutchings Street past the gas station to go talk to the Quinns about the murders from the day before.

Golubski went first to see Doniel's aunt Josephine, whose house was directly across from where the Cadillac had been parked. Josephine told him that she did not see the suspect well enough to make an identification. But she said her daughter Stacey had, and Stacey knew who committed the crime. Stacey was not home at the moment, Josephine told Golubski and Ware.

The detectives then walked two doors down the street to talk to Josephine's other daughter, Niko.

Niko became distraught as she viewed the five photographs the detective handed her. Golubski wrote a report later that day stating that Niko "began shaking, became teary eyed" when looking at Lamonte's photo and told Golubski that she "thought this might be him," but could not say for sure. The detective left, leaving behind a still-distraught Niko.

He next went one block over, to Hiawatha, to visit the resident who had spotted the murderer climb into the getaway car. She looked at the photos Golubski had taken that morning of the parked car outside of Lamonte's aunt's house and told the detective that the car in the photo was definitely not the getaway car.

Golubski prepared a report that day, writing of the "possibility" that Josephine Quinn's brother John, or her daughter Stacey, could identify the gunman, although neither of them were interviewed at the time. His report added, "Also, it is very obvious that Niko Quinn knows exactly who the shooter is, but being highly traumatized at this time is reluctant to provide that information."

Golubski prepared a second report that day, far more succinct. "This case is cleared with the arrest of LAMONTE MCINTYRE, B/M, 7-28-76." The facts and details, he added, were being sent to the district attorney's office for review.

At that point, the case was based completely on the shaky identification of Ruby Mitchell. Golubski cleared the case without ever taking several basic investigatory steps. He never sought to search Lamonte's house for the all-black outfit witnesses described the shooter wearing, or the murder weapon, which was never recovered. Nor did he obtain any information suggesting that Lamonte knew the victims or had a motive to murder them.

And his assigned partner, W. K. Smith, did even less.

No matter. Two days after Golubski submitted his report, Wyandotte County assistant district attorney Victoria Meyer filed a complaint charging Lamonte with two counts of murder. Regardless of how little evidence the detectives had developed.

6

The City Is Wide Open

After his three-day stint on suicide watch, two guards handcuffed Lamonte and shackled his legs before taking him up the prison elevator to the fourth floor of the courthouse to D-4, the section that held juveniles accused of the most serious of charges. The pod had ten cells, each with two young men locked up, and Lamonte would spend most of the next two months locked up inside his cell.

At some moments, Lamonte considered suicide, but he quickly dismissed the idea when he thought about the pain it would cause his mother. He just really wanted to get out and could not wait for a court hearing when he fully expected the mistake to be cleared up.

While Lamonte waited in his cell, the dismal reputation of Kansas City, Kansas, took a turn for the worse, if that was possible.

The popular mayor, Joseph Steineger, became the first mayor in KCK history to be indicted while in office. Steineger, his top aide, and a chief building inspector all were charged by U.S. Attorney Barry Grissom with bribery. A strip club owner had worn a wire and taped conversations with all three men about money he gave them to get around zoning restrictions and potential building code violations.

The case was "seen as a blow to KCK image," *The Kansas City Star* headline warned. A columnist noted that when Steineger ran for reelection three years earlier, the columnist had written then, "It is remarkable, perhaps unprecedented that a Kansas City, Kan. mayor seeking reelection isn't under attack for corruption, malfeasance, or stumbling incompetence in his nepotism-riddled administration." Sadly, the same columnist added in retrospect: "It just took Steineger a little longer than the usual four years to get to that point."

Certainly, corruption had its roots planted deep in Kansas history. In the 1800s, saloons provided liquor, women, and gambling to the unskilled meatpacking and railroad workers, many of them immigrants, and to the cowboys delivering cattle from Texas along the Chisholm Trail. Many of the early transplants from New England who came to the territory with strong antislavery sentiments found the array of vices as abhorrent as the concept of enslaved people.

In 1880, Kansas voters approved a state constitutional amendment that declared, "The manufacture and sale of intoxicating liquors shall be forever prohibited in this state, except for medical, scientific, and mechanical purposes." The amendment remained the law of the land for decades; Kansans could not legally buy bottled liquor until three years after the end of World War II, long after the failed national experiment in prohibition ended in 1933. Liquor by the drink in Kansas restaurants, taverns, and other public establishments only became legal in Wyandotte County in 1987, after voters amended the state constitution.

It was in Kansas that Caroline Amelia Moore Gloyd Nation, soon to be known to the world as Carrie Nation, achieved fame. She began her prohibition campaign after her first husband, a Union physician, died from alcoholism he developed during the Civil War. Her crusade took her to saloon after saloon, axe in hand, destroying bottles of liquor and the bars that housed them.

Neither the restrictive constitution nor the spectacles produced by Carrie Nation put a stop to drinking in Kansas. But the law did serve to invite corruption among public officials in Wyandotte County who were willing to wink at the effort to legislate all manner of public morality, and drinking, prostitution, and gambling all flourished. Over the years, corruption became endemic to the region.

When Al Jennerich transferred to the Kansas City FBI office in 1986, he was surprised to discover that KCK was a "Little Chicago," as he later described it.

Al was raised in New Jersey, went into the army after college and then started his career working for Government Accounting Office. But the job put him constantly on the road, and away from his wife more than he liked. Al left GAO for the FBI and was assigned to the public corruption squad of the Chicago field office.

Until Al arrived in Chicago, he naively believed that all police officers were good people. That quickly passed. He was part of a team that built a successful case against ten Chicago Police Department officers who were taking bribes to protect a heroin market—an operation so flagrant that uniformed officers directed traffic. Then he worked on one of the largest public corruption cases in bureau history, Operation Greylord, which led to the indictment of seventeen Cook County judges, forty-eight lawyers, eight policemen, ten deputy sheriffs, eight court officials, and one state legislator.

Al Jennerich left Chicago for the Kansas City office, which was the region his wife was from; the FBI office there oversaw western

Missouri and all of Kansas. He was quickly struck by how much Kansas City, Kansas, felt like Chicago. Those in power were all connected to each other, and both cities were run with an insular power structure. Corruption was pervasive and deeply ingrained, dating back almost to the city's founding. One early KCK mayor was voted out of office, and another forced to resign, over their failures to enforce the state liquor ban. A third mayor resigned in disgrace in 1926 over accusations of "official misconduct" that included profiting off bootlegging. *The Kansas City Times* splashed the allegations of the Kansas attorney general on its front page: THE CITY IS WIDE OPEN.

More than three decades later, the *Star* reported that KCK police officers had complained to the state attorney general that the mayor and police chief were permitting unrestrained liquor and gambling violations. Echoing the past, one of the officers was quoted as saying, "The town is wide open."

The U.S. attorney for Kansas warned in 1973 that organized crime was moving into Wyandotte County, adding that could not occur "without corrupt or sympathetic public officials, including judges, policemen, and prosecutors who cover up the activities." Soon after, a *Kansas City Star* investigation documented that prostitution, liquor, and gambling were pervasive in KCK. "Against a backdrop of political influence, permissive courts, and ineffective intervention, such operations run wide open in Kansas City, Kansas," the newspaper reported. "Present city officials appear no more determined to change that tradition than preceding administrations."

Within months of that report, a federal grand jury indicted the commander of the vice squad, KCK police captain Thomas Dailey, on charges of bribery to promote prostitution. Two others indicted, a massage parlor owner and a patrolman, pleaded guilty and testified at the subsequent trial that they paid regular bribes to Dailey and a lawyer who was allegedly turning the money over to Dailey to win police protection of two massage parlors and two apartments.

Dailey's first trial ended in a mistrial. After the case was retried, the jury convicted the attorney but found Captain Dailey not guilty. The officer was welcomed back to the force as vice commander and given back pay for the months he had been suspended awaiting trial.

Al Jennerich arrived just as the state's voters finally passed an amendment to permit the legal sale of liquor by the drink in public establishments, effective January 1, 1987. Crack cocaine was by then a far greater danger to the community than bootlegged liquor or gambling, and illegal drug money was a greater enticement to corruptible public officials. And that was the scene when Al began working with Assistant U.S. Attorney Julie Robinson.

Robinson was a fourth generation Kansan, a descendant of one of the early families lured to Kansas in the Black exodus from the South after the Civil War. She was an army brat. Her father was stationed in a series of posts overseas and in the U.S. before the family settled back in Kansas. She went to the University of Kansas as an undergraduate and on through law school before clerking for two years for a U.S. Bankruptcy Court judge.

At the end of her clerkship in 1983, Robinson served as an assistant U.S. attorney for the Kansas district. The main office was in Topeka; Robinson was assigned to be what was called a "floater" in the KCK courthouse, handling a mix of civil and criminal cases. Criminal cases did not interest Julie Robinson much, but she wanted the job and was happy to take whatever assignments came her way.

Four years into the job, Robinson prosecuted a case after an FBI raid on a prefabricated building where 128 patrons gathered around six blackjack tables, a craps table, and two poker tables. The customers had paid $25.00 admission and were being served food and drinks by what the newspaper called "scantily dressed women." Two uniformed deputies guarded the door.

Not surprising, perhaps. The gambling enterprise was run by John L. Quinn Jr., the son of the Wyandotte County sheriff. "Smokey" Quinn,* as he was known, was convicted on charges of conspiring with owners of topless bars to operate the gambling operation.

Federal agents were tipped off to the operation by Joseph Cantalupo, a former Colombo crime family associate in New York who was relocated to Wyandotte County after he flipped and testified in several Mafia trials.

"Highway patrolmen, judges, prosecutors, they all reported in to Smokey, they all took care of his problems," Cantalupo would later write in his book *Body Mike*, recounting his life of crime:** "There was a redneck mafia that used political clout and backwoods justice to peddle crime and line its pockets in a way that put the nearby city mafioso to shame."

He added, "Drugs, prostitution, gambling, extortion, loan sharking and murder were all a part of a way of life."

---

* The sheriff and his son were not related to the family of Doniel Quinn, one of the two men shot dead in the Cadillac.

** It was coauthored with the *Newsday* organized crime reporter Tom Renner.

7
"Historically Corrupt"

Al Jennerich, upon arriving in town, was soon building cases with Julie Robinson against illegal drug traffickers. It didn't take long before the pair discovered their targets were in cahoots with members of the KCK police to protect corrupt operations.

It began with the prosecution of Hernan Velasquez, who told authorities after his arrest that he had been paying KCK Police Detective Bernie Smith for information about impending raids. Velasquez agreed to wear a wire and recorded the detective visiting him in jail, where Velasquez was awaiting trial. On tape, Smith referred to $1,900 that the drug trafficker had paid him.

Smith was indicted for extortion and was confronted at trial with the tapes as well as Velasquez's testimony. The jurors also heard that Jennerich tracked down where the $1,900 was spent, all the way down to ski lift tickets purchased as part of a Smith family vacation.

Smith contended the money had nothing to do with protection, testifying that in any event, he had returned it to Velasquez. The jury acquitted him, and the officer was welcomed back to the force. But FBI agent Jennerich and Assistant U.S. Attorney Robinson had gotten a whiff of the rotten core within the KCK police force.

They teamed with DEA agent Harley Sparks, who had been encountering a series of failures each time he laid a trap to build evidence against a drug trafficker named Carl Marshall. Marshall had been buying large quantities of cocaine in Los Angeles which were then transported to KCK in secret compartments welded to the undercarriages of vans. Once in KCK, a team of people cooked the cocaine into crack, and the finished product flooded the streets. Marshall's ability to elude the traps convinced Sparks there could only be one reason: A leak from a dirty cop.

To Jennerich and Robinson, the stakes could not have been higher. Crack was destroying lives, especially in Black neighborhoods, and police were doing nothing about it. As Jennerich wrote in an internal memo, "The reason that there is such an extensive crack cocaine problem in Kansas City, Kansas, is because of the fact that the KCKPD virtually ignores the drug problem in that city. The problem is as bad as it is because of corruption with the police department and general investigative incompetence."

Making matters worse, a new KCK police chief had taken office as the DEA investigation was getting started, one whom Jennerich and Robinson discovered had antipathy to the FBI. That new boss was Tom Dailey, the same Tom Dailey who had been indicted by the Organized Crime Strike Force in 1973 on charges he took bribes from a strip club owner, charges that ended with his acquittal. When the screening committee chose Dailey from forty-five applicants, one member said Dailey's past legal troubles were not held against him, explaining, "He's faced the fire and been made stronger for it."

Federal officials had a different perspective. As one agent* described it in an internal memorandum: "Historically, the KCKPD has been

* Name whited out on publicly available records

labeled 'corrupt' from the police chief, who was acquitted from a public corruption charge, down through a certain few ranking officers within the chain of command."

As Jennerich and Robinson dug into the corruption, they felt Dailey was obstructing their efforts at every turn.

At one point, Robinson called police headquarters to speak to a major, one of the few in the department whom they found cooperative. A receptionist announced over the loudspeaker that Robinson was on the line. The major later reported that Dailey chewed him out for talking to them. From then on, they arranged covert meetings with him, away from the office.

When Jennerich and Robinson sought to review complaints that citizens filed against officers, they were told the complaints were routinely discarded. When they sought photographs of patrol officers to show to jailed suspects who complained of corrupt officers, they were told the department did not have officers' photographs.

The rift between the federal authorities and local police was no longer subtle or a secret. Robinson obtained a subpoena, ordering each patrol officer to sit for a photograph, which Jennerich used to build a photo board to show to potential witnesses who knew the abusive officers by sight, but not by name. Robinson obtained a second subpoena, requiring the police to turn over official complaints on a continuing basis before they were destroyed. Both those steps served to further outrage Dailey and, for that matter, his entire department.

Jennerich met repeatedly with the local district attorney, Nick Tomasic, who told him that the KCKPD did not bring drug cases to him for prosecution, except when drugs were discovered during a traffic stop or some other contact. Tomasic told Jennerich that he was barely on speaking terms with Dailey and had almost no professional relationship with the chief.

Jennerich shared DEA agent Sparks's worry about leaks. Back when Robinson was presenting the case against Bernie Smith to the grand jury, one panel member was said to have relayed the grand jury evidence to the police. Jennerich and Sparks agreed to cut the police out of the drug investigation.

The pair got a break in their new investigation when a cab driver was stopped with kilos of cocaine in his trunk. The cabbie agreed to work as an informant, and Jennerich and Sparks soon learned that Carl Marshall's brother-in-law, veteran KCK patrol officer Edward Dryden, was feeding the drug ring information about upcoming raids.

But that still left a nagging question in the minds of the investigators: How would Dryden, assigned to the traffic division, have access to inside information about drug investigations? Jennerich would later point out to a local reporter the easy access that Dryden had to the KCK police brass. "Dryden was in and out of the chief's office at will," he said.

By late 1992, more than four years into the investigation that Sparks had launched, Jennerich wrote a memo expressing concern about how slowly the investigation was proceeding. "Until this office does convict several police officers and hopefully gain the cooperation of some of these police officers, the situation in Kansas City, Kansas will only deteriorate."

Five months later, the grand jury indicted Marshall, Dryden, and several others. They were finally convicted of conspiring to traffic drugs after a September 1993 trial.

The Kansas City Star headline reporting on the trial summed up the situation: POLICE ACCUSED OF AIDING CRIME.

By now, Jennerich and Robinson had gathered boxes of evidence, as the continuing subpoena required the police to regularly deliver copies of fresh complaints of police misconduct before they would be destroyed by the police. Jail inmates were identifying officers who engaged in misconduct, officers they often only knew by street names, by studying the poster board of photographs Jennerich brought them on visits to the jail.

But the police investigation was stalling after Dryden's conviction. There was, for one thing, the issue of manpower. It required a massive undertaking to expose systemic corruption. Jennerich's boss told his bosses in Washington that it would take four to eight agents, working for a year or more, to substantiate the widespread allegations Jennerich was developing.

The issue was not just the commitment that would be required. Not everyone in the office shared Robinson's and Jennerich's fervor. Chief Dailey had stepped up his attacks, complaining to Jennerich's boss and others of the intrusive investigation.

On top of all that were the demands from other pressing cases. A new U.S. attorney had been sworn in after Bill Clinton took office in 1993, a Wichita lawyer named Randy Rathbun, who held political ambitions of his own.

Following the conviction of Marshall and Dryden, Robinson was pressed to devote attention to the other high-profile investigation—the strip club owner's allegations that Mayor Steineger was taking bribes.

But before that case fully developed, President Clinton nominated Robinson to a seat on the U.S. Bankruptcy Court in Kansas. It was a vacancy created by the death of Robinson's mentor. Robinson handed off her investigation of Mayor Steineger—along with the rest of her caseload, including the deep probe of police corruption.

The assistant who took over Robinson's cases quickly dropped the continuing subpoena for complaints against officers. The probe into police misconduct was effectively ended. At the time it was shut down, there remained more than a dozen officers Jennerich had identified as suspects, and even more officers about whom Jennerich had heard damaging information that remained to be developed.

That included allegations that one detective was using his badge to sexually abuse vulnerable Black women in the poorest parts of Kansas City, Kansas. That detective was Roger Golubski.

8
Being Black in KCK

If Kansas had ever really been a beacon of opportunity and equality, that idea had long vanished for Black residents of KCK by the late twentieth century. Jobs were scarce, while crack was plentiful.

Many older Black residents had grown up without the right to attend public school with white students. Kansas legislators enacted a law in 1879 to segregate elementary schools across the state, though the high schools across the state were integrated. There was one exception. After a Black child allegedly killed a white child in a KCK park in 1905, the state legislature responded to community outrage by enacting a new state law to segregate the high schools in exactly one place: Kansas City, Kansas.

Originally, the Black school was to be called Manual Training High School. After residents objected, it opened in 1906 as Charles S. Sumner High School, honoring the fiercely antislavery senator from Massachusetts whose name would adorn schools in Black neighborhoods across the country. The KCK schools, from elementary through high school, remained segregated until 1954, when a Topeka parent named Oliver Brown, who opposed enrolling his daughter Linda in a segregated elementary school in the Kansas capital, won his lawsuit in the U.S. Supreme Court. The case, *Brown v. Board of Education*, ended the system of "separate but equal" education in Kansas and throughout the nation.

As in so many American cities, the neighborhoods of KCK were largely segregated as well. Over time, the residents of the largely Black neighborhoods of Kansas City were disadvantaged by a series of official actions, actions such as redlining and zoning codes, that kept Black people out of many neighborhoods over decades. In the 1930s, as many residents were left desperate by the Great Depression, a federal program was created to encourage banks to refinance loans to those in economic distress. The program was not available to residents of neighborhoods where assessors deemed the risk too great.

The notes made by KCK assessors in that period prove why loans in the Black neighborhoods were denied: "Negroes," the notes state, dominated the neighborhood. That was enough: just skin color. Housing discrimination set up a cascade of other obstacles: Lesser schools, lead paint that harmed children, and decreased generational wealth.

Until the federal government sued in 1972, even the Wyandotte County jail was segregated, with white and Black inmates held separately.

Even amid the widespread and systematic bias, the KCK police stood out. Officers piled abuse on the city's Black citizenry regularly. Often these abuses were known to superiors, who tolerated it and let it go unpunished.

This was the world Lamonte grew up in, the world Black residents of KCK endured. The most common victims of it, as elsewhere, were a particular segment of the population: young Black males.

In 1992, Donald Wilkins was being transported to the jail in the back of a police van. Along the way the transporting officers fired seven bullets into Wilkins, killing him. It was the kind of incident that, a generation later, might have caused national attention and outrage; but that was not KCK in the 1990s. Instead, the incident attracted no attention.

Officers Golubski and Smith, the same pair assigned two years later to the double murder on Hutchings Street, were assigned to investigate. The detectives accepted the version of the arresting officers: Wilkins had reached over from the back seat, grabbed a police baton, and prompted an altercation that only ended with the fatal shots.

Chief Dailey suspended the officers who transported Wilkins for two weeks. Their violation? Their failure to handcuff the suspect before putting him in the van. Period.

Many other cases came to light through Jennerich's work before the federal investigation was shut down. He identified a core group of eighteen officers who were the subject of multiple complaints. One officer was the subject of seventeen complaints of excessive force, and twelve more of threatening conduct. Another of the eighteen had been the subject of ten complaints of excessive force, and fifteen complaints about his conduct.

Many complaints appeared unfounded, but plenty of others that had substance were quickly dismissed, if they were even considered at all. In one case the families of several children and the local NAACP chapter complained about the conduct of white officers who came upon a group, ages seven to sixteen, walking down the street on a rainy day. The officers ordered them to lie on the wet pavement and searched them. When one of the kids questioned the command, according to the complaints, an officer stepped on and kicked him and used a racial slur. The police internal investigation ended with the offending officer being given a written "counseling form," advising him that he could have let the youth up sooner once it was determined no one in the group was armed. The officer was advised to show more tact in the future.

In another case, a man went into his backyard to see why his dogs were barking and ended up needing hospital treatment afterward. He filed a complaint that he had been knocked to the ground and beaten with nightsticks by officers who had entered his yard chasing an escaped fugitive.

The FBI review identified a series of other cases where department officials accepted officers' alternate explanations for injuries that complainants said were caused by excessive force. One man said an officer beat him with a nightstick, breaking his jaw, while he was on his bicycle. The officer's explanation: the man got hurt when he rode into the curb and fell off.

A diabetic man said he was kicked twice by an officer as he got out of his car. According to the officer, the man was drunk and fell to the ground. A third man complained that an arresting officer beat him on the head with a flashlight. The officer responded that the man hit his head on a stud in an unfinished part of the basement.

The report exposes, through case after case, a police force where officers could act with impunity. "The KCKPD does not investigate civil rights violations against its officers any more than it investigates allegations of drug dealing or robberies committed by officers," Jennerich wrote in an internal memo at the time.

But after patrolman Dryden was convicted along with members of Carl Thompson's drug ring, and then Julie Robinson departed from the U.S. attorney's office, the federal investigation into the KCK police effectively ended. Dailey remained the chief, and the many officers whom the federal probe had identified continued in their roles, undeterred.

9

"That's the Man"

Wyandotte County officials sounded an alarm in June 1994, hosting a public forum to discuss the rise in juvenile crime, which Assistant District Attorney Victoria Meyer warned was "pretty much out of control." KCK Police Lt. Jim Stevens agreed, saying there had already been eleven juveniles arrested for homicides just a little more than five months into the year. "That's going to break all kinds of records compared to the past," Stevens said.*

One of those eleven, of course, was Lamonte McIntyre. He remained locked up in the juvenile detention facility.

The wait in Pod D-4 was agonizing for Lamonte, who continued to believe he just needed his day in court for the judge to see that a mistake was made and he could go home. He had no doubt that

---

* As they struggled to reduce the incidents of crimes by juveniles, Wyandotte County officials came up with bizarre initiatives in response. Ten teenagers who had been put on probation were ordered, for example, to take part in a program designed by the warden of Lansing prison as his master's thesis: They were taken to the prison for a day, and forced to wear ill-fitting tan and orange prison uniforms and leg shackles and then endure shouted orders from prison guards, jeers from inmates, and a strip search.

this woman who was accusing him of murder would realize her mistake once she saw him in the courtroom. In the meantime, being confined day after day to D-4 was torture. The inactivity and the routine seemed endless.

Another teenager there, Corey, was always ready to pick fights. Lamonte was not looking for fights, but he was not about to back down, either. The violence often started over nothing. Lamonte's first fight in custody erupted between him and Corey over which channel to watch on the only television in the pod.

Showing the others that he was willing to fight was the only way Lamonte knew how to keep himself safe. He was, after all, only 140 pounds and had quickly been given the name "Short Dog" by other inmates.

After several weeks, Lamonte received a visit from Gary Long, the lawyer appointed to represent him. Like most communities across the country, Wyandotte County had no public defender office despite the significant number of prosecutions being handled in the courthouse. Instead, judges appointed private lawyers to handle cases of defendants who lacked the funds to pay for their own lawyer. Such appointments are not necessarily based on merit, and too often are the result of connections of some sort to the judges who appoint them. In communities where judges are elected, those connections frequently include donations to the judges' political campaigns.

The pay for appointed representation was $40.00 an hour in 1994, and most skilled attorneys avoided such appointments altogether. Many of those who took such cases made a living by relying on judges to send them several cases at a time.

Long had been appointed by District Judge Podrebarac, who earlier presided over Lamonte's pizza case and now was assigned the double murder.

The son of a Yugoslavian immigrant who spent years working at the Armour plant, Matthew Podrebarac's lifelong ambition had been to become a judge. After law school and the army, he entered public service, working as an assistant Wyandotte County attorney, then assistant KCK solicitor. When a seat opened in 1972 on the Wyandotte County Commission, Podrebarac ran for and won the seat. Six years later, he won election for Wyandotte County district judge.

Podrebarac scheduled a hearing for late June for two purposes. It would serve as a preliminary hearing, at which prosecutors would have to present sufficient evidence to hold Lamonte for trial on murder charges. And the proceeding also would serve as a waiver hearing, to consider the prosecution request that Lamonte's case be transferred to adult court, where the consequences for a guilty verdict would be far more severe.

The nation's first juvenile court opened in Cook County, Illinois, in 1899, dedicated to the concept of rehabilitation rather than punishment, and by 1925 all but two states had followed suit. But by the second half of the twentieth century, as the public became fearful of a perceived rise in juvenile crime, states across the country, including Kansas, began trying more accused juveniles in adult court.

By 1994, the Kansas legislature had established a series of factors that would permit judges to transfer the cases of juveniles as young as ten years old to adult court upon request of the district attorney.

In appointing Long to be Lamonte's lawyer, Judge Podrebarac chose an attorney whose legal record was already wanting. The son of a foreman at the General Motors plant, Long had opened his law practice after passing the bar in 1987. One year later, he botched a federal case, failing to ever serve the defendant with a copy of the lawsuit he had been appointed to handle on behalf of a woman claiming discrimination based on her age and disability.

In the next three years, Long mishandled two more cases, one a bankruptcy and one a criminal appeal, by not filing the required papers to launch the proceedings. His performance was so substandard that he was given an informal reprimand and barred from representing anyone in the federal appeals court. The Kansas state attorney disciplinary board had already launched its own investigation into Long's performance even before Podrebarac appointed him to represent Lamonte.

Lamonte knew none of that. At the time, he was so sure of the rightness of his cause that he may not have cared. "Why would I need a lawyer to prove that I am innocent?" he thought as he welcomed the visit from Long, since it meant his day in court was approaching.

Lamonte did not recognize the slippery slope he was already on: A young Black kid caught up in the system, without a fierce advocate to fight the legal machinery that was geared to convict him and others like him.

On the morning of June 28, 1994, two guards showed up at Lamonte's cell. Again, they handcuffed and shackled him and led him to the prisoner elevator. This time his destination was a courtroom. It was his first time out of the cells in more than two months.

The juvenile courtroom was mostly empty for his hearing, not counting the court personnel and deputy sheriffs. But in the audience was Lamonte's mother, Rosie, and his long-absent father, James. Also in the audience was a woman Lamonte did not recognize—the mother of victim Doniel Quinn, Saundra Sublett Newsome. Years earlier, she had divorced John Quinn.

Lamonte was directed to sit at the defense table with his appointed lawyer, Gary Long, and an inexperienced young colleague with whom Long worked. Across the way were two assistants in the office of District Attorney Nick A. Tomasic: A. J. Stecklein and Terra Morehead.

The Kansas legislature established the Wyandotte County District Attorney's Office in 1972, replacing the old system of part-time prosecutors handling criminal cases. Tomasic, who had been the first assistant under the old system, was elected without opposition that year as the county's first district attorney.

He came from the same circle of local political power as Judge Podrebarac. The two had been classmates at Bishop Ward High School and again at the local Jesuit institution, Rockhurst College, which would later become Rockhurst University. Both attended St. John's, the grand church that served as a hub for the Croatian community that now dominated Strawberry Hill, and both were members of the church's Catholic Club, headquartered in the church basement and featuring a six-lane bowling alley and bar.

Tomasic had gone to law school and served in the army, just like his old classmate, but had then played minor league baseball for a time and worked as an in-house lawyer handling claims for an insurance company before entering public service.

He was immensely popular and powerful: Elected without opposition, Tomasic would go on to win eight four-year terms as district attorney,* running unopposed in six elections before he finally stepped down in 2005. He cared about his community and was proud of his role in ensuring public safety.

He also, of course, was one of the pillars of the ruling establishment. Tomasic took steps to keep politics out of the office, putting an end to the Christmas turkeys and gifts being sent to the office by the political insiders, though he faced a delicate balancing act. The longtime prosecutor cooperated with Al Jennerich and Julie Robinson in their investigation, passing along information he might learn about allegations of police misconduct. But he did so quietly, doing his best to maintain relations with the police and judges, relations that were critical as his office went about the job of public safety. Passing along information to Jennerich was one thing, but Tomasic's office was not launching its own investigations of police misconduct.

Starting from scratch, Tomasic had built up the office to a staff of more than twenty attorneys in 1994, dedicated to convicting offenders and ensuring they were locked up. Stecklein, who was taking the lead at the hearing, had just joined the office a month earlier, his first job

---

* In his first term Tomasic infuriated some powerful figures when he sought to oust two members of the municipally owned utility board for wrongdoing. He also angered members of the Black community when he brought involuntary manslaughter, not murder, charges against a white man who shot and killed a Black youth who had stoned his house on Halloween. (The man was later acquitted by a jury of even the reduced charge.) When Tomasic ran for reelection in 1976 and again in 1980, a brash lawyer named J. R. Russell challenged him, contending Tomasic had looked the other way at the embezzlement of $600,000 from the utility. The suggestion that he lacked integrity infuriated Tomasic, who called the allegations "the worst thing that has happened to me in my entire life." Tomasic brought attorney disciplinary charges against Russell for false accusations, and won more than 60 percent of the vote in beating Russell in the primaries both in 1976 and 1980. After that, until he retired, Tomasic ran unopposed.

as an attorney. Morehead had come aboard in 1988 and now handled some of the office's most serious cases.

She was known in the office for her tenacity and determination.

Long asked Lamonte moments before the hearing if he was sure no one could place him at the scene of the crime. "I'm sure," he responded. How could anyone? He wasn't there.

But then the courtroom was called to order, and Assistant District Attorney Stecklein called Ruby Mitchell to the stand. Lamonte watched as a "big-eyed skinny woman with a sad expression on her face," as he would remember her, walked into the courtroom and took her seat in the witness chair. Lamonte looked right at her because he wanted Ruby to get a full-on, clear look and see the mistake she had made. If she could just get a good look at him, this nightmare could be over.

Stecklein began by asking Mitchell about the scene that day, and what she had seen, before asking:

> Q: Did you get a close look at that shooter that day?
> A: Yes.
> Q: Do you see that shooter in this courtroom today?
> A: Yes.
> Q: Could you point him out please?

And then, to Lamonte's horror, she looked at him and pointed directly at him.

That was all Stecklein needed to ask.

Lamonte would later describe this moment in a journal into which he recorded his thoughts while he sat in his prison cell. Ruby's testimony felt "like someone was choking me and I didn't have the strength to fight them off. Who is this woman, and why was she lying on me?"

On cross-examination, Ruby Mitchell testified that she did not know Lamonte McIntyre and had never seen him before witnessing the murder. She described being with her son in her house when she was attracted outside by the noise of the Quinns' arguing. "And then that's when I seen the guy coming down the hill, and I was about to call out 'Lamont,' cause I know a Lamonte, and I was about to call out his name and that's when I seen him shoot the two down." But she did not call out, Ruby Mitchell testified, as she watched the gunman shoot the two men in the parked car.

At the police station, she said, she was shown photographs and identified "Number 3" as the shooter, without knowing his name.

Lamonte could not understand what was happening. It only got worse when Niko Quinn followed Ruby Mitchell to the stand. She didn't look familiar to him, either. Stecklein repeated his questions, and Niko testified that the killer was "right there," pointing at Lamonte, whom she said she never had seen before the day of the shootings.

Lamonte's chest got tight and he felt like he stopped breathing. What was happening? Had he blacked out and killed two strangers and just had no memory of it?

On cross-examination, Niko Quinn testified that when Golubski had come to her house the day after the shootings, she had recognized Lamonte's photograph but had been afraid to pick him out at the time. Golubski then followed Niko to the stand and described Niko's reaction that day: "She just continually held onto the picture, and I had to physically take the picture from her hand, and she became physically upset and began to cry."

That was enough for Judge Podrebarac. He ordered Lamonte to stand trial on two charges of first-degree murder. As an adult.

10
Becoming Muggz

Lamonte was led out in handcuffs and shackles, but not back to D-4.

The juvenile lockup was a paradise compared to where he was taken. In jails across the country, the men who remain locked up in county jails awaiting trial are those charged with the most serious crimes, or are poor defendants who cannot make bail. In these cells were "some of the meanest people in that place," Lamonte later recalled, men whose anger was fueled by the tension of long delays for court dates. It was enough to make men snap.

The county agreed to build the 352-cell jail after a federal judge ruled in a lawsuit brought by the ACLU in 1987 that conditions in the old jail were unconstitutionally bad, amounting to cruel and unusual punishment. The old jail, housed in the courthouse built in 1927, had long been notorious. In the 1970s, the Department of Justice sued to end the unconstitutional segregation that jailers imposed. It also cited overcrowded conditions and evidence of "numerous abuses, including beatings, homosexual attacks, and kangaroo courts."

The new jail was opened in 1990 with no bars, just secure windows. It was superficially more humane and certainly more comfortable. Each seventy-two-square-foot cell had a steel desk, a bunk, a toilet-sink combination, and hooks for clothing. But it was a dangerous place, where violence flared over nothing.

One day as Lamonte was on the phone with his grandmother, Maxine Crowder, he noticed another inmate "staring a hole in my soul," as Lamonte put it. The man recognized Lamonte for having once had relations with the woman who now carried his child.

Lamonte's frustration boiled over: "There I was waiting to go to trial for killing two people I never seen before, and I got this little ugly guy in my face talking to me about a woman I bonked before he even met her," Lamonte wrote in his diary. He began pounding on the man because "I was so angry about being in that situation that I took some of my frustration out on him."

Lamonte was no longer Short Dog. He now was known as Muggz, for the dour face he wore constantly.

Once it was transferred to adult court, Lamonte's case was assigned to J. Dexter Burdette, who six years earlier became the second Black man in history to serve on the Wyandotte County district court. Like so many judges across America, Burdette had been a former assistant district attorney, joining District Attorney Nick Tomasic's office straight out of law school. He specialized in prosecuting serious felony cases for most of his eight years there before becoming an attorney for the city, representing KCK in civil matters for three years. Then longtime Wyandotte County district judge Leo Moroney retired, and Burdette was appointed to fill the vacancy.

His appointment to the vacancy lasted only months before Burdette had to run in a contested primary against Moroney's son, Michael. Burdette won the primary, and then ran and won seven more times, without an opponent, before retiring in 2018.*

As Lamonte sat in the adult lockup, U.S. Attorney Rathbun told reporters that he had taken the "first step in cleaning up corruption in Wyandotte County," after the city's deputy chief building inspector was convicted in the U.S. District Court on bribery charges. It was the first of a series of cases that Rathbun was building based on the tape recordings and testimony of the strip club owner who testified that he had paid off the mayor and other city officials. The next step for Rathbun would be the trial of Mayor Steineger, who still enjoyed popular support. *The Kansas City Star,* incredibly, published the address where readers could contribute to a fund to pay for his legal defense.

Lamonte's case, in contrast, was receiving far less public attention, and certainly less legal support. The crime had earned three paragraphs in *The Kansas City Star* on the day following the murders, reporting Lamonte's initial arrest but nothing more. He had no legal defense fund to help hire a fancy attorney.

On July 6, 1994, Lamonte was still three weeks shy of his eighteenth birthday when he was taken for the first time into Wyandotte County adult court. The proceeding was brief; Lamonte was formally arraigned and entered his not guilty plea. Judge Burdette ordered the young defendant to be held in the adult jail on $100,000 bond, an

---

* The defeated younger Moroney would go on to win his own seat on the bench two years later.

impossibility for Lamonte's mother to raise, and appointed Gary Long to continue representing him.

Long and Burdette had been acquainted through functions of the local bar association, and had both been on the campaign trail a few years earlier. In 1988, when Burdette ran for judge the first time, Long was one of three Democratic candidates for an open seat on the Wyandotte County Commission.* After he lost that primary, Long returned his focus to the courtroom and bolstered his law practice with court appointments.

Two days after Burdette appointed him to represent Lamonte, the Kansas Supreme Court handed down its ruling that Long had violated the disciplinary rules when he botched those three federal cases. Rather than suspend Long's license, the justices imposed two years of supervised probation to give him the opportunity to show he could practice law without further errors. The court noted that Long had begun using a computer to keep track of deadlines and was now referring files that he was not experienced enough to handle to other attorneys. The court noted that Long had told state bar authorities he had "confined his practice to matters he feels qualified to handle."

Though Gary Long had little experience representing defendants in murder cases, he was willing and allowed to take on the case of Lamonte McIntyre.

Soon the summer was vanishing and September had arrived. KCK mayor Steineger and his chief of staff went on trial in federal court

* The Wyandotte County election board responded to a Freedom of Information Act request that it could not find any record of paperwork that both candidates would have been required to file, detailing their committees and contributors to their campaigns.

over the strip club owner's bribery allegations. U.S. Attorney Rathbun tried the case personally. Just like the case of the chief building inspector, the case was built on the testimony of the strip club owner and tape recordings of his conversations. After hearing it all, the jury voted to acquit both the mayor and his chief of staff. The verdict prompted the crowded courtroom audience to erupt in cheers.

City officials attended a raucous celebration at a downtown KCK nightspot afterward that went into the early morning hours. Judge Michael Moroney became highly intoxicated, got into a shouting match with another celebrant, went to the trunk of his car and pulled out a handgun before being restrained.

Police Chief Dailey told reporters that officers were investigating. No charges were ever filed.

11
"I Don't Believe This"

Days after the raucous celebration of the mayor's acquittal, Lamonte's grandmother Maxine brought a pair of tan slacks and a white shirt to the county jail. The U.S. Supreme Court had recognized two decades earlier that jurors may be prejudiced if they see a defendant in prison clothes. And the fate of her grandson was about to be decided by a jury.

The day the trial opened the local Wyandotte County newspaper, *The Kansan,* prominently displayed on its front page the news that Mayor Steineger would celebrate his acquittal by serving as the grand marshal of a parade in the neighborhood in south KCK known as the Argentine.

Lamonte's trial, in contrast, received no public attention.

Escorted by guards through a back entrance, Lamonte entered the courtroom still confident that truth would prevail. Prosecutors had two witnesses who said he committed the crime; but he had seven cousins and aunts and uncles ready to say where he actually was that day. "I was calm and confident," he wrote in his journal, "because I knew there was no way the state could convict an innocent man."

Judge Burdette took the bench. Assistant District Attorney Morehead was the assigned prosecutor, inheriting the case from Stecklein once it was transferred to adult court. Morehead had joined Tomasic's office after serving for two years as the county attorney for rural Kiowa County, which was closer geographically to Dodge City and the Old West than it was to Kansas City. After she joined Tomasic's office, Morehead had spent a few months handling juvenile cases before being assigned to adult court, where she handled sex crimes, homicides, and other serious felonies.

Lamonte's mother and the relatives who could say what Lamonte was actually doing on the day of the murders hung outside in the courthouse hallway. As prospective witnesses, they were not allowed in the courtroom, ensuring that their testimony would not be shaped by what they heard from other witnesses.

The first morning, the room filled with more than forty prospective jurors. The two attorneys chose from that group a panel of eight men and four women, plus a male alternate juror. Four Black jurors were selected.*

The pace of the proceedings was fast, as if the legal apparatus could not wait to dispense with Lamonte and move on. The jury took their seats after lunch. By the end of the day, Ruby Mitchell and Niko Quinn had completed their testimony.

* There had been nine Black people in the original pool, but one was excused for cause, and Morehead used her peremptory challenges to strike four others. Under U.S. Supreme Court precedent, Morehead cited nonracial reasons for her objections to the four: One was a mental health professional and might be sympathetic to Lamonte, one had dozed off during the selection, and two others had family members who had in the past been charged with drug crimes.

Morehead faced a strategic decision on where to start, a decision that highlights how weak the prosecution case really was. The case was built, after all, on two women who witnessed the murderer. But which one to put on first, when both had flaws? The identification by Ruby Mitchell was the basis for even arresting Lamonte in the first place. But there was a downside: Ruby settled on Lamonte McIntyre because she had the wrong Lamont stuck in her head. Alternatively, Morehead could put on Niko Quinn, the second eyewitness. But Niko's testimony was also flawed, since she had not even identified Lamonte McIntyre when she first was shown his picture. Morehead chose Niko first, then Ruby.

Both testified they were certain that Lamonte was the man they watched approach the car and pull the trigger. Ruby reiterated that she "recognized" the shooter as the Lamonte who "used to talk to my niece," but then realized, as police were creating the composite from her description, "I knew they wasn't sketching Lamonte that I knew." Niko Quinn testified that she had not identified Lamonte when Golubski came to her house the day after the shooting because she was afraid to do so.

On the second day of trial Morehead called a series of witnesses in rapid fire: Two pathologists; the witness on Hiawatha who saw the murderer get in a waiting blue sedan; and eight patrolmen and detectives who had duties the day of the murders. The lengthiest testimony came from Roger Golubski.

While the detective was on the stand, Morehead told the judge outside the presence of the jury that she wanted to elicit testimony from Golubski that the detectives focused on Lamonte because of "street talk," not because of Ruby Mitchell's identification. Golubski was prepared to testify the information "came from confidential informants, numerous confidential informants, numerous police officers obtained information with the name Lamonte McIntyre that he was responsible for that shooting. It wasn't Nikki Quinn," as the transcript reflects Morehead called her. "It wasn't Ruby Mitchell."

The claim seems implausible, given that the detectives focused on Lamonte within a couple hours of the shooting and charged him within hours. *Numerous confidential informants?* Morehead appeared determined to guard against the likely defense argument that the whole case developed because Ruby Mitchell confused Lamonte for the young man who was seeing her niece.

Judge Burdette ruled that he would permit Golubski to go part way down the road Morehead sought. The detective could testify that Lamonte's name had surfaced "from various sources." But Golubski would not be allowed to offer any more detail in direct testimony. That left unexplained who those sources were, when and where they were interviewed, and whether any notes even existed to substantiate Golubski's testimony. They were questions defense attorney Long could have asked on cross-examination, but, like so many other points, did not.

Morehead also surprised Long with another piece of testimony: About a week after Golubski first interviewed Niko Quinn, she contacted the detective and told him she wanted to meet with him again and once more view the photographs. The two met by Wyandotte High School, where Golubski again showed her the photographs and "she made a positive ID of the suspect . . . She was adamant about it."

Golubski had not written any report detailing that Niko Quinn had become a second witness who positively identified Lamonte; in fact, he never documented in writing anything about a second meeting with Niko, a significant deviation from proper police procedure. Nor had either Niko Quinn or Golubski mentioned a second meeting when they testified at the preliminary hearing, even when the detective was questioned about Quinn's failure to positively identify Lamonte when he first interviewed her. Golubski testified at Lamonte's trial that he had told prosecutor Morehead about the second meeting only *after* the preliminary hearing.

Morehead told the judge in a sidebar conversation that she had no obligation to relay what Golubski had told her about that second meeting to Long, and that Long, in any event, had never contacted her about the case or sought to review her file. "And I want the court to know that I'm under no duty or obligation to be in the habit of contacting Mr. Long to come and review this case."

By midafternoon, Morehead announced she was done, and she rested her case. That was it. The prosecution case beyond Ruby Mitchell and Niko Quinn, who both testified on the first day, was so brief the judge sent the jury home early.

The next morning it was the defense's turn. Long put on a series of cousins and aunts to testify that Lamonte was with them all day, not out shooting two men in a car on Hutchings Street. Morehead's cross-examination brought out a series of contradictions about what time of day Lamonte was at the house and what time he left. There was confusion when events such as Lamonte's calls to the cab company occurred, and who came and went during the day, though neither side apparently bothered to check with the cab company to corroborate that anyone had ordered cabs from the home of Lamonte's aunt.

The final witness was Lamonte, who testified of his memory of how he had spent the day from the time he woke up at his aunt's house the morning of April 15, 1994, through to the time police arrested him at FiFi's parking lot. He never dated Ruby Mitchell's niece, and did not know her. He did not know Niko Quinn nor Donald Ewing nor Doniel Quinn. He was not at Hutchings Street on April 15. He never owned a gun and had never fired a shotgun.

And that was the end of the case. Morehead closed by telling jurors to believe the two eyewitnesses. She told the jury she could not prove why Lamonte killed Doniel Ewing and Donald Quinn. Nevertheless, despite the lack of any evidence, Long made no objection as Morehead said, "He had a vendetta against one of them, both of them, there to settle a score."

A vendetta, of course, requires some previous connection between two parties. But the prosecution offered nothing to counter Lamonte's testimony that he did not know the two victims and had no idea who they were.

Morehead brushed off the lack of any physical evidence. "Clothes can be changed; shotguns can be thrown away." But, she noted, "I have two eyewitnesses."

The jury had no way of knowing how unreliable eyewitness testimony often is, and that thousands of convictions have been overturned after the testimony of eyewitnesses was later discovered to be mistaken. Many states permit experts in the field to take the stand and warn jurors about the many factors that make eyewitness testimony fallible, no matter how certain the eyewitness may say they are of their identifications: The inherent stress of witnessing a violent crime, especially if a weapon is involved, makes identifications less reliable; eyewitnesses tend to focus on the weapon and the crime, not necessarily on the face of the culprit. The incidents are often sudden, and quick. What witnesses are told as they try to reconstruct what they saw and how they put those pieces together also impact their identification. Factors such as lighting, distance, and the ability to observe all impact the reliability as well. Kansas is one of the dwindling number of states that prohibits experts from explaining these limitations to jurors, even in 2025.

But years before Lamonte's case, the Kansas Supreme Court ruled that in cases where the eyewitness testimony is an important part of the prosecution, and there is a "serious question" of the reliability of the identification, the jury "shall be given" a cautionary warning, during the judge's instructions, about eyewitness unreliability. Long did not ask the judge to give that instruction and Burdette ruled that, absent such a request, he was not going to do so.

That ruling was so favorable to Morehead that she feared it could lead later to a reversal by the appellate court; Morehead guarded against that risk by asking, outside the jury's presence, for Burdette to detail on the record his legal reasoning for not giving the instruction. Burdette responded that both Ruby Mitchell and Niko Quinn had a good opportunity to view the shooter, adding, "Here in court their identification of the defendant was absolute, positive, no mistake, no doubt at all."

The jury began deliberating, but soon after sent in a note: The jurors wanted to read for themselves the transcript of the testimony of Ruby Mitchell and Niko Quinn. Burdette told the jury that was "totally out of the question," but agreed the jurors could have their entire testimony read back again to them.

The jurors were sent home, and the next morning the eyewitnesses' testimony was read to them. They retired to continue to deliberate and came back with their verdicts later that morning: Guilty of first-degree murder of Doniel Sublette Quinn. Guilty of first-degree murder of Donald Ewing.

Lamonte's mother, Rosie, had been barred from sitting in the trial, even though she ended up not being called to testify. But she was inside the courtroom and burst out crying as the jury verdict was read and Burdette began polling the jurors. "I don't believe this, man," Lamonte called out, over and over again. Burdette warned him to be silent or he would be removed from the courtroom.

In his prison journal, Lamonte wrote that when he heard the jury verdict, "I went into shock and started yelling. I felt someone grab me by behind. It was my mother crying and screaming, 'Please don't take my baby away from me.' To see her in so much pain really broke my heart."

The guards led him back to his cell. The other prisoners were surprised to see him. Lamonte had not convinced the jury he was innocent, but he had persuaded *them.* They had all expected that Muggz was going to be acquitted and sent home. He later wrote, "I cried that night until I fell asleep."

12

"I'm Innocent. That's It."

The months in county jail after the conviction brought more torture. Lamonte had prayed God would fix what the State of Kansas and two witnesses' flawed identifications had broken. When that did not happen, he wrote, "God and I weren't speaking for a while. It would be a long time before God and I would have a heart-to-heart conversation."

In November 1994, Judge Burdette rejected a post-verdict motion for a new trial based on the contention of Lamonte's defense attorney, Gary Long, that the eyewitness testimony was dubious. Burdette commented he had given Long great leeway to try to undercut the testimony of Ruby and Niko, but "obviously," he wrote, the jury believed them and so did he. He set the date of January 6, 1995, for sentencing.

Lamonte's mother had seen enough of Gary Long. She was outraged by her son's conviction and determined to fix the injustice. She begged and borrowed the money to hire a real lawyer—not some court-appointed attorney who wasn't up to the job.

After Judge Burdette refused the motion by Long for a new trial and set a sentencing date, Rosie hired Carl Cornwell, one of the most well-known criminal defense attorneys in Wyandotte County, to take on the case.

Nor was Rosie leaving her son's fate to lawyers. She dressed up in men's clothing for safety and went at night into the neighborhoods off Quindaro Boulevard to find out what happened, sometimes alone and sometimes with her eldest son, James. It was scary, but what else could she do? At least one resident on Hutchings Street offered Rosie a false claim that he had witnessed the shooting and it was another man, not Lamonte, who committed the crime—a claim, Rosie would later conclude, driven not by facts but by the man's desire to make himself attractive to her.

Rosie also grabbed her Yellow Pages and found a listing high up in the alphabetized list of private investigators, the firm Action Investigations. It was run by Carolyn Adams, a former deputy sheriff in Solano County, California. She mostly stayed afloat doing background checks of potential employees for local KCK businesses.

When Rosie showed up at Caroline's office, the investigator was struck by how much this mother believed in her son's innocence and how hard she was fighting for him. Caroline was not given to just falling for a sad story from a stricken mom. She assumed Lamonte was guilty and Rosie was merely overzealous in her belief in her son's innocence, but she agreed to help. As Caroline began interviewing witnesses, she changed her view about the case. In the end, she never sent Rosie a bill.

Caroline's conversion began in the days before Lamonte's sentencing, as she interviewed Josephine Quinn, who was right there on the day of the murder, and her daughter Niko, who had testified in court that she was sure Lamonte was the man she saw shoot her cousin. Josephine told Caroline that when she went to the courtroom and saw Lamonte, she knew he was not the man who murdered her nephew.

Why had Josephine not told the prosecutor this? Josephine told Caroline that she had done so when she saw Lamonte in the courtroom during the trial. But Morehead told her it was up to the jury to decide, that her testimony was not needed, and that she could just go home.

In a separate interview two days later, Niko told Caroline that when she saw Lamonte in court she was sure he was *not* the shooter. Morehead's reaction was simple and direct: "Just go ahead" and identify Lamonte.

Lamonte's sentencing was the next day. His new lawyer, Cornwell, was at the defense table, along with Lindsey Erickson, a young associate who had recently joined his firm.

Cornwell did not mention the new evidence gathered by Carolyn Adams and simply told the judge they were not yet ready to challenge the conviction. "We've been doing some investigation," he said. He noted that he had not tried the case, and the "jury has already ruled, and whether I agree with that is not the point right now." Instead, Cornwell said, it was time to sentence Lamonte and "move on to the next phase," when they might be able to vindicate Lamonte.

Lamonte still hoped Judge Burdette would see him as "young and full of life," with his family sitting behind him. He hoped Burdette would somehow send him home with his family. As Judge Burdette asked Lamonte if he had anything to say, he swallowed the words he really wanted to say, "I hope you burn in Hell." Instead, he merely said, "Judge, I would like to tell the court that I'm innocent. That's it."

Under the strict sentencing law Kansas had adopted, Burdette faced only one decision: whether to sentence Lamonte to two consecutive life terms, or whether to let them be served concurrently, which would make him eligible for parole years sooner. Burdette said he found the decision "extremely difficult," given Lamonte's age. On the other hand, he noted, were Lamonte's past robbery conviction in the pizza case, and the fact that the murders were "one of the more savage and brutal murders" he had ever seen.

He sentenced Lamonte to two consecutive life terms in prison. That meant fifteen years per each count, before Lamonte could even ask for parole. He would be forty-eight years old by then.

PART II
TRAPPED INSIDE

13

Fresh Meat on the Block

It took about three hours for Lamonte and a couple dozen other prisoners, handcuffed and shackled, to be taken by bus from central processing in Topeka to the Hutchinson Correctional Facility. Lamonte had never been so far from home on his own.

It was cold as hell on that February day and he was wearing only his prison-issued brown pullover with matching pants. Entering B2 Cellhouse felt like walking into hell without the fire. He felt like he was outside his body looking at himself. People were screaming "fresh meat on the block" and "new booty" as he made his way to the single-person cell, about fifteen feet by about ten feet.

Lamonte was put in one of the three cells closest to the guard station so that he could be watched closely. Each time the phone rang in the guard station he thought it was the court system, calling to say they discovered that they had made a mistake in convicting him.

It was a call that never came.

Lamonte's only idea of prisons was from movies, and so he feared being raped. Even while still in county lockup Lamonte had determined that he would never be one of "those people." He began doing push-ups and lifting weights, and "conditioning my mind to survive."

The facility in Hutchinson, Kansas, 220 miles southwest of KCK, was opened in 1895 as the Kansas State Industrial Reformatory, designed to provide vocational training and education for first-time offenders under the age of thirty. It was supposed to represent the progressive ideal of rehabilitation over punishment, an idea that had originated at an institution in Elmira, New York.

Just like Quindaro, over time the idealism vanished, and five years before Lamonte arrived there the facility was renamed the Hutchinson Correctional Facility, a maximum-security prison enclosing almost 2,000 men behind a double-perimeter fence reinforced with barbed wire.

When Lamonte arrived, he found Hutchinson was filled with young, out of control gangbangers. The prisoners confined there gave the institution the nickname "Gladiator School" because of the many fights that transpired. It was, Lamonte thought to himself, an appropriate nickname.

Thrown into that violence-ridden environment, Lamonte was ready to fight to keep from getting robbed, raped, or extorted. "Other prisoners try to extort you, they take advantage of you sexually," he much later recalled. "I don't like that stuff. You see people getting raped, see people getting stabbed. Just me, sent to a place of people I didn't know. I was afraid. I was scared to death. Once I went through the gates, I couldn't go home. I didn't eat. And I was innocent."

On his first full day, Lamonte headed for the shower room. He kept on his boots and underwear: The boxers because he "didn't want perverts staring at me like I was a big piece of chocolate"; the boots, "just in case I had to prove to everyone that I wasn't a big piece of chocolate." It would be several months before Lamonte washed his hair, fearing that the water and shampoo might blind him and leave him vulnerable.

On his second day Lamonte was standing in the shower, boxers and boots on, when he saw an older inmate, balding with a full beard, looking his way with a smirk on his face. Lamonte started after him ready to tear a hole in the man. "What the hell are you looking at?" Lamonte called out. He caught himself as the man responded, "Little Brother, I don't want no troubles, I was just in a daze and you caught me deep in thought."

The next day, Lamonte was in the gym working out when three gang members stood nearby, trying to rile him. One said something about Lamonte's supposed ability to "hear a conversation in China." Lamonte was used to jokes about his big ears from friends, but not from the three Bloods making fun of him. He approached the loudest one, whom the others called Quack. Without a word, Lamonte turned and began throwing punches at Quack, knocking him to the ground.

The other two stood there, startled, as Quack warned of retribution: "I'm going to get your ass." But Lamonte did not care. The only thing flashing through his mind was that he was doomed to stay in this place for decades more, so best to show from the start that he could stand up for himself.

After several days under the guard's watchful eye, Lamonte was assigned to a cell one floor up. A fellow inmate who worked as a porter,

Lafayette Gayden, helped him carry his things up the stairs, and was struck by the sincerity of Lamonte's tone as the cell doors slammed shut: "Forget this. I'm here for something I didn't do." Not only did his complaint ring true to Gayden; Lamonte had avoided swearing over his predicament, which caught Gayden's notice.

Gayden gave Lamonte two presents that day: A porn magazine, and a rolled cigarette of Bugler tobacco. After all, Lamonte may have been old enough to be sent to jail for two lifetimes; but he was not yet old enough to buy his own pack of cigarettes at the commissary.

The cells were small, barely enough room for a single prisoner, and there was no air. It turned miserably hot in the summer, and inmates devised a system: They would fill their trash cans with ice and put a fan on top to blow the cool air.

Lamonte hated the dehumanization of the prison. The first week he ripped his number—60558—from his clothing, because that was not his name; his action earned him two weeks in solitary confinement, where he found blood and urine lining the walls. Lamonte was given one hour a day outside "the hole."

He tried every way he could think of to reject the arbitrary rules. He was sent to the mental health counselor who asked what the problem was. But she was not prepared to accept his answer: He was innocent and did not belong there. She put him on medication that dulled his senses, so he stopped taking it.

Lamonte took up writing while in custody, and before long he would write obsessively. He wrote poetry. He wrote songs. He kept a journal. He wrote about anything and everything. He also would write *on* anything; at times, he ran out of money to buy paper from the commissary and would just keep writing on toilet paper, if need be. Twice the guards took away his journals, and he would start anew.

Lamonte recorded in his journal how different prison was for him than other inmates. “When you are doing time for something you are responsible for, you can make peace with it,” he explained. “But if you don’t belong there, that is something different. Every day you wake up you feel torment. There is no way to make peace with it. You don’t feel like you’re being punished; you feel like you’re being tortured.”

He seldom spoke, but now his words were filled with curses and fury. He directed all of the hatred and anger he had for the State of Kansas toward the people he was around. Lamonte knew not to fight a guard, which would only add more time to his sentence. Time was the only thing he feared. Time was the thing he could not beat in a fight. He was facing thirty years before he could even ask for parole.

“You become something different,” he thought to himself. “I was a kid, and I was on my own. I was no longer Lamonte. I was Muggz.”

Lamonte was in Hutchinson as his nineteenth birthday came and went. Eleven months after Lamonte arrived at the prison, his lawyer Lindsey Erickson stood before the Kansas Supreme Court in January 1996, to present her oral argument why Lamonte’s appeal should be granted. Erickson was still in law school when Doniel Quinn and Donald Ewing were murdered. She had not yet been admitted to the Kansas State Bar when the jury found Lamonte guilty of two murders.

Nevertheless, Lamonte’s retained lawyer, Carl Cornwell, put his young associate in charge of challenging Lamonte’s conviction, both in a direct appeal to the Kansas Supreme Court and in a separate motion for a new trial that would be considered by Burdette.*

Erickson and Cornwell jointly signed the written legal brief on the direct appeal, outlining all the reasons the Kansas Supreme Court should overturn the verdict, and seven months later Erickson stood before the justices to present the oral argument, while prosecutor Morehead was there to defend the verdict.

Just six weeks later, in March 1996, the court unanimously brushed aside every one of Erickson's arguments and upheld Lamonte's conviction. Burdette had not erred in failing to instruct the jury about eyewitness identification since Lamonte's trial attorney, Gary Long, did not object at the time, the justices ruled. Morehead had no duty to tell Long before trial about the second meeting Niko Quinn had with Golubski in the detective's van, where Niko first identified Lamonte. There was sufficient evidence for Judge Podrebarac to order Lamonte to be tried as an adult. "We are convinced that a rational factfinder could have found the defendant guilty beyond a reasonable doubt," Justice Edward Larson concluded.

But no rational factfinder had yet even heard that Niko Quinn and her mother had sworn—even before Lamonte was sentenced—that he was not the killer.

---

* Defendants can challenge their convictions on direct appeal only by challenging errors that are part of the record from the proceedings below; in separate post-conviction proceedings, defendants can offer collateral attacks, presenting new evidence and issues that call into question the verdict.

14
Curb Your Anger

After striking out on Lamonte's direct appeal, his young lawyer put her mind to a motion for a new trial, based on affidavits from the Quinn sisters. Niko recanted her testimony that Lamonte was the shooter. Stacey provided evidence for the first time, stating in her affidavit that the detectives had never questioned her even though they were told from the start that she had seen the murders and could identify the killer.

Burdette scheduled a hearing for April 1996 to consider Erickson's motion. Lamonte, still just nineteen years old, was not brought back from Hutchinson to attend. Erickson began the hearing by telling Burdette that both sisters were "adamant" that the wrong man had been convicted of killing their cousin.

Stacey, who was serving time for violating parole over a theft conviction, was brought to court in her prison uniform. Her cousin's shooting "messed me up," she explained of her delay in coming forward, testifying that she had been terrified that the killer might come after her to ensure her silence.

After hearing from Stacey, Burdette said he was prepared to rule without hearing anything more from Niko. He did not accept Stacey's testimony, explaining, "She is a felon. She is a habitual drug user. I find it incredible, frankly, and in effect not believable that someone who watched their relatives murdered (would) not say anything about who the perpetrator was until now."

As for Niko, Burdette said he recalled Niko's trial testimony clearly, and was confident it had been reliable; he considered it implausible that she, too, waited so long to come forward if she thought Lamonte was innocent. "I find no credibility whatsoever to her recantation."

Burdette was not aware as he ruled that Niko *had* come forward and recanted in an affidavit to investigator Carolyn Adams even before Lamonte was sentenced. And he had no way of knowing that as soon as Niko had walked off the stand during the trial, she was heard sobbing outside the courtroom that authorities had forced her to falsely identify Lamonte. That information would only be known much later.

Burdette saw no reason to doubt that Lamonte was a murderer.

Lamonte quickly discovered that Hutchinson State Penitentiary was run by a strict set of rules. Prisoners had limited time out of their cells: Inmates were given only fifteen minutes at the chow hall to get their food, eat, and be back in their cell block before the door shut; if they failed, they were written up. Guards did not cut breaks for those who missed the deadline.

Meals were among the most stressful times. Seating was rigid: The Crips sat together, the Bloods sat elsewhere; Aryan Brotherhood, Mexicans, Gangster Disciples, each had their own area. Because prisoners were locked up, away from each other for most of the day, meals were where fights erupted.

Lamonte sat at a "neutral table" from the time he arrived at Hutchinson; he had sat there for months before "Baby Smooth," a Crips leader, arrived in the prison. Baby Smooth went to Lamonte's table and told him that he had to move. The table was Crips territory. Lamonte told Baby Smooth that he was not leaving. "We'll see about that," Baby Smooth replied, as he picked up his tray and walked away.

If Lamonte thought that ended things, he was wrong.

Lamonte went to work as a porter, sweeping and mopping hallways, cleaning empty cells. The job only paid $9.00 a month, but it wasn't about the money—it got him out of his cell. He could leave and patrol hallways. He could also shower on his own.

But as he lathered up days later, Lamonte noticed two Crips sent by Baby Smooth standing in the doorway of both entrances to the shower room. Lamonte was still wearing his boots and boxers for just such a moment. Seeing no choice, he told the Crips to "come on in." The two looked at each other, and back at Lamonte, and walked away. "Since both of these guys were much bigger than me, I couldn't say they were afraid of me," Lamonte wrote in the journal he kept. What protected him, he felt, was God. "In retrospect, I know now that they were terrified of what was inside of me."

Hutchinson had factory buildings where select prisoners worked for private industry, and another building for classrooms. The classes were not of interest to everyone, but Lamonte seized the opportunity. He completed high school in late 1995 and then took and completed some vocational training classes.

He largely kept to himself. He was always angry and had no interest in talking to others. When in the yard, Lamonte often chose basketball. And he was quick to battle on the court. He received advice from Mumba, a wheelchair-bound inmate who had been locked up for decades for shooting a man who had hurled a racial slur at him. After watching Lamonte on the court, Mumba could see him seething as he played aggressively. Mumba had advice for the younger man: "You have got to curb your anger."

It was difficult advice to accept.

Lamonte developed some routines to cope with the boredom. When alone in his cell, Lamonte learned to play chess the same way other prisoners did. He would start a game with someone in a neighboring cell, and they would call out moves like "A4 to G5," each move ringing out in the cellblock. Before long, Lamonte was playing for money.

Even worse than the threat of violence to Lamonte was the separation from everyone he knew and cared for. "Being alone is one of the hardest things a man can deal with while doing time," he wrote. "No one seems to understand my level of loneliness." The driving distance kept his mother away for many weeks, and his only other visitors were a brother and an aunt who came on rare occasions. In between, Lamonte was by himself with only his thoughts and dreams as company.

Lamonte shrugged off his mother's repeated advice to pray. "What kind of God would allow this much pain in someone's life?" he wrote in his journal. "I respect God but I don't mess with him. I'm too busy trying to keep my sanity. Plus, I prayed before I got convicted for a crime I didn't commit, and nothing changed. So I don't deal with God."

15

On Their Own

Rosie McIntyre had searched high and low for ways to help her son as soon as the jury had convicted him, and regularly sought the intervention of God and anyone on Earth who might be so inclined.

Even as the new defense attorneys she hired, Carl Cornwell and Lindsey Erickson, were trying to overturn the conviction, Rosie wrote to an organization she heard about named Centurion Ministries, a New Jersey–based organization run by a Princeton seminary graduate that was dedicated to helping exonerate prisoners wrongly convicted of the most serious of crimes. Rosie contacted Centurion and its founder, Jim McCloskey, and told Lamonte to follow up.

Lamonte's appeal was still pending before the state Supreme Court when he wrote to Centurion Ministries in late 1995, "Hello. My name is Lamonte McIntyre and on the day of April 15, 1994, I was accused of murdering two people in cold blood."

Lamonte then described his experience of being wrongly convicted, concluding, "So you see I am in prison for something I knew nothing about at all, and I hope that someone would see the mistakes the courts, police, and the witnesses have made."

He closed with "Write back and let me know how I did."

Centurion Ministries in those days was really just Jim and a woman named Kate Germond, who became Jim's close associate after she heard about the organization and contacted Jim out of the blue, offering to help.

To meet the deluge of letters flowing in from prisoners seeking help, they developed criteria to determine which cases to undertake. Centurion Ministries would only take on murder or rape cases—charges that led to life sentences. Before he would commit to a case Jim needed sufficient evidence that the prisoner was likely innocent, had exhausted the legal avenues, and also that the prisoner was someone whose character warranted the enormous effort required to overturn a conviction.

A part-time volunteer who helped Jim and Kate screen the letters began corresponding with Lamonte, asking for more information. Lamonte responded with details of his past record, with the unlikely identification by Ruby Mitchell of the wrong Lamont, and with Judge Burdette's rejection of the recantation by Niko Quinn. He then wrote again in August 1996: "Are you helping me with my case or do you not believe me? I have nowhere to go, no one to help. I know it's kind of hard to believe, but trust me, I didn't do this crime and don't know who did."

Lamonte heard back that Centurion was not prepared to take on his case. While he should stay in touch, the organization would only consider taking on the case once all of Lamonte's legal avenues had been exhausted.

At that point, Lamonte still had hope that the court system might do the right thing.

One day in October 1996, a guard came up to Lamonte and told him to "pack your box." He had been in Hutchinson for almost two years.

Now Lamonte was being moved to the Lansing Correctional Facility, less than thirty miles away from home.

Lansing was a far more dangerous place for inmates than Hutchinson. The state legislature approved building the Kansas State Penitentiary, as it originally was known, in 1859. Marred by delays caused by the Civil War, Lansing was opened to prisoners in 1868.

It was, for most of its existence, a maximum-security prison, the place where defendants sentenced to death were hanged, where murderers like Perry Smith and Dick Hickock whose crime became infamous in Truman Capote's book, *In Cold Blood*, were sent. In the 1980s new prison buildings went up nearby, adding not just maximum security but new medium- and minimum-security units. By the time Lamonte arrived, the population had swelled to almost 3,000 prisoners.

Gangs were rampant at Lansing just as they were at Hutchinson. But the guards at Hutchinson had been in control. Prisoners faced more restrictions at Hutchinson on when and where they could go. At Hutchinson strict rules had been more rigidly enforced, even if arbitrarily. In Lansing, Lamonte soon discovered, the prisoners were far more in control. They had more freedom to leave their cells, and knifings and rapes occurred in poorly monitored rooms.

While mealtimes were a tinderbox at Hutchinson, at Lansing trouble could erupt any time. Lamonte quickly discovered the prisoners sentenced to the maximum-security unit, where he was sent, were older and more hardened than the population at Hutchinson. Many were doing life sentences, so they had much less fear of penalties for violent conduct as there was no parole to lose.

Still, Lansing was filled mostly with prisoners from the streets of KCK, not the western part of the state. Many knew of Lamonte or his older cousins and uncles, some of whom were gang members and involved in the drug trade.

It was, Lamonte thought, like returning to the United States from a foreign country. And best of all, Rosie could now see her son weekly.

Lamonte had been in Lansing just a couple of months when word arrived that the Kansas Supreme Court had upheld Judge Burdette's decision denying a new trial despite the Quinn sisters' affidavits rescinding their eyewitness testimony. His mother was out of money. Erickson and Cornwall were done representing Lamonte; there was nothing more they could do for him.

He was heartbroken. "What am I going to do?" kept playing in his head. The images of his mother crying, and of spending years in an institution where inmates were stabbed over 21¢ soups, were more than he could bear.

Every time he closed his eyes, Lamonte had recurring visions of the day he was arrested. What he was doing that day. The last time he saw his mother. And then, once he fell asleep, Lamonte would dream he was getting out.

But each morning, Lamonte awoke to the truth that nothing had changed. He was in prison, facing the same routine. Sleep was always going to be a problem, because he wanted to avoid those recurring images.

Some prisoners, like "Lil C" whom Lamonte befriended, could not cope. "Lil C," the moniker of Marcus Clemons, was serving ninety-nine years for one count each of murder and attempted murder. He fought his case as long as he could; but one morning guards found "Lil C" dead in his cell with a sheet wrapped around his neck. That night, Lamonte cried in his cell.

None of it made sense. Niko, her mother, and her sister—who all saw their close relative murdered—were insisting that Lamonte was not the killer, and yet Lamonte remained locked in Hell and authorities were not doing anything about it. Lamonte and his mother became increasingly desperate to find a way out.

Rosie wrote an article about the case that was published in *Cry Justice*, a journal of an evangelistic church dedicated to helping expose injustice. "I have paid every dime I could make, over $9,000, and still owe more," she wrote. "And now my lawyer said there is nothing more we can do." Her article concludes, "My son and I are again on our own."

Lamonte quickly discovered that at Lansing, as at Hutchinson, the guards were generally "horrible." Many were racist and meted out punishment for no apparent reason. Like other prisoners, Lamonte was treated as though he had no rights; anything, big or small, could be taken from him at any time.

Within weeks of being sent to Lansing, he was disciplined for too much noise from the music he played on the radio in his cell. It felt like a joke. "Too much noise!" Lamonte would later reflect. "There was noise everywhere in that place. And they write me up for that?"

Saturdays in the chow line, the menu was always cheeseburger and fries. Disgusting cheeseburgers, Lamonte thought, but cheeseburgers all the same. One day, a guard noticed another prisoner passing his own cheeseburger over to Lamonte for him eat. The guard ordered Lamonte to throw the second cheeseburger away, for no good reason. It was like that all day every day.

Guards would block prisoners from even getting ice in the summer, saying that the machine was broken. For months.

As Lamonte saw it, the guards make you think you're not a human being.

Not all of the guards were so cruel. But Lamonte had no use for the ones who whispered their sympathy upon seeing abuses inflicted by other guards, because despite their kind words they would say there was nothing that they would do to intervene. "That's not helpful," Lamonte thought. "That's nothing. When you see something wrong, do something about it."

Drugs were everywhere. So was "hooch," the moonshine whiskey that prisoners made.

Getting ahold of drugs was easy. The prisoner next to him would get weed from guards. Lamonte took full advantage, smoking grass regularly. For a time, that was how he got through the day, smoking joints from the time he woke up until he went to sleep. It was the only way he could avoid the reality of being in prison for a crime he did not commit.

Lamonte never did anything more than smoke marijuana, but plenty of other drugs flowed through the prison. "You go into a certain room and guys were shooting up. People would OD. There was heroin and crystal meth," Lamonte recalled. "I couldn't be there all my life."

16
Another Door Closed

The clock was ticking.

Under Kansas law, once convictions have been upheld and the post-verdict appeals completed, prisoners have a year to file any habeas corpus petitions, which permit convicted prisoners to challenge their convictions by proving some constitutional error or a manifest injustice. Strict time limits were becoming common across the country in the late twentieth century as judges and politicians fretted about endless appeals. In 1996, Bill Clinton signed into law the Antiterrorism and Effective Death Penalty Act, which made it considerably more difficult to get cases before a federal judge. Getting the petition to state court was everything.

But time was running out. Lamonte had no lawyer and was certainly no expert on the law. He just knew he was innocent of the crime and that this was his chance to fix on his own the injustice that his lawyers had been unable to fix. For a time, Lamonte's bunk was covered in legal documents. He would sit on an overturned trash can, trying to make sense of the legal papers scattered over his mattress. He needed to amass a filing that would make it clear to everyone that he had been wronged.

He was not yet twenty-one, still too young to buy a bottle of liquor, and the pressure was intense. This was his one shot, he needed to get it right, and he needed to file on time. Several "jailhouse lawyers," who had been locked up for years, and had learned plenty about the legal system, some of it accurate and some of it not, "graciously" offered just the help he needed, for a price.

There was all this pressure to file stuff quickly. "Hurry, hurry, the law has time limits," Lamonte would later recall. One veteran prisoner offered his legal expertise for $1,000; another could add his own insight for $800. Everybody had an idea, and everybody wanted money. Where does that money come from?

So he did what he knew best; he began hustling. He would win money from betting on himself in basketball games, on dominoes, on chess. He would scrape together money to buy things—cigarettes, chips, whatever commodity prisoners wanted—and resell it on credit.

He struck up relations with a female guard, a guard who seemed sympathetic to him and whom he sensed he could persuade to help him. Enlisting her was about the most dangerous thing Lamonte could do. The prison system acted most harshly against prisoners who subverted the disciplinary system by involving guards, especially female guards, in their illicit behavior. But Lamonte was desperate, and soon the guard was smuggling in contraband in Big Mac containers for Lamonte to sell. She brought in cologne, an item prisoners widely sought for those cherished weekends when visitors showed up; and drugs, the gold standard of goods for sale.

"It was a commodity for me. I didn't do it for comforts," he wrote of the contraband in his journal. "I did it because I needed money to fight for my freedom."

Lamonte was not afraid his drug dealing would result in criminal charges, adding more time to his prison time, the same way he feared the results if he punched out a guard. After all, a drug charge would expose the guards, so nobody was going to prosecute him for selling the drugs; it felt safe. At worst, he might end up in the hole on a disciplinary charge.

By the spring of 1997, Lamonte was ready. He had cobbled together a habeas petition that he sent to be filed in Wyandotte County. The petition reflected the limits of jailhouse lawyering.

It presented as "Issue 1" that the court failed to instruct the jury on lesser offenses to first degree murder. But that wasn't really an issue in Lamonte's case, because whoever committed the crime almost certainly had committed a premeditated double murder. The issue in Lamonte's case was whether he was the killer. But jailhouse lawyers knew that defendants were entitled to instructions on lesser-included offenses, and so they sold Lamonte that advice.

The petition did not include any other enumerated issues, but contended police should have questioned Lamont Drain, the "other Lamonte" who was seeing Ruby Mitchell's niece. The petition also contended Lamonte's trial attorney, Gary Long, engaged in a "lack of diligence" by not putting on more of a defense, failing to call two witnesses who seem unlikely, in retrospect, to have been of much value to Lamonte's defense.* And it cited Long's failure to ask that the judge instruct the jury about eyewitness identification. "The defendant is

* One was the man Rosie McIntyre talked to, who gave her bogus information when she went into the neighborhood following her son's conviction; the other was Ruby Mitchell's niece, who could have said she did not know Lamonte McIntyre.

not the guilty party in this case, he's been accused of something that he did not do," the petition Lamonte wrote about himself concludes.

The American legal system was changed forever after a Florida prison inmate named Clarence Earl Gideon wrote a five-page habeas corpus petition to the U.S. Supreme Court in 1963. Gideon had been convicted of breaking and entering into a Panama City pool hall and taking wine, beer, and a pocketful of quarters. Gideon had no money for a lawyer and represented himself at the 1961 trial after the judge refused to appoint a lawyer for him; Florida law at the time only provided state-paid lawyers in capital cases, when the death penalty was at stake.

The U.S. Supreme Court took up Gideon's petition and unanimously ruled that the Sixth Amendment right to assistance of counsel applied not only to federal trials but to state prosecutions as well, under the 14th Amendment guarantee of due process. Gideon was entitled to a lawyer paid by the state.

In another case two decades later, the U.S. Supreme Court ruled that defendants had the right not just to an attorney, but to *effective* representation. After all, Lady Justice cannot succeed in an adversarial system if the scales of justice are totally lopsided. Inherently, the system is weighted against the defense. Defense attorneys do not have the same investigative ability as prosecutors, who have at their disposal an entire police force supplemented by the prosecutor's own investigators. On top of that, many defense lawyers work on their own or in small offices, without the training and supervision afforded prosecutors.

Judges are loath to overturn convictions based on defense missteps. They are not about to second-guess strategic decisions that seemed reasonable at the time but proved unsuccessful. They particularly defer to jury decisions and favor finality over letting courts be bogged down endlessly with challenges.

To win a new trial because of incompetent representation, the U.S. Supreme Court has said that a defendant must show not just ineffective representation, but also that the bad lawyering likely affected the outcome of the case. That has proven to be a high bar for defendants to clear. Courts have upheld convictions even when the defendants present evidence that their lawyers slept through portions of the trial. They have upheld convictions even if the defense lawyers were proven to be drunk or high on drugs throughout trials.

And there certainly is no bright line that establishes a defense lawyer's ineffectiveness if the attorney fails to fully examine crime scenes, to track down witnesses, to adequately prepare alibi witnesses, or to ensure jurors understand the unreliability of eyewitness identification. In other words, the kinds of issues that were raised in Lamonte's case.

Weeks after Lamonte filed his petition, he found himself in new trouble. Guards came to his cell and accused him of stealing the radio, tapes, and headphones in his cell. They took him to the Intelligence and Investigations Unit at Lansing, known to the prisoners as I & I.

He was questioned there about a break-in by inmates to the prison property room, during which the intruders did thousands of dollars' worth of damage to televisions and other equipment and stole several radios.

Lamonte insisted he knew nothing about the break-in, but the case was referred to the local district attorney. He was criminally charged and sent to solitary. Lamonte later learned the crime had been committed by three other inmates with whom he was close. But none of them came to his aid, and he was left to face the charges on his own. From that moment on, he stopped trusting even those he had thought of as "friends" and "partners."

Lamonte produced receipts that proved he purchased each of the items from the prison store. This time, finally, Lamonte was cleared of charges for a crime he did not commit. He wrote a note in his journal: "Why would they charge me with something I had nothing to do with? It seems to be the recurring theme of my life."

Despite being cleared of wrongdoing, Lamonte was sent back to Hutchinson, farther away from both Rosie and the court system where his habeas petition was to be considered.

Inartful as it was, Lamonte's petition was sent back to Judge Burdette, who scheduled a hearing and appointed a private attorney named Mark Sachse to the case.

Sachse had once been a respected local criminal defense attorney. Back when KCK Mayor Steineger was put on trial three years earlier, Sachse had represented his codefendant, the chief of staff. But by the time Burdette assigned him to Lamonte's petition, Sachse was mishandling one case after another.

Lamonte, who was still just twenty-one years old, was victimized for a second time by a system that is supposed to protect the rights of indigent defendants. Lamonte never heard from the lawyer the entire time he was being paid by the state to represent him.

Judge Burdette scheduled a hearing on the petition for October 1997. It was three years since the trial, and Lamonte remained locked up in Hutchinson, hundreds of miles away. Rosie had learned the hearing was upcoming and talked about it with Niko Quinn, who agreed to have her mother, Josephine Quinn, show up at the courtroom that day. Rosie hoped Josephine could repeat in court what she had told the investigator that Rosie picked out of the Yellow Pages years earlier: That Josephine saw as soon as she arrived at the courtroom for the trial that Lamonte was not the man she had seen commit murder. Josephine told Sachse of that memory and added that she had told prosecutor Morehead of the mistake at the time, but that Morehead responded by telling Josephine Quinn that the matter was in the jury's hands, and she could go home. Sachse assisted Josephine in writing a statement that the attorney made sure was notarized right there in the courthouse that day.

But the hearing did not go on that day. When the rescheduled hearing took place, Josephine Quinn was not present and Sachse did not tell Judge Burdette about her affidavit or any other new evidence. Instead, the judge heard arguments by Sachse and Morehead on whether, based on the evidence already in the record, Gary Long had failed to effectively represent Lamonte, especially by failing to seek an instruction on eyewitness identification.

Burdette was unpersuaded by Sachse's argument. "I can find absolutely nothing in Mr. Long's efforts on behalf of Mr. McIntyre that would rise to the level of ineffective assistance of counsel," Burdette ruled. "Defendant's not entitled to the best attorney available, he's not entitled to the worst attorney available. He's entitled to adequate assistance of counsel and under the circumstances and facts and demands of this case, he got that, and I am convinced he got that."

Neither Lamonte nor his mother Rosie knew the rescheduled hearing was even taking place that day, and word of Burdette's latest denial apparently was slow to get to Lamonte. Weeks after the hearing,

Lamonte mailed from Hutchinson a motion asking that he be transported to Wyandotte County so he could be present at the hearing, apparently unaware it was already decided. He also submitted a second motion asking for a different appointed lawyer, complaining that Sachse was not in contact with him about the hearing that Lamonte believed was still upcoming.* And he asked that the proceedings be delayed until his requests could be considered.

Several weeks later, Burdette huddled with Morehead and Sachse about Lamonte's requests. They agreed that, since the habeas motion had already been decided, Lamonte's new requests should be denied as "moot."** Another door had slammed shut.

---

* Sachse would later give an affidavit saying that was just the way things were done in those days in Wyandotte County.

** When Lamonte received Burdette's ruling, he was puzzled; he had never heard the word "moot."

17
Not the Finest

When Judge Burdette was considering whether attorney Gary Long had failed to provide Lamonte with effective representation during the initial trial, the State of Kansas was considering whether he should be practicing law at all. His poor representation had received a private admonition in 1992, and then the state Supreme Court had put him on probation in 1994 after new complaints were filed against him.

Long served out that probation, but complaints about his representation were continuing to arrive at the Kansas Disciplinary Board. A U.S. district judge filed a complaint after Long had twice failed to appear for hearings that the judge scheduled to consider Long's motion to suppress evidence in a drug case. An attorney filed a separate complaint about Long's mishandling of a case concerning a contract to sell land.

Once a complaint is filed against an attorney, the state disciplinary board undertakes a preliminary investigation and holds hearings, if necessary. For cases not dismissed nor resolved informally, the board recommends discipline to the Kansas Supreme Court. The Court metes out discipline that can range from public censure to probation to suspension to disbarment.

The standard for whether an attorney is subject to discipline is completely separate from the requirement that attorneys provide their clients facing criminal charges with effective representation. The disciplinary process is based instead on the Model Rules of Professional Conduct, developed by the American Bar Association and adopted in some form by Kansas and most states, that cover everything from how attorneys handle clients' money to whether they display proper decorum in the courthouse.

The vast majority of the 8,000 or so Kansas lawyers spend their career without ever facing public discipline. An original review undertaken for this book establishes just how badly attorneys have to act to put their licenses in jeopardy.*

The review revealed a forgiving system, with the disciplinary board and the courts often struggling to safeguard the livelihood of errant lawyers while also trying to accomplish the overriding responsibility to protect the public from shoddy attorneys. Many of those who receive public discipline, like Long, are repeat offenders. Fewer than ten lawyers a year face disbarment statewide.

The review documented that attorneys who steal or misappropriate their clients' money, especially those charged with crimes of dishonesty, are likely to face harsh discipline. Attorneys who fail their clients by missing deadlines, failing to show up in court, or not telling their clients what is going on in their cases tend to face significant trouble

---

* That review involved every disciplinary case identifiable in a search of the Kansas Supreme Court over a period of nearly two decades, from late 1996 to late 2015, a period largely covering Lamonte's legal case. The published cases represent only a small fraction of the complaints; most, of course, are handled informally or simply dismissed. Of the 525 cases that resulted in public discipline—roughly 27 per year—the Supreme Court issued 171 suspensions ranging from one month to indefinite, and the court disbarred 166 lawyers. Another 112 complaints ended in probation or public censure.

only if they commit those failures repeatedly. Little regard is given to the client, who likely only had this one chance at mounting an effective defense.

At times the courts appeared to show greater concern to matters involving money than about the representation of those facing criminal charges; in one case the court ruled against suspending an errant lawyer; instead, he was barred from taking more civil matters while on probation. But the lawyer was permitted to continue to represent defendants in criminal cases, as if the risk of losing one's liberty was less weighty than losing one's money.

Criminal defense attorneys who show up when they are supposed to and present their cases are unlikely to be disciplined, no matter how poorly they serve their clients. It took a level of atrocious lawyering accomplished by a lawyer named Ira Hawver to get the state Supreme Court to step in over an attorney's dreadful criminal representation. Hawver represented a client in a capital murder case, though he had never before handled a death penalty case and later admitted he had no appreciation for the effort required in such cases. He did no pretrial investigation and did not prepare for jury selection. At trial, he told the jurors about his client's prior manslaughter conviction, and then told them, in the penalty phase, that whoever committed the murders deserved the death sentence. Hawver undoubtedly did not help his cause by showing up for the state Supreme Court disciplinary hearing dressed as Thomas Jefferson. But Hawver's was the only case identified of a criminal defense attorney disciplined for incompetent courtroom representation throughout the twenty-four years covered by the review.

In contrast, Long's 1997 board hearing was over not one botched case but repeated failures to follow judges' directives, like showing up for a hearing even after his earlier probation. This time, the disciplinary panel concluded that enough was enough, and recommended that the state Supreme Court suspend Long for a year from practicing law. While that recommendation was pending, two *more* complaints were filed against Long. At that point, he voluntarily surrendered his license to practice law. Weeks later, the state Supreme Court unanimously voted to disbar him from practicing law; he would be one of nine Kansas attorneys to be disbarred in 1998.

The decision to disbar Long over his pattern of poor representation did not even include Lamonte's case. No one had filed a complaint about Long's performance in the double murder case, and Judge Burdette had after all ruled it was quite adequate.

Mark Sachse, appointed by Judge Burdette to handle Lamonte's post-conviction claim of ineffective assistance of counsel had, if anything, a string of mishandled cases that was even more disturbing than Long's. When he was appointed to Lamonte's case, Sachse was representing the family of a seven-year-old boy who had been hit by a car while his family was visiting KCK from their home 150 miles away. Sachse filed a lawsuit on behalf of the family members, but then he failed to respond to a series of requests for discovery by the defendants, even after he was ordered to respond by the judge. The case was finally dismissed because of Sachse's neglect, a fact Sachse did not tell the family. When the family rented a car and came to town two months later for a scheduled pretrial hearing, Sachse met them at the courthouse and told them only that the hearing was "canceled," not that the entire case had been dismissed weeks earlier.

Sachse also had been appointed, while he represented Lamonte, to represent another defendant in his direct appeal of a first-degree murder conviction. But Sachse never contacted his client, nor file the required appellate brief with the Supreme Court.

Those two cases were among several in which the state disciplinary board found the attorney had violated his ethical obligations to adequately represent his clients. He repeatedly harmed clients by failing to file necessary documents or to show up in court on their behalf, the court found. And in each of the cases, just like in Lamonte's case, Sachse failed to communicate with his clients.*

In July 2000, the Kansas Supreme Court ordered Sachse to be placed on supervised probation for his mishandling of seven cases. Less than a year after Sachse served out that probation, the disciplinary board scheduled a hearing in seventeen different new complaints about Sachse failing to perform work he was hired to do, and failing to respond to phone calls and letters from clients trying to learn what was going on in their cases. As that hearing was pending, Sachse voluntarily surrendered his license. The state Supreme Court finally voted, in September 2007, to disbar Mark Sachse from the practice of law.**

The odds of a judge appointing an attorney whose representation across multiple cases would prove so inadequate that it justified disbarment are very small, in Kansas or anywhere. It would be extraordinarily unlikely that a judge would appoint, at different stages in one case, two different attorneys whose woeful representation would lead to their disbarment.

And yet that was Lamonte's luck.

---

* In Lamonte's case, of course, no one complained about Sachse's failure to stay in touch with his client; Burdette was satisfied to write it off as "moot" when it was clear that Lamonte had not been informed of the hearing that would decide his appeal.

** Once disbarred, Sachse found a new career as a licensed stockbroker. But following a client's complaint that Sachse defrauded him, Sachse was barred from serving as a broker.

18
Dead in the Water

Prisoners had no privacy. The guards opened and read their mail. They listened to their telephone calls. As they heard Lamonte constantly discussing his innocence with Rosie, they set out to do something about it.

They came to his cell and took his legal papers from him to examine them. They told him they wanted him to take a lie detector test.

But they did not want him to do so to help his case. They wanted to prove that he was guilty, that he could *not* pass a lie detector test, so his mother could move on with her life. "Give her some peace," a guard said. "Let's see how innocent you are."

Lamonte refused to take part in their game.

In December 1998, guards came into his cell in the middle of the night. Another prisoner had told the guards that Lamonte was high on drugs.

He was taken to a room and forced to give a urine sample. Afterward, he was sent to the hole for twenty-one days for the "use of stimulants," in this case marijuana. The penalty also carried sixty days of restricted time, which curtailed the right of prisoners to make telephone calls, to have visits, to shop at the commissary.

Sitting in the hole for that long, Lamonte had time to do major soul-searching. He was in "the worst place on earth." As long as he was stuck there, he was never going to get high again.

Lamonte was still in his early twenties and was unprepared for the reality that his life was stuck in place while everyone else moved on. Brothers had babies. Cousins got married. His sister built a house from the ground up. That reality left him depressed and angry. The state had taken his life, and he felt family members turned their backs on him. He expected to see them marching in front of the courthouse with signs that said, FREE LAMONTE. HE IS INNOCENT. But that never happened. It left him feeling abandoned.

In February 2000—about a year after Lamonte had last been in the hole—he was told he was being moved back to Lansing. He got a job as a wood router for the cabinet maker Prime Wood, one of the companies that had a factory inside Lansing. Like the other prison workers, he would get paid $7.00 an hour to build cabinets for retail sale.

Out of that modest sum, there were a series of deductions for room and board, for a victim's fund, for mandatory savings. By the time the deductions were done, Lamonte was getting a check for about $150.00 every ten days.

The prisoners who received the jobs also were required to sign papers waiving their right to sue over the arrangement. It was a bad deal, but still better than the $9.00 a month that working as a porter paid. And besides, the point of the job was not the money. It was to get out of the prison cell in which he was trapped.

Before too long, Lamonte wrote a letter, "To whom it may concern," explaining that he was convicted of a double homicide and sentenced to two life terms. "The problem with this conviction is I'm not the person who committed this crime I'm doing time for," he wrote.

He sent the letter to anyone and everyone he could think of: The University of Kansas law school, Oprah Winfrey, *60 Minutes*, the Innocence Project. He saw an article in *Jet* magazine featuring the New Jersey seminary graduate, Jim McCloskey, and he wrote once again to Centurion Ministries. Most of the letters he mailed went unanswered, but that was not true of Centurion Ministries, which as a policy answered every one of the thousands of prisoners who wrote to the organization.

Lamonte began corresponding anew with Centurion Ministries, reminding them of his earlier correspondence. He had now exhausted his legal avenues, he wrote, and his case was "dead in the water." He had been locked up for eight years, and had nowhere else turn. As he wrote to Centurion in early 2003, "I have no money and I don't know where to go from here, so I'm asking for your help. If you could just look at my case you would see that I shouldn't be here."

Lamonte's case was assigned to a volunteer named Jock McFarlane, a retired physicist at RCA headquarters with a keenly analytic mind.* McFarlane had heard Jim McCloskey speak about Centurion Ministries at their church and signed up to help; Lamonte's was his first case.

McFarlane began asking Lamonte for a series of documents as well as for him to write about his background, and to answer questions about the case, questions that helped the organization determine which cases were most worth the incredible time required to prove innocence. Getting answers wasn't always easy; Lamonte encountered trouble getting some court documents from inside his cell. His mother, Rosie, went repeatedly to the courthouse to help gather what he needed; but the emotional toll and mental strain on Rosie were tremendous.

Lamonte became concerned when, at one point, Rosie did not answer several telephone calls he placed to her. He called his grandmother, Maxine, to ask how everybody was doing, and could tell by the sound of her voice that something was wrong.

"Your mother is in a mental hospital," his grandmother said. Lamonte felt like he had died; he knew there was nothing he could do about the strain his imprisonment had on his mother. His mother, the strongest woman he knew, had raised five children with no help from his father and had done so without complaint. But his imprisonment had put an unbearable strain on her and there was nothing he could do about it. As Lamonte put it, "That thought hurt me to the core because it was all because of me."

* For years Lamonte believed Jock's last name was Hanford, because the volunteer had initially felt the need to use a fake last name when corresponding with prisoners.

Unable to trust any fellow prisoners and with his mother ill, Lamonte struggled with loneliness. And with each year, Lamonte became increasingly focused on the lack specifically of female companionship. He thought about women. He talked about women. He dreamt about women.

One young woman especially caught Lamonte's eye. She was a teenager about the age he had been when he first was locked up. Corisha Josenberger would come each weekend to visit her brother, Cortez, who was convicted on charges of murder and robbery. She occasionally brought along her infant son Marvieon, who otherwise stayed with Corisha's mother while she visited.

The first time they talked, Lamonte was standing in front of her in line at the concession stand. He asked how she was, and they started talking. Lamonte was twenty-seven, but Corisha felt it was as if they were the same age, how easy it was to talk to him.

They became friends. When Corisha visited Cortez, Lamonte would ask how Marvieon was doing. He seemed generally concerned about Corisha and her life. Before too long, Lamonte told Cortez, "I'm going to marry your sister."

Transfers between prisons occurred quickly and unceremoniously. Prisoners were rarely given a reason. They were just told to pack up and leave.

When Cortez was transferred out of Lansing, that left Corisha with a decision: She could not be on Lamonte's visitation list at one facility, and on her brother's list at another. She told her brother that she was not going to remain on his list.

Within weeks, Corisha became a regular, visiting Lamonte twice a week without fail. She knew nothing about Lamonte's legal case, and did not care. Now when she came to visit, they could greet each other with a brief hug and kiss. And, similarly, when the stay ended.

Their relationship developed, despite the barriers. A full decade since he first was wrongly convicted, Lamonte's improbable dream was realized; a pastor from Leavenworth whom the prison arranged for, improbably named Tom Sawyer, came to Lansing prison in November 2004, and married them. The prison rules that limited prisoners' touching visitors were loosened in the chapel. That day, the hugging and kissing lasted longer.

In his letter to Jock that month Lamonte wrote of seeing television shows about other prisoners who were exonerated, which would make him ponder, "When will it be my time to feel that kind of joy? Ten years is a long time. But I can see the ending of my story. That's a good thing. I know I shouldn't be here and when the time is right, I know this nightmare will end . . . Hopefully this road to the truth is a short one."

That optimism was short-lived.

Holidays are the worst time, Lamonte wrote in his journal, the time when "memories of being with family and friends are covered with harsh realities of loneliness and despair."

Deep into winter, Lamonte felt that he had made a horrible mistake asking Corisha to marry him. She was going to waste her life waiting.

When she and Marvieon came to visit, Lamonte told her not to come back anymore. Corisha wanted to know what happened, but Lamonte would not offer an explanation. He told her she needed to leave and not come back.

With that, he got up and left her sitting in the visiting room, devastated. She vowed to herself never to return. Years later, divorce papers arrived for Lamonte in prison.

One result of the nationwide push in the 1980s for tougher sentencing laws to combat crime has been the aging of so many prisoners. Men locked up for decades grow sick and die while in custody.

In the back of the clinic section of Lansing prison was the hospice section. A prison social worker who heard from Lamonte that he was desperate to spend less time in his cell recommended that he begin volunteering to help in that section. It was there that Lamonte met Shorty, a prisoner from Mississippi who was dying from lung disease and had trouble breathing.

Shorty was on a breathing machine. Yet, to Lamonte's amazement, he kept a tremendously positive attitude. Shorty knew the Bible from front to back, and Lamonte began sitting with Shorty to talk about life, about God, and about regrets. Spending time with Shorty brought Lamonte a new way of looking at things.

About two months went by, with Lamonte visiting regularly and absorbing Shorty's message. Shorty then was transferred to another prison. But his serenity, even knowing he might die any day, stayed with Lamonte. And Lamonte prized his copy of the Bible that was filled with stick-on notes and passages annotated from the time they spent together.

Despite the extreme tests his faith had already endured, after his time with Shorty, Lamonte became even more dedicated both to God and to fighting for his freedom.

Lamonte used to go into the prison barber shop when there was no barber working and give himself shaves and haircuts.

He became pretty good at it. Before long, other prisoners would ask him to cut their hair. Weekends, after all, were the time when loved ones came to visit, and everyone wanted to look their best for those visits.

Lamonte charged $5.00 for a haircut. And though he didn't have a state license—and wasn't legally cutting hair—suddenly he found he could make way more money cutting hair than what he could earn at the prison factories of private industry.

So he went to one of the corrections officials with whom he had a relationship. And though Lamonte hadn't gone through the formal training, he was given authority to put on a barber's uniform and cut inmates' hair.

He was in business.

19

No One Gets to Skate Through Life

Lamonte kept up his correspondence with the Centurion volunteer, Jock McFarlane. Often, he would hear things in the prison and pass them on to Jock, though Lamonte had no way to establish what was true and what was bullshit. There was the information Lamonte passed on in September 2005, that he heard from another prisoner that Lamont Drain had confessed to the murders.* Often Jock would write back seeking more information, some of which Lamonte could answer and some of which involved documents that Rosie, who had recovered from her breakdown, had to track down.

Following that note about Lamont Drain, Jock heard nothing from Lamonte for three months, a period when Lamonte was feeling hopeless. Finally Lamonte wrote again, explaining the delay to Jock: "I been going through a lot since you heard from me last. I been really trying to focus on my purpose in life according to God . . . Jesus warned that we would have problems in this world. No one gets to skate through life 'Problem Free'! Knowing this, it's easy for me to understand some of what I'm experiencing. But it's hard to walk in Christ when the

---

* There was no truth to that tale.

pain is constant. I just find it difficult at times being the person I was created to be."

Jock sent a series of additional questions: What was the jury composition? What was that juvenile armed robbery guilty plea? What was his involvement in drugs?

Lamonte turned thirty years old in June 2006, and birthdays, like other holidays, were losing their meaning. He answered Jock the following month: "I was not someone you would consider 'big time' in the drug trade. I was just a kid selling pieces of cocaine to buy stuff like shoes and whatever else a teenager might find interesting. I smoked weed almost every day." He concluded, "The only thing I have on my side is God and the truth. No matter how bad that truth may make me look."

The correspondence slowed. The day after Christmas that year, Lamonte wrote to Jock again: "I know it's been some time since I wrote but you did tell me to watch for the mail. My faith is still in place and God is still working on my spirit. I understand the importance of patience now that I'm living according to God's will. I'm not saying it's easy. Hopefully this will be the last year of this experience."

Nine months went by. In August 2007, Lamonte wrote to Jock, "I'm learning to be still and allow God to be God. I'm not saying I'm happy to be here . . . I know something is going to happen on my behalf concerning my case and I know Centurion Ministries will have a lot to do with it."

Six more months elapsed. In February 2008, Lamonte answered more questions from Jock. "The only thing I can tell you about Lamont Drain is what I told you before. I'm not saying he's the shooter because I don't know that for certain. However, the evidence points more to him than me."

Three more months went by, but then a possible breakthrough appeared. In May 2008, Rosie wrote Centurion Ministries a typed letter headlined, NEW INFORMATION REGARDING A STATEMENT FROM A WITNESS ABOUT THE CASE OF LAMONTE MCINTYRE. Rosie reported that Doniel Quinn's mother, Saundra Sublett Newsome, had reached out to her. Saundra's ex-husband, John Quinn, told Saundra that he knew Lamonte had not killed their son. Instead, John said, Doniel was killed because of drugs that John had stolen from a drug dealer and given his son to hold.

In her letter to Centurion, Rosie wrote that Saundra said she "was going to help me get my son Lamonte McIntyre out because she doesn't want the wrong person in jail." Saundra said she was willing to go jointly with Rosie to talk to John, and Saundra was even willing to tape-record the conversation.

This was one more stunning development, the type of information, if provable, that could help bring life to a dormant and seemingly hopeless case. Jock wrote back to Lamonte with the question Lamonte and Rosie had been praying for ever since Lamonte first wrote to Centurion Ministries more than a dozen years earlier: Could Lamonte make arrangements for Jim McCloskey, the Centurion Ministries director, to come to Lansing prison to visit?

PART III
UNCOVERING INNOCENCE

20

Winning the Lottery

Jim McCloskey flew from Philadelphia to Kansas City in March 2009, to finally meet Lamonte and deliver in person what Lamonte had been waiting for years to hear: Centurion Ministries was taking on his case. Lamonte was thirty-three years old and had spent almost half his life locked up, and all that time waiting for someone, anyone, to help end his nightmare.

Jim was struck by how subdued Lamonte seemed to his arrival, the thing Lamonte had wanted for so long. As they sat together in the prison waiting room at Lansing, Lamonte was, at least outwardly, emotionless. "Do you understand what I'm telling you?" Jim asked. "You just won the lottery."

His comment reflected his confidence, built on the strong record of success that Centurion Ministries had accomplished both by being selective in which cases to embrace, and by the doggedness Jim brought to ferreting out the truth.

By 2009, when that first meeting took place, Centurion Ministries was receiving more than a thousand letters a year from prisoners all over the country, and even some from other countries. Its success was astonishing. By the time Jim was prepared to commit to take on Lamonte's case, Centurion had built the evidence that led to the exoneration of dozens of wrongly convicted men. Just between February 2003, when Lamonte reinitiated contact with the organization, and late 2008, when Centurion had decided to take on his case, eleven different prisoners were freed based on proof that Jim had developed.

It was an extraordinary number, to be sure, but a tiny fraction of the number of prisoners who sought help.

Born in 1942, Jim grew up on Philadelphia's Main Line. His great uncle Matt was the owner of a major construction company, McCloskey & Co., that had helped shape the Philadelphia skyline and built both Veterans Stadium in Philadelphia and RFK Stadium in Washington. Great-uncle Matt also was politically connected, serving at one point as the chairman of the Democratic National Committee, and winning appointment by President John F. Kennedy as ambassador to Ireland.

Jim's father was a civil engineer who enjoyed a position as a McCloskey & Company executive. But Jim's childhood was not entirely one of privilege and comfort. Jim's mother was stricken with polio and paralyzed from the waist down when Jim was five years old. The selflessness Jim's father displayed in caring for his mother, Jim wrote in his 2020 autobiography,* provided an example for him on how to serve others, an example it would take him years to embrace.

He was an athlete in high school—captain of the baseball team—and drove a series of what Jim considered cool cars, starting with a 1957 Ford Fairlane 500 with fender skirts and low tail fins. He went to

* *When Truth Is All You Have: A Memoir of Faith, Justice, and Freedom for the Wrongly Convicted.*

Bucknell University in Pennsylvania's Lehigh Valley, a couple of hours north of where he grew up, where he joined a hard-partying fraternity along with his best friend from back home. Jim could not later figure out how he managed to graduate on time.

But the Vietnam War marked the end of his revelry. Jim experienced combat serving on a navy vessel that patrolled the Mekong Delta and South China Sea and was awarded a Bronze Star Medal with Combat "V," a designation recognizing Jim's valor. He returned home to find that his father was facing criminal charges for alleged improprieties in the construction of Veterans Stadium.

His father considered the charges bogus and political payback, and a judge ultimately ruled that the evidence was illegally obtained and threw the case out. But the episode had shamed his father. "When I look back on it now, watching my dad live through the horror of being falsely accused of a crime he didn't commit must have stayed with me," Jim wrote.

He joined a corporate consulting firm and was stationed in Tokyo, where he had served in the navy before Vietnam. He engaged in an affair with a woman he fell madly in love with, unaware she was already married. After Jim returned to New York, his life was adrift. He had affairs, and also spent many nights with prostitutes in seedy hotels with hourly rates.

In 1979, at age thirty-seven, Jim told his parents he needed to find more meaning in his life and enrolled at the Princeton Theological Seminary, intending to become a minister. As much as he was hoping to help others, he was trying to save himself.

The program required field work, and Jim was assigned to counsel prisoners at the nearby state prison complex in Trenton, NJ. The seminary students assigned to the state prison are strictly warned that their job is only to minister to the prisoners, not get involved in their legal cases. Truth be told, Jim had no legal knowledge or training to do so.

On his first day, he met a prisoner named Jorge De Los Santos who insisted that he had been wrongly convicted of murder. De Los Santos, who went by the nickname Chiefie, told Jim that his conviction was built on the word of two men who gave false testimony in return for breaks from the prosecutor. Chiefie said that the prosecutor knew the stories were concocted but didn't care.

To Jim, the idea that prosecutors would knowingly tolerate false testimony to win a conviction seemed outlandish. But he could not help himself from diving in.

The more he learned the more Jim came to believe Chiefie. Before long Jim took a leave from the seminary. Working with an attorney named Paul Casteliero, Jim developed evidence that proved the conviction was built on false testimony with the full knowledge of the detective and prosecutor.

Chiefie was exonerated in 1983, by which time Jim graduated from the seminary.

He began having a recurring dream after helping Chiefie, one that took him back to Vietnam. He was standing on a riverbank in the Mekong Delta with a friend. They watched as a boat loaded with refugees, some hanging on the side, sailed by them. Jim watched from afar as the boat sank, helpless and unable to rescue them. Suddenly a helicopter of Navy SEALS arrived and saved them, one by one, as Jim watched.

Those people, Jim realized, were the innocent men and women in prison. They are all going to die unless someone jumped in and saved them. He did not want to stay stuck on the shore. He wanted to be his own kind of SEAL. He had found his life's work, to investigate and work to overturn wrongful convictions. "For the first time in my life, I knew my purpose, my mission, and it was an important one," he would write. "It was to take the most horrible injustice there is—putting an innocent man in prison—and make it right."

At the time, Jim was a pioneer. The Innocence Project and the network of law school clinics nationwide devoted to such endeavors would come years later. "It was a pretty lonely road I was walking," he said. "At that time there was no one else anywhere in the United States, or elsewhere in the world for that matter, committed to freeing the imprisoned innocent." He had no idea how he would possibly be able to raise money to sustain Centurion Ministries, yet he had no intention of giving up.*

Elizabeth Yeatman, a widow who lived in a stately Princeton house once owned by Woodrow Wilson, let Jim have a bedroom rent free in return for whatever help he could offer her with household upkeep. That arrangement made the idea of Centurion Ministries possible, though the early years were still a struggle.

Jim took on a second New Jersey case, a prisoner he met through Chiefie, and then a third one, a man named Nate Walker. He found that by hearing prisoners out, carefully reading court transcripts, and then going out and talking to witnesses and families, he could uncover the truth. It did not hurt that for some interviews he wore his clerical collar.

When Nate Walker was exonerated in 1986, a *New York Times* reporter was in the courtroom. Suddenly Bryant Gumbel was interviewing McCloskey on *Today*, and *60 Minutes* was talking to him, as were *People*, *Jet*, and *Ebony* magazines. A philanthropic organization, the Public Welfare Foundation, gave Centurion Ministries a $15,000 grant.

As prisoners from all over began writing to seek help, Jim heard from a woman named Kate Germond. She had moved with her husband to New York City from Mendocino, California, and had not

* The organization's name came from Luke 23, a passage in which a Roman centurion is said to have looked up at Jesus on the cross and said, "Certainly, this man was innocent." In recent years the organization has been rebranded, simply as "Centurion."

yet decided what she would do in their new surroundings. Kate was in their cramped Manhattan apartment reading *The New York Times* when she came upon a feature about Jim, following the exoneration of Nate Walker. There was a photograph of Jim on what looked like an old Princess telephone, surrounded by piles of paper.

Kate knew nothing about criminal justice, but she was struck by Jim's story. She had some experience organizing businesses back in Mendocino. Her immediate thought as she looked at the photograph was, *This guy needs help.* She called 411, as one did before the Internet, got Jim's phone number in Princeton, but got a busy signal when she dialed it. She called it again. And again. Finally, Jim answered and Kate began talking. It took a minute or two of conversation before Jim realized Kate was looking to *offer*, not *seek*, Jim's help. He drove up to Manhattan and met Kate at a bar. Suddenly Jim had a colleague.

Before long, Kate was commuting to Princeton to work out of Jim's room on Library Place. The mail pouring in soon became too much for Mrs. Yeatman, and Kate found the fledgling organization a modest office in Princeton.

She went on to become Centurion's senior advocate and investigator, and later executive director, as the organization moved again when it grew to a staff of fifteen including an investigator, lawyers, a social worker, and an intake coordinator, supplemented by a team of volunteers including Jock McFarlane, who scoured the mail for possible cases to take on.

When Jim took on the case of a St. Louis woman convicted of murder named Ellen Reasonover, he turned for help to the senior partner of Kansas City law firm, Wyrsch Hobbs & Mirakian, who assigned an associate in the firm, Cheryl Pilate. The case against Reasonover was largely based on testimony from two other inmates who said that Reasonover made incriminating statements as they were locked up together. Cheryl and Jim discovered that the police had withheld exculpatory evidence, on top of evidence Jim was gathering that discredited the testimony of the jailhouse inmates. In 1999, after Ellen Reasonover had spent sixteen years in prison, a U.S. District Court judge overturned her guilty verdict as Jim and Cheryl stood by her side.

It was a transformative moment for Cheryl, who had devoted her life to exposing and attacking societal problems. Cheryl had gone to college at the University of Michigan, where she became coeditor of the student newspaper. She and another member of the editing staff, Gordon Atcheson, became a couple, and moved after graduation to Wichita, where both went to work on the staff of *The Wichita Eagle.* It was not long before Atcheson left the paper and went to law school, launching a legal career that, in 2010, would land him a seat on the Kansas appellate court.

The two married while Gordon was in law school, and before long had two children. Cheryl left the paper and obtained a master's degree in Social Work and then enrolled at the University of Kansas law school. She was a star there, and upon graduation she received a prestigious two-year clerkship for a U.S. Appeals Court judge before joining the Wyrsch firm.

Ellen Reasonover's case opened Cheryl's eyes. Despite her journalistic skepticism, she was shocked to discover the justice system acting in such a reckless and deceitful manner.

After winning Ellen Reasonover's exoneration, Cheryl was intrigued when she heard from Darryl Burton, a St. Louis man who also was convicted on dubious evidence of murdering a customer in a St. Louis gas station. Cheryl brought the case to Jim's attention, and they debunked the testimony of two eyewitnesses who said they recognized Burton as the murderer.

In 2002, the Eighth Circuit U.S. Court of Appeals issued an opinion that was devastating to Darryl, Jim, and Cheryl, even as the court acknowledged the significant likelihood of Burton's innocence. "A layperson would have little trouble concluding Burton should be permitted to present his evidence of innocence in *some* forum," states the opinion, written by U.S. Circuit Judge Kermit Bye. "Unfortunately, Burton's claims and evidence run headlong into the thicket of impediments erected by courts and by Congress."

The federal appeals court concluded it could not act upon the "considerable" evidence of Burton's innocence but expressed hope that Missouri state courts would permit a review. It took six more years of work before, in 2008, a Cole County, Missouri, judge held the long-sought hearing on the evidence of Burton's innocence that Jim and Cheryl and investigator Dan Clark had assembled.

While the three were in Jefferson City, Missouri, for the hearing that would lead to Darryl Burton's exoneration, Jim told Cheryl and Dan the details of another case he hoped three could soon work on together—the case of Kansas City, Kansas man Lamonte McIntyre.

There were several things that helped convince Jim and the Centurion volunteer, Jock McFarlane, of Lamonte's innocence: The brevity and flaws in the police investigation. The pathetic weakness of Ruby Mitchell's identification of the shooter as the "Lamont" who had visited her niece. The alibi. Lamonte's spontaneous outburst when he was convicted: "I don't believe this, man."

On top of it all were the continuing efforts by members of the Quinn family—relatives of one of the murder victims—to help Rosie McIntyre prove her son's innocence. Niko Quinn and her sister and mother had all long maintained that they had seen the murderer and it was not Lamonte. Niko Quinn had called Rosie to describe what happened when she saw Golubski on the street and confronted him about Lamonte's innocence; Golubski's response was to "Let it go."

Doniel Quinn's own mother, Saundra Sublett Newsome, had separately contacted Rosie after becoming convinced of Lamonte's innocence. Jim found that powerful. Loved ones of murder victims do not normally stand up on behalf of those convicted of the crimes. They have heard police and prosecutors speak confidently of the defendant's guilt, and quickly come to share that view. So for Doniel's relatives to instead be worrying about Lamonte spoke volumes to Jim. They had seen Doniel lose his life senselessly; they did not want to see another man lose his life.

Jim had developed the practice of preparing a report detailing why he was convinced to take on a case before he met with the prisoner he intended to help. That way, he felt, the personality of the prisoner would not sway his judgment.

And so in January 2009, Jim crafted "The Murder of Donald Ewing and Doniel Quinn and the Wrongful Conviction of Lamonte McIntyre," a twenty-one-page report that detailed the weak investigation. He wrote, "When April 2009 arrives, Lamonte McIntyre will have spent 15 years in prison for a double homicide that he had absolutely nothing to do with." The report concludes, using the initials of his organization: "CM is determined to free and exonerate this innocent man."

21

Peeling the Onion

Jim recognized that proving Lamonte's innocence would require him to unpeel several layers of the onion in which the truth was wrapped. It was obvious to him the inadequacy of the police investigation, if you could call it that. Authorities never established a motive for the murders, much less who really committed the crimes. And while prosecutors do not have to establish a motive, showing *why* the defendant committed a murder helps convince a jury of the defendant's guilt. Lacking a motive, on the other hand, opens the door to a wrongful conviction. Why were Doniel Quinn and Donald Ewing gunned down in broad daylight in front of several witnesses? The KCK authorities had no curiosity about that. It was just the same lack of concern that so often is thrown into solving murders of Black people from impoverished neighborhoods.

When Jim arrived in Kansas City, one of his first steps was to sign a contract with Cheryl Pilate, who had left her old law firm to join attorney Melanie Morgan in a new partnership, Morgan Pilate, just over state line in downtown Kansas City, Missouri. The two were a dynamic partnership: Cheryl, a woman of fierce tenacity who stands almost six feet tall, and Melanie Morgan, an engaging presence who stands 5'4" and is skilled at persuading prosecutors, judges, and juries to the rightness of her cause. The two shared, above all, a sense of justice. The contract called for Centurion Ministries to pay Morgan Pilate $125.00 per hour for each hour the firm spent on Lamonte's case, as well as whatever expenses the firm incurred, to build a case for a new trial.

After Cheryl was done with Reasonover's case, she was contacted by Barry Scheck, the famed cofounder of the Innocence Project in New York, to work together on a civil lawsuit of two men, Ron Williamson and Dennis Fritz, whom Scheck had helped exonerate of murder in Ada, Oklahoma. Together with investigator Dan Clark, Cheryl and Barry developed evidence that officials had charged Williamson and Fritz rather than the real killer, Glenn Gore, who dealt drugs and seemed to have enjoyed protection from the police.* To Cheryl, the Oklahoma case demonstrated how the justice system can be subverted by powerful local interests, a lesson she saw unfolding closer to home.

The Morgan Pilate firm was located on the Missouri side of the river. Cheryl and Gordon lived in nearby Johnson County, Kansas. Their county had boomed after the U.S. Supreme Court, in 1954, ruled in *Brown v. Board of Education* that "separate but equal" education was illegal. Many white families, seeking "quality schooling," moved to Johnson County, which became the most populous and most prosperous county in the state of Kansas. Between the wealth of Johnson

* The case became the basis for a nonfiction book by John Grisham, *An Innocent Man*.

County to the south and Kansas City, Missouri, across the river to the east, lay Wyandotte County and its principal city, KCK.

Wyandotte County offered little economic opportunity but all of the urban problems that poverty brings. KCK functioned so badly that, in 1997, its residents would vote to disband the city government and have it absorbed as the Unified Government of Wyandotte County and Kansas City, Kansas, overseen by one mayor and an elected board of commissioners. Not only would the streamlined government cut costs, its supporters urged, it also would help shed the county of the longstanding image of poverty and corruption.* While many services were combined, the KCK police force remained intact.

While Cheryl lived in Johnson County, she knew plenty about KCK corruption. She was in the midst of representing a man named Barron Bowling in a lawsuit that stemmed from events following a car accident between Bowling and an undercover DEA agent. The lawsuit contended that KCK police commanders were part of a conspiracy to cover up the agent's misconduct, thereby subverting justice and protecting friends and those with power. To Cheryl, it was the same kind of unequal justice that she had just observed in Ada, Oklahoma; the same kind of inequities that she and Melanie Morgan had dedicated their practice to challenge.

The lawsuit was assigned, by chance, to Judge Julie Robinson. The same Julie Robinson who, years before she was appointed to the federal

* How successful that consolidation proved remains a matter of dispute. Supporters cite improvements; but almost three decades later, in October 2023, Mayor Tyrone Garner pushed to break up the combined government, saying the benefits had not reached the poorer neighborhoods. While proponents had argued for consolidation to break up the machine, Garner said, "it appears that the machine has been replaced by an even bigger machine."

bench, worked as the assistant U.S. attorney with FBI agent Jennerich to prosecute corruption in the KCK police department.*

Two weeks before Jim McCloskey first arrived in town to begin investigating Lamonte's case, Judge Robinson refused a motion to dismiss the county and its officers from the case. Her ruling meant that Bowling's case against the county and the federal government would be going to trial within months. It also meant that Cheryl's plate was overflowing, developing cases that were directly attacking the local justice system, including Lamonte's.

Once Jim arrived in town, he began knocking on doors with investigator Dan Clark. Starting with that first trip in April 2009, he made five trips to KCK that calendar year and three more in 2010. He would generally spend a week or more, interviewing a dozen or more people each visit.

The door-knocking met with mixed success. Sometimes the interviews took place in living rooms. Other times they got no farther than the front door, where they stood outside and asked what questions they could. It was not unusual for them to be told the person they were seeking wasn't home, even when that was an obvious lie. It was a measure of Jim's dedication that he was never deterred.

He and Cheryl understood the reticence of so many of the Black people in the community. Many people were afraid to talk. After a

* Judge Robinson was first appointed in 1994 to a vacancy on bankruptcy court, but in 2001 was elevated to the district court. (That latter appointment was somewhat delayed, as the phone call Judge Robinson had been told to expect from then-President George W. Bush on 9/11/01 was postponed by the catastrophic events of the day.)

lifetime of seeing how things worked, of being on the bad end of every outcome, they saw no reason to trust that anything good would come from talking to these white strangers.

Jim, along with Dan and Cheryl, worked to erase that distrust by returning again and again, gradually winning confidences. Even so, there were limits to how far many of their sources would go, no matter how hard Lamonte's team pushed.

22
A Detective's Obsession

Jim McCloskey returned to KCK in late April 2009, three weeks after his first trip, and checked into Room 515 of the Hilton Garden Inn. He was man of regular routines about everything—from when he ate lunch to his daily walk to where he stayed when he traveled. He made a point of asking to stay in room 515 each of the eighteen times he returned to work on Lamonte's case.*

On this second trip, he had a list of leads he wanted to pursue. He needed to gather evidence that showed Lamonte was not the killer, to identify the flaws in the police case—and try to find who *did* commit the murder.

Most exonerations across the nation involve identifying and testing DNA evidence, which goes a long way to irrefutable proof of innocence.**

---

* Jim actually was successful on seventeen of those trips; one time, he had to settle for a different room in the hotel with an identical layout.

** Even so, not all prosecutors willingly acknowledge the evidence of innocence. Former Cook County Illinois, state's attorney Anita Alvarez famously suggested on *60 Minutes* that the five teenagers convicted of the rape and murder of a sex worker might still be guilty, even when DNA on the victim was matched to another convicted rapist. She shrugged off her unwillingness to acknowledge the teen's innocence, suggesting it was "possible" the DNA may have been left by someone who happened on the corpse and engaged in intercourse with the body.

But taking on cases without DNA evidence, as Jim McCloskey routinely did for Lamonte McIntyre and so many others, was a much taller order. It requires intensive digging to convince courts not just that the conviction was based on weak evidence, but that there is enough evidence to *prove innocence.*

Jim and investigator Dan Clark started at the beginning, going over to Hutchings Street to see the crime scene and knock on doors. Jim spent time with Rosie, who introduced Jim to her oldest son, James. He knew the characters in the troubled parts of KCK, and was willing to help Jim with introductions to that world.

Cheryl introduced Jim to Max Seifert, a former detective who became the key figure in the lawsuit that Cheryl was handling on behalf of Barron Bowling over the events that followed Bowling's collision with the agent's car.

Max Seifert had plenty to say about the Kansas City, Kansas police. He had shared an office with Golubski for a time and then worked under Golubski's command once Golubski was promoted to captain. Max told Jim that Golubski was "famous for hitting on Black women." It would be a description that became central to Jim's digging.

Over the next few days, Jim would hear story after story of Golubski's lust for Black women, even accounts in which he abused his badge to satisfy his appetite. Saundra Sublett Newsome, the mother of Doniel Quinn, told of Golubski asking her, after the murder, if she dated white men. Freda Quinn, an aunt of Stacey and Niko Quinn, told Jim and Cheryl that Golubski "had a thing" for Black women, and would "hit on" anyone at any time. Freda Quinn said that Golubski had a sexual relationship with her niece, Stacey Quinn, the eyewitness who oddly was never interviewed about the murders. Freda Quinn said the relationship began when Stacey was just sixteen years old and lasted up until Stacey herself was murdered in 2000.

Rosie McIntyre offered her own chilling account. A few years before the murders of Doniel Quinn and Donald Ewing, she was sitting in a parked car with a boyfriend when Golubski showed up and told her, but not the boyfriend, to come back to his car. Once she was alone with him, Golubski told Rosie he would file charges against her boyfriend unless she came to the station the next night.

When Rosie met with him in the detective room the following evening, as directed, Golubski had Rosie remove her clothes and he engaged in oral sex with her. When Golubski was finished, he told Rosie she could leave and there would be no charges against her boyfriend. She left, humiliated.

Golubski then began calling her repeatedly, talking of his personal life and his desires. She stopped taking his calls and moved and changed her phone number before he finally quit calling. Rosie secretly feared that her rejection was the reason that a lineup would have been created that included in a group of five photographs both James and Lamonte McIntyre as well as her nephew.

It was astonishing. Just within his first month working on Lamonte's case, Jim heard stories about Golubski's sexual harassment from a former colleague of Golubski's; from the mother of the victim; and from the mother of the suspect. And he learned that Golubski had a longstanding sexual relationship with an eyewitness to the murder who mysteriously never was interviewed about what she saw.

Jim had heard a lot of stories of prosecutorial and police abuse in the course of his work, but this one was especially awful. Golubski may not have charged Rosie's boyfriend the night he first encountered them. But he later took her son from her.

It was injustice on top of injustice, breathtaking in its utter horror.

The misconduct of the lead detective was only one thread that Jim and his team followed. They went to work to gather evidence of who murdered the victims, and why, but there were many dead ends. Potential sources had moved in the years since the murder, and some appeared to have vanished. And there was that continued reluctance of so many people to share what they knew. They were afraid of Golubski and his allies on the force, of the gangs, and so much else. After so many years of misconduct being tolerated, they had no reason to think anything good might come of talking.

Ruby Mitchell was a case in point. Jim was eager on his first trip to talk to Ruby. After all, her identification of Lamonte drove so much of what followed. If Ruby did not stand behind it, nothing buttressed the conviction.

Ruby had moved, but Jim and Dan tracked her down through Ruby's niece, the young woman who had dated Lamont Drain. When Ruby met Jim and Dan at a friend's apartment on the Missouri side of the river, she explained she had been so frightened by having witnessed the murder that she moved right after the trial. Jim would write in his report that he found Ruby "very friendly, seemingly straightforward and non-defensive." She said she would never forget that day, and repeated that when she first saw the killer, he looked to her like Lamont Drain. She was sure the killer had French-braided hair—though back on the day of the crime, Detective Krstolich recorded her saying the murderer had short hair.

She reiterated to Jim and Dan that she had never said "McIntyre" to police, since she did not know Lamonte McIntyre, and could not explain why the transcript prepared by police showed that she said his name.

At the end of the interview, Jim asked if she might have made a mistake in her identification of Lamonte McIntyre. She replied, "It could be a mistake."

That was a step, but just one. No court was going to overturn a jury verdict based on a mere nod to the unproven possibility of an error. Several months later Jim and Cheryl tracked Ruby down to an apartment in a public housing complex, where she said again the shooter had braids. She was certain the shooter did not have short hair.

Both Jim and Cheryl were struck by this detail. They knew from Rosie and Lamonte that as a teenager before his arrest, Lamonte never had braids and always had very short hair.

Ruby told them of her identification, "I could have made a mistake, but I'm not changing my story" of what she said in court.

Jim mentioned Golubski's reputation for harassing Black women, and she told him of her experience on the day of the murders, when the detective commented on her "nice body and nice breasts" and asked if she liked to date white men as he drove her to the station.

Her response then had been to move closer to the passenger door and grip the handle.

Jim and Cheryl needed Ruby to go further but knew better than to push too hard right away. Jim visited Ruby in April 2010, and showed photographs of Lamonte, one taken the year before the murders and one after he had been arrested. Both showed him with short hair. She said she wanted to see the photograph she had seen in the station that night but reiterated that the shooter had braids.

Months later, Jim and Cheryl tracked Ruby down at a house in KCK to which she had moved and showed her the five photographs from the original array. She studied them and said that the photo of James McIntyre, Lamonte's brother, looked most like the shooter, though she said she was uncertain.

Jim sensed they were winning her trust. A few days later he dropped off copies of her testimony for her review. Ruby agreed that once she had the chance to do so, she would meet with Cheryl to discuss giving an affidavit.

It took several more months, but finally, in June 2011, Ruby was ready to provide that sworn affidavit. In it, she recounted seeing the murders and telling the detectives that the shooter "looked exactly like my niece's former boyfriend whose first name was Lamont. I didn't know his last name. From the beginning I told the police that the person who did the shooting had French braids . . . the same as the hairstyle of this Lamont who dated my niece."

Ruby also swore in the affidavit that when Jim showed her the photo array, as well as the composite that was created from her description, it was "very puzzling and of grave concern" to her that the suspect she identified did not have French braids. "I am positive the person who shot those men in the car had French braids that went down the back of his neck," she said. "If I made a mistake in the identification of Lamonte McIntyre as the person who did this double homicide, I am truly sorry for this occurrence."

It was another step the right direction, but it still fell short of the kind of renunciation of her identification that might make authorities take notice. Jim hoped he could persuade Ruby to go further, but she was no longer interested in talking. On his next visit Jim tracked Ruby down to a house back on the Missouri side of the river, but she did not answer his calls.

When Jim and Cheryl tried dropping in unannounced, Ruby met them at the door and asked if they could return the next day at 1:00 P.M. When they did so, she was not there. She left them a note of apology, asked them to call the following day to reschedule. They did, but she did not answer the call.

They got no further. Ruby's brother slammed the door in Jim's face on one visit. Jim and Cheryl visited Ruby's sister at the hair salon where she worked, and she put them in touch with Ruby by phone. "What more is there to talk about?" Ruby asked when she got on the phone.

She said she would call Jim to let him know when she could meet with them. Unsurprisingly, that call never took place.

As much work as Jim and Cheryl were putting in on Lamonte's behalf, there were other matters, other cases, that took up their time. Jim had obtained key documents that had been withheld before trial from a Dallas murder defendant, Richard Miles. After the Dallas district attorney conducted a reexamination, the case went back to the courtroom, where Miles was released after fifteen years in prison.* In the summer of 2009, a few months after Jim took on Lamonte's case, he also committed to the case of the so-called Savannah Three, three soldiers who drove to Savannah for a bachelor party in 1992 and were mistakenly identified as the men who committed a murder.**

Cheryl, meanwhile, was deep into representing Barron Bowling in his own federal lawsuit over the incident that developed after Bowling sideswiped the DEA agent's car.

The case quickly turned into far more than a simple dispute over a car accident. Max Seifert, the KCK police detective, had been assigned to investigate and concluded that after the initial accident, Bowling

---

* Miles was released from prison in October 2009 and found factually innocent by the Texas Court of Appeals in 2012.

** The three soldiers would finally be exonerated of the murders in 2018, based on Centurion's work. The case is among those recounted in *Framed*, a book coauthored by Jim and John Grisham that recounts a series of wrongful convictions.

had been beaten by at least one federal agent. Max also felt he was experiencing improper interference from two top KCK police commanders, Colonel Steven Culp and Major Dennis Ware, who did not welcome evidence that agents of the DEA had committed an unprovoked beating of Bowling. Those names would be noticed by Cheryl; both Ware and Culp years earlier had been directly involved in the wrongful arrest of Lamonte McIntyre.

23

The Shunning of Max Seifert

Max Seifert was twenty-four years old when he joined the KCK police force in 1975, where his older brother already had gone to work. He joined a class at the academy that included, coincidentally, Roger Golubski and the first Black woman to join the force, Ruby Ellington.

Max spent more than seventeen years as a patrol officer before becoming a detective in 1991, and he would spend fourteen more years in that role. It was a job, Max would say, that he loved "the way you love a beautiful woman."

Max rubbed many on the force the wrong way, and some officers whispered behind his back. He was a sort of Midwest version of the NYPD officer Frank Serpico, a man who wanted nothing more than to be a policeman but found himself ostracized for trying to be an honest cop.

His troubles began back when he was still a rookie on the force and arrested a politically connected lawyer. The two had words after Max arrested a client of the lawyer's. Max then discovered the lawyer did not have a driver's license and, on top of that, was driving a car with tags registered to a different vehicle. Days later, a supervisor advised Max that he was going to face trouble over the arrest. After all, the supervisor told Max, there are two kinds of people in KCK: Those you can arrest and those you had better not. The lawyer was in that second category.

Sure enough, a major called Max in and told him he was being fired; Max's job was saved only when his direct superior intervened.

Max ran into trouble again years later when he investigated former police lieutenant Bernie Smith, who long had struggled with a drug problem, both while he was on the force and even afterward.*

Max and other officers went to a KCK dwelling owned by Smith, who lived on the first floor and rented out an upstairs apartment. The officers arrived to arrest the upstairs tenant on outstanding warrants. While there, they found a second man outside the building in possession of cocaine.

Max learned the next day from an informant that Smith not only was using drugs, he was selling KCKPD uniforms, badges, identification cards, and even a gas mask and bulletproof vest to support his addiction. Max prepared an affidavit for a search warrant for Smith's house, which a district judge approved.

But Max encountered "a lot of interference," as he put it, from his boss. He was ordered not to conduct the search even though the judge had found probable cause and issued the warrant. To Max, it was the "blue code" in action. Smith would later admit just how much the

---

* Years earlier, Smith was the first officer indicted and tried by then–Assistant U.S. Attorney Julie Robinson in the investigation into police corruption she worked on with FBI agent Al Jennerich. That case against Smith was based on evidence that he had been tipping off a drug kingpin of pending raids. Once Smith was acquitted by a jury, he had been welcomed back to the force. By Smith's own admission his drug use caused continuing problems, and he was ultimately permitted to retire on medical disability because of his addiction. Smith would concede in an affidavit years later that he struggled with a "serious substance-abuse addiction" after he had left the force as he was "hellbent on self-destruction."

department was out to undercut Max's effort to do honest policing: Max's superior called him to offer a heads-up that Max had gotten a warrant to search the house.*

The tipping point for Max came after he was assigned to investigate the report that Barron Bowling had assaulted a federal agent. At issue were the events that unfolded after Bowling's car collided with one driven by plainclothes DEA agent Timothy McCue as a second car of DEA agents trailed behind. McCue called into 911 that he had been the victim of an assault, contending Bowling sped up and rammed the unmarked government car McCue was driving.

It was a case that, seven years later, would end Max's career, leave him ostracized and pushed off the force because he worked to establish facts even when they pointed to wrongdoing by those in power. Several of those who turned on Max would be the very same officials who played roles in the conviction of Lamonte McIntyre.

Max and his partner found Bowling badly bruised when they arrived at the jail on the day after the collision. Bowling told them his version of what had transpired: McCue tried to pass Bowling on his right as the right lane was ending, and Bowling failed to slow down. Bowling said that after the collision, he heard a siren, pulled over, and got out of the car, where he then was handcuffed and beaten by the enraged DEA agent, McCue.

To the surprise of Max and his partner, as Bowling tearfully recounted what had occurred, he reached into his sock and pulled

* Smith said in an affidavit the supervisor was, at that time, trying to curry favor with him to convince Smith to privately sell him land at a discount price.

out the business card of another KCKPD detective, Bobby Lane. Bowling said Lane had been at the scene and had assured Bowling of his assistance; Bowling said Lane told him he also had spoken to two bystanders who had witnessed the beating.

Max and his partner were shocked; they had no idea another KCKPD detective had been at the scene ahead of them and talked not only to Bowling but also to two bystanders who described Bowling as the victim, not the aggressor. Max called Lane, and learned Lane had not taken formal statements from the witnesses because those reports would be bad for the federal agents. "DEA agents do a lot for us and we should help them," Lane told Max. The KCKPD officers needed "to cover for them," Lane said of the DEA agents.

As Max investigated, he quickly discovered that two top police officials, Major Dennis Ware and Colonel Steven Culp, were taking an unusual interest in his investigation.*

Max tracked down the eyewitnesses Lane had spoken with and both confirmed Bowling's account in interviews that Lane recorded. But when Max returned to the station, Major Ware hardly patted Max on the back; instead, he expressed concern that Max had tape-recorded witnesses accusing DEA agents of misconduct. Ware took the recordings away from Max.

Max completed the investigation and sent his reports to the district attorney's office. Days later he received a letter informing him that the assistant district attorney for charging decisions, as well as District

---

* Major Ware had been the detective who accompanied Golubski to Hutchings Street on the day after the murders to interview Niko and Josephine Quinn. Colonel Culp was the supervisor who assigned Golubski and Smith to investigate the murders of Doniel Quinn and Donald Ewing and supervised the investigation that led to Lamonte's arrest.

Attorney Tomasic personally, had decided not to charge Bowling in connection with the case. It was the outcome he anticipated.

But that was hardly where things ended. Colonel Culp was a friend of the special agent in charge of the DEA Kansas City office. After they played golf together, Culp contacted District Attorney Tomasic to urge that prosecutors take a second look. He did so without even talking about it with Seifert, the investigating officer.

After Culp intervened, the district attorney's office decided to prosecute Bowling with one felony, criminal damage to property, and two misdemeanors, leaving the scene of an accident and possession of a marijuana pipe. Before trial, Bowling's criminal defense attorney contacted Max, curious that the detective had been the assigned investigator but was not on the list of prosecution witnesses. Max told the defense attorney what had transpired, and when the case finally went to trial, Max was subpoenaed as a defense, not prosecution witness.

The jury acquitted Bowling of the felony after hearing Max's testimony. Incensed, Assistant District Attorney Renee Henry* complained to Colonel Culp.

Max's supervisor at the time was none other than Roger Golubski, then captain of detectives. Golubski told Max to report to Internal Affairs because a complaint had been filed against him by prosecutor Henry and Colonel Culp, accusing him of improperly providing the defense with the initial decision by prosecutors against charging Bowling.

Internal Affairs was then headed by Terry Zeigler, who had been Golubski's partner and was on his way to becoming chief. Max told Zeigler that he thought it very wrong that *he* was being investigated for misconduct, when he was blameless and the public officials who

---

* Henry was elected to a seat on the district court in 2016.

needed investigation were Lane, Ware, Culp, the DEA agents, and Henry, the prosecutor.

By the time Bowling's criminal trial occurred, Cheryl Pilate already had brought a lawsuit on his behalf against Culp, Ware, Lane, Chief Ron Miller, the KCK/Wyandotte County Consolidated Government, and the DEA agents and federal government.

Cheryl spent two days taking a deposition from Max in preparation for Bowling's civil lawsuit. Though Max was subpoenaed to testify, his supervisor, Golubski, not only disapproved; he told other detectives that Max and his partner were "poor examples" of detectives.

Max was called into a meeting with KCKPD brass up to and including Chief Miller. By the end of the meeting Max concluded that he was in a hostile work environment.

In his last weeks on the job, he ended up in a foot pursuit of a suspect he had seen attempt to flee after causing a serious car accident. As Max, then fifty-five, gave chase on foot to a much younger man, he called in for help, and the dispatcher issued an alert for any nearby units to help him.

No officers responded. Max was able to catch the suspect on his own, but he realized he was isolated on the force. Feeling he had no choice, he retired in December 2005 from the only job he ever wanted.

Max's troubles did not end there. When he bumped into Internal Affairs Captain Zeigler in a store, he was shocked to learn that Chief Miller sustained the Internal Affairs complaint against Max the day after he retired. Miller ruled that Max had violated department rules by his interactions with Barron Bowling's criminal defense attorney, but since Max had retired, no further discipline was necessary.*

Max had not even been told of Miller's decision, which left Max the only government official found by the department to have engaged in wrongdoing in connection with the incident.** Since he was retired, Max could not even contest the ruling.

Shockingly, the troubles Max encountered did not even end there.

Miller refused to provide Max the reserve commission commonly given to retired officers, enabling them to continue work in law enforcement. When Miller refused the routine request, Max turned to the sheriff's office, which gave him a reserve commission and put him to work helping on investigations for the sheriff.

That did not last long. Sheriff LeRoy Green Jr. lost his reelection bid within weeks of Max's appointment as a reserve on the sheriff's department. The new sheriff, and his undersheriff, both had been officers in the KCK police force, where Max was viewed by many as a traitor. Max was called in and told that District Attorney Jerome Gorman, Tomasic's successor, had notified the sheriff's office that Gorman had determined Max was not credible and would not prosecute criminal cases if Max was the investigator.

Gorman's explanation was that a federal judge had discredited Max's testimony in a federal drug case. That explanation made no sense to

---

* Miller, who would go on to become the U.S. Marshal for Kansas, contended in an interview that he had no alternative to sustaining the complaint, since Max had not contested Henry's complaint.

** Months later, the state attorney general indicted Lane on unrelated corruption charges. In addition to being a KCK detective, Lane simultaneously was serving on the City Council of suburban Edwardsville. Lane was charged with taking bribes in return for fixing DUI tickets of local businessmen. In a negotiated plea, the felony charges were dismissed in 2007 as Lane pleaded no contest to four misdemeanors and resigned from the KCK police force.

Max. The federal judge's ruling had been a full decade earlier. The district attorney had since prosecuted a multitude of cases investigated by Max, and that old case had never come up. Furthermore, the judge who suppressed Max's testimony in the drug case had not found Max deliberately lied, and Max was adamant he had not.

Where did Gorman come up with the idea that Max was not credible, because of that federal judge's ruling from long ago? His source was Terra Morehead, who years earlier had prosecuted the case of Lamonte McIntyre. Morehead had since moved on to become an assistant U.S. attorney, where she now worked closely with the DEA agents.

Even worse, Max learned that he was cited as an example of an officer whose untrustworthy testimony made him unfit to be used as a prosecution witness, as Morehead and Gorman jointly conducted a session at the annual training for active police. That news broke Max's heart.

In early 2010, Bowling's lawsuit finally went to trial. By then it was only against the DEA agents and the federal government; Wyandotte County officials had already settled their part of the case. Judge Robinson heard the evidence over nineteen days, without a jury. Cheryl, who was Bowling's attorney, couldn't help but notice that Assistant U.S. Attorney Terra Morehead sat in as a spectator through portions of the trial, though she had no official connection to the case.

Cheryl called Max to the stand, and he tearfully described what the case had done to him. He testified there was no merit to the complaint against him. "In 1998 I did not lie in court," Max testified. "I'm not lying now. You know, I don't want my grandkids to think I was a bad cop."

Robinson awarded Bowling $833,250 against the federal government for the injuries he incurred. She noted in her decision that Max was the most credible of all the witnesses to testify in those nineteen days, and said it was "shameful" the way he was treated by his department.

In a footnote to her opinion Judge Robinson wrote that Max was wrongly "castigated by his superiors" for trying to "fully and objectively investigate" the case. He was "shunned, subjected to gossip and defamation by his police colleagues, and treated as a pariah," she wrote, adding he was "balkanized for crossing the 'thin blue line.'"

It was a line that kept officers on one side, no matter what, and the rest of the world on the other. And it was a line that Jim and Cheryl were up against as they investigated who really killed Doniel Quinn and Donald Ewing.

24

"It Doesn't Satisfy My Heart"

On a Sunday afternoon in his first month on the case, Jim McCloskey drove out to the West Heights neighborhood to meet Saundra Sublett Newsome. Saundra, after all, had approached Rosie to express her concern that Lamonte was wrongly locked up even before Jim had taken on the case. She had even told Rosie she was willing to tape her ex-husband talking about their son's murder, if it would help.

Jim and Saundra talked for two hours. Saundra, a longtime employee of the regional U.S. Environmental Protection Agency office, where she worked as photographer and graphics designer, poured out her frustration at the tragedy that unfolded: Two young men murdered. An innocent boy locked up for life. And public officials having no concern for any of it. None of the lives mattered one bit to them, as she saw it.

No official even bothered to even tell her of her son's death. She heard about it only from members of the Quinn family. She had been so incensed by the lack of respect that she went to a City Council meeting to complain. Rather than having the issue aired in public, Mayor Steineger arranged for her to meet privately with him and Chief Dailey.

The mayor fidgeted with a pencil, and Chief Dailey made a reference to Saundra living in the Quindaro neighborhood, the most blighted, impoverished part of town. Saundra keenly felt the disregard being shown her and her murdered boy. She corrected him: She was from West Heights, a stable neighborhood, not Quindaro.

As Saundra corrected the chief, the pencil snapped in the mayor's hands. Throughout the rest of the meeting the two officials at least pretended to care about her complaint. But the sting of that disrespect had stayed with Saundra.

She told Jim that soon after the murders, she began hearing from members of the Quinn family that police had the wrong man. Saundra made it clear she held her ex-husband responsible for their son's murder, even if he didn't pull the trigger.

The two were high school sweethearts, but John began using drugs soon after they married and, she said, turned violent. She left him when Doniel was still an infant, and decades later, she said, he still had a drug addiction.

Saundra had warned John not to involve Doniel in his drug dealings, but he had managed to worm his way back into Doniel's life. After the murders John came to her, distraught, and said he could not attend his son's funeral. Saundra told Jim that she responded to John, "It's your fault he's dead. I don't care if you go naked, you're going."

Saundra raised again with Jim that she could engage John in a conversation about the murder of their son and secretly record it. She said of Lamonte, "It doesn't satisfy my heart to have him locked up, because he's not the right one."

Two days later Jim and Cheryl paid a visit to John's sister, Freda Quinn, who told them that her brother had been tortured about his son's death for fifteen years and likely was ready to talk about it. That evening,

Cheryl and Jim knocked at John's door. A young boy and a woman who answered insisted he was not home. Jim and Cheryl doubted them, but there was little they could do. They were certain they would only get John to cooperate through Saundra or Freda.

On his next trip to KCK Jim went to see Saundra, this time accompanied by Lamonte's brother James McIntyre, who knew the streets and was eager to help convince hesitant residents to cooperate in any way he could. Saundra was still willing to go see her ex-husband and try to capture his words on tape, but said Jim should not come along. Her ex-husband, she explained, "hates white people."

Saundra and James McIntyre brought along a tape recorder, kept discreetly out of sight.* As they talked, John told his ex-wife that before the murder, he knew "something was bothering" their son. But Doniel had told his father not to worry, that whatever it was, he could take care of it.

John Quinn then provided something the prosecution had never obtained: a motive for the murder. He said Doniel and Donald were killed after a contract had been put out on Doniel because of "something that had been taken." John said the contract was supposedly issued by a man named Cecil Brooks, though John added that Brooks was not at the scene.

James McIntyre and Saundra turned the tape over to Jim McCloskey. As Jim listened to the tape, he heard for the first time the name "Cecil Brooks." It would not be the last time.

---

* Kansas is among the states that permits individuals to record conversations legally without the consent of the other party.

25

A Monster Enters

Jim McCloskey had been struck from the start that the family of a victim was eager to right the injustice suffered by the man convicted of the murders. Normally, family members resist any idea that the system failed. Guilty verdicts provide solace, of a sort, that someone has paid a price for the crime.

Getting Saundra's cooperation reinforced Jim's belief in not just Lamonte's innocence, but his conviction that the investigation and trial were a sham. Three days after Saundra confronted her ex-husband, Jim met with Niko Quinn, who had been on Hutchings Street when the shootings took place and testified against Lamonte at trial.

By the time Jim met with her, Niko had since recanted her testimony, but Judge Burdette had rejected her recantation more than a decade earlier as not credible. Jim was not sure what to expect as he and Dan Clark approached her house. But she was willing to talk, offering so many details that Jim called her the next day and talked for another forty-five minutes.

She said she knew at the preliminary hearing that Lamonte was not the murderer and alerted prosecutor Terra Morehead. But, she told Jim, Morehead warned her that she could be held in contempt if she changed her story. She tried again before trial, but Morehead warned Niko that changing her story carried consequences. Morehead told her that she could be charged criminally, and have her children removed from her.

Niko told Jim that Cecil Brooks had operated a drug house near the murder scene on Hutchings Street. The spot was run by his cousin and close friend, Aaron Robinson, and Doniel served as a "doorman" at the house.

Days before the murder, Doniel showed up badly bruised at her house, she continued. He said he had been beaten by several members of Cecil's gang, including Aaron Robinson and a man named Neil Edgar Jr., because they suspected him of stealing their drugs.

That account, Jim realized, would explain bruises observed on Doniel's body at the autopsy—which were never of any interest to detectives. And they would help establish a motive.

At the time of the murders, Neil Edgar Jr. was just fifteen years old but already had a reputation for violence. He was someone eager to prove himself to Cecil Brooks and Aaron Robinson, part of a gang of teenagers who prided themselves on being known as ThunderCats in appreciation of the cartoon series featuring alien invaders. Edgar went by the street name "Monster."

Niko told Jim the word on the street was that Monster had been paid to murder Doniel, an act of punishment because Aaron Robinson and his cousin Cecil Brooks believed Doniel had stolen drugs from the house that Aaron ran. Niko recounted that after the murders she bumped into Monster, who asked her a question she took as a threat. "Do you know who I am?" he asked. Niko was terrified of what might happen to her for having witnessed the murders, a fear that had caused her to welcome whatever protection Detective Golubski might have provided.

By the time Jim heard all this, Edgar was locked up for an unrelated murder in Missouri, and Aaron Robinson was dead—killed by one of his associates who accidentally fired his gun inside a Church's fried chicken restaurant on Quindaro Boulevard.

All of that information would itself have made the trip successful for Jim. But on top of all that, he talked by telephone during that trip with Donald Ewing's aunt, Gloria Labat. Gloria, who worked for years as a case manager at the Social Security office, had been Saundra Newsome's best friend since grade school.

She attended the trial and watched Niko on the stand, and afterward, witnessed her sobbing in the hallway as she explained she had been forced to wrongly identify Lamonte, under the threat that her children would be taken from her.

This was a major development. Judge Burdette had said back when he rejected Niko's effort to recant her testimony that it was not credible because it came so belatedly. But here was the evidence that put the lie to that logic. Niko was saying from the moment she got off the stand that her testimony against Lamonte was not truthful.

When Jim returned to Princeton, he filled Lamonte in on everything he had learned. Lamonte had some information of his own—that some years back, another prisoner told him that someone known as Monster had something to do with Doniel's death. He disregarded it at the time, however, having never heard that name.

By coincidence, Lamonte was locked up at Lansing with Neil Edgar Sr., the father of the violence-prone teenager. Neil Edgar Sr. had been pastor of the God's Creation Outreach Ministry, where his wife was considered a prophet who spoke the word of God. Local authorities considered the church a cult.

The Edgars adopted four children. They homeschooled them and their discipline amounted to criminal abuse. Edgar Sr. and his wife were convicted of murder and sentenced to life in prison after one of their foster sons, age nine, died of asphyxiation while bound with duct tape from head to toe.

At Jim's suggestion, Lamonte struck up a conversation with Monster's father, who said he could not understand why his son had adopted a life of violence and drugs. "Every time my son would kill someone; he'd tell me about it," Edgar Sr. told Lamonte. His son had been convicted in Missouri of murdering a man he believed had stolen money from him.*

Edgar Sr. said Lamonte reminded him of his son, except that Edgar Jr. wore his hair in French braids. When Jim heard this from Lamonte he instantly realized the importance of that detail. Monster's hairstyle was just as Ruby Mitchell had described the killer to him.

Lamonte told Neil Edgar Sr. that he was in prison because he had been wrongly convicted of murdering two men, Doniel Quinn and Donald Ewing. Edgar's answer gave no hint whether he knew anything

---

* That 2000 murder involved a man named Anthony Conley, whom Monster shot and killed at point blank range as Conley sat with others at a dining room table, according to court records. Conley's body was dumped in the trunk of his aging white Cadillac, which was set on fire.

to connect his son to the double murder: "Leave it in God's hands," was all he told Lamonte.

God's hands had not provided much help to Lamonte, who remained trapped inside the locked doors and barbed wire of Lansing State prison.

Lamonte spent July 26, 2009, his thirty-third birthday, behind bars, just as he had the fifteen birthdays before then. The same month back in Princeton, Jim wrote a report for Cheryl, investigator Dan Clark, Centurion volunteer Jock McFarlane, and Lamonte that summarized the interviews and concluded by identifying the likely killer: "The brazen double homicide of Donald Ewing and Doniel Quinn in broad daylight and in front of many witnesses seems to fit the profile of a young 'Monster,'" he wrote, "who has no compunction about killing and who is happy to do so for money, reputation, status, and the cold-blooded thrill of it."

26

"This Case Cannot Die"

Proving someone innocent after they have been found guilty is enormously difficult and requires relentless work. Jim was driven to get Lamonte out of prison and outraged at what increasingly appeared to be a case that went well beyond a series of errors. He never tired of the task. It was clear to Jim that Lamonte's conviction amounted to the deliberate railroading of an innocent teenager.

Each trip provided new leads and additional people to interview. Cheryl told Jim that defense lawyer Michael Redmon knew all the local players in the court system, and many of those who were involved in Lamonte's case. Redmon had long ago represented the McIntyres in the pizza case—the armed robbery of the delivery man that first got Lamonte caught up in the system—and had more recently represented Cecil Brooks and Aaron Robinson.

In early 2010 Jim went to a modest office building, a block from the county courthouse, where Redmon and several other local attorneys had offices. Redmon did, indeed, know a lot. He was both an experienced lawyer within the local criminal justice system and also an observer of its flaws.

Redmon told Jim that Golubski was "out of control," and had engaged in sex with a large number of vulnerable women. And an additional bombshell: Judge Burdette had previously had an affair with Terra Morehead that was the talk at the time of the courthouse.

Redmon cautioned Jim that he had known Wyandotte County District Attorney Jerome Gorman for more than two decades, warning he tended to discount the possible innocence of anyone charged with crimes. But Redmon said he would help any way he could, and offered the names of more residents who were part of the KCK world of crack cocaine and might know things that could advance Jim's investigation.

Plenty of those who talked to Jim had things to say about Roger Golubski; in fact, it seemed like the entire Black community of KCK had stories to tell about the notorious detective. Of course, many people were too scared to talk. Even so, more than a dozen people Jim and Cheryl talked to in their first year of reinvestigation talked of Golubski's obsession with Black women and his abuse of them. It appeared common knowledge that Golubski frequently had sex with Black female prostitutes and drug addicts. Some of the stories were secondhand, but some people offered more direct details.

One man told them of Golubski ostensibly investigating the murder of the man's brother but instead the detective was "hellbent on hitting" on their sister. Rather than investigate the murder, Golubski was "interested only in trying to get her to have sex with him," as Jim described it in his report.

He had supposedly fathered several children on the streets he worked.*

* Years later, in a court proceeding, he pleaded the Fifth Amendment when asked how many children he had.

One woman who talked to Jim and Cheryl was Ethel Abbott, who was one of Golubski's ex-wives. Ethel, who is Black, met Golubski in the early 1990s, when she was working at a gas station. One night, a murder occurred at the station while Ethel was not there; she had called in sick. Golubski contended that her absence was suspicious and kept showing up to grill her about what she knew, which was nothing.

Golubski was in his late thirties, and Ethel was thirteen years younger; his interests quickly shifted from investigating murder. Golubski stalked her and pestered her when he knew her boyfriend was away until finally Ethel agreed to go out with him. He promised to take care of her, to pay her bills, and he convinced Ethel to pack up, move in with him and, before long, marry him.

Ethel already had two sons and Golubski had a son from his previous marriage. For a time, Ethel thought of it as an ideal union. Golubski kept his rosary in his pocket and prayed every day. On Sunday, the family went to church together, and weekends were devoted to activities like baseball and fishing with the boys.

But there were signs of trouble that Ethel was noticing, starting with the bigotry of his parents. Golubski told Ethel his father, who was deceased, had been a racist; his mother treated Golubski's son differently from the way she treated Ethel's sons, even signing Christmas gifts to them as "Mrs. Golubski."

Roger Golubski was controlling. He kept the checkbook locked away from his wife, giving her one check at a time as needed. On one occasion, he locked the garage door to try to keep her from leaving to visit a friend.

When Ethel asked Golubski why he seemed attracted to her and other Black women, his answer stunned and angered her: "Because they're uneducated."

Over time, she became doubtful of his fidelity. One young woman called the house asking for "Dad," which shocked Ethel, who only knew of a son of Golubski's. She noticed evidence the detective was unfaithful to her. (Only after they were divorced did Ethel begin hearing, over and over, that Golubski was known for picking up and having sex with Black women who were drug addicts and streetwalkers.)

She finally moved out and filed for divorce, despite his protests to her that he "bought your ass." Even after she was gone, Golubski still was not ready to concede. He stalked Ethel for years, placing repeated telephone calls during which he detailed that he knew her comings and goings. He got physical in one instance, when he showed up while Ethel was with friends and, after words were exchanged, he grabbed onto the necklace she was wearing and pressed it against her neck. He left only when Ethel's companions called 911.

But the worst parts were the break-ins to her house, two in four days, when her valuables and furniture were stolen. Ethel said Golubski "tried to rise to the rescue like a knight in shining armor," accompanying a police unit that dusted for prints. Only later did Ethel learn that Golubski had hired a teenage boy to do the intrusions.

In early 2010, Jim put officials on notice that he was looking into Lamonte's conviction. He sent an email to District Attorney Gorman, who had first taken office five years earlier after being Nick Tomasic's longtime first assistant. Back when Tomasic had decided to retire in 2004 after thirty-two years in office, Gorman was the logical successor. He won the election that year without opposition to be Wyandotte County's top prosecutor, the same way Tomasic had won his election so many times over thirty-two years, from the time position was created.

While Jim waited for Gorman to review the file and provide some responses, Cheryl was pulled away to try Barron Bowling's lawsuit before Judge Robinson, the case that would expose so much about how the local law enforcement community operated.

That same month, Golubski, then the captain of the homicide unit in KCK, retired with full pension. His transgressions were well-known in the neighborhoods he worked and to many in the department, but not to the wider public. He received the reserve commission that was denied to Max Seifert and would soon go to work as a captain in the police department of suburban Edwardsville, where he lived.

Once the trial before Judge Robinson of the civil lawsuit brought by motorist Barron Bowling ended, Jim returned to KCK, his seventh trip on behalf of Lamonte.

Armed with Redmon's endorsement, Jim showed up at the door of Joe Robinson, who was a brother to Cecil Brooks and a cousin to the now-deceased Aaron Robinson; Joe welcomed Jim inside when he heard Redmon had sent him. Redmon was, Joe Robinson explained, "like our father," handling problems for the Brooks and Robinson families.

The interview lasted about an hour. As Jim laid out what he believed—that Monster had committed the murders under orders from Aaron Robinson—Joe Robinson repeatedly told Jim that he was on the right track. Monster was Aaron's enforcer, and Doniel Quinn was suspected of stealing from the drug stash. More than likely, Aaron ordered the murder without Cecil's involvement. But Cecil would know what happened and would cooperate with Jim if that was what Mike Redmon wanted. "Whatever we can do for Mike we will do," Joe Robinson told Jim.

So Jim went back the next day to again visit Redmon, who told Jim that he had often represented Cecil Brooks and knew him well. Despite Cecil's criminal record, Redmon considered him bright and personable.

Three years earlier, Cecil was arrested at a drug stash house after he had become the target of a massive joint investigation that involved local authorities as well as the FBI and DEA. His case was prosecuted by Terra Morehead, who by then had left the Wyandotte County district attorney for a position as an assistant U.S. attorney.

The evidence showed that Cecil and his associate operated with an extreme level of brutality. Cecil had tortured one associate with a hot iron for losing $1,000 worth of cocaine. The case never went to trial; Cecil agreed to plead guilty to conspiracy to distribute crack cocaine within 1,000 feet of a Topeka high school. When he was sentenced in July 2009, the U.S. attorney's office issued a press release with the headline: HOT IRON DRUG TRAFFICKER SENTENCED TO EIGHTEEN YEARS IN FEDERAL PRISON.

Cecil was being held at a federal prison in Yazoo City, Mississippi. Redmon agreed to write a letter of introduction to Cecil on behalf of Jim, explaining the Centurion director was trying to correct the injustice dealt to Lamonte. "I would strongly urge you to cooperate with him as best you can to help determine what really happened, and free this innocent man," the letter states. "I will consider this to be a personal favor."

District Attorney Gorman ignored repeated phone calls and emails from both Jim and Cheryl, so they decided on Jim's next trip that they would just drop in on the prosecutor. But first Jim went to revisit

Saundra Newsome and seek her permission to tell Gorman that she believed in Lamonte's innocence.

Saundra's answer surprised Jim. She would do more than that. She wanted to talk to Gorman directly to ask, "How do you decide who is free and who is in jail in the face of two mothers that are convinced that the wrong man is in prison for the murder of my son?"

She considered herself an ongoing victim and would remain so "until the innocent is freed and the guilty party is brought to justice. This case cannot die until the boy is out."

She had one request for Jim: To make sure Gorman knew she lived in West Heights, not Quindaro. She was still mindful of the treatment years earlier from city officials, and their disregard for Doniel's murder considering what neighborhood they presumed, wrongly, that he was raised in.

When Jim and Cheryl went to Gorman's office, the prosecutor promised to provide Cheryl with access to whatever files and evidence his office maintained on Lamonte's case. He seemed irritated as Jim pressed him to reach out to Saundra Newsome but agreed to do so.

Jim made another unannounced visit that trip, to Edwardsville, a community of 4,700 residents on the southwestern edge of Wyandotte County. When KCK merged its government with the county, Edwardsville was one of the two small jurisdictions in Wyandotte County that remained independent after Kansas City, Kansas, and the county merged governments. The neighborhood was a cluster of modest single-family homes nestled on two sides against interstate highways. Three of every four residents were white, and only one in twelve were Black residents, a sharp contrast to the much larger population of KCK.

Jim arrived at his destination, an unadorned one-story house with fewer than 1,100 square feet of floor space. When the white-haired mustachioed man answered the door, Jim was face to face with Roger Golubski.

Jim introduced himself and said that he was investigating the case of Lamonte McIntyre and his potential wrongful conviction. Golubski said that he remembered the case and remembered that it was solved quickly. He commented that there were so many murders going on in KCK in those days that the department sent officers inexperienced in homicides to help. One of those, Golubski told Jim, was Detective Krstolich.

Jim showed Golubski the statement from Josephine Quinn that her daughter, Stacey, knew the identity of the killer. Golubski responded, curiously, that it could be "cultural generic knowledge," a phrase that Jim did not ask Golubski to explain. The detective said he did not recall if Stacey was asked if she knew the killer's identity.

Jim told Golubski that Stacey's sister, Niko, contended she had been pressured by "law enforcement" to falsely identify Lamonte. Golubski said he had run across Niko several times over the years, and she never mentioned that she thought the wrong person had been convicted.

Golubski said he had not heard until Jim showed up that there were any questions about the conviction at all. But, the detective said, Jim had "got his curiosity up." Mistakes sometimes occur, Golubski commented, and "if the wrong man is in prison, we need to own up to it."

Jim did not push back but he was not impressed or fooled. He wrote in his report that Golubski "is a classic case of a wolf in sheep's clothing."

As his months behind bars came and went, Lamonte continued taking business courses, working toward a degree that would make his grandfather, David Crowder, proud. He had read more than 300 books in prison, reading authors as varied as Robert Frost, Faulkner, Hemingway, George Bernard Shaw. Some authors, like the California evangelical preacher Rick Warren, particularly spoke to him. He absorbed the Greek philosophers, Aristotle and Socrates and Plato.

And he was writing, as well—about himself, about the prison experience, about Corisha and his mother. Writing was a way to look back and to try to figure out how his life and gone so wrong.

> *For my own personal reasons I write, because I know it's emotionally healthy for me to express myself. I just wish it didn't make me so sad. I'm tired of being reminded of how much life I missed out on. And I'm really tired of people telling me to be patient. That's like asking a man not to move while his body is on fire.*

27

"Everybody Knows Muggz Did Not Do This"

The puzzle pieces were fitting into place.

Doniel Quinn was suspected of stealing drugs and was the intended victim. Donald Ewing was a "freebie," in the wrong place at the wrong time. The drugs belonged to Aaron Robinson, now dead as well from the accidental shooting. And a teenager known as Monster likely pulled the trigger.

A former friend of Monster's who had spent time with Lamonte in Hutchinson prison told Jim, "Everybody knows Muggz did not do this. He had nothing close to that in him."

Having a sense of what really happened on that April day on Hutchings Street and proving it were two different things, and Jim and Cheryl had a long way to go to win freedom for Lamonte. The key was Aaron Robinson's cousin, Cecil Brooks, who was locked up in Mississippi.

One week after Jim returned from Kansas City, he wrote a letter to Cecil and attached the letter of introduction from attorney Redmon.

"My name is Jim McCloskey," he began. "I believe I know who the shooter is and why [Doniel Quinn and Donald Ewing] were killed. I think this was a drug-related execution. I would very much like to visit with you in order to see if you might be able to shed any light on the truth of the matter."

Cecil sent back Jim's letter with a note hand-printed on the bottom: "Feel free to come and talk with me on this matter."

Jim arranged the meeting for the morning of June 21, 2010. The day before, he boarded a plane from Philadelphia to Jackson, Mississippi, rented a car and headed about sixty miles north. Yazoo City was once the site where the Confederacy built battleships and much later the home of the writer Willie Morris. But the city more recently became known for the prison complex that opened in 2005 and two decades later held more than 4,000 prisoners.

At 8:30 on the morning of June 21, Jim took a seat in a private room arranged by Cecil's counselor, and the one-time drug ringleader was escorted by guards to a chair across from him. The meeting began cautiously but went on for more than three hours.

Cecil declared at the start: "If I help you, you have to help me." He said he had been reluctant to even meet because he could not see how it would be to his benefit. He then decided to "play it by ear," figuring the visit would at least break up the boredom of prison life.

Cecil had information that he hoped could help him win a reduction in his eighteen-year sentence. He said that he had witnessed a murder of a police informant committed by two gang members. But prosecutors had showed little interest in doing anything to help him win freedom any sooner. Cecil said that his reputation worked against him, and the authorities were out to throw the book at him.

Jim worked to establish rapport, telling Cecil that theology teaches that those who commit horrible deeds can win forgiveness. He talked of Moses in the Old Testament and Paul in the New Testament, both having committed murders before they did great things.

After they talked for a while, when Jim turned the conversation from the scripture to the murders of Doniel Quinn and Donald Ewing, Cecil told Jim that he knew Lamonte "didn't do it." He described his relationship with his cousin Aaron Robinson: "I trained him in the business. I taught him the drug game."

Cecil said Aaron Robinson broke out on his own, and before he was killed in 1996, had created his own operation, where "Aaron ran the house and made the calls." He said he retained love and respect for his dead cousin and would not go against him.

But he confirmed that Doniel Quinn was a doorman at Aaron Robinson's drug house, and that he had stolen something. "Your man didn't do it," Cecil said again of Lamonte. "Monster got paid to do it. Aaron told me Monster did it." When Lamonte was arrested "we all knew that Monster" was the killer, he continued. "Maybe we should have stepped up and did something, but that wasn't how it worked."

Cecil told Jim that he regretted how he spent his life and wanted to rehabilitate his name for the sake of his children.

By the end of the meeting, Cecil told Jim that he would be willing to sign an affidavit against Monster, but not one that said Aaron Robinson had ordered the hit.

Weeks later, Jim sent Cecil Brooks a handwritten thank-you note. The note added, "If you don't mind, I might want to visit you another time in the fall as a follow-up to our initial discussion. Before doing so, I will ask you for your permission by letter."

More than 500 miles north of Yazoo City, Lamonte remained locked up in Lansing as his thirty-fourth birthday approached. Though he had told her years ago to get out of his life, he could not stop thinking about Corisha.

In recent years, after Lamonte left her sitting alone in the Lansing visitation room, Corisha had set out to rebuild her life. She had two sons with a man whom she left because she said he was abusive. Then, through friends, she met a man who did not mind that she had children, and they married and had a daughter. But while they liked each other and cared about each other, Corisha did not love him.

Lamonte called her every year on her birthday, and each time she hung up on him. But even long after he had told her to move on, she still thought about him. They each had their own hurt and anger.

Lamonte wrote a poem that summed up his feelings.

I got a freezer where my heart was
cause that's the side effects
of what that penitentiary love does.

It still sucks to know I love her
like Cupid shot me.
I tried to be the good guy
but look where that thinking got me.
A heart that's barely beating
with issues of people leaving . . .

When Jim next returned to Kansas City, he had lunch with attorney Redmon to fill him in on his conversation with Cecil Brooks. Redmon told Jim news that showed the challenge ahead: Redmon had run into prosecutor Jerry Gorman and passed along word that many of

Redmon's clients were saying Lamonte was innocent. That news had not impressed Gorman, who assured Redmon that he was cooperating with McCloskey, but, after all, a jury had convicted Lamonte and the state Supreme Court affirmed the decision.

It was just as Mike Redmon had warned Jim in their first meeting. Jerry Gorman was not someone who gave much thought to the potential innocence of defendants. A conviction by a jury, affirmed on appeal, only reinforced the idea of guilt.

On that same trip Jim went to see Maxine Crowder, Lamonte's grandmother, in the home where Maxine and her husband, David, had settled more than fifty years earlier. A grandson, Montre Johnson, had just been killed—her third grandson to meet a violent death. Her advice to young members of her family: "There ain't nothing here." There are too many feuds, too many bullets in the air. Get out of KCK.

28
Collecting Affidavits

Two years into their investigation, Jim and Cheryl had established the shoddiness of the police investigation. They knew a lot about the KCK police department, the tight circle of the law enforcement community and its tolerance for corruption within the ranks. They now even knew what had really been behind the murders of the two men in the parked Cadillac in April 1994—and who was responsible. All of this was because they had done the detective work authorities failed to do at the time Doniel Quinn and Donald Ewing were killed, or in the seventeen years since.

By early 2011, it was time to start gathering affidavits to make the case in court. Jim came to Kansas City and began knocking on doors. Some affidavits were easy; in other cases, getting people to sign a sworn statement was a challenge. It was one thing to give information to Jim or Cheryl; it was something else to sign a document that was going to be introduced in court.

Saundra Sublett Newsome, Doniel Quinn's mother, was one of the first to sign. "I am convinced beyond a shadow of a doubt that Lamonte McIntyre is completely innocent of the murder of my son," she said in her affidavit. She described hearing that Lamonte was not the killer from, among others, her ex-husband, John Quinn, and niece, Niko Quinn, who both were on the street that day.

Saundra also described in the affidavit how Golubski came to her door after his investigation was over, to ask her if she ever did "go out with white men."

Jim began gathering other affidavits—about Golubski, about Monster and about the rotten core of the Kansas City, Kansas, criminal justice system. Joe Robinson, Cecil's brother, signed an affidavit repeating what he had told Jim months earlier; that is, Monster, a violent teenager eager to curry favor with Aaron Robinson, killed Doniel Quinn after Doniel had stolen drugs from Aaron's drug house; Donald Ewing was unlucky to be in the wrong place at the wrong time.

Joe's account was secondhand; the key was still Cecil Brooks. When Jim returned to Princeton in late February, he wrote to Cecil in the Yazoo City prison, saying he wanted to meet with him again. Jim reminded Cecil that he had agreed, in their meeting seven months earlier, to at least consider signing an affidavit. Now, he hoped to meet with Cecil again to show him a draft version—one they could discuss and edit together when they met.

Days later, Jim learned that Cecil had been transferred out of Yazoo City to a prison in Arkansas, so Jim tinkered with his letter and sent the revised version to his new address. A month later, when Cecil didn't answer, Jim wrote to him that Cheryl would contact the prison to arrange a meeting between Jim and Cecil, one where Jim could go over a draft affidavit with him.

But when Cheryl tried to arrange the interview, she learned it was not possible. Cecil Brooks had denied permission for Jim to visit.

Jim went back to see attorney Redmon on his next visit, and the next day Redmon sent Cecil another letter. "As you are very much aware, being away from your family and having to spend time in prison is a difficult thing," he wrote. "I think it would be even more difficult if the circumstances were such that you were totally innocent of the crime for which you were convicted. I believe that to be the case with Mr. McIntyre."

Redmon wrote that he was not getting paid to represent anyone to work on the case; he was merely asking for Cecil Brooks's help because of his belief in Lamonte's innocence. Redmon repeated what he had told Cecil a year earlier, that he would "consider it to be a personal favor if you would continue to assist Jim McCloskey."

Jim sent the letter along with one of his own, writing that he hoped Cecil "might have a change of mind."

Cecil Brooks never answered that letter.

Lamonte turned thirty-five in July 2011, his seventeenth birthday behind bars.

Even without Cecil Brooks, the case for a new trial was moving forward.

By the end of 2011, Jim and Cheryl had eleven signed affidavits. Ruby Mitchell signed hers, as did Doniel's aunt, Freda Quinn, and Donald Ewing's aunt, Gloria Labat. Rosie McIntyre's old boyfriend detailed the incident when Golubski first directed Rosie to his car. Mike Redmon signed one, and even Greg Lauber, a juror who felt grave misgivings about his acquiescence in the guilty verdict years earlier, put his signature on an affidavit.

Jim and Cheryl made sure to circle back to people who had cooperated to keep them on board. Winning a hearing would only be a first step; they needed to make sure they had witnesses once such a hearing took place. But they kept hearing more stories from more people. Corruption in KCK was a way of life, and former detective Golubski seemed at the center of much of it.

After Jim arrived on one trip in early 2012, Jim and Cheryl, along with her husband, Gordon, had dinner together at a Chinese restaurant after attending church. Jim opened a fortune cookie that read, ALL THE PREPARATION YOU'VE DONE WILL BE PAYING OFF. Jim opened it and shared it with his tablemates, amazed at what the message portended.

29

No Place for Honest Cops

By now, Jim and Cheryl had heard plenty of tales of Golubski misconduct, and his behavior was clearly well-known within KCK's Black community. But they also were learning that the conduct was no secret within the police department.

When Jim met Sonny Callahan, a Black KCKPD officer since 1977, he was helping lead an anti-gang task force and nearing retirement. He had gotten to know Doniel Quinn as the teenager had struggled to get off drugs. Callahan even served as his drug counselor for a time, and was a pallbearer at Quinn's funeral.

Callahan also knew Golubski well, and for a time had ridden with him when both were assigned years earlier to the vice squad. He said Golubski's conduct was well-known throughout the department. Top officers thought Golubski's obsession with Black women was "funny and saw no harm in it," Callahan told Jim. "They don't see how predatory and corrupt it is."

But Jim and Cheryl were hearing plenty of stories that were anything but funny, about Golubski taking drugs off dealers, and using the cocaine to entice vulnerable women to provide him with information or sex. They heard about a department that showed too little concern for crimes that victimized impoverished people, about "misdemeanor murders," where less weight was given to solving murders against Black people. But that same department, they heard, treated some people in the community as untouchable, their crimes to be ignored. Golubski seemed to be one of them.

It was a place, the interviews collectively demonstrated, that disrespected justice and winked at corrupt behavior, a place that would open the door to the miscarriage of justice that befell Lamonte.

After Barron Bowling won his large civil verdict, Cheryl took on representing the star witness, former police officer Max Seifert. She filed a lawsuit on his behalf against the sheriff and the unified city-county government, contending that Max had been subjected to harassment and lost his job as punishment for his honesty. The unified government officials included both the police department and sheriff's department, and the lawsuit contended that in both "there is a long-standing unwritten policy and custom of covering up and failing to punish law enforcement misconduct."

At the very time Seifert was forced out and "branded a 'liar'" for "truthfully reporting facts," the complaint stated, the unified government "continues not only to harbor but also to promote and reward officers who have been investigated for domestic incidents, steroid use, stealing from citizens, and for using and trafficking in drugs. Numerous officers and commanders have been involved with domestic incidents or sexual misconduct and their wrongs continued to be covered up."

The top officers and the unified government contended the actions they took against Seifert were justified, and initially U.S. Dist. Judge J. Thomas Marten dismissed the case before trial. But Marten was reversed on appeal to a panel of the 10th Circuit U.S. Court of Appeals, which noted that the sheriff removed Seifert from undertaking investigations less than a week after the unified government agreed to settle Barron Bowling's claims. Following the appellate ruling, the unified government settled Seifert's lawsuit as well.

But before it was settled, the lawsuit opened the door for Cheryl to subpoena the KCK police department's top officials to depose them about their alleged tolerance of wrongdoing by officers in general and Golubski in particular. The command officers insisted, during the depositions and in more recent interviews, that if Golubski was committing outrageous crimes he did so without their knowledge.

Former top officers acknowledged they knew of Golubski's fetish for Black women even as they insisted that they knew nothing about allegations that Golubski engaged in outrageous crimes. Former chief Rick Armstrong called it "common knowledge that Detective Golubski liked African American women." Asked about Golubski's relationship with Black women in the poor neighborhoods of KCK, former chief Ron Miller testified: "That's not foreign to me. I can't say I've never heard that before." Michael York, at the time the captain of internal affairs, and later promoted to the top ranks of the department, called it well-known within the department that Golubski had "an affinity" toward Black women he was not married to.

York testified having heard of a detective who walked into the detective room one night while Golubski was engaged in a sexual act—the kind of situation that Rosie McIntyre had described being forced into.

The chiefs said Golubski was known within the department for his ability to clear cases. "He had a vast number of informants," Armstrong testified. "If you needed some information, he was someone you could go to and he could find that information out."

In their testimony neither Armstrong, Miller, nor York expressed any doubts about whether the informants were credible, whether those arrested were guilty, nor how Golubski had built his network of informants.*

All three of the former commanders denied learning that Golubski was engaged in sexual acts with women who were being exploited by Golubski because they were vulnerable to arrest for drugs, prostitution or other illegal acts. Years later, the former chiefs insisted there never were any reports of complaints about Golubski, and the allegations never reached them. Ron Miller said the allegations raised in Barron Bowling's lawsuit had been thoroughly vetted before he was confirmed by the U.S. Senate as U.S. Marshal. The larger issue, said Miller, is that over many decades KCK police officers were held accountable, disciplined, terminated and, on occasion, prosecuted. "It defies logic that somehow Golubski escaped that accountability because of his 'connections' within the police department." Rick Armstrong, who would become president of the Metro Kansas City Crime Commission, said in 2025 the allegations of longstanding corruption in the Kansas City Kansas police were

---

* That is not to say such doubts did not exist among Golubski's colleagues. There were plenty of officers down in the ranks who shared the views offered in an affidavit by retired detective named Tim Maskil: "I believe that the administration of the Kansas City police department turned a blind eye to Golubski's activities because the information that Golubski appeared to be obtaining from these black prostitutes/informants seemed to get results in terms of getting cases cleared." In recent interviews, former chief Miller, now the U.S. Marshal, and former chief Armstrong both reject the accusation from Maskil, or a series of other former officers that Golubski's misconduct was widely known. Both Miller and Armstrong note that there is no record of any complaints about Golubski's conduct—and had there been any complaints, they said in separate interviews, they would have been followed up.

false. The department command, he said, never heard reports of corruption by Golubski.

And yet, Jim and Cheryl were hearing that over and over again from victimized residents of the community and, even, from current and former members of the force. The problem was convincing those officers to be willing to voice their complaints publicly, to cross the blue line that Judge Robinson had referred to as she ruled in the case of the motorist, Barron Bowling.

When Tim Hausback read news accounts of police officials denying knowledge of Golubski's misdeeds, he was incensed. Hausback stopped reading the news and contacted Cheryl Pilate to report his own story. He had joined the KCK police force in 1972, driven by idealism to help protect crime victims. A few years into his service, he observed Golubski parked while on duty in an area outside his district frequented by sex workers. Hausback consulted the women and then filed a report to internal affairs: "We've got an officer down here out of his district on duty getting blow jobs."

When nothing happened, Hausback reported him again.

Days later, Hausback was called into internal affairs, but it was not to keep him informed on the results of his investigation; instead, it was to put him on notice that a pimp had filed a complaint that Hausback was extorting money from him. The accusation vanished after Hausback hired a lawyer who accused the pimp of slander; to this day Hausback is certain that Golubski arranged the false complaint against him.*

* Hausback described the incident both in an interview and in a sworn affidavit. Former police officials interviewed recently discount Hausback's allegation, insisting no such reports were filed.

It was only one of many moments during Hausback's eighteen years on the job that challenged his idealism. Even before he graduated the academy, he witnessed a former school classmate dragged to the booking desk, his torso covered with wounds that appeared the result of police blackjacks. Years later, he would witness a suspect's death that Hausback feared was the result of improper force. In one case that haunts him, a confidential informant of his was found dead soon after Hausback was ordered to reveal his name to his superiors.

But when Hausback filed reports upon observing apparent misconduct, he found himself estranged and ostracized. As a young officer he was assigned to the vice squad and made repeated arrests at a strip club that was flouting the laws. The owner confronted him and asked what he wanted. Money? A woman? Two women? The strip club owner assured Hausback that other officers were accepting his largesse.

Hausback reported the corruption to his captain, who directed him to the chief's office. Almost immediately, Hausback found, word spread that Hausback had crossed the blue line and reported them. He was left to solve on his own threats he learned that the club owner had made.*

Hausback spent seventeen years on the force before he was forced to retire on medical disability in 1990 as a result of an injury incurred while on duty.

Hausback and Seifert had landed in a department that rewarded officers who were part of the inner circle and drove away officers who were

* Hausback described the incident at length in an interview, and said he ultimately took care of it himself. He confronted the bar owner, telling him that if anything happened to him, another officer was prepared to blow the club owner's head off, and the matter was put to rest.

not. An insular place where officers who went to Bishop Ward High School, grew up in the parish of St. John's, or who had the right uncle or brother-in-law could do most anything—and those who lacked such insider connections were distrusted.

Doug Parisi joined the force in 1995, months after Lamonte McIntyre first was sent to prison. He was an air force brat, the son of a soldier who moved from base to base before finally settling in suburban St. Louis. He then attended the University of Kansas where he met his future wife, and after graduation, followed her to KCK, where she entered medical school. He worked at the Wyandotte County juvenile detention center before entering the KCK police academy.

Back when Doug graduated from Parkway Central High School in St. Louis, the St. Louis Cardinals' head coach, Gene Stallings, offered the class advice that stuck with him: "Spend fifteen minutes a day reading something about the career you're in."* Once Doug joined the force, he stuck his nose into law books, general orders, standard operating procedures, anything that would increase his knowledge. He graduated first in his class at the academy and quickly gained a reputation as a by-the-book officer.

And an outsider.

While still a rookie, he was called in one night at 2:00 A.M., four hours ahead of his normal shift. On his way in, Doug responded to a call that officers were in pursuit of a suspect.

Doug headed off the suspect, handcuffed him, and called on the radio that he had him in custody. "Don't cuff him," the officers in

---

* A classmate of Doug's was Stallings's daughter Martha Kate, perhaps explaining why the College Football Hall of Fame inductee was available to speak at commencement.

pursuit responded. "Don't cuff him," they called again frantically. Whether the suspect got in the car or not, Doug was not sticking around.

The suspect dove into the back seat. As Doug began to drive away, two officers from the night shift arrived and urged the rookie officer to release the prisoner to them. He declined. Hours later, on the day shift, a veteran colleague explained to Doug: "They do things differently on the midnight shift."

Doug worked his way up the department, from sergeant to captain, assigned at various points to the chief's office, where he helped develop policy; to communications; and to patrol. He was for a time commander of the academy. He helped develop programs to deescalate incidents involving the mentally ill, an issue of special importance to him.

He quickly developed the reputation as a guy who knew the rules inside and out and abided by them. Also rising through the ranks was a former partner of Golubski's, Terry Zeigler. As Doug describes it, "Terry Zeigler and I were just in different factions." Doug was not a fan of how the other faction worked.*

Doug had an unblemished record and received a series of commendations. But that changed after Zeigler became chief of police. Doug had been assigned, as acting major, to investigate whether the animal control commander had been submitting inaccurate and incomplete reports regarding thousands of dollars in misspent county money. Doug documented the financial irregularities as well as his concerns

* Zeigler authored a book on leadership, *Popcorn Fridays*, in which he wrote that being linked in news accounts as Golubski's former partner did "irreparable damage to my reputation and image." Zeigler noted he only had been Golubski's partner for three years, and not during the time Lamonte McIntyre was arrested.

that the commander had an inappropriate relationship with the animal shelter director while the alleged misspending was occurring.

Normally such allegations would go to the internal affairs unit. But by the time Doug began his investigation, the commander had been reassigned to take charge of internal affairs. So Doug submitted his report to his supervisor, not to internal affairs.

He heard nothing more about the allegations he raised. But weeks after Doug submitted his report, an internal affairs investigation was launched into whether Doug was living improperly outside the county.

Before long Terry Zeigler was promoted to be the new chief of police. Within weeks, Zeigler called Doug into his office and fired him, based on the internal affairs conclusion that Doug had committed "major violations" of county regulations by living outside the county.

Doug contended the firing was retaliation. Doug denied violating any written department regulations. He also contended plenty of other officers, presumably the "insiders," lived openly outside the county with no repercussions. He tried to sue, but the case was dismissed because Doug missed the filing deadline. The merits of the case were left unresolved.*

But Zeigler would, within a few years, face more accusations that he and the department he ran had long been willing to tolerate misconduct and to obstruct efforts to investigate corrupt practices. And it would take the case of Lamonte McIntyre to pry open practices that long had been covered over.

---

* Oddly, in his book *Popcorn Fridays*, Zeigler described his opposition to the county's residency requirement, which he maintained was an obstacle to recruiting and maintaining the best police officers.

30
Righting Wrongs

Lamonte was feeling increasingly hopeful. He spent days in school, studying business-related courses toward a degree from Donnelly College, a small local Catholic university that offered a program within the prison. He was working. He was reading the Bible and everything else he could get his hands on.

He was determined to right all the wrongs he had committed, all acts that he knew Jesus would not be happy about. He could not stop thinking about Corisha. He wrote her letters from prison, all of them ignored. She changed her phone number but Lamonte got the new number from her younger brother.

He wrote her and called again. This time, Corisha took the call, and they began catching each other up on the nine years that were lost between them. Before he hung up, Lamonte asked for and won Corisha's permission to call again.

On the third call, he asked her if she was happy. She answered that it was funny that he asked, because she was going through a divorce. Her new husband, Patrick, and she had recognized that they were just incompatible, and started divorce proceedings. At the final hearing, Patrick had a divorce lawyer, and Corisha went on her own. The lawyer sat between them, and told the judge that it could not have been more amicable.

Lamonte and Corisha discovered they had both turned to God. They exchanged spiritual books and continued their telephone conversations. Finally, at the end of one conversation, Lamonte asked Corisha if she wanted to come visit him. She reminded him that the process of getting on a visitor's list was slow, and any visit would be months away.

No, he said, it would not be that difficult. He had never taken her off his visitor's list.

As they gathered stories, Jim McCloskey and Dan Clark heard the story of one woman they knew they had to track down who had long ago left town. They spread the word throughout the community and through social media. It took several weeks, but then one day Rosie McIntyre, Lamonte's mother, called and left her phone number for Jim.

Her story was chilling: When she was a teenager, two friends were murdered. She gave Golubski the names of the men who had committed the crime. Soon after, the woman started hearing on the street that Golubski had alerted the murderers that she had identified them. "That made me a target of those killers," as she put it in an affidavit that Cheryl was later able to secure.

Her mother gave her $800 and told her to leave town. She moved with her toddler to a new home, out of state, and had remained away ever since.

Corisha was nervous as she got in the car to go visit Lamonte. It was strange, being nervous about going to the prison, the same prison she had visited for years to see Lamonte, a man to whom she had been married.

Lamonte had cut her off before so abruptly and without explanation, leaving her in pain for years. She knew the road to Lansing, up US 73, by memory. As she got closer, her stomach began jumping.

Inside, Lamonte was equally excited. Visits were his escape from a world he could not relate to. He thought about the other prisoners who were addicted to hooch or drugs to escape prison's harsh realities, and a thought crossed his mind: His addiction was human contact by way of visits.

Finally, the guards came and escorted him to the prison waiting room. Corisha was waiting for him. They hugged, tightly. And kissed, for the first time in forever.

That day they talked about spirituality. They talked about their lives apart. They talked about loneliness. It seemed Lamonte knew Corisha in a way no one else did. The time flew by. It seemed like her visit ended just as it was getting started.

Before they parted, he made her promise that she would visit again. He wrote in his journal, *Now I understand how important visits are. I enjoy every moment, every minute and every second because I know that once this visit is over, I'm going back to fighting for sanity. I find myself struggling through the week just to get to the weekend for visits. Some people say that's the only time they see me smile.*

He added what he hated most about the visits: *I never got used to the act of getting naked at the end of visit to be searched for drugs. I hate standing there naked in front of a stranger suspected of having drugs. The entire process is humiliating. I'm sure when the first prison was created the creator didn't have people like me in mind.*

31
A "Good Trick"

Lamonte was nearing his thirty-seventh birthday and had now spent more than half his life behind bars.

In March 2013, Jim and Cheryl returned to see Jerry Gorman, the district attorney. They intended to file the new petition on Lamonte's behalf by summertime, Cheryl told Gorman, and it would be "explosive and ugly." Cheryl made clear to him that they would omit nothing. About Golubski. About prosecutor Terra Morehead. Because of the allegations of an affair between Judge Burdette and Morehead, she made clear they would ask for an out-of-county judge.

Gorman listened attentively but took no notes. He noted that the case had been reviewed by twelve jurors and the appellate courts. He asked what Cheryl and Jim expected him to do, and said he would like the courtesy of receiving whatever motion Cheryl filed in advance of it being filed, to offer him the chance to review it before it went public.

After the meeting Cheryl and Jim divided up tasks and agreed that the petition, the key to Lamonte finally being freed, should be filed no later than the end of that summer. On Mother's Day, 2013, Cheryl promised Rosie that her son would be home by the next Mother's Day.

Cheryl's promise did not work out. There were more people to talk to, more affidavits to gather, and investigator Dan Clark had stepped away to tend to his ailing wife.

Six months after Mother's Day, the motion still had not been filed, but Jim wrote a memo making clear that he believed the investigation was complete. After recounting what was accomplished on his seventeenth trip to KCK, Jim concluded by writing of himself, "For all practical purposes, McCloskey's investigation of Lamonte McIntyre's case has concluded."

Cheryl, however, did not share Jim's view, and on top of that was facing the pressure of other matters. The Democratic attorney general of Missouri had his eye on the governor's seat and was pressing for more and faster executions of the state's death row prisoners.

Like so many places around the country, Missouri's effort to execute prisoners was hobbled by legal challenges over whether the method of lethal injections amounted to cruel and unusual punishment that violated the Constitution. Missouri had moved to break through that morass in May 2013 by creating a new cocktail of lethal drugs, and the attorney general now was pushing to execute twenty-one prisoners under the new protocol. Cheryl had been appointed to represent two of them.

The state set an execution date of January 29, 2014, for Herbert Smulls, convicted of murdering a jeweler while robbing his suburban St. Louis store. Another five months later, her other client, Russell Bucklew, convicted of kidnapping and raping his ex-girlfriend, and murdering the man she was with when Bucklew arrived, was also scheduled for execution.

As is typical in death penalty cases, the impending executions set off a flurry of last-ditch efforts to prevent the men from being put to death. Smulls was executed as the state ignored a series of frantic letters and calls from Cheryl and Lindsay Runnels protesting that all of Smulls's legal challenges had not been exhausted. Cheryl won delays in the execution of Bucklew as she filed appeals up and down the legal system.

Weeks after Smulls's execution, and just as Bucklew's case was becoming more desperate, Cheryl visited Lamonte and apologized to him for the delays in filing his petition. He was her top priority, she assured him, and her job was to make the petition reflect the strength of his case. She promised to be back to him in sixty days, petition in hand. Lamonte wrote a note to Cheryl saying, "I'll see you in 56 days, 13 hours and 29 minutes."

Cheryl developed more interviews, more affidavits, more evidence of the corruption of Roger Golubski in particular and the KCK police force in general. She shared the eagerness of Lamonte, his mother Rosie, and Jim for Lamonte to get out of prison. But she also felt she still was developing new information that would be so explosive officials would have no choice but to release Lamonte. She understood everyone's impatience, but she also could not risk any chance of failure. Cheryl was the attorney of record for Lamonte, the one with the responsibility for the legal decisions on Lamonte's behalf; and she was determined to take the time to make the case for Lamonte's freedom to be airtight.

After Cheryl visited Lamonte, Morgan Pilate associate Lindsay Runnels went to the Topeka Correctional Facility, armed with the draft of an affidavit that reflected all the things a woman named Natasha Hodge had told Cheryl and Lindsay over a series of interviews. Hodge was serving an eleven-year sentence for killing her boyfriend who had physically abused her, including incidents when he beat her with a lead pipe and broke a beer bottle on her head.

It had taken several visits to Topeka before Natasha was ready to sign an affidavit. Now that day was at hand, and the information Natasha had been providing over months was reduced to writing: Hodge had left home when she was sixteen, only after she had been physically abused by her mother and sexually abused by her father. She ended up developing a crack cocaine habit and became a sex worker to raise money to feed her addiction.

Hodge said that one day Detective Golubski pulled her over on the street to question her, saying she matched a battery suspect. Golubski took her cell phone number before letting her leave his car.

Before long, Golubski was among the KCK police force members who were her clients. Another was Bobby Lane, the detective who had been involved in the incident that grew out of Barron Bowling colliding with the DEA agent's car.

Hodge called Golubski a "good trick," never physically abusive and always willing to pay her for her services. He also paid her money for tips regarding crimes he was working.

Not all officers were so good to her. Hodge told of one officer who ordered her to leave the U-Haul truck in which she was sitting with a friend at a gas station. That officer handcuffed her, ordered her into the back seat of his squad car, and drove her to an abandoned house off Quindaro Boulevard and forced her to give him oral sex. Hodge said that she reported the incident and internal affairs officers accompanied her back to the abandoned house, where they found her nose ring and his boot prints. And yet, nothing came of it; no charges were filed.*

Her affidavit, notarized by a prison staff member, states: *When Det. Golubski, Det. Lane or other officers came to my house for sexual services they generally wore their uniforms, if they were street cops, or their typical work clothes if they were detectives. They also drove their official police cars. They did not think anything of it, and neither did anyone else. It was a common occurrence for Kansas City, Kansas, cops to frequent prostitutes. The cops were all powerful, and if they wanted to go to a prostitute's house in the middle of the afternoon, that's what they did.*

Cheryl sent the affidavit on to Jim with a note that Natasha was "solid, sympathetic and cooperative."

Mother's Day in 2014 fell on May 11. Not only was Lamonte not going to be home as promised, but the long-awaited petition was still not yet filed.

The State of Missouri scheduled an execution of Russell Bucklew for May 21, and two days before Mother's Day, Cheryl filed an urgent lawsuit in U.S. District Court, contending the new cocktail the state intended to use would amount to cruel and unusual punishment because of Bucklew's unique medical condition.** Two days before the execution date, U.S. District Chief Judge Beth Phillips dismissed the lawsuit and refused to grant a stay of execution.

---

* Melinda Henneberger wrote of Hodge's experiences in a *Kansas City Star* article published June 27, 2021, headlined in print, DA DECLINED TO PROSECUTE KCK COP ACCUSED OF RAPE, and republished online under the headline ROGER GOLUBSKI WASN'T THE ONLY ALLEGED RAPIST IN KCKPD, BUT DA "DECLINED TO PROSECUTE." The incident occurred in 1996, back when Tomasic was still district attorney. After her first column was published, Henneberger wrote a second column, EX-KCK COP: COLLEAGUE ALSO ASSAULTED ME, republished online as: HE'S DEFINITELY A SEXUAL PREDATOR: FORMER KCK COP SAYS COLLEAGUE ASSAULTED HER, TOO.

** Bucklew suffered since infancy with a vascular tumor that covered much of his face.

In the frantic hours before Bucklew was to be executed, a divided three-judge panel of the Eighth U.S. Circuit Court of Appeals agreed to stay the execution until Bucklew's appeal of Judge Phillips's decision dismissing his lawsuit could be heard. Hours later, the full Eighth Circuit agreed to consider the appeal en banc, but lifted the stay in the meantime, meaning the execution could take place even before the panel considered the merits of the appeal. At the eleventh hour, the U.S. Supreme Court ordered the execution to be postponed until the appeal was resolved.

It was, literally, a case of life and death importance. The full Eighth Circuit Court set a schedule for its review of the appeal that demanded Cheryl's attention that summer. Over the course of two months she had to file a brief, which totaled sixty pages; then a response to the state's brief; and then prepare to orally argue the case before the full court in St. Louis at the start of September.

Not only had Mother's Day come and gone, so too had Lamonte's thirty-eighth birthday, as well as the sixty-day deadline that Cheryl had committed to Lamonte.

But Cheryl was not yet done gathering information and was undeniably moving the ball forward. In one new affidavit, a woman accused Golubski of trying to coerce her into falsely saying she witnessed a man commit murder when she had seen no such thing.

Cheryl obtained an affidavit from Ethel Abbott, Golubski's ex-wife, and from Gary Long, Lamonte's appointed lawyer, who said prosecutor Terra Morehead never informed him that Niko Quinn or anyone else ever told her that Lamonte was the wrong man. Mark Sachse, the ineffective post-conviction lawyer, provided an affidavit acknowledging that he had never talked to or communicated with Lamonte while being paid to represent him. "This was not unusual in Wyandotte County during that time period," he said.

32

"A Very Corrupt Place"

As the months flew past, Jim McCloskey, like Lamonte, was growing increasingly anxious. He made one last trip to KCK in early November 2014 and spent the day in a work session with Cheryl, taking stock of where things stood.

Cheryl had begun feeding information as she developed it to FBI agents, information on witnesses who claimed that Golubski abused them, witnesses who alleged Golubski was using drugs as currency for sex and information, witnesses who alleged Golubski was protecting drug dealers who were behind much of the violence on the very streets that Golubski was supposed to be protecting. She promised Jim that she would write the petition that month.

She told Lamonte's mother, Rosie, that her son would be home by Valentine's Day, just months away. When Rosie told that to Jim, he was left to tell Rosie the awkward news that it would not happen that quickly.

Cheryl believed that the petition would be so rich in detail, an atom bomb on the justice system, that District Attorney Gorman would support freeing Lamonte once he appreciated the magnitude of their motion. Jim agreed with Cheryl that the petition, and the resulting media attention, would provide a powerful jolt. "I don't think its explosiveness is an exaggeration," he told her.

But Jim had been disappointed by prosecutors too many times. He told her that Gorman would instinctively oppose the motion to protect the "integrity" of Wyandotte County, such as it was.

As the end of the year neared, Jim wrote Cheryl that he had a conversation with Lamonte, and said the repeated delays were "depressing him and wearing him to the nub." He added, "What he doesn't understand and what frustrates him is that given the past assurances of filing and coming-home dates that have come and gone over the last year and a half and everyone agreeing that we have more than enough to proceed to court, why haven't we done so?"

Jim conceded the affidavits Cheryl continued to collect were "very important." Even so, he added, "Let's let go of our obsession with building the case against Golubski. Our cup runneth over with affidavits against him. With the infinite number of Black women who have been abused by him over the last thirty+ years, it is an endless enterprise that can only end when we ourselves decide to end it."

Jim and Cheryl, of course, had history together that predated Lamonte McIntyre. They had worked together successfully to free Ellen Reasonover, and then Darryl Burton. Now they had worked together for five years on Lamonte's case and had become close friends as well as colleagues.

Though he couched his email in praise for Cheryl's work, she did not take kindly to it. "I am doing my best," she wrote. "You and Lamonte will have to trust me to judge the legal environment. I know what it takes to win this, and I am doing it. Lamonte can discuss all of this next week with me if he likes. He is generally depressed and has been for years. I am not pursuing things that do not need to be done. And what I am doing on Golubski at this point is generally giving information to the FBI. I am indeed wrapping up the affidavits and am getting to the petition. There is no need for an 'intervention.'"

A few days later, Jim received a letter from Lamonte describing his phone conversation with Cheryl that followed Jim's prodding. "She said we are almost there and I should be patient," Lamonte recounted. "She also said that she is being careful because she doesn't want to lose this case."

Jim wrote again to Cheryl. "I urge you to NOW set aside everything else in Lamonte's case, and with singular purpose and focus WRITE the petition as only you can do . . . [P]lease, it's time to do what we're all waiting for you to do."

Two weeks later, Cheryl sent Jim an email with an update. She listed a considerable amount of work she had done, interviewing new witnesses about Golubski and sharing her information with the FBI. Her list said nothing about the petition, further alarming Jim.

ABOVE: Doniel Quinn and Donald Ewing were sitting in this blue Cadillac on Hutchings Street when a man dressed in black and wielding a shotgun appeared. *Police photo of crime scene, introduced as court exhibit.* BELOW: When Jim McCloskey took on Lamonte McIntyre's case, he quickly determined the difficulty seeing details from where eyewitness Ruby Mitchell lived to the Cadillac up Hutchings Street. *Photograph taken by McCloskey in 2009.*

ABOVE: A man dressed in black carrying a gun walked through the empty lot from Hiawatha to Hutchings Street, as part of the reenactment conducted by the team working to prove Lamonte innocent. BELOW: Josephine Quinn was sorting clothes in the yard of her Hutchings Street home, and not paying attention to her nephew sitting with another man in a car across the street, when the shotgun-wielding assailant arrived.

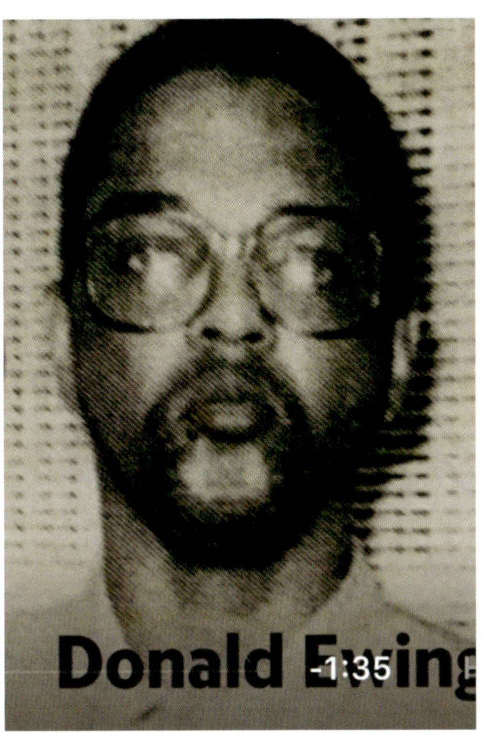

Donald Ewing, thirty-five, was one of two men sitting in the parked Cadillac, the unlucky extra victim when the man in black walked up to the car with a shotgun.

A few years before he was murdered, Doniel Sublett Quinn was photographed at the Sweetheart Dance at Washington High School in Kansas City, Kansas.

Kansas City, Kansas, police detective Roger Golubski put together five photographs to show witnesses of the April 1994 shooting. Oddly, they included Lamonte, suspect number 3, as well as his brother and his cousin.

An undated photograph of Rosie McIntyre, Lamonte's mother, who spent years fighting to overturn the unjust conviction of her son.

All Colored People
THAT WANT TO
GO TO KANSAS!
On September 5th, 1877,
Can do so for $5.00

IMMIGRATION.

WHEREAS, We, the colored people of Lexington, Ky., knowing that there is an abundance of choice lands now belonging to the Government, have assembled ourselves together for the purpose of locating on said lands. Therefore,

BE IT RESOLVED, That we do now organize ourselves into a Colony, as follows: — Any person wishing to become a member of this Colony can do so by paying the sum of one dollar ($1.00), and this money is to be paid by the first of September, 1877, in installments of twenty-five cents at a time, or otherwise as may be desired.

RESOLVED, That this Colony has agreed to consolidate itself with the Nicodemus Towns, Solomon Valley, Graham County, Kansas, and can only do so by entering the vacant lands now in their midst, which costs $5.00.

RESOLVED, That this Colony shall consist of seven officers —President, Vice-Pres dent, Secretary, Treasurer, and three Trustees. President — M. M. Bell; Vice-Preside — Isaac Talbott; Secretary — W. J. Niles; Treasurer — Daniel Clarke; Trustees — Je Lee, William Jones, and Abner Webster.

RESOLVED, That this Colony shall have from one to two hundred militia, mo less, as the case may require, to keep peace and order, and any member failing n his dues, as aforesaid, or failing to comply with the above rules in any particul ot be recognized or protected by the Colony.

The poster encouraging the migration of Exodusters to Kansas was part of the collection of civil rights activist and historian Chester Owens, the first Black man elected to Kansas City, Kansas, City Council.

Tom Dailey was indicted by the U.S. Organized Crime Strike Force for taking bribes in 1973, but, after he was acquitted, Dailey was welcomed back to the force and rose to become police chief at the time of the murders on Hutchings Street.

Don't worry PAPA everythings going to be ok. The lord is going to work it out and we can be together once more. So don't worry and be happy. your grandson, LOVES YOU

I'll be home SOON!

Lamonte McIntyre

After his arrest, Lamonte McIntyre sent a card to his grandfather, David Crowder, assuring him that he would soon be coming home. *Courtesy of the McIntyre family.*

Terra Morehead prosecuted the cases of many of Wyandotte County's most serious cases, including the murder charges of Lamonte McIntyre. Only long after Morehead had left the district attorney for the prestigious U.S. attorney's office did her aggressive style of prosecution become an issue.

Gary Long was appointed to represent Lamonte McIntyre in the 1994 murder trial. Long's failures to competently represent his clients would soon become a recurring issue, though Long nevertheless served as president of the Wyandotte County Bar Association in 2021.

J. Dexter Burdette served as a Wyandotte County district judge from the time of his election in 1988 until his retirement 30 years later. Burdette was the trial judge in Lamonte McIntyre's murder trial and later repeatedly rejected motions to overturn the verdict based on evidence Lamonte was innocent. *Photograph courtesy of Kansas Judiciary Branch.*

As soon as Niko Quinn left the witness stand at Lamonte McIntyre's 1994 trial, she tearfully insisted she had been forced to falsely identify an innocent man. Niko kept fighting on Lamonte's behalf until he finally was acquitted more than two decades later. *Photograph courtesy of Carlos Moreno/KCUR.*

The Kansas State Penitentiary opened in 1868 and, over the next century and a half, housed many convicted of serious crimes. Later renamed Lansing Correctional Facility, it is where Perry Smith and Dick Hickock, made famous in *In Cold Blood*, were hanged, and where, for years, Lamonte McIntyre was incarcerated. *Photograph by Rick Tulsky.*

As a young assistant U.S. attorney, Julie Robinson took on corruption in the Kansas City, Kansas, police force. Years later, after being appointed to as U.S. district judge in 1991, Robinson took on corruption in law enforcement and among federal prosecutors. *Photograph courtesy of Deusen Photography.*

Portraits of two men who presided over the local criminal justice system for decades are displayed in the lobby of the Wyandotte County District Attorney's Office. Nicholas A. Tomasic served for 32 years, from 1972 until 2005; his successor, Jerome A. Gorman, then served until 2017. *Photograph by Rick Tulsky.*

Jim McCloskey was a student at Princeton Theological Seminary when he first became determined to help prisoners who were wrongly convicted of serious crimes. In 2009, McCloskey and his organization, Centurion Ministries, took on the case of Lamonte McIntyre. *Photograph by Diane Bladecki for Centurion Ministries.*

Once he took on Lamonte's case, Jim McCloskey hired attorney Cheryl Pilate, with whom he had worked to free two previous wrongly-convicted prisoners, to work with him. Cheryl would spend years working to develop evidence of Lamonte's innocence, and of the darker corruption of Wyandotte County that had entrapped the innocent teenager. *Photograph by Rick Tulsky.*

Wyandotte County District Attorney Jerome Gorman, (bottom photo) gave no indication he took seriously the claim that Lamonte McIntyre was innocent. Soon after the motion to overturn Lamonte's conviction was filed, Gorman lost his reelection to Mark Dupree (top photo) a lawyer and pastor who built his campaign on justice for the long-underserved Black community. *Photograph courtesy of Allison Long,* The Kansas City Star.

Darryl Burton was wrongly convicted of a St. Louis murder, and was ultimately exonerated through the work of Jim McCloskey and Cheryl Pilate. Darryl moved to Kansas, went through the seminary and provided counsel to Lamonte as he agonized over the delay in being exonerated. *Photograph by Rick Tulsky.*

Upon finally winning his freedom in October, 2017, an elated Lamonte McInytre hugged his lawyer, Cheryl Pilate, in the courtroom; then, once outside, hugged his mother, Rosie McIntyre. *Left photograph courtesy of Midwest Innocence Project. Right photograph by Rick Tulsky.*

Moments after Lamonte (second from right) was freed, he posed for a photograph with Darryl Burton (far left) and the team that won freedom for both of them, Cheryl Pilate and Jim McCloskey. *Photograph courtesy of Midwest Innocence Project.*

As a Kansas City, Kansas, police detective, Roger Golubski developed a reputation with the Black community for abusing women, using his badge and the offer of drugs to get what he wanted. It took Lamonte's case to bring him to account for his actions. *Photograph courtesy of Carlos Moreno/KCUR.*

Lamonte and his mother Rosie, who never lost faith. *Photograph by Rich Sugg,* The Kansas City Star, *Tribune News Service/Getty Images.*

ABOVE: Darryl Burton and Melissa Testrake, the Morgan Pilate paralegal who helped Lamonte cope with prison, celebrate Lamonte's exoneration together. *Photograph courtesy of Midwest Innocence Project.*

LEFT: Lamonte and Corisha Josenberger, at a fundraiser for the Miracle of Innocence. The two were twice married, but discovered tremendous challenges to living together once Lamonte was freed. *Photograph by Rick Tulsky.*

At a rally sponsored by Team Roc, Lamonte told the crowd that for those who felt like they didn't get justice, "this is what it looks like." *Photograph by Rick Tulsky.*

OPPOSITE PAGE, TOP: Lamonte with his grandmother, Maxine Crowder, and his mother, Rosie McIntyre. The two women were powerful forces in Lamonte's upbringing. *Courtesy of the McIntyre family.* OPPOSITE PAGE, BOTTOM: Mark Dupree, left, the first Black person to be elected district attorney in the state of Kansas, with Tyrone Garner, right, the first Black person to be elected mayor of Kansas City, Kansas. They huddled in 2022, prior to the county agreeing to Dupree's request for funding to digitize the court records. *Photograph by Rick Tulsky.*

Lamonte walks through the barber shop that he co-founded and co-owns in Kansas City, Kansas. *Photograph by Rick Tulsky.*

33

Winking at Misconduct

The calendar turned to 2015, two full decades since Lamonte was first sent to prison at Hutchinson. And much as Lamonte's case mattered to Jim, it was not the only issue on Jim's mind.

He had spent the past thirty-five years fighting to free more than one hundred wrongly convicted men and women across the country, one case at a time. The time had come to give up the day-to-day responsibility of budgets, of fundraising, of personnel. Jim had built up Centurion from the fledgling days in Mrs. Yeatman's house. Kate Germond, his longtime colleague, was more than ready to step into the executive director position, and Centurion now had its first legal director, Paul Casteliero. Paul had been connected with Jim a long time. He was the pro bono lawyer who had worked with Jim on his first exoneration, the case of Chiefie, even before Centurion Ministries existed.

On top of all that, Jim had his own longstanding dream of writing a book that could combine his own personal memoir with the story of Centurion over forty years, a book that could raise the organization's profile, even help raise money to secure the organization's future. There were still seven cases, including Lamonte's, that Jim would continue to see through, seven more wrongly convicted men whom Jim had embraced but whose cases were still unresolved. But the work of running the organization would be passed on to Kate and Paul.

While Jim prepared for his retirement, Cheryl continued building the case. This was Lamonte's best shot, she was certain. Retired agent Al Jennerich provided an affidavit based on his long-ago investigation with Julie Robinson, then the assistant U.S. attorney. Years before Doniel Quinn and Donald Ewing were murdered, Jennerich had heard repeatedly that Golubski was using his badge to exploit vulnerable women. As Jennerich described it, the women had nowhere to complain: "Corruption at the KCKPD was longstanding and systemic, and many of the commanding officers swept wrongdoing under the rug rather than confronting and rooting it out." They had no choice but to submit to whatever Golubski demanded. And as Jim and Cheryl were discovering, Golubski did not use that power only to force submission into sexual acts; he also would close cases based on obtaining information from these women, reliable or not.

Anxious for the petition to be filed before he retired, Jim suggested in March 2015 that he and Paul go to KCK to meet with Cheryl. But Cheryl replied that was not needed. She would block off all of April to write and file the petition before his retirement gala.

That plan, like others before it, went awry. In March, the Eighth Circuit Court of Appeals ruled that Judge Phillips was wrong to dismiss without a hearing the death penalty case of Cheryl's client, Russell Bucklew, and sent the case back to the district judge.

Judge Phillips gave Cheryl until April 1 to file an amended complaint and then, after a telephone conference, gave Cheryl until April 30 to file a second amended complaint. So much for blocking out April.

Even so, Cheryl continued her work on Lamonte's behalf. It took weeks and several canceled appointments, but Cheryl secured a sworn statement from Ruby Ellington, the first Black woman to ever serve in KCKPD, who was in poor health. Ruby had been in the academy years earlier with Max Seifert and Roger Golubski, and she had plenty to say about Golubski and a department that looked the other way. "Everyone in the department knew that when Golubski would go out on calls that any Black female involved would likely end up in his police car."

But because Golubski was "part of the 'in' group at the department," the misconduct went unpunished, she added.

To Cheryl, the fact that Golubski's abusive conduct over many years was so widely known without any repercussions was exactly why it took so much time and energy to build trust. Those who lived in the community felt they had no reason to expect anything to come of talking about it, and there was plenty of reason to expect the worst.

Ruby Ellington added one other troubling detail: In her years working in vice and narcotics, her squads tried many times to bring charges against Cecil Brooks. But their search warrants always came up empty. "We had strong reason to suspect that unknown officers within the department were working against our efforts and were warning Brooks about planned raids or stings," the affidavit concludes.

In an email cover sheet, Cheryl wrote to Jim, "You don't know how happy I am," noting, "Ruby has outstanding credibility, and she has shown real courage here." Still, the email was not all great to Jim. Cheryl wrote that "we are working hard on the petition," but were hampered by the resignation from her office of a key staff member.

"Anyway," concludes the email, which was sent the day before Jim's retirement gala, "I am flying out in the morning. Looking forward to celebrating with you."

Jim had always taken the position that Centurion Ministries needed to keep paying Cheryl's bills because the most critical issue was getting Lamonte home. That central mission could not get caught up in a dispute over money. But as Kate took over from Jim, she worried not just about the delays in accomplishing justice but about the bills. They had paid Cheryl more than $180,000 to represent Lamonte and new invoices were still arriving, without a sign of the petition being filed.

Kate, Paul Casteliero, and Jim agreed. It was taking too long and costing way too much; they had more than enough evidence to go forward. More than five years earlier, the outline of the case was clear: Corrupt detective with an outrageous sexual appetite; unscrupulous prosecutor willing to hide exculpatory evidence; and evidence of who committed the murders and why. Cheryl had helped uncover valuable details. *But how could it take this long?*

The group decided that, retired or not, it was up to Jim, given his long relationship with Cheryl, to deliver the news that Centurion Ministries would not pay any more for her work until the petition was filed. But Paul and Kate corresponded further with Cheryl, and some ambiguities developed: Were they intending to *never* pay her for continuing work? Or were they intending to delay payment until after the petition was filed? And if they intended for her to complete the petition, how did they think that work would be paid for?

34
Building the Atom Bomb

From Cheryl's point of view, her duty was to press forward on Lamonte's behalf. She had significant experience in building cases on behalf of defendants, and Centurion Ministries had hired her more than six years earlier to make legal judgments. From the time Cheryl filed her entry of appearance on behalf of Lamonte in April 2009, it was her job to build the strongest case, one that would win his freedom by exposing a corrupt system. She knew how unlikely it was to get Wyandotte County officials to acknowledge a grievous mistake. It had to be an atom bomb of a petition.

She also felt that Jim had moved too quickly in doing interviews and taking affidavits. Many of the current and former residents of KCK whose information was at the heart of their case had long been traumatized by a system in which justice was a farce. Maybe Jim had stepped away and Centurion Ministries did not want even more investigation, but Cheryl believed more was needed.

Weeks after the Centurion gala, Cheryl went back to interview a woman with whom she and Jim had long been talking. The woman had been involved in gang activity, including drug dealing, in her youth. Everyone in the group, she said, knew the way to be successful was to pay off police. Her new affidavit states: "Basically, Golubski was a member of the criminal community, and he also had the power of his badge. Everyone knew how powerful Golubski was. He protected the drug dealers but was never investigated for his illegal activities."

In July 2015, Lamonte turned thirty-nine. He had been incarcerated now for two decades. Even as Cheryl was pushing forward on his behalf, she was still battling to keep her death row client Russell Bucklew alive. Judge Phillips continued to reject Cheryl's petition and set a new deadline for an amended complaint. In June. Then October.

Bucklew's life rested in the balance while Lamonte McIntyre's life was being spent behind bars.

Cheryl had brought a retired suburban police detective, Mike Bussell, to join the team in 2014 as Jim stepped away. Bussell had been skeptical of Lamonte's innocence at first, but as he discovered how many people were telling the same stories, he became convinced.

Among those Bussell interviewed was a retired KCK homicide detective who had been among the throng of police investigating in the hours after the murders of Doniel Quinn and Donald Ewing.

Timothy Maskil was in his thirtieth year on the force the day that Doniel Quinn and Donald Ewing were murdered; he would retire nine months later. Two decades later, he was in declining health as Bussell interviewed him. Just as Ruby Ellington had a few months earlier, Maskil stated in his affidavit that "the entire department" knew Golubski was "having sex with Black drug-addicted prostitutes," and also used those same women as his informants. Maskil said he knew top officials had confronted Golubski about his conduct, but added that he believed they "turned a blind eye" because of Golubski's success in using those informants to "solve" cases.

Whether they were properly solved, apparently, was less a matter of concern.

Maskil described the KCKPD as highly political, an institution where politicians and community members of influence could help decide who in the department got ahead and who did not.

With that, Maskil had crossed the blue line. It was a line that had safeguarded Golubski for decades, but through tenacity Cheryl succeeded in overcoming it.

By this time, justice, or more precisely injustice, was on the minds of a growing number of Americans. Weeks before Jim McCloskey's gala, a twenty-five-year-old Black man, Freddie Gray Jr., died after Baltimore police officers on bike patrol took him into custody and he was placed in a police van. The circumstances remained unclear, and after his funeral violence broke out in Baltimore and elsewhere.

Gray's death came a year after Michael Brown, eighteen, a young Black man, was shot to death by a policeman. The shooting followed an altercation that began when Brown was walking with a friend in the street near his grandmother's house in Ferguson, Missouri. Six weeks earlier, Eric Garner died on a New York City sidewalk after he called out, "I can't breathe," while an officer held him in a chokehold.

No government agency keeps authoritative numbers on how many Americans die at the hands of the police each year. *The Washington Post* kept such records for a decade, through the end of 2024, and found 1,000 people were shot to death by police each year across the country, regardless of the circumstances, and Black men are killed at a rate disproportionate to the population.

The deaths of Eric Garner, Michael Brown, and Freddie Gray generated public outcry and heightened attention to the imperfections of a criminal justice system that Black Americans had long known too often victimized them. The dangers to young Black men who encountered police, even when they had done nothing wrong, caused generations of Black parents to give careful instructions to their sons about what to do if stopped by law officers: Be compliant. Make no sudden moves. Keep your hands in sight.

The issue was not just people dying at the hands of the police. There was the Exoneration Registry, which recorded the growing number of documented cases of innocent people, mostly men, who were wrongly convicted—an outcome that threw significant shade on William Blackstone's 500-year-old doctrine that it is better that ten guilty persons escape than that one innocent suffer. There was the growing realization of the failures of the American prison system, locking up far more of the nation's population than any other democratic nation—and especially Americans without the means to hire skilled defense attorneys. There were, as well, people accused of crimes, even nonviolent crimes, who were locked up only because they could not afford bail.

And all of those issues left prosecutors across the country, like Jerry Gorman, who had long held their powerful offices without opposition, facing unprecedented challenges. The last thing Gorman needed was for a legal bomb to explode in Wyandotte County.

35
Time for Change

In the fall of 2015, Mark Dupree decided it was time that he answer the call to take on Jerry Gorman in the 2016 election. Nobody had ever run against him, and only one man even challenged Gorman's predecessor, Nick Tomasic, dating all the way back to when the office first was created in 1972.

Dupree, thirty-four, a Black man, grew up in a house with seven children, three of them adopted, and not a lot of money. Religion was everything: Mark's father was pastor and his mother Linda co-pastor of Grace Tabernacle Family Life Outreach Center, one of the many small churches around KCK. Dupree served the church for years, and by 2025 was senior pastor there.

Early in high school Dupree spent a day shadowing Wyandotte County District Judge Cordell Meeks Jr., the son and namesake of the first Black district judge in the state of Kansas, who was succeeded upon his retirement by his son.

After shadowing Meeks for a day, Dupree went home and told his father he aspired to become a lawyer when he grew up, and for the next several years Judge Meeks served as his mentor. It was a big deal when Dupree, like an older brother, went to college at all. Neither of their parents had done so.

While in college at the University of Kansas, Dupree and some friends went to a movie theatre and, as they were in the lobby, off-duty police stopped and accused them of having entered the theatre without paying. A couple friends left, but Dupree and a friend who were held back insisted they had paid their way inside. More officers were called, and before it was over they used batons and pepper spray on Dupree and his friend. The two spent three days in jail before being bailed out.

The case ultimately went to trial and the judge threw out the more serious charges but convicted Dupree of misdemeanor trespass. It was a lesson to Dupree on how innocent young Black men can be caught up in the system for no reason. "I was the perfect minority college student; chaplain of the choir, dean's honor roll, and I was beat on by six cops," he said in recalling the incident.

Dupree told his father he was determined to use the law to help ensure people are treated equally. He went from KU to Washburn University School of Law in Topeka, and married Shanelle Elaine Gunn, a classmate who shared his devotion to both the law and the Bible. Dupree took on some criminal defense work on his own before forming a partnership with Shanelle, whose focus was family law and child rights.

The only thing he knew about prosecutors, at that point, was "that they lock people up, that they were hard on crime and that they separated families." But then Dupree read the book *Smart on Crime*, written by Kamala Harris as she prepared to run for California state attorney general, and it opened his eyes. The book made him conclude prosecutors could be intentional and community-oriented. As he prayed, he felt the Holy Spirit was directing him to become the elected district attorney for Wyandotte County, a job at which he could enact all the progressive policies that Harris had espoused.

Dupree temporarily shrugged off that feeling and supported Jerry Gorman's 2012 reelection campaign. But four years later, Dupree decided he could no longer ignore the spirit that he felt was commanding him to do more. By late 2015, he was knocking on doors to urge voters to elect him to office.

Telling supporters that "God told me to run this race so we can help Wyandotte County," Dupree didn't talk about locking up more people. Instead, he vowed, "We will work on prevention as well as prosecution, be proactive rather than reactive."

He talked of working with specific categories of defendants—young people, those who committed nonviolent drug crimes, people with mental health issues, and veterans—and to explore alternatives to incarceration for them.

If Cheryl and her team hoped that talk would make Jerry Gorman rethink his policies as the August 2016 Democratic primary approached, that hope was quickly dashed. Gorman had been elected to prosecute dangerous criminals and that was what he intended to do. He listened when Cheryl and other supporters of Lamonte explained the flaws of Lamonte's prosecution but made no commitments about revisiting a conviction that the police department's detectives considered solid.

As Dupree was preparing to launch his campaign, Cheryl hired a new paralegal, Melissa Testrake, who was eager and committed to their now-shared cause of tackling injustice and righting wrongs. She began reading Lamonte's file and was incredulous. Then one day she answered the office phone and it was Lamonte, calling from prison.

Melissa was nervous at first and quickly turned the call over to Cheryl. Cheryl told Lamonte that Melissa was the new paralegal and he could talk to her. They began talking regularly. Each time, Melissa would ask Lamonte how he was doing, and call him out when he responded, "I'm good." She knew Lamonte was not comfortable enough to confide to a stranger, especially a white woman from the suburbs.

The first time Melissa came to prison to visit, they met in the parole room. They talked about the case and so much more. They bonded over music and books. Lamonte, to be sure, was better read than Melissa or most anyone, but Melissa loved reading, especially biographies.

Melissa left that visit moved. Lamonte's struggle and tenacity had a hold on her. Her life's mission became helping to win his freedom.

In the mid-1990s Kansas lawmakers, just like the Missouri attorney general's office, were eager to shut the door on endless appeals of criminal cases, a concept that would make great sense if justice worked flawlessly. But the growing number of defendants who establish their innocence years later showed that not to be the case. Across the country, every day, many prosecutors and judges shrug off the reality that the system is less than flawless, erring more often than many Americans care to believe.

The concept of a defendant being "presumed innocent" is often an empty phrase, and one that too many prosecutors and judges easily shrug off.

In 2014 the Kansas Supreme Court gave the state's trial courts broader latitude to consider habeas corpus petitions filed belatedly in those instances when the facts suggest a manifest injustice. The ruling jolted Kansas lawmakers into action to keep that door from opening too widely. Acting at the request of the Kansas attorney general, Derek Schmidt, the House Committee on Corrections and Juvenile Justice introduced HB 2502 in January 2016. The bill restricted the rights of courts to consider such petitions from prisoners if they were not promptly filed.

The Kansas House of Representatives passed the bill and sent it on to the Senate, where assistant attorney general Lee J. Davidson testified that the bill would "promote judicial efficiency and accuracy by requiring the resolution of issues while the record is fresh, to conserve judicial resources, and to lend finality to convictions within a reasonable time." Otherwise, Davidson warned, prisoners would wait to file their petitions, providing time "for witnesses to die and evidence to disappear and degrade."

The Senate, too, passed the bill, and it was signed into law by Gov. Sam Brownback on May 11, 2016—with an effective date of July 1.

Suddenly the pressure to file the petition intensified. After July 1, the bar would be raised to get a court to even consider the evidence that Jim and Cheryl spent years assembling. The new law would make it that much more challenging.

Even as the deadline for Lamonte drew closer, Cheryl was facing new pressure related to her representation of Russell Bucklew. U.S. District Judge Beth Phillips announced in May that she wanted to set deadlines and resolve Cheryl's lawsuits seeking to block Missouri from injecting Bucklew with its new lethal cocktail.

Judge Phillips also questioned whether Cheryl should temporarily postpone submitting any more bills for her work on behalf of Bucklew until the Eighth Circuit Court of Appeals considered new limits on what the courts should and should not pay for. Like so many lawyers who devote their practices to defense work in wrongful convictions and death penalties, Cheryl was accustomed to both the strain of handling the cases and the financial pressures that can accompany such work. Now, Cheryl was at key junctures in representing both Russell Bucklew and Lamonte McIntyre, and getting paid for her work was an issue in both cases.

She filed a motion before Judge Phillips saying that she could not litigate Bucklew's claims without being paid appropriately. "Counsel cannot conceive of a way to represent Mr. Bucklew's most important interest—his life—without adequate compensation, and funds to retain and pay experts. It is an impossible challenge to meet."

And with that, Cheryl turned her attention to the flurry of activity needed to set off the bomb on Lamonte's behalf.

36
Boom

As July 1 approached, there was still much to do.

Cheryl's investigator, Mike Bussell, went to the crime scene with paralegal Melissa Testrake and investigator Dan Clark in April 2016—when the sunlight would be similar to how it was on the date of the double murders. They rented an old blue Cadillac DeVille—resembling the car that Doniel Quinn and Donald Ewing were in that day—and parked it on the street. They arranged for a few Black men to take part in a reenactment. Two of the men sat in the car, and the shooter, armed with a toy shotgun, followed the path taken years earlier by the actual murderer. Clark stood where Ruby Mitchell would have been standing to document the unlikelihood of making out the features of the shooter from that distance.

In the final weeks before the new law would take effect, the efforts to gather affidavits that would accompany the explosive petition became more desperate. Clark and Bussell gave affidavits about the reenactment, and Bussell provided another affidavit about an interview he had with a former boss of Golubski's, who said "there were a lot of things that were not kosher" going on in the department in 1994.

In addition, Randy Eskina, a retired police captain, reviewed the entire case file and provided a seventeen-page affidavit that detailed how Golubski's investigation was riddled with "glaring failures and omissions" that left the evidence against Lamonte McIntyre so weak he would not have submitted the case to the district attorney for prosecution.

Eskina's affidavit noted the "shortcomings span several categories," but highlighted the failures in dealing with eyewitnesses—including the dubious identification by Ruby Mitchell, the unusual photo array she was shown, and the failure to ever interview Stacey Quinn or to record the second interview Golubski had with Stacey's sister Niko. The review highlighted a multitude of other areas, including the failure to search Lamonte's house for a murder weapon or the black clothing witnesses described.

Cheryl gathered affidavits to explain that the motion was being filed years after the fact because so many Black residents had long feared reprisals if they spoke up. Niko Quinn, for one, had told her Aunt Freda that she had lied on the stand because she was afraid of what would happen if she told the truth. Freda explained in a new affidavit that such fear was commonplace: "In Kansas City, Kansas, I knew it was not unusual for people to be scared of the police or prosecutors. It is well-known in the community that police and prosecutors have used threats and improper and coercive tactics to gain compliance from witnesses."

And Jim McCloskey reinforced that point in an affidavit from Princeton. Jim called the investigation "one of the most challenging" he ever undertook "because of many witnesses' fears of retaliation from law enforcement."

Jim added, "Without question, many of the witnesses we interviewed have a real fear of Roger Golubski specifically and law enforcement in general based on their own experiences in the community."

⁂

The investigation had gone about as far as it could. But Mike Bussell persuaded Cheryl there was one more piece to pursue: they still only had Jim McCloskey's word for Cecil Brooks's account of Doniel's murder, since Cecil had never signed the draft affidavit following Jim's visit to Mississippi.

Cheryl knew how much effort Jim had put into getting Cecil to sign, and did not see much hope in revisiting it with everything else there was to do. But she relented and Melissa Testrake emailed Cecil at the U.S. Medical Center for Federal Prisons in Springfield, Missouri. Cecil had been transferred there, closer to home, after applying to work as an HVAC technician at the prison.

Cecil was curious what evidence Lamonte's team had developed since his last correspondence with Jim. He also wondered if there might be something in it for him to cooperate.

He agreed to be interviewed, and the visit was arranged for June 22, 2016, nine days before the new law was to take effect. Mike and Melissa met at the parking lot of Morgan Pilate while it was still dark and headed south in Mike's Ford Edge, Elvis Presley songs blaring, for the prison 170 miles away. They were armed with the affidavit that Jim McCloskey had prepared six years earlier, still unsigned.

The massive prison hospital in Springfield, known as Fed Med, opened on the day Franklin D. Roosevelt took office in 1933. Over the years it has housed prisoners who included Robert Stroud, known as the Birdman of Alcatraz; *Hustler* magazine publisher Larry Flynt; and Mafia bosses Joe Bonanno and John Gotti, the latter of whom died there of throat cancer.

Mike and Melissa were ushered to a square table in the prison cafeteria, where they sat opposite each other. Cecil was lead in and sat between them. Mike was a seasoned investigator, and now was paired with Melissa, who had an uncanny ability to make people open up and reveal details about themselves. Mike pulled out the affidavit and a legal pad. Melissa started chatting with Cecil about his life.

He had been a promising basketball player, Cecil told them, and had entered college playing ball. But after he blew out his knee, Cecil had to give up basketball and find a job. He ended up in the kitchen at a hotel, where other workers introduced him to crack cocaine. Brooks did not enjoy the drug, but quickly realized he could make far more money selling it than working in the kitchen.

They talked for less than an hour. Cecil asked about being paid for the information, and they insisted they couldn't. What was at stake, they stressed, was getting an innocent man out of prison.

Cecil was not ready to sign until Melissa challenged him: What would he want if his son was an innocent man locked in prison? The question brought Cecil to tears, and soon Mike was adding four paragraphs to add to the draft affidavit Jim McCloskey had prepared years before.

Doniel Quinn was the doorman at Aaron's dope house, the addendum states. Everyone fell asleep, and when they awakened, $3,500 and Doniel were missing. Everyone assumed he had taken the drugs. Days later another member of the gang picked up Monster in a dark blue Oldsmobile Delta 88, and they parked on the next street over from where Doniel Quinn and Donald Ewing sat in the car. Monster walked over with a pump shotgun and killed the two men.

They disassembled the shotgun and threw it in the Missouri River. Brooks said when he was told about the murders, he became angry, because he did not need any heat from authorities.

Bussell wrote one more paragraph for Cecil: "I'm deciding to sign this affidavit because I know it is the right thing to do. I know I have done things to deserve to be in prison, but Lamonte McIntyre did not commit the homicides of Doniel Quinn and Donald Ewing."

Mike tried for one last piece: Would Cecil say anything about Golubski? But Cecil made it clear: No. He was not going to say anything about the former detective, no matter how many stories Bussell may have heard about Golubski working with Cecil.

Cecil Brooks signed the pages drafted by Jim McCloskey, as well as the handwritten addendum. The affidavit reflected what Cecil had told McCloskey years before about Lamonte, "None of us had ever heard of him."

Melissa pulled out her notary stamp, formalizing the sworn declaration.

She and Mike walked out of the prison, got in the car, and took in what had just happened. "Holy shit," Melissa shouted. "We fucking did it. We fucking did it."

Mike called Cheryl on the Bluetooth device in the car to tell her the news. They had met with Cecil, Mike told her, and "We got him to sign the affidavit." Cheryl could not believe it: "You're lying! You're lying!" And Melissa and Mike yelled back, "No! We fucking did it!"

When she returned to the Kansas City, Missouri, office of Morgan Pilate, Melissa wrote an email to Cecil to thank him for his help in righting a horrible injustice. Melissa could not send that email, though. In the time it took to return from Springfield, Cecil had removed her from his list of authorized email contacts.

He did not care to hear from her ever again.

With hours to go before the new law took effect, on June 30, 2016, Lindsay Runnels and Melissa Testrake filled the back seat of their car with copies of the petition, 180 pages long, together with boxes of the affidavits and other documents to be included as exhibits. The petition exploded on the local court system from the opening paragraphs:

> Lamonte McIntyre stands before this Court seeking justice and release from his wrongful conviction and confinement. Arrested when he was just 17 years old, McIntyre has now served 22 years in prison for a double homicide he did not commit and knew nothing about. McIntyre did not even know the two victims and was nowhere near the scene when they were shot. After an eyewitness told police the shooter looked like a man she knew named 'Lamonte,' they arrested a different 'Lamonte'—Lamonte McIntyre.
>
> The arrest of Lamonte McIntyre was the beginning of a nightmare in which virtually nothing happened as it should have. Police and the prosecutor manipulated and threatened witnesses and forced them to testify falsely while concealing exculpatory evidence. Police failed to gather or analyze physical evidence, never looked for a motive, and ignored obvious leads suggesting the homicides were connected with the victims' drug activities. Five months later, McIntyre was convicted of two counts of first-degree murder in a trial studded with prosecutorial abuses and devoid of due process.
>
> Throughout the investigation and trial, the police and prosecutor failed to seek the truth, indeed, they consistently subverted and concealed the truth—manufacturing evidence and presenting testimony that they knew to be false.

The petition took on the entire Wyandotte County law enforcement community. Cheryl wrote of Golubski's lust for Black prostitutes upon whom he relied for information as well as sex. Golubski was widely viewed as "crooked" and "corrupt," the petition states, and many in the department were aware of his practices.

The prosecutor, Terra Morehead, "engaged in deceitful and illicit practices throughout the proceedings that were 'calculated to bring about a wrongful conviction.' Morehead coerced false testimony from Niko Quinn and elicited false testimony from Ruby Mitchell. She failed to disclose that both Niko and her mother, Josephine, told her that Lamonte was not the shooter."

The filing took on Judge Burdette, who had overseen the trial and the posttrial motions, writing that the failure to disclose his former romance with prosecutor Morehead deprived Lamonte of his right to be tried before an impartial tribunal. "The critical point is that Judge Burdette, the former romantic partner of the prosecutor, was the sole decision-maker in critical posttrial proceedings, including a hearing on a motion for a new trial based on newly discovered evidence. Virtually every time Judge Burdette had the opportunity to exercise his discretion, he did so in favor of the prosecutor's position."

The petition took on Gary Long, the court-appointed attorney; Lindsey Erickson, the appellate attorney; and Mark Sachse, the court-appointed post-conviction attorney, contending they all failed to offer Lamonte the representation he was guaranteed by the Constitution.

> The evidence of Lamonte McIntyre's innocence is overwhelming. The newly discovered evidence demolishes the State's flimsy, falsehood-laden case and exposes the murders to be just what they appeared to be—a retaliatory, drug-related hit.

Under state law, a new petition would normally go back to Judge Burdette, the trial judge, for consideration. But Cheryl filed a motion that not just Burdette, but the entire Wyandotte County bench, disqualify itself from considering the case. The county's justice system, after all, was going to be put on trial. The judges agreed within days, and an out-of-county judge, Edward Bouker of Hays, in rural Ellis County, was assigned to hear the case.

Weeks after the petition was filed, Rosie McIntyre drove to Lansing to visit her son on his fortieth birthday. Rosie was shocked by what she realized that day. The man she was looking at was not the boy she had raised. He did not have the same sparkle and joy of her Monte. He had grown up and changed in the years in prison. She felt it that day in a way she never had.

37
A New Day

Cheryl's legal filing could not have come at a worse time for Jerry Gorman, the face of the county's criminal justice system. He had never faced a contested election. Now Gorman faced his first test, against Mark Dupree, who was seeking to become the first elected Black district attorney in Kansas history.

Dupree ran on a platform of reforming the office and pushing for alternative programs to help divert more defendants from prison for nonviolent crimes. He spoke of being a role model for youth, as Judge Meeks had been for him, to show them they could be judges and lawyers as readily as defendants. And he emphasized that he would ensure the office sought justice, not convictions.

"History has shown that when folks get in office and try to pursue convictions rather than justice, mistakes are made. Wrong people are prosecuted," Dupree said as he campaigned.

Once the petition exploded on the court system, the issue was now more than just an abstract matter. As he went knocking on doors, residents asked Dupree what he intended to do about Lamonte's case.

All of this was contrary to the way Gorman and thousands of prosecutors across the country had been taught to think. They were elected to keep their residents safe, to be partners with the police in locking up dangerous criminals. They enjoyed the support of the police, the sheriff, and business owners who had long fostered the status quo. The idea that the office could be run by someone who had himself *been convicted of criminal trespass* after a disruption in a movie theatre seemed preposterous.

As Dupree would later reflect on it, Gorman thought that Dupree's past would be a weapon against him. But having been an innocent victim made him more, not less, connected to the community. "This criminal justice system has screwed over so many people that the people in this community said, 'It's time that someone finally realized that it is flawed.'"

The Kansas City Star, the newspaper that served as the main source of information for the region, made its position known: *Incumbent Jerome Gorman has earned a reputation as a strong prosecutor since taking office in 2005, particularly while he and his staff deal with violent crime cases that afflict parts of Kansas City, Kan. He has earned reelection. The challenger is Mark Dupree.* Period.

Gorman was not about to embrace a case that challenged the way law enforcement operated in Wyandotte County.

Cheryl's petition did not immediately draw media attention, though talk of Lamonte's case was percolating in the predominantly Black north end of Kansas City, Kansas. Then, as the election approached, news accounts began to trickle out. The local ABC affiliate aired interviews with Cheryl, Saundra Newsome, and Rosie McIntyre—and also juror Greg Lauber, who long had felt regrets about his guilty vote, which he cast despite his personal doubts.

The results of the primary election were staggering. Dupree won with 59–41 percent. Given the overwhelming Democratic tilt of the county, Kansas was about to have its first Black district attorney.

The next day, *The Kansas City Star* finally published a story on Lamonte's case, its first. MAN CONVICTED OF KCK DOUBLE MURDER SEEKS EXONERATION, the headline stated.

After filing the motion, Cheryl still had plenty of work to finally get Lamonte home. There also was the matter of being paid for the work she had performed after the time Centurion Ministries said it would stop paying her.

Melanie Morgan, Cheryl's partner, wrote Centurion Ministries to point out language of the contract Jim had signed with Cheryl long ago, and demanded payment for work Cheryl had provided since the money was cut off. The new bill was for more than $129,000, a significant amount for Centurion, an organization with an operating budget of about $1 million a year.

Kate, Paul, and Jim all felt the charges were excessive, especially since they felt the motion had taken years too long to prepare. It was all unfortunate and sad. Jim and Cheryl had been friends, dedicated to justice and the difficult work in attaining it, and now, with a long-awaited victory seeming in reach, a chasm divided them.

Morgan Pilate sued Centurion, the first time *that* ever happened to the organization, and both sides felt morally wronged. Jim went to his board speaking of "righteous indignation." To Cheryl and Melanie, Centurion was reneging on its promise to pay Cheryl for work that she had poured herself into and that she deemed essential to establish Lamonte's innocence.

The case ended up in the hands of a mediator and was settled for an undisclosed sum that Centurion Ministries only would describe as "substantial." But the price was more than money. The dispute was the final rupture in Jim and Cheryl's relationship.

More than fourteen years after Lamonte began corresponding with Centurion Ministries, when no one else would give him the time of day, the organization's role on his behalf was over. The Midwest Innocence Project, one of the organizations that had sprouted up around the country to take on wrongful convictions, agreed to give Cheryl the support she needed to keep fighting on Lamonte's behalf.

Lamonte was beside himself with the long delays. He talked with Melissa Testrake regularly on the phone and she paid several visits to the prison. He felt like she was one of the few people on the outside, other than his mother, whom he could trust. He told her about Corisha and his increasing desperation for freedom.

The wait for justice was agony. Cheryl beseeched Darryl Burton, the previous exoneree on whose case she and Jim had worked together, to get in touch and try to bring Lamonte some calm. Darryl had moved to the Kansas City area, attended theological seminary, and become associate pastor of Church of the Resurrection, which has 19,000 members and calls itself the largest United Methodist church in the country. Darryl had some reservations about going back inside a prison, but he agreed and went to Lansing. There, he connected with Lamonte and gave him the best advice he could. Be patient.

Melissa set up an account to email Lamonte. Prisoners pay for email they send with stamps, and Melissa started buying stamps and sending them to Lamonte so they could correspond.

She told him about little things, about her son Mason's soccer games and her son Parker's fourth birthday party. She sent him books, *Men Are from Mars, Women Are from Venus,* and one of her favorites, *Tuesdays with Morrie.* Lamonte sent her a longer list of books he hoped she could send to him. Just as so many others felt after talking with Lamonte, Melissa agonized over how the years were wearing on him.

Corisha had overcome her initial fears and was eager each weekend as she headed to the prison. He was the only person who really knew her, who understood her, the person she could talk to about anything. Her secrets were safe with Lamonte; he was her soulmate.

Her mother, who had disapproved of their union, remained a skeptic. "You need to slow down," she would say. "You need to think about the big picture." But Corisha told her mother she was going to do what felt right to her.

Cheryl arranged a prison visit for a *Kansas City Star* reporter who wanted to write a feature story. The publicity could only help push Dupree, the incoming DA. After the reporter visited, Lamonte told Corisha in a telephone conversation to be ready, that there was going to be news coming about his case. Then, one day she was in the convenience store, and there was his picture on the front page of the paper.

In early November, Melissa had a different kind of news for Lamonte: She was leaving her job at Morgan Pilate, feeling the long hours more than she could handle with young children. She feared he would feel abandoned and assured him that she was staying involved in his case. She said she hoped this would be his last Thanksgiving away from his loved ones; then, a few weeks later, offered the same hope about Christmas.

After he handily defeated Jerry Gorman in the 2016 Wyandotte County Democratic primary, Mark Dupree had to wait five months until after the November general election, when he faced no opposition, before he would finally be sworn in.

Not everyone was in support, to put it mildly. Before his inauguration Dupree interviewed all the members of the staff and decided to dismiss six veteran assistant district attorneys. *The Kansas City Star* reported that those who were fired included "some of Wyandotte County's most experienced prosecutors," who handle "murders and other serious cases."*

It quickly became obvious that the old guard had no faith in what would happen after Dupree took office. After a tragedy struck at what was billed as the world's biggest waterslide, Gorman made clear his own mistrust.

A ten-year-old boy was decapitated when the raft he was riding at Schlitterbahn Waterpark flew off its track. The boy's father was a Republican state senator. Instead of launching an investigation, which would be handed off to Dupree's administration, Gorman turned the case over to the state attorney general, explaining that he considered the case too complex for Dupree's incoming office to handle. With so

---

* One of the three cited by name in the article was Ed Brancart, who had received the "Nick A. Tomasic Prosecutor of the Year" award from Gorman in 2014. In 2020 Brancart, who went on to work in the office of state attorney general Derek Schmidt, was cited for misconduct in his days as prosecutor; Brancart had elicited testimony from an unreliable jailhouse informant and failed to disclose the tactics he used in the prosecution, leading to a wrongful murder conviction of a Wyandotte County mail carrier. In overturning the verdict, the judge accused Brancart of suborning perjury from the informant.

many experienced prosecutors leaving, Gorman said he and Schmidt agreed it was best to have the attorney general's office review the case and prosecute if appropriate.*

The first Black district attorney anywhere in Kansas took office facing an openly disdainful establishment.

---

* That alleged superior expertise turned out to be overrated. District Judge Robert Burns threw out the criminal charges Schmidt's office brought against the park owners and ride designer. Burns found Schmidt's office had misled the grand jury, taking quotes out of context. "The court has grave doubts as to whether the irregularities and improprieties improperly influenced the grand jury and ultimately bolstered its decision to indict these defendants," Burns said as he threw out the murder charge. "Quite simply, these defendants were not afforded the due process protections and fundamental fairness Kansas law requires."

38

A Fresh Look

Cheryl raised Lamonte's case with Dupree even before he took office. As soon as he was sworn in, Cheryl was in his office pushing him to review the record.

Dupree was on the cutting edge of a national movement away from the presumption that more prisons and longer jail time for anyone who "seems dangerous" was the way to protect people. There started appearing, in Seattle and Brooklyn and Baltimore after Freddie Gray, prosecutors who believed in focusing on prison for the most serious offenders, and alternatives for nonviolent offenders. It was a concept that went completely against the traditional way things were done. Local prosecutors almost everywhere are elected by voters, and voters mostly favor prosecutors whom they can count on to win guilty verdicts and put away criminals. Prosecutors rely on the support and cooperation of the police. The result was a system that led to overcharging, long sentences, and little scrutiny of police misconduct.

But the shooting of Michael Brown and the protests that followed in Ferguson raised new doubts about the system, and residents in impoverished communities began to loudly voice their complaints about aggressive policing and prosecution. And that unrest gave birth to the new wave of prosecutors, among whom Dupree was one of the earliest.

"The mentality was, 'Lock them up,'" Dupree said of the office he took over. "If you lock up everybody who seems dangerous, we'll all be safe." But stepping into the office and making big changes was difficult. Dupree inherited a staff that included veteran prosecutors who were accustomed to earning praise for winning convictions, especially in cases with weaker evidence, and suddenly were being told to approach the job differently. The county's judges had their own reservations about whether Dupree was engendering public safety. Many of the judges had started their careers as assistant prosecutors and appreciated the traditional prosecutors' way of thinking. On top of that was their own self-interest: The biggest threat to being reelected as a judge was publicity that might accompany the release of a suspect who seemed dangerous. And God forbid those released commit a crime afterward and invite critical news reports.

The KCKPD was no happier about this turn of events. Dupree's election certainly didn't sit well with Terry Zeigler, Golubski's former partner, who had risen to become chief of the department a year before Dupree was elected. "I'll say a lot of arrows were shot from them to us," Dupree would recall of the response from the police department once he took office. "And that was really affecting how we could bring about justice for some of our cases."*

So while Dupree welcomed Cheryl's presentation and took it seriously, he intended to be thoughtful and careful in his approach. The fierceness of Cheryl's petition made it a more politically charged decision. Supporting a move to overturn the conviction would likely put

---

* For his part, Zeigler wrote of Dupree becoming the district attorney, "Just because someone is elected to office does not mean that they know what is best for your organization or the community."

him at odds with the police and the assistant prosecutors whose work would determine whether he succeeded or not. Nor would it be likely to win him favor with the county officials who set the budget for his office.

Dupree launched an examination of what had occurred, including a review of the facts presented in the petition. He undertook new interviews from the case that was nearly twenty-three years old.

Cheryl sent Saundra Sublett Newsome, the mother of Doniel Quinn, to tell Dupree that even the victims' families believed him to be innocent. She came away discouraged by his caution. Dupree made no commitments, and Saundra felt he was just another politician who talked a good game but would not do anything that required real courage.

Cautious as Dupree may have been, the reinvestigation immediately met with opposition from members of the police department headed by Golubski's old partner. Dupree began getting calls telling him to stay away from the case, that Lamonte was guilty, that officers had done nothing wrong. "It was a call to stand down," Dupree said of that time. It created "a solid standoff" between the two departments which, after all, have to work together.

Dupree later described his response: "So is this what you guys do?" He told them he would stick to his job, and they should stick to theirs. And he pushed forward, regardless of the cost.

The district attorney arranged for Cecil Brooks, the former drug kingpin, to be brought from Springfield to KCK, so that Dupree could interview him personally. Cecil repeated to Dupree what he said in the deposition, that he sat in conversations before and after the murders in which Aaron Robinson and others discussed the need to get revenge on Doniel Quinn, whom they believed had stolen drugs from them. Cecil told Dupree that Neil Edgar Jr., not Lamonte McIntyre, had committed the double murder, and that he had never heard of Lamonte before the murders.

Melissa's phone rang one night while she was already in bed, at the hour when a call usually brings some kind of bad news. Her husband thought something must be wrong. It was Lamonte calling. Though Melissa had left Morgan Pilate months before, she and Lamonte remained in regular contact, though not usually so late at night.

Lamonte was emotional. He had been brought back to the Wyandotte County jail, his first time out of a state penitentiary in more than two decades. Nobody had given him a heads up, and he was shaken by the unexpected upending of his normal routine.

He had waited years for some official, somewhere, to realize the wrong that had been done to him. But now he was to face an interview with the new district attorney that could make or break his future, and he felt spooked. Abruptly transported without his toothbrush or even a change of clothes. Lamonte felt once again like he had no control of his surroundings. He felt the pressure to say the right things to Dupree. He felt unprepared. The smell of WyCo jail, the sounds, it was more than he could bear. He cried on the phone to Melissa.

The interview the next day went fine; Lamonte's anxiety had been needless. The district attorney was straightforward in his questions, and Lamonte did his best to answer truthfully. The truth was, of course, he did not know much about the murders or how he had come to be identified by two women as the killer.

Lamonte was sent back to Lansing that afternoon, and then there was nothing to do but wait.

Weeks later, District Attorney Dupree gave Cheryl disappointing news: He would not join a motion to overturn the verdict. She needed to go to court to present the case to a judge. He did not, however, intend to stand in the way. He would let Cheryl put on her evidence and then let the out-of-county judge, Edward Bouker, make the decision.

It wasn't that Dupree disbelieved Lamonte. He concluded, instead, that overturning the jury's verdict was better left to a judge.

The hearing was scheduled for October 2017. The delay rankled both Lamonte and Cheryl. Even after twenty-three years, another six months mattered. His time behind bars did not make him more patient; it made him less so. He would spend his forty-first birthday still locked up.

39

"It's Nice Outside"

As the summer turned to fall, there was plenty of preparation to do. Cheryl was busy, working with Lindsay Runnels as well as Tricia Bushnell, director of the Midwest Innocent Project, to plan the presentation and line up witnesses.

Though Melissa was no longer at the firm, she made plans for clothing that Lamonte could wear in court; after all, he had not needed anything other than prison garb since he was seventeen.

Her brother in Montana was a fashionista, about Lamonte's size, and, like Lamonte, favored purple. Melissa arranged for her brother to send a package of outfits.

Judge Bouker set aside seven days for the hearing, but it turned out it would not take nearly that long. Lamonte was brought from Lansing back to the Wyandotte County jail and was escorted by sheriff's deputies into the courtroom wearing a gray suit and a purple tie.

Outside the courthouse a few dozen supporters held signs that said FREE LAMONTE MCINTYRE and other slogans. Lamonte's father, whom Lamonte had not seen or heard from in decades, was among those in the crowd.

Inside the first-floor courtroom were the lawyers and reporters and about sixty-five spectators, who included family members of Lamonte's and members of the victim's family as well. Unlike virtually any other case, where the victims' families are convinced of the defendant's guilt, all of them were pulling for Lamonte to win his freedom.

Lamonte's grandmother, Maxine Crowder, was there but not Rosie nor Saundra Sublett Newsome; both were on the list of witnesses to be called, and were required to wait outside the courtroom, on the wooden benches in the hallway, so that their testimony would not be colored by what they heard from other witnesses.

The first witness Cheryl called was Donald Ewing's aunt, Gloria Labat. She had no reason to be anything but honest, so it rang true as she described seeing Niko Quinn outside the courtroom during the trial, in tears as she said that she had been forced to wrongly implicate Lamonte.

As Gloria Labat testified that day, the assistant district attorneys assigned to the hearing, Jennifer Tatum and Francis Gipson, did not object to the testimony by Gloria or any other witness. While Dupree did not join in the motion for Lamonte's conviction to be overturned, he wanted Lamonte's team to present its case unhindered.

Gloria testified that she repeated to Terra Morehead and to Lamonte's trial lawyer, Gary Long, what Niko had told her, but nobody seemed to care. From the witness stand, she looked at Lamonte and said, "I'm sorry you had to go through this."

Dupree came in and out of the courtroom as different witnesses testified. He had stipulated to his conversation with Cecil Brooks, putting it into the official record and eliminating the need for him to be called as a witness.

Cheryl called Jim McCloskey to the stand, and neither gave any clue that their relationship had fractured. Nothing was more important to either of them at that moment than Lamonte's freedom.

Jim testified that of the ninety cases that Centurion Ministries had taken on in his time there, he had never seen another case in which members of the victims' families witnessed the crime and insisted the wrong man was convicted. "I've not seen that. It stunned me," he testified.

He called Golubski the "dirtiest cop I ever saw," and described the steps he took to uncover the truth: More than 100 interviews over almost seven years. In that time, Jim testified, many people told him of the brazen criminality of Golubski: coercing sex with numerous women; planting drugs on suspects; confiscating drugs and using drugs as an incentive to trade for sex.

Doniel Quinn's mother, Saundra, tearfully recounted the pain she felt from knowing the wrong man was convicted. As she spoke, Lamonte and others in the audience were in tears.

Saundra described the disregard from authorities after her son was murdered. She described Golubski coming to her house after the funeral and asking if she dated white men. She turned in the witness chair to look directly at Judge Bouker at the end of her testimony and implored him: "Look at all the reasons why and do the right thing." The judge could not "give me back my boy," she said, but he could return Rosie McIntyre's to her. "All we want is justice. Just do what's right."

The next morning began with Yale University Law School professor Lawrence J. Fox testifying, "This was not a fair trial." Fox, an ethics expert, said the undisclosed former relationship between Judge Burdette and Terra Morehead represented "serious, serious misconduct," adding, "Nothing could taint a trial more than that kind of relationship."

It was irrelevant that the relationship had ended three years before Lamonte went on trial, Fox testified. "The very fact that it went undisclosed," he said, suggested there was something to hide. "I don't think you can cure this without having a new trial."

The last witness actually called to the stand was Rosie McIntyre. It was late morning, and Judge Bouker called a lunch recess. The afternoon promised to be explosive. Not only was Rosie prepared to publicly describe for the first time her encounters with Golubski, Judge Burdette was to be called afterward to answer questions about his relationship with Terra Morehead. Over the lunch break and out of public view, however, there was chaos in the chambers. Scheduled or not, Burdette was suddenly saying he could not show up. He was too occupied with cases to oversee in his own courtroom. The judge who presided over Lamonte's sham of a trial was insisting that he could not be available to take the stand and answer questions under oath about his own behavior.

As the crowd filed back into the courtroom after lunch, Judge Bouker and the lawyers were missing. They remained in the backroom, sorting out what to do. Lamonte's future hung in the balance.

When everyone emerged from the chambers, Dupree was with them. He had seen enough. He stood before the judge and read a prepared statement. Enough evidence had already been presented, he said, to show that Lamonte had been dealt a manifest injustice. The time had come to reverse it, and he asked Judge Bouker to overturn the conviction.

The motion was granted, and Dupree immediately announced that he was dropping the charges. He would not retry Lamonte. It was over.

Cheers rang out in the courtroom. Lamonte hugged his attorneys. He hugged his mother and other family members and then was taken back into custody to await his formal release. A half hour later, the secured door to the jail swung open and Lamonte emerged into the sunshine. A crowd of family, supporters, and reporters gathered around.

He was free. Finally. His first words were an understatement. "It's nice outside."

PART IV
SEEKING JUSTICE

40
On His Own

The crowd lingered for almost an hour outside the courthouse to celebrate. Lamonte's mother and grandmother and sister and brothers were there, and, of course, Corisha. Cheryl and the legal team were there. So was Jim. He got it started, did much of the work, and without him, Lamonte would surely still be in prison.

The sun was shining brightly, and there was a glare from the television cameras representing all the local stations. Reporters pushed in close with their microphones and writing pads. Saundra Newsome had stayed to watch. So had Greg Lauber, the juror who had first expressed his misgivings to Jim, and members of churches and community groups carrying signs who saw Lamonte's freedom as a victory for justice.

It was all a blur for Lamonte, and disorienting. He was besieged with hugs and congratulations from people he cared about and people he barely knew, and suddenly he was being bombarded with questions about how it felt and what he planned next.

When it broke up, a smaller group of family and friends and lawyers headed over to the Homesteader, one of Cheryl's favorite spots. The restaurant was in the River Market area, near where the ships carrying members of the Wyandotte tribe had arrived 180 years earlier.

Champagne flowed, and people made speeches about how special the moment was. People mingled and said how glad they were for Lamonte, whose head was spinning.

And then it was over. Lamonte left with Corisha to spend the night at a motel that Corisha had arranged. Lamonte had been locked up for twenty-three years in a world without women. He had not had the chance to touch women other than the brief hugs and kisses at the start and end of prison visits from his mother or Corisha. And now, finally, came a moment he had dreamed about forever, satisfying his longing for Corisha that had blossomed over years of notes and calls.

When they awoke the next morning, Corisha went home to her three children and Lamonte went back to the house of his younger brother, Reggie. He just wanted to be away from everyone to process everything. But then Cheryl called. All the TV and newspaper reporters wanted to hear from him.

Lamonte first took a brief walk through his brother's neighborhood, marveling at the sights and sounds, before he arrived at Cheryl's office. Lamonte described for reporters what it was like to walk freely, after twenty-three years, with no one telling him which direction to turn in, when to get back to his cell, when he could talk, and when he had to keep his mouth shut. It was a "great feeling," he said, explaining, "Nobody told me I can't go there."

Like many people released after a lengthy incarceration, Lamonte would soon discover a series of obstacles, small and large. He had little more than the few clothes sent by Melissa's brother, and some meager savings from his work in prison. He had to rely on handouts from supporters to pay his expenses. A generous donor in New York agreed to provide monthly payments for a time. A law professor set up GoFundMe campaigns, one of the many ways Lamonte was introduced to the world that had developed online while he was locked away.

Still, there were all kinds of bureaucratic obstacles. He could not even deposit the money sent to him because he had no bank account. He could not get a bank account without a state ID, and to get that, he needed not only a birth certificate, but additional proof of identity to show that he was in fact the name on the birth certificate. But since he been locked in state custody since he was seventeen, he had no utility bill, no driver's license, no credit card statement.

Had Lamonte been released on parole after serving his sentence, there would have been a variety of services to help him return to life on the outside. A caseworker would have been assigned to assist in everything from ensuring adequate housing to getting needed identification. But because he was released to correct an unjust conviction, those services were not available to him.

"They told me to go to the parole and probation office for help," said Lindsay Runnels, the attorney in Cheryl's office who was spending her time trying to help Lamonte become acclimated. "I told them he wasn't on parole or probation."

The state of Kansas had housed Lamonte for decades, but it was not willing to recognize his identity on the outside. Frustrated, Lindsay told them how they could verify Lamonte's identity, given the publicity around his release: "Google him," she suggested.

Lindsay finally persuaded legal counsel for the Department of Corrections to give Lamonte his prison identification badge—something that officials consider state property and do not normally release. She took him to the state capitol to pick it up, then they headed back to KCK to meet with Reggie, who could provide proof of his residence.

"This is not something they train us to do" in law school, Lindsay said of the bureaucratic struggle.

He had a million other hassles, some of them technological, like learning how to use devices like a smartphone. But he also faced many emotional challenges learning how to be free from captivity. Despite all the people who came to his side, he felt lost and alone. The world had moved on and he had been left behind. It was exhilarating and terrifying.

A used car dealer who had read Lamonte's story donated an old car, a Ford Bronco. Mike Bussell, the investigator who had worked for years helping to prove Lamonte's innocence, took Lamonte to a parking lot to give him driving instructions. Lamonte got in the car, turned on the radio, and put on Celine Dion. They drove around the parking lot, but Mike quickly arranged for Lamonte to take driving lessons from a certified instructor, a retired police colleague.

Lamonte came back from the first class and mentioned the obvious to Mike: all his classmates were sixteen. Mike told him to stick it out. The last thing Lamonte needed was to be caught driving without a license. The KCK police were almost certainly itching to catch Lamonte breaking the law. Lamonte was not going to find it easy living in Wyandotte County.

Mike knew what he was talking about. Once he went to work for Cheryl on Lamonte's case, former colleagues in law enforcement shunned him. His own brother, a KCK cop, stopped talking to him.

Mike knew that Lamonte had no way to sustain himself. But he had been cutting hair for years in prison, and so Mike had an idea. The Headlines Barber Academy was said to be the best barber school in Wyandotte County. Mike met with the two owners and asked for help. Lamonte had no cash to pay for their course and had no equipment but needed to get certified. Could they help? The owners had read about Lamonte, and said they would talk it over and let Mike know.

Before Mike had even gotten back to his home in Johnson County, he heard from George Jacobs, one of the academy owners. Not only would they give Lamonte a scholarship to attend; they would also provide him with the equipment he would need.

Lamonte graduated from the academy, became an instructor and before long was a partner in the business. His presence attracted customers, as Lamonte was a local celebrity of sorts. He soon became a partner in a second business that he and George set up together, a barber shop where graduates of the academy could work.

Darryl Burton, the exoneree who now served as associate pastor of United Methodist Church of the Resurrection, stayed in touch following Lamonte's release. Burton had spent a month homeless when he got out of prison, and he came to Lamonte with an idea: Together they could create an organization not only to help those wrongly convicted prove their innocence, but also help them adjust upon release. Lamonte responded quickly: "Let's do it."

Best of all, Lamonte and Corisha were seeing each other regularly, and every Friday night they went to a Chinese restaurant, Evergreen Lin's. Lamonte was a particular fan of their shrimp fried rice. Twenty-three years was a long time between good meals.

Rosie McIntyre, ever protective of her son, did not trust Corisha. *She got married to him while he was in prison. Then she divorced him, and had children with someone else? And now that Lamonte was out she was suddenly back with him?* None of it seemed right to Rosie.

Despite his mother's misgivings, Lamonte was just thankful that Corisha was back in his life. She was the woman he had dreamed about, cared about, thought about, and loved all those years he was locked up.

He cared deeply about what his mother thought, but he was finally with Corisha, on the outside.

Six months after Lamonte finally set foot outside of prison, he and Corisha invited Rosie, his siblings, Corisha's mom and brother, and a handful of close friends, including Melissa Testrake, to join them on a Friday night at Evergreen Lin's. When the guests arrived, they found Lamonte wearing a sharp new navy blue suit, and a minister was on hand.

Lamonte had spent years dreaming of this moment, even when it seemed like a fantasy. Corisha had been on his mind for years, even after he broke off their relationship when things looked hopeless. He was overcome with emotion when the minister pronounced them man and wife.

Lamonte had gone from almost complete isolation to having a family of five.

41
"Sick and Tired" of Injustice

Three weeks after Lamonte's release, voters elected a member of local royalty, David Alvey, as mayor. Lamonte's family, like so many Black families, had struggled to try to stay above water. Alvey's family, on the other hand, had held power for generations.

His great-grandfather, John Gibbs Jr., first came to Kansas from Michigan in 1855, soon after the passage of the Kansas-Nebraska Act opened the land for purchase by European immigrants. He mined in Colorado and Montana before returning after the Civil War with $30,000 in gold dust that he used to purchase a large section of land in what would become KCK. Gibbs's daughter, Katie, married Andrew Leo Alvey, and their six children and their grandchildren were born into local prominence.

David Alvey's father, Lloyd G. Alvey Sr., was the youngest of the children born to Katie Gibbs and Andrew Leo Alvey. Lloyd served as an assistant county attorney, a justice of the peace, and then Wyandotte County judge pro tem. One of his brothers, Edmond Alvey, served on the old KCK City Council, and plenty of other family members were on one public payroll or another. A park in KCK bears the family name.

David's sister Constance became a state court judge in Wyandotte County. A brother, Andrew, joined the KCK police force and became the president of the KCK police union before leaving the force and joining the FBI. David held a position on the board of the public utility at the time he decided to run for mayor.

David became incensed during that campaign when a *Kansas City Star* reporter asked if "only a handful of politically connected families, including his, are typically allowed to govern" in KCK. "My family has never, ever taken advantage of its position or its power," he responded.

Maybe not, but the family's political power was no secret. David's father, Lloyd, had demonstrated that years earlier, when he flexed his political muscles to help his brother-in-law, William J. Burns.* Burns, a lawyer, had first won a seat on the District Court when he upended a longstanding tradition that helped ensure the parties' chosen candidates would run opposed for judgeships in Wyandotte County.

The parties had long honored their agreement to divide the judicial seats between them, ensuring chosen candidates would not face opposition. But Burns decided that rather than wait for a Democratic seat to open, he would run as a Democrat for a Republican-held seat. He won despite opposition from the county bar association and even from the chairman of the county Democratic Party, who was dismayed by Burns's intrusion into the parties' arrangement.

Four years later, when Burns was up for reelection, the Democratic Party plotted to run a strong candidate against him in the primary. Democrat or not, Burns had gone against the way things were done. That is when David's father, Lloyd, stepped in and filed to run for county attorney against the candidate who was the party's choice for that office. Lloyd then announced his price for withdrawing his

---

* Lloyd Alvey and Burns were married to two sisters.

candidacy for county attorney: The Democrats needed to drop their plan to run a judicial candidate against his brother-in-law. Burns ended up reelected without opposition.

Years later, as David Alvey announced his plan to run for mayor, his cousin William J. Burns Jr. was the district court administrator, a position that Burns Jr. held until, more recently, he ran and won a seat on the board of the KCK/Wyandotte County unified government.

It meant something in Wyandotte County to be part of that family.

The corruption exposed in Lamonte's case seemed not to reverberate in the mayoral race, and local reporters did not ask much about it. Alvey was seeking to defeat the reelection bid of the incumbent mayor, Mark Holland, a United Methodist pastor who was finishing his first term. Holland and Alvey quarreled about redevelopment for the poorest areas of KCK, and about the high property tax rate. Firefighters had issues with Holland, who they said was planning to lay some of them off. David painted Holland as a mayor who cut deals with "special interests," citing the city's willingness to pay half the utility bill for the financially floundering minor league baseball team's use of the stadium that the city had purchased from the team a few years before, in a desperate effort to keep the team afloat.*

In a county in which 60 percent of the budget was devoted to public safety, the candidates were not asked much about their views of the

* After consolidation the mayor of the unified government, Carol Marinovich, had worked to bring economic development to the west side of the county, separated by a few miles and highways from the poorer sections of town. The baseball stadium, an auto speedway, hotels and restaurants, and a large mall sprung up. But they did not improve the lives of the inner-city part of KCK noticeably and soon were struggling themselves.

justice system in general—or about the corruption that spilled out into the public view in Lamonte's case. It was as if none of that ever happened.

The voters unseated Holland in favor of the challenger, David Alvey. At his swearing in, three rows of seats at the front of Memorial Hall were set aside for the Alvey family. An Alvey sang the national anthem, another played "Amazing Grace" on the violin, and a third family member administered the oath of office.

A family that long had wielded power now had even more. The new mayor, whose brother Andrew had fought against greater police accountability when he was head of the police union, was by no means ready to concede that Lamonte was innocent.

Kansas was one of eighteen states that by 2018 had not yet passed a law to compensate wrongly imprisoned people for the years they spent behind bars. After Lamonte was freed, the Innocence Project and Cheryl pushed legislators to do something. Soon after the start of the session that year, Lamonte and the two other Kansas exonerees, Floyd Bledsoe and Richard Jones, went before the Senate Judiciary Committee to make their case.

Lamonte testified the cost to him: "The state of Kansas took away twenty-three years of my life and has given me nothing to rebuild. The state took away my youth. It took away every birthday and Christmas with my family, and every hard time when they needed me and I couldn't be there. I missed joyful occasions and I missed sad ones, too.

"I had nieces and nephews born while I was in custody who are young men and women now. I missed their entire childhoods. I was not able to comfort my mother when she buried her father, my beloved grandfather. The state also took financially from my family and me. My mother took what little money she had saved from working multiple jobs and paid lawyers to appeal my conviction in 1996. I was crushed when their efforts did not succeed.

"After that, I spent two more decades in prison. During that time, I had no opportunity to establish a career, build a family, buy a home, or save money for my retirement. At the same time, the state took thousands of dollars that I earned from years of working in prison to cover fees like room and board. I paid to keep myself locked up in a place where I never should have been. Meanwhile, my family suffered greatly as well. My mother broke down emotionally and was hospitalized. My brothers and sisters struggled to cope with losing my presence, and family celebrations and holidays became a time of pain, not joy. It was not just me who was imprisoned; my entire family paid an incredible price and the years of pain have taken their toll on all of us."

The bill moved through the legislature, offering $65,000 to the victims for each year of wrongful incarceration. If the exonerees won any court settlement for their wrongful conviction, they were to repay the state.

As he signed the bill into law, Governor Jeff Colyer turned to the wrongly convicted Kansans who were at his side as he said, "I want to say to Lamonte McIntyre, to Floyd Bledsoe, to Richard Jones, we believe in you, we apologize to you . . . we will make it right."

But that turned out to be easier said than done. The state attorney general, Derek Schmidt, opposed a December 2019 motion for Lamonte to be paid. Judge Bouker had overturned the guilty verdict after Dupree cited the "manifest injustice" of the case, and Dupree then agreed that the case did not merit a retrial.

But nobody said Lamonte had been proven innocent, Schmidt argued.

The attorney general was not alone. Many KCK police officers saw Lamonte's case as an attack on their department and the criminal justice system. Even more upsetting to the police was that District Attorney Dupree had acquiesced and not fought against Lamonte's freedom. The department, including Chief Terry Zeigler, Golubski's former partner, shrugged off the miscarriage of justice. Mayor Alvey shared his department's skepticism. He told a *Kansas City Star* columnist that he believed the facts of the murders had not yet come out.

Schmidt basically told Lamonte: Prove it if you want to be paid.

Lamonte, Cheryl, Lindsey, and the Midwest Innocence Project staff were all flabbergasted. They believed that Cheryl *had* already proven his innocence, and the court system had agreed. His case was the whole reason the Kansas legislature had finally passed the compensation law. Now, Lamonte was left to fight some more to get officials to do what was right.

It was politics, pure and simple, and Lamonte's team went to work.

Dupree issued an "open letter" that blasted officials for still obstructing justice. "The act of silence by those in power [has] continued to perpetuate the mistakes of the past on the backs of the less fortunate and powerless," Dupree wrote. He added that those "everyday people," as he put it, simply "want a fair shake and are sick and tired of people in positions using their power to help their friends and screw everyday citizens."

Others shared Dupree's frustration with the establishment's intransigence. Gov. Colyer, who had signed the compensation law but whose term ended a few months before Schmidt refused to pay Lamonte, said, "I think this is exactly the kind of case the law was intended for. And frankly, it's just past due. It's time for him to be compensated."

Several other elected officials chimed in as well, though they acknowledged that the decision was not up to them but to Schmidt.

Under increasing pressure, in February 2020, Schmidt caved and agreed to pay Lamonte. The next month, Lamonte received a check for $1.5 million from the state of Kansas.

The state compensation was to repay Lamonte for the State of Kansas's act of wrongfully imprisoning him. Lamonte could still sue the county and its police officers for compensation for the injustice of the wrongful arrest and conviction.* That lawsuit would not only help him be financially secure; it also offered a chance to highlight for the world the underlying corruption that infected the police department.**

The most successful of such cases do not just expose the bad acts of errant individual officers, they also expose failures of their departments to appropriately train and supervise their officers, giving exonerees access to deeper pockets that can compensate them more fully for the injuries they suffered.

Across America, the law gives judges, prosecutors, and police varying degrees of protection from being sued individually for official acts, no matter how egregious the conduct. The immunity is designed to protect officials' independence and spare them from endless complaints.***

Judge Burdette was absolutely immune from being sued even if Lamonte could have shown his judge's rulings were intended to deny a fair trial. Terra Morehead was similarly immune even if she hid

---

* The state compensation law required that if exonerees like Lamonte won a later legal verdict, the compensation from the state would be repaid.

** Such lawsuits, if successful, also provide significant awards for the attorneys, who earn a percentage of the award. That money provides a major source of funding for innocence projects around the country to take on additional cases.

*** The concept has its roots in medieval English common law, under the theory the king could do no wrong.

evidence and invited false testimony.* Golubski and other officers, on the other hand, only enjoy *qualified immunity* that left them liable if their actions violated clearly established standards. The departments that employ the officers may also be liable for failing to take proper steps to train and supervise them.

In October 2018, as the one-year deadline following Lamonte's exoneration approached, a civil lawsuit was filed on behalf of Lamonte and his mother Rosie against Golubski and other officers, as well as against the KCK/Wyandotte unified government. The lawsuit echoed Lamonte's heart-wrenching statement before the state legislature about the emotional and psychological costs to him and his mother. It also demanded compensation for all Lamonte had been put through.

A small army of lawyers represented Lamonte and his mother. The team included not just Cheryl and Lindsay but also Barry Scheck, the cofounder of the Innocence Project, and his partners in his New York law firm; and attorneys at Lathrop Gage, a national firm that established roots in Kansas City more than 140 years earlier.

Scheck had, of course, worked with Cheryl in Ada, Oklahoma, and was happy to provide his firm's resources to bolster Lamonte's case. He saw the civil case not only as a way to get some form of justice for Lamonte and Rosie; but also to help expose the civil rights violations that were rampant in the KCK police department.

The opening lines of the suit were explosive:

> For decades, the Kansas City Police Department (KCKPD) permitted Detective Roger Golubski to terrorize an entire community—by using his badge to extort sexual favors from

* Prosecutors lose their immunity if they go beyond prosecuting cases and take part in the investigative phase, such as taking part in interviews.

> poor [B]lack women and by coercing and manipulating those women into providing fabricated evidence to close his cases. With the full knowledge of KCKPD supervisors, including his former partner, current KCKPD police chief Terry Zeigler, Golubski forced his victims to submit to sexual acts, through physical force or with threats of arrest or harm to them or their loved ones. He also manipulated his victims by promising favors, like clearing arrest warrants, or by providing illegal drugs to those who were addicted. Golubski's practice was to gain leverage over vulnerable women and force them to provide fabricated information that he would use to close cases without any proper investigation. Throughout the community, and among the women he manipulated, Golubski had a reputation for being corrupt and for "putting cases on people."

The fifty-one-page complaint included all the information compiled over the years by Jim and Cheryl, and the bigger picture of Golubski's corruption. It alleged his "close and continuing association with high-level drug dealers," including Cecil Brooks and, until he died, Aaron Robinson. And it included the stories of women who said Golubski had abused them over the years, including his ex-wife, Ethel Abbott. The list amounted to a highlight reel of the women who had given affidavits. The lawsuit used only their initials:

- Golubski met E. A. in the early 1990s while he was investigating a murder at her workplace. He became obsessed with her, falsely accused her of being involved with the murder (as a pretense to talk to her), and repeatedly called her at home, once pretending to be a rapist. He stalked her continually until she agreed to marry him if he took care of her financially. She divorced him after learning about his sexual involvement with witnesses. Following the divorce, he stalked her for 10 years. When he later assaulted her in her car, in defiance of an order of protection, the KCKPD refused to discipline him.

- Golubski had a regular relationship with D. L. and used her for sex and information. She knew, as most other women in KCK knew, that when Golubski came around the "Bottoms" in KCK, they either had to provide sexual services to Golubski or get arrested.
- C. R., a prostitute in the early 1990s, tried for a long time to avoid Golubski, but ended up having sex with him on several occasions. Golubski provided protection from arrest in return for frequent sexual favors. In an affidavit, she stated: "I did what I had to do to stay out of jail. . . . I provided him with sexual favors in his vehicle."
- T. B. was the friend of a murder victim whom Golubski attempted to coerce into giving information related to the crime. T. B. knew nothing about the murder, but Golubski interrogated her anyway, frightening her with sexual advances. He later stalked her at home and work.
- Golubski stopped N. H. under the guise that she looked like an aggravated battery suspect. He began paying her for sex and information on a regular basis. Golubski introduced N. H. to other KCKPD officers, who also paid her for sex. When an officer raped her at gunpoint after an arrest, she complained to the KCKPD; but to her knowledge, the officer was never disciplined.

- K. D., who used to sell drugs, encountered Golubski in the course of her dealing in the late 1990s. Although Golubski typically shook down street-level dealers and took their inventory, he sometimes purchased drugs. K. D. once sold crack cocaine to Golubski through an intermediary, and then saw him enter the back room of a house to have sex with the woman who received the drugs. Sometime later, Golubski approached K. D. for sex, telling her that he had "pull" and could get rid of any tickets for her.

The lawsuit was not about just the money; no amount of money could really make up to Lamonte the twenty-three years that had been stolen from him. Lamonte had been up and down through the court system, and yet the corrupt system that had captured him had been untouched. Golubski, who was now retired, had never been brought to justice, nor had the deeply rooted corruption that existed been forced to answer to its victims. Lamonte saw this as his chance to put the system on trial, to make sure that the detective who put him in prison for twenty-three years, and abused so many others, would face the consequences.

42

"Amazing," "Disgusting," and "Nasty," Too

Terra Morehead had not attracted much public notice until the 2017 hearing that led to Lamonte's freedom, when witnesses first testified that she brushed aside their warnings both before and during the 1994 trial that she was prosecuting an innocent man. Long before that evidence emerged, Morehead had moved from the Wyandotte County District Attorney's Office to a coveted position as an assistant U.S. attorney.

Over the seven years that followed the revelations at Lamonte's hearing, Morehead's reputation would be destroyed by a whole series of cases in which she would be accused of conduct that crossed the line from aggressive to unethical. Even a former boss in the U.S. attorney's office described her courtroom tactics as "disgusting." The most startling of the accusations came during a scandal that befell the KCK office of the U.S. attorney, which the Department of Justice did its best to keep from public view.

By the time all was said and done, Judge Julie Robinson, who somehow seemed to be involved in all matters exposing the underbelly of corruption in KCK's criminal justice system, had found the entire U.S. attorney's office in contempt for its refusal to reveal the evidence of misconduct. She specifically called out Morehead and several other senior prosecutors for unethical conduct.

Just weeks after Lamonte's exoneration in the Wyandotte County courthouse, a suspected drug dealer's conviction was overturned blocks away in the Robert J. Dole Federal Courthouse because of Morehead's threats to a witness in *that* case. Gregory Orozco had been sitting in the driver's seat of a parked maroon pickup truck with three other people inside when agents arrested him on drug trafficking charges. A search of the vehicle turned up a gun under his seat and methamphetamine inside a pink pouch in the console armrest, and he was charged in connection with those items as well.

The morning that the trial was scheduled to begin, Morehead had a couple of late surprises that, Judge Robinson would later note, demonstrated bad faith. Morehead said she was seeking enhancements that would double the mandatory minimum prison term from ten to twenty years if Orozco were found guilty. And she belatedly turned over to Orozco's attorney a flash drive that was found with the drugs inside the pink pouch.

Morehead told Judge Robinson the delay in turning over the flash drive was inadvertent, that she had just gotten physical access to the pouch, but she assured the judge the device did not contain anything she intended to use at trial, just some "random, discrete photos" of "normal things" that "didn't appear to be anything related to drugs or guns or anything like that."

Judge Robinson granted a two-month delay in the start of the trial, to offer the defense a chance to review the new evidence.

Morehead certainly did not reveal that the evidence belatedly turned over was potentially exculpatory evidence, the kind of evidence she was supposed to disclose well before the day of trial. The flash drive was filled with more than 200 photos of a woman who was one of the passengers in the truck. The logical conclusion was that the pouch containing both the flash drive and the methamphetamine belonged to her, not to Orozco.

But that was hardly the only issue. Orozco's lawyer was prepared to call to the stand the brother of a prosecution witness, to challenge the testimony of his own brother about whether Orozco had bought methamphetamine in quantities larger than he would have been buying for personal use. At the eleventh hour the potential defense witness, who had his own pending drug case in Missouri, changed his mind about testifying.

The jury convicted Orozco of drug trafficking, while acquitting him of the charges related to the items found in the truck. At a posttrial hearing, Judge Robinson heard why the potential witness had a change of heart and decided not to testify: Terra Morehead had told his attorney that if he took the stand he might be charged with perjury, and might also suffer consequences in how his own pending drug charges were resolved.

Weeks later, Judge Robinson overturned the verdict, ruling that Morehead had obstructed Orozco's right to a fair trial.

Morehead's warning to the attorney amounted to a "veiled threat" that "substantially interfered" with the defense witness's testimony.

Judge Robinson noted the similarities to what had just been exposed, weeks earlier, in Lamonte's case, and wrote, "This prosecutor should have had a heightened awareness of the bounds of fair play and the gravity of witness intimidation."*

---

* Judge Robinson was so outraged by Morehead's conduct that she ruled the prosecution was barred from retrying Orozco on the overturned drug charges. A panel of the 10th Circuit U.S. Court of Appeals later upheld Judge Robinson's finding that Morehead committed misconduct but ruled the government should be afforded the chance to retry Orozco. An internal DOJ investigation was more forgiving, concluding that Morehead had done nothing more than exhibit "poor judgment" by not adopting a "more measured and less aggressive tone." The public version of the OPR report, following department practice, does not name Morehead by name; but as *The Kansas City Star* and local NPR station noted, the details in the report mirrored the Orozco case.

The Orozco case, it would turn out, was only the start of Terra Morehead's fall from grace. The veteran prosecutor's reputation unraveled in the most likely of venues, Judge Robinson's courtroom.

Morehead's troubles would be magnified by what unfolded in a much larger scandal, involving the Kansas City office of the U.S. Attorney, where Morehead was a senior prosecutor. The scandal began to unfold on primary election day, 2016, the day Mark Dupree toppled Jerry Gorman; Lamonte's hearing was still more than a year away.

Two U.S. attorneys called defense attorney Jackie Rokusek to their office to confront her with their suspicions that she had slipped a confidential document to one of her clients who was being held at a pretrial detention facility in Leavenworth. The document had information about an ongoing investigation into a network that was smuggling drugs, alcohol, and tobacco into the detention center, which was managed by the Corrections Corporation of America (CCA).* The massive investigation involved a collaboration of federal and state officials and targeted more than 100 people, including detained suspects, guards, and suppliers on the outside. The two federal prosecutors, Erin Slinker Tomasic and Kim Flannigan, said a federal agent would review video recordings made in the rooms where attorneys met with their clients to determine if Rokusek had passed the confidential document to her client.** They mentioned

* The CCA had contracts with the federal government to house criminal defendants and immigrants in its facilities across the country. The corporation would later change its name to CoreCivic, mostly maintaining the acronym.

** Erin Slinker Tomasic was a "special assistant U.S. attorney." She had joined the Shawnee County District Attorney's Office after law school and a judicial clerkship, and was promptly detailed to work in the KCK office of the U.S. attorney on drug cases. Federal rules permit government attorneys from other agencies to be designated as "special assistants" to work on federal cases connected to the agency.

possible obstruction of justice charges. At the least, the prosecutors said, Rokusek should not be serving as one of the defense lawyers in the case.

Rokusek left the federal courthouse that day alarmed, not just at the accusation, but also at the unexpected news that meetings between attorneys and clients were not confidential.

She immediately alerted the office of the Federal Public Defender.

With sixteen staff attorneys and many additional paralegals, investigators, and administrative staff, the office headed by Federal Public Defender Melody Brannon was the primary source for representation of defendants unable to afford lawyers in federal criminal cases across Kansas. Brannon had worked in the Federal Public Defender office since 1996 and had been chief of the office since 2014. Brannon was galled by what she considered the ethical failings that accompanied the cutthroat approach of the local assistant U.S. attorneys and was alarmed by what Rokusek reported. *Confidential meetings between attorneys and clients were being recorded! The recordings were turned over to the prosecutors!*

Brannon quickly filed a motion to intervene in the contraband case, warning that defendants' right to consult privately with their attorneys was "essential to secure the fundamental right to due process and the protections of the Sixth Amendment."

The right of accused suspects to meet privately with their attorneys is among the oldest of legal privileges, woven into English law more than five hundred years ago. The Sixth Amendment to the Constitution includes the right to counsel, and that right depends on open communications between accused suspects and their clients. Prosecutors have the burden to prove their case beyond a reasonable doubt and cannot satisfy that burden with information overheard surreptitiously during privileged attorney-client communications, whether the defendant is guilty or not.

The danger of such eavesdropping is significant. Listening to conversations, prosecutors might also overhear discussions about whether defendants would be willing to plead guilty and what might influence those decisions, as well as other discussions that would deny defendants a fair proceeding.

Judge Robinson quickly arranged the first of a series of hearings on Brannon's emergency motion that quickly became the talk of the courthouse. Erin Tomasic and other prosecutors *had* been provided video recordings, without sound, from cameras throughout the courthouse, even where attorneys conferred with their clients. On top of that, detainees' calls to their attorneys from the 121 pay phones in Leavenworth CCA were routinely included in what the detention center turned over when prosecutors asked for recordings.

Despite a recording played at the start of every call warning that calls may be monitored, defense attorneys routinely assured their clients not to worry, that the calls between attorneys and clients were privileged.

Those assurances proved misguided. The detention center had a protocol to protect calls to attorneys from being included in telephone calls turned over to prosecutors. But many attorneys did not know the protocol, and calls were turned over to prosecutors even when the protocol was followed.

What occurred over the next two years was extraordinary, a legal scandal that undoubtedly would have attracted major national news had it unfolded in New York or Los Angeles or other cities that were a focus of intense media attention.

Judge Robinson held a series of hearings trying to get to the bottom of things, and before long appointed a special master, David R. Cohen of Cleveland, to help her determine the facts.

At first the U.S. attorney's office insisted it had done nothing wrong. Then when it turned out she had learned the contents of private conversations between defendants and their attorneys in two cases, the office fired her and insisted there was no widespread scandal. Nevertheless, attorneys for dozens of suspects detained at the Leavenworth facility began filing motions seeking recordings that prosecutors may have obtained between themselves and their clients, and the issue threatened to overwhelm the Kansas federal courts.

The U.S. attorney's office insisted that the issue was a big legal nothingburger, that if anything an inexperienced prosecutor had erred in isolated incidents and the office had appropriately responded.

Things became more confrontational as the hearings progressed. The Department of Justice specially assigned Assistant U.S. Attorney Steven Clymer, who had a reputation as a hard-charging but fair prosecutor. Clymer, who once served as colead counsel in the trial of officers involved in the beating of Rodney King, had become a professor at Cornell Law School and went back and forth between teaching law and high-level positions with the U.S. attorney in Syracuse.

Clymer resisted turning over to Cohen everything the master asked for, insisting neither he nor Judge Robinson had the authority to poke their noses into the internal affairs of the U.S. attorney. What the government would turn over would be done voluntarily, Clymer wrote.

That was the final straw for Federal Public Defender Brannon, who filed a motion to hold the U.S. attorney in contempt. Months of delays then followed. First Clymer tried without success to win an appellate ruling that Robinson lacked authority to even hold the contempt hearing. More delay followed as a new U.S. attorney, Stephen

McAllister, took office* and tried to resolve the controversy with Brannon; his effort blew up when Rod Rosenstein, the controversial deputy attorney general during the first Trump administration, rejected the agreement McAllister had sought to accomplish.

That left matters back in Judge Robinson's courtroom for the long-delayed hearing on Brannon's contempt motion.

The ten days of testimony revealed a shocking variety of problems within the KCK office of the U.S. attorney, an office beset by backbiting and the routine crossing of ethical lines in pursuit of winning cases. Winning was all that mattered.

There was testimony that the prosecutors sat around the lunchroom making disparaging comments about Judge Robinson, the only Black federal judge in Kansas—suggesting, for example, that she had fallen in with Black Lives Matter.

One prosecutor described distrusting her supervisors so much that she recorded her end of internal conversations and even brought home copies of emails she sent internally, just to safeguard her version of events. Things were so bad that an employee put a copy of the manual to diagnose mental disorders in the reception area and sent an internal email encouraging everyone to read it.

Erin Tomasic, who had moved back to Kentucky and no longer was practicing law, described the working conditions of the office as a "mean-spirited, angry environment."

---

* McAllister, a former law clerk for U.S. Supreme Court Justices Byron White and Clarence Thomas, served for several years as the solicitor general for the Kansas attorney general. He sought the U.S. attorney position, he would later say, seeking to be a moderating voice.

The most damaging account came from former First Assistant U.S. Attorney Kenneth Michael Warner. Warner, who supervised the federal prosecutors' offices throughout Kansas, testified that he was concerned from the start about assigning Erin Tomasic, the young special assistant U.S. attorney, to the KCK office. The veteran prosecutors who worked there, including Morehead, had created a disturbing and distinct culture. They were far more confrontational toward, and contemptuous of, the attorneys in the defense bar than were prosecutors in other offices of the Kansas division of the U.S. Attorney. He warned Tomasic to stay away from them, and described from the witness stand his assessment of the office: "We're talking about a group of folks that were extremely fervent, like-minded, punishment-oriented, very insular, did not like to be supervised and were extremely oppositional to the administration that was then in office . . ."

The aggressive conduct, Warner testified, was accompanied by "nasty behavior" toward defense attorneys, and also supervisors in the office, including himself. And top on his list of the offenders, he said, was Terra Morehead.

He described prosecutors as gaining tactical advantage by delaying turning over evidence relevant to their cases for as long as they could, pushing defendants to plead guilty while holding back on revealing evidence that might have gotten in the way of a plea deal. The argument, said Warner, was that "hard-nosed prosecution," withholding the best evidence to the end, provided a tactical advantage. To Warner, it "reeked of ambush prosecution."

Warner said Morehead viewed the detention of suspects until trial as "a war to be won," and if "somehow somebody wasn't detained, that was a defeat and evil prevailed." Warner said Morehead abused the law permitting enhanced sentences of defendants convicted of drug crimes who had a prior conviction, threatening to invoke the enhancement if a defendant sought to be released from custody before trial. He considered the tactic "disgusting," and had ordered Morehead and other prosecutors to stop doing so.

If defendants remained locked up before trial, of course, they would be in Leavenworth CCA, where their recorded phone calls would then be available to prosecutors.*

Warner took one marijuana case with multiple defendants away from Morehead after he received complaints about her tactics, which he described as "onerous as hell." The complaints were not just that Morehead was trying to impose an excessive sentence; defense attorneys complained that she was treating them "like dogs." They were the enemy, and she was out to win at all costs.

A string of assistant U.S. attorneys shrugged off the accusations, insisting that concerns over prosecutors intruding on attorney-client conversations were overblown. One by one, they testified that they believed the calls were not privileged—and that the recorded warning message at the start of calls waived any privilege. Even so, they said they would not have listened to them, privilege or not.

They had only heard of prosecutors listening to calls in rare cases, and denied knowing, before it spilled out in court, that Tomasic was listening to privileged calls. They never would have condoned such conduct, the procession of prosecutors testified.

Tomasic offered a sharply different account and disputed her portrayal as a "young rogue attorney." She testified that she repeatedly

---

* In the case of Gregory Orozco, of course, Judge Robinson had seen for herself and called out Morehead for both turning over exculpatory evidence belatedly and seeking to use the sentencing enhancement on a defendant who did not plead guilty.

sought advice from her colleagues on what to do when calls to attorneys were mixed in with other calls made by the detainees. The response was clear: "If the defense attorney is stupid enough to make a call on a recorded line, then that's on them."

The hearings made clear that it was not just one inexperienced attorney on her own. One veteran prosecutor, Tanya Treadway, was confronted at the hearings with legal pads containing notes she had taken documenting what was said on telephone calls between a defendant she was prosecuting in Kansas, and attorneys representing the defendant in Texas on separate DUI and child custody disputes.

Treadway was asked why she previously denied to U.S. District Judge Daniel Crabtree, when the issue arose during the defendant's case, that she had listened to these calls. The legal pads in her handwriting, after all, proved otherwise.

Her answer: The conversations to the Texas attorneys were so unimportant that she forgot about them. "That's the only way I can reconcile it," she testified.*

How often were prosecutors gathering conversations from the prison and then using that information? Only the prosecutors knew for sure. But an analysis by Assistant Federal Public Defender Rich Federico suggested it was far more often than prosecutors claimed. Federico found that U.S. attorneys regularly asked the detention center to turn over recordings of all the calls made by specific defendants from the pay phones.

* The week after Treadway's testimony in Judge Robinson's courtroom, Judge Crabtree approved a joint motion to reduce the defendant's sentence to the time she already had served because Treadway "may have violated the defendant's constitutional rights."

Of the sample he examined, calls between those suspects and their attorneys, calls that the prosecutors were not supposed to have, were turned over about a quarter of the time.

While Federico had no way to know how many times the prosecutors listened to those calls, he observed that such calls had been turned over again and again to some prosecutors. At some point, it became reasonable to assume those prosecutors knew what they were being given and found it useful.

Studying just the period between late May 2013 and September 2016, Federico found that Terra Morehead had requested calls thirty-three times, for twenty-eight different defendants. At least nine times, the calls turned over to Morehead included conversations between the defendants and their attorneys. Morehead testified at the hearing that she was not aware of any calls that were between attorneys and their clients that were turned over to her, no matter how many times it happened.

Clymer maintained, on behalf of the government, that without evidence the recordings were used against individual defendants, there was no real issue. He argued that there was no duty to inform the defense that their calls had ended up in the hands of the prosecutors; and, certainly, there was no constitutional violation.

After that, it was up to Judge Robinson to decide.

43
A Pattern of Misconduct

It took months before Robinson handed down a 188-page opinion that laid out the widespread misconduct that permeated her old office. She chastised the government for employing a "wholesale strategy to delay, diffuse, and deflect." Prosecutors had permitted evidence to be destroyed and ignored orders from Special Master Cohen to promptly turn over calls that had been recorded. The government had demonstrated its intention to frustrate her quest to discover the extent and scope of the Sixth Amendment violations.

Her language extinguished any ambiguity. Judge Robinson called out individual prosecutors for dishonest testimony, clearly and directly.

Tanya Treadway "lied" to Judge Crabtree when she denied listening to conversations for which she had taken notes. Judge Robinson rejected Kim Flannigan's denials that she and Tomasic had threatened defense attorney Jackie Rokusek that an agent would review the video recordings, the accusation that sparked the whole scandal. "None of this testimony is credible," Judge Robinson wrote of Flannigan's testimony.

She did not spare Terra Morehead. The judge rejected the testimony of Morehead and another prosecutor that they were unaware they had been provided recordings of defendants talking to their attorneys in case after case. The evidence showed they knew that they could listen to recordings between detainees and attorneys simply by asking for all the calls placed by a defendant being held at Leavenworth CCA, Robinson found.

In deciding credibility, Judge Robinson noted that she took into consideration the culture of the office, and the KCK prosecutors' conduct in other cases. The judge specifically cited her finding of misconduct by Terra Morehead in the prosecution of suspected drug dealer Gregory Orozco.

Morehead, Kim Flannigan, and two other prosecutors singled out by Judge Robinson in her opinion jointly appealed to the 10th Circuit U.S. Court of Appeals, but the appellate court offered no relief.*

As evidence of Morehead's misconduct spooled out, the U.S. attorney, Stephen McAllister, wanted to fire her, but his Justice Department superiors told him that was too harsh a response. By that time, Joe Biden had been elected and McAllister's time was up. On his last day in office, he directed that Morehead be removed from handling any more criminal cases and be assigned to only civil cases. It would prove to be another step downward in the shocking downfall for the embattled prosecutor.

* Ten days after Judge Robinson issued her sweeping decision, the detention center and the company that provided the phone system jointly settled a class-action lawsuit on behalf of all the inmates whose calls had been recorded. CoreCivic, as the company now was known, and Securus Technologies agreed to create a $1.8 million fund to be paid out to potentially hundreds of detained defendants. The largest payments, up to $10,000 each, would go to the 73 defendants whose calls to their attorneys had been recorded after either the defendant or their attorney had taken steps to ensure that would not happen.

That reassignment came years too late for Jay Giannukos, who was convicted by a jury of four counts of drug, gun, and counterfeit charges and sentenced to twenty-six years in prison. Evidence later emerged that Morehead made false representations in court and withheld evidence that could have helped Giannukos's defense. It was one more case in which Morehead had crossed the line to win the conviction.

The conviction was thrown out, a new federal prosecutor took over the case and agreed to let Giannukos plead guilty to only one count, possessing counterfeit money. Before Judge Crabtree imposed a new sentence, he asked Giannukos if he wished to say anything. That normally is the time that defendants express regret and apologize for their conduct.

That is not how Giannukos responded. Instead, he complained that he had been locked up for more than six years "due to fraudulent, outrageous, and flagrant prosecutorial misconduct." He added, "When someone in Morehead's unchecked and powerful position . . . when the power she yields is dirty, just like cancer in a live body, it taints and contaminates, corrupting any and everyone around them."

The judge called Giannukos's presentation unlike any sentencing statement he ever heard before. He acknowledged that Morehead "failed in her duty to do justice" and reduced the sentence from twenty-six years to the time Giannukos already had served. He was released that day.

Not long before, Terra Morehead had been a star prosecutor, a crime-fighting hero in the local court system. But the case of Lamonte McIntyre had brought an earthquake to criminal justice in Wyandotte County, Kansas, and the aftershocks continued to ripple through the system.

44
The Empire Starts to Crack

In the weeks after Lamonte was exonerated, Wyandotte County District Attorney Dupree announced he wanted to create a conviction integrity unit within his office that would review cases involving allegations of wrongful conviction. It was a proposal that shook the orthodox view that the system *works,* and that the appeals process provided the necessary route to correct errors.

Such units began to appear at the start of the twenty-first century in jurisdictions as widespread as Santa Clara County, California, and Dallas, Texas, after cases of wrongful convictions came to light in those cities. Those exonerations caused a few pioneering district attorneys to reconsider how their offices responded to credible claims of a wrongful conviction. Traditionally, any suggestion of a wrongful outcome would be sent back to the trial prosecutor, the very attorney who worked with police to build the cases and then advocate for convictions. Along the way, those attorneys develop certainty of guilt, leaving them unlikely to objectively reconsider the innocence of a defendant no matter what comes to light after the conviction. Opening, instead, a new unit reporting to different supervisors, who could offer fresh looks at cases, was a new and somewhat revolutionary concept.*

Across the river, the prosecutor in Jackson County, which included Kansas City, Missouri, had a conviction review unit, but there were none in any Kansas county. Lamonte's case sped up planning for such a unit for Wyandotte County.

While the case exposed the importance of such a unit, not everyone got the message. When Dupree sought $300,000 from the county to fund the new unit with one attorney, an investigator, and a staff assistant, he faced opposition from the sheriff, the police chief, and the presidents of the two local police unions. The four sent a letter to the members of the board that ran the unified government and to Attorney General Schmidt, hoping to block the funding. If there ever was a need to reopen an old case, they contended, such a decision should be left to Schmidt, not Dupree.

And why not Dupree? He had proven that he was not up to the task, by failing in his duty "as an advocate for homicide victim(s) and the state" in how he handled Lamonte's case. Dupree had botched the case of the murders of Doniel Quinn and Donald Ewing, they wrote, resulting in the "potential mishandling of a case purporting to be a wrongful conviction."

The police chief who signed that letter, of course, was Golubski's former partner, Zeigler. He and the others were *not* willing to accept that Lamonte had been wrongly convicted. *Potential mishandling of a case*, they called Dupree's failure to work to keep Lamonte locked away.**

---

* Having the district attorney acknowledge a wrongful conviction is not the final step; a judge would have to ultimately agree to overturn a jury verdict. But, as Jim and Cheryl knew as they represented Lamonte, having the district attorney's office at least not vigorously opposing the motion can make a tremendous difference.

** In a book on leadership that Zeigler published in 2021, he complained "irreparable damage to my reputation and image" was done by a reporter who linked Zeigler to the nefarious conduct of Golubski. Zeigler noted he was Golubski's partner for a three year period, and was not involved in the case of Lamonte McIntyre.

Their position was remarkable considering that there was never any physical evidence that Lamonte committed the crime; no DNA, no motive, and no history of Lamonte ever engaging in that kind of violence. Witnesses had not just recanted but had tried to, right from the start! Layered over that was Golubski's unspeakable corruption, Morehead's lack of ethics, and the complete incompetence of Lamonte's appointed defense lawyers.

A young Black man was sentenced to life based on all of this and spent more than two decades locked away. And now that he was finally out, these four men in positions of power were asserting that the real injustice was that a Black district attorney had helped set him free.

To say that it was unbelievable would not be accurate, because based on KCK's racist history, it was not. But it was shameful.

The unified government board voted to fund the unit, with a budget of $162,000. It was meager, but it was a start.

The evidence laid out during the hearing that led to Lamonte's freedom was no surprise to many in the Black community. Zeigler's position opposing a conviction integrity unit only further alienated them. But the last straw came in May 2019, when a former police cadet sued the county and Steven Rios, former police training officer, contending that she had been wrongly fired after she had filed a complaint of sexual abuse against Rios.

The cadet had complained within the department more than a year earlier. The department corroborated her accusation and referred it to Dupree, whose office charged Rios with one count of sexual battery based on the cadet's complaint that Rios had harassed and assaulted her.

Rios pleaded guilty and resigned, but the cadet was then fired by Zeigler on what she contended were trumped-up charges. The lawsuit she filed over her firing, together with the resulting publicity, became one more flash point. A coalition of clergy and activists marched to police headquarters, demanding that Zeigler be fired. The lawsuit showed that nothing had changed since Lamonte's case, the protesters contended.

Within weeks, Zeigler announced his plans to retire. Ironically, the decision may not have been the result of the revelations from Lamonte or Rios or any of the other cases that had stirred the community. Zeigler was also under increasing public criticism for a sweetheart deal he had received from the county: He was living in a county-owned house inside the Wyandotte County Lake Park, with geese and ducks for his neighbors.

Just the way the insiders helped each other.

The news was broken by TV station KSHB, which questioned, "Too Sweet A Deal?" Zeigler was to pay a total of $19,000 in rent for the two years he would live in the long-vacant two-bedroom house, but the chief was given credit for any work he put into it. He claimed expenses that cut his rent to less than $1,300 over the two-year lease. The expenses included bills for mileage as well as $21.92 he billed for each of the 263 hours he *or his mother* spent working on the house.*

The deal was negotiated on a handshake between Zeigler and the longtime county chief executive, Doug Bach, and only put in writing when the arrangement became public. "I guess handshakes aren't always good enough for people," *The Kansas City Star* quoted the chief as saying.

Bach then provided a memo to the county commissioners, saying that, "This arrangement is working out quite well for both the Chief

* Zeigler noted in the book he wrote after leaving office that the "barrage of new stories failed to mention the disrepair of the house, the fact that no one wanted to rent it for nearly a decade, or that I had sunk my own money into the property upfront which would be credited toward rent payment. It wasn't that sweet of a deal."

and our Park," since a building that hand long been vacant was being fixed up. Janice Witt, a community activist who had run unsuccessfully against Alvey for mayor, saw it otherwise. She and her husband filed a lawsuit contending that the chief had been given a covert benefit not afforded to other residents.

Mayor Alvey told the *Star* that he was untroubled by the deal, calling it a "good-faith agreement." "It is my opinion that some individuals in our community continue to amplify this story in what seems to be an effort to discredit our county administrator and our police chief," said a statement he put out, "and they are doing so for their own political purposes."

The Kansas Bureau of Investigation (KBI) got involved and reviewed whether Zeigler had double-dipped the county, charging for work on the house while he was on the job. The agency turned over its findings to Dupree in May 2019.*

Whatever the motivation, Zeigler announced his retirement weeks later. The announcement caused Alvey to comment, "Our city is a better place because of Chief Zeigler's commitment to protect and serve."

Zeigler's retirement did nothing to reduce the tension between the old guard and the growing restlessness of the Black community. In late 2019, Kristiane Bryant announced she would contest Dupree's reelection. She had been Wyandotte County deputy district attorney but was one of the attorneys dismissed by Dupree back when he took office in 2016. As she entered the race, criticizing Dupree for alleged

* Zeigler contended in his book that the district attorney had asked for the KBI investigation because of politics, not anything illegal. The KBI concluded there was no probable cause to believe a crime, even a misdemeanor, had occurred, Zeigler wrote.

inexperience evident in his "inconsistent" treatment of cases, Bryant drew support from many among the political establishment.

The campaign was just beginning to heat up in the spring of 2020 when George Floyd was murdered in Minneapolis by police officer Derek Chauvin. Across the country, citizens took to the streets, and Kansas City, Kansas, was no different. "No Justice, No Peace" was the rallying cry at the Wyandotte Courthouse door.

Amidst the heightened attention to police abuses, Dupree announced he was seeking funds to rebrand and expand the Conviction Integrity Unit. It would be called the Community Integrity Unit and examine not only potential wrongful convictions but also instances of misconduct by police and other law enforcement. "If we are to really bring about systemic change, we must change the systems that allowed the acts of a few bad to go unseen and unchecked," he said.

He hoped to add three investigators and a hotline for complaints. Concerned about the community outrage that washed across Wyandotte County just like so much of the country, the Unified Government board approved the plan. But first some commissioners suggested putting the new unit outside of Dupree's office, just like they had talked about with the Conviction Integrity Unit.

Dupree, amid his reelection contest, worked to assure residents that he was the voice of reform. "We must move from anger to action," he said in one video, adding that change had to occur in all parts of the system and not just in the police force. "Prosecutors' offices across America share in the responsibility for the injustices we have seen in this country. It falls on all of us: Prosecutors, judges, deputies" to enact reform.

As Dupree was focused on building a team to review allegations of misconduct, the mayor was devising his own response to the protests. David Alvey, the unified government mayor with the KCK royalty pedigree, announced he was forming a ten-member task force on police and community relations. He named himself cochair. Other members included the sheriff; the acting KCK police chief, Michael York, who had been serving in an interim role since Zeigler's retirement months earlier; a Wyandotte County commissioner; and several residents.*

One name was conspicuously missing from the list: Mark Dupree. Alvey explained that he left Dupree off the task force because he was seeking an "objective" panel, whatever that meant. It was unthinkable to create a task force on criminal justice reform *without* the district attorney, but that is how things had often gone in Wyandotte County. And, of course, the election for district attorney was just weeks away.

As Alvey announced his task force, the calls of "No Justice, No Peace" by protesters at the county building included specific demands. Top of the list was an investigation into the allegations against Golubski that had been left unresolved after Lamonte was exonerated. As Kansas State Representative Cindy Holscher said of the former detective: "Today, he is a free man. Despite numerous allegations, he is able to roam the streets."

Nor was Holscher a lonely voice. As the protests continued, a coalition of twenty-seven lawmakers, religious leaders, and racial justice advocates called for the KBI to investigate Golubski and other members

---

* In the insular ways of Wyandotte County, Chief York's wife, Delia York, has been a Wyandotte County District Court judge since 2013; before that, she was an assistant district attorney, and then served as an attorney for Wyandotte County, where her duties included representing the county and its officers in lawsuits such as the one brought by the aggrieved motorist, Barron Bowling.

of the force who were involved in allegations of "sexual abuse of women, malicious actions toward citizens, and framing of individuals for crimes they did not commit." At a press conference, one KCK state senator said that local officials had "allowed this seedy underbelly of abuse of people of color, of those who have been downtrodden, to be perpetuated and continued for decades, maybe even a century."

Cheryl had been passing on information to the KBI and the FBI for years about all kinds of allegations about Golubski, from sexual abuse to conspiring with drug dealers to framing innocent victims. There were even questions about the unsolved murders of a series of sex workers, several of whom appeared to have some connection to the detective. But nothing much seemed to come of her tips, and the agencies shrugged off the dated evidence. The same day state lawmakers held a press conference calling for a state investigation, a KBI spokeswoman told *The Kansas City Star* that Dupree had asked the state agency to investigate Golubski nearly three years earlier when Lamonte's conviction was overturned. The spokeswoman said the agency had reviewed thousands of pages of documents but concluded then that there was nothing their agency could do because the statute of limitations had long since run out on any possible state crimes.

But, the official said, the office had turned over information to federal authorities. The U.S. attorney's office told the *Star* they could not confirm or deny information about the matter. And that is where things stood.

If being left off the task force were not troubling enough, Dupree would face another gut punch days later, with the primary now less than two weeks away. The editorial board of *The Kansas City Star* took on the

Wyandotte County district attorney in a two-part investigative editorial. The first part was headlined, without subtlety:

> 'CRIME IS NOT BEING PROSECUTED': WYANDOTTE COUNTY DA MARK DUPREE ENDANGERS PUBLIC SAFETY.

And it began with this chilling pronouncement:

> Something is wrong, dangerously wrong, in Wyandotte County. And it's spilling out into the entire Kansas City region.
>
> Whether through incompetence or inexperience, the Wyandotte County District Attorney's Office is inarguably playing Russian roulette with the public's safety. And people may be dying as a result.

The *Star* editorial board reported that it had identified "nearly 50" cases that "local legal experts found poorly handled," stating: "Multiple people have been murdered after their alleged killers slipped out of the Wyandotte County District Attorney's grasp."

Shockingly, even defense attorneys were complaining about Dupree, contending their clients were being offered plea bargains that were too lenient.*

The following day the next installment, no less chilling, appeared under the headline:

---

* An odd circumstance, to be sure: Attorneys have an obligation to work on behalf of their clients, and attorneys' complaints to journalists that their clients were being treated too well belongs in the man-bites-dog category. The article quoted one defense lawyer, KiAnn Caprice, saying, "I started getting plea deals on cases that went from being a happy surprise to making me feel like, 'I can't believe I'm getting these deals.' I was talking to attorneys who were getting the same deals."

'SORRY FOR PEOPLE IN WYANDOTTE COUNTY': CRIME VICTIMS DENIED JUSTICE, EMPATHY BY DA.

The article was built in large part on the conclusions of a former Wyandotte County prosecutor whom the newspaper had asked to review and evaluate how the district attorney's office had handled ten cases. The review, as one might guess, was not favorable.

Left unsaid in the article: The newspaper's expert was among the attorneys whom Dupree had not retained when he took office. Back while she was still a part of the office, the expert was a colleague of Kristiane Bryant, Dupree's challenger.

The paper the next day published a commentary by Dupree, who wrote, "This office has endured three-and-a-half years of attacks, bullying, and half-truths, and the recent misleading *The Kansas City Star* editorial attacking my record is just the latest example. My opponents have influence, and they apparently influenced the writing of that editorial. My reforms threaten the status quo in Wyandotte County, and that's the only reason so many people who benefit from the status quo want to derail my office's progress."

He added, "They don't want me digging into past wrongs because they know what I'll find—more corruption."

And then, days later, Dupree was given the space to write a guest column offering a rebuttal to the editorial. "Our office is an anomaly," he wrote. "We give fair pleas. We charge crimes accurately. We don't play the game of 'upcharging' to boost conviction rates." He added, "Justice loses every time we hammer people who do not have political connections, every time someone with connections gets a special favor, and every time a secret agreement is forged."

He concluded by reminding readers that he had grown up impoverished and had seen his share of crime. "I'm one of you," he wrote. "I don't want your child to see and experience what I did as a child . . . We aren't trash. But unless we stand together, people in this community will continue to treat us that way."

Days later, Dupree easily defeated Bryant and essentially won a second term; he was assured reelection, since no Republican had filed to oppose him.

The Conviction Integrity Unit's first test came when Dupree asked the team to review the conviction of a retired letter carrier, Olin L. Coones, better known as "Pete." He had been convicted of murdering his grandfather's former caretaker, but after Lamonte's exoneration Pete wrote to Cheryl, to the Midwest Innocence Project, and to Dupree, contending he had been wrongly convicted.

Kathleen Schroll and her husband Carl were found dead of gunshot wounds inside their home in April 2008. The gun used in the shootings belonged to Kathleen. Pete was a likely suspect; after all, police found the bodies after Kathleen's mother received an alarming call from her daughter. "Pete is in the house," Kathleen told her mother, adding, "He said he is going to kill Carl and he said he is going to kill me and he said he has got his tracks covered where no one will find out." Then the phone went dead, Kathleen's mother told police.

The police arrested Pete within hours of the incident. Pete had recently fired Kathleen after he discovered she had been neglecting Pete's grandfather and stealing from him.

Pete insisted that he had been home all night, and family members vouched for him. The prosecution was assigned to Edmond Brancart, a veteran in the Wyandotte County District Attorney's Office. Brancart was a former president of the statewide association of prosecutors, and one year won the annual award given by District Attorney Gorman to one Wyandotte County assistant district attorney in recognition of outstanding work. There was his name on a plaque visible to any visitors. Brancart was a star in Gorman's office.

The jury convicted Pete at trial of murdering Kathleen Schroll but not her husband, and he was sentenced to spend fifty years to life in prison. The conviction was overturned, however, when it was belatedly discovered that Brancart had withheld evidence that supported Pete's alibi.

The case was set for retrial, this time only on the charge of murdering Kathleen, and this time Pete's attorney was armed with the previously withheld evidence. But days before trial, Brancart revealed he also was armed with new evidence: Pete's cellmate in the Butler County jail, where Pete was held awaiting trial, was prepared to testify that Pete had confessed in prison. Brancart insisted before the retrial that he only recently had learned that the informant was even willing to testify.

Jailhouse informants, known derisively as "snitches," have inherent credibility problems. Providing information about other inmates can be a ticket out of prison, or at least for reduced charges. Skilled inmates find it relatively simple to learn key details, reading other inmates' legal papers or news accounts for details that they can sprinkle into invented confessions to make them seem believable.*

---

* Perhaps the most notorious of such prisoners was Leslie Vernon White, who had time after time after time gone to Los Angeles County prosecutors back in the 1980s saying that some other inmate had confessed to him. White's skill was such that he could learn non-public details about an inmate, armed only with an inmate's last name and a telephone, which he would use to impersonate an officer. *The Los Angeles Times*, and then *60 Minutes*, exposed White's exploits in investigative reports, raising concerns not just about a series of prosecutions in which White testified but also to other prisoners' claims of hearing confessions from cellmates in other jurisdictions.

Because of the inherent unreliability of such confessions, some prosecutors will not use jailhouse informants at all, and some jurisdictions have even barred or strictly limited their use. Prosecutors tend to use jailhouse informants' testimony when their evidence is weak and they are desperate for something to bolster their case; if the case is strong, prosecutors tend to shy away from adding dubious testimony that could leave jurors with credibility doubts. That leaves weaker cases most vulnerable to wrongful convictions from the dubious testimony of jailhouse informants. Nationwide the Exoneration Registry reported in 2024 that 247 cases of exonerations in its database involved testimony from jailhouse informants. Those cases commonly involved the most serious charges, especially murder.

After a new jury convicted Pete at the retrial, defense lawyer Brandon Bell agreed to take on the case, certain that his client was innocent. Pete was not a criminal and never had been. The prosecution theory actually made no sense at all to Brandon. The murder happened in the middle of the night. The murder weapon was a gun that belonged to Kathleen. The prosecution theory meant that Pete went over to his grandfather's former caretaker's house in the middle of the night, unarmed, and then committed premeditated murder with a gun that was already in her house? What sense did that make?

Bell thought it far more likely that Kathleen had decided to stage a suicide and make it look like murder.

When the judge rejected Bell's posttrial arguments and sentenced Pete to twenty-five-to-life in prison, Bell was so despondent he contemplated giving up his law license.

But after Dupree agreed to give the case a second look, the Conviction Integrity Unit found the smoking gun. In the prosecutors' files were a series of letters between Brancart and the jailhouse informant that showed Brancart had actively worked to win the informant's testimony, contrary to the prosecutor's representations before trial.

The unit's review showed other details that would have made the informant's allegations less credible. He got some details of the crime scene wrong when he was interviewed. He had even suggested to Brancart that he had knowledge that would help the prosecution of another Wyandotte prisoner, a telltale warning for prosecutors. In fact, Brancart had been warned by Butler County prosecutors from the start that the informant was not credible.

On top of that, Brancart withheld evidence that contradicted his assertion that there was "no evidence" to suggest Kathleen had a motive to kill herself. In truth, the walls were closing in on her. She had stolen significant sums from both Pete's grandfather and from the credit union where she worked. The police found forged checks in her purse that she had written on Pete's grandfather's account.

But all that information had remained hidden away during Pete's trial.

Within weeks of an expansive motion by Bell to overturn the verdict, Wyandotte County District Judge Bill Klapper agreed, ruling that the evidence showed Pete had been framed by a desperate former housekeeper, and that the prosecutor won the conviction of an innocent man through misconduct.

"The state suborned perjury," Klapper said, calling testimony that Brancart introduced "patently untrue."

Dupree, who was in the courtroom for the ruling, told reporters, "Prosecutors have two jobs, that the guilty not go free and that the innocent not suffer. And I think for a century, prosecutors have gotten so caught up on that first prong; but when there is innocence, we must do the second duty."

The next day, the director of Miracle of Innocence, the organization created by Darryl Burton and Lamonte, showed up at Pete's house with a new iPhone, to help him adjust to everything that had changed while he was locked away, and a promise to help him in any way possible.

While he was in prison, Pete had developed cancer that had gone undetected; his last years were stolen from him. He died 108 days after his release while visiting his sister in Alabama. Miracle of Innocence paid for Pete's family to travel there to be with him.

As for Brancart? After Dupree was elected, Brancart was among the old guard who moved on, becoming a senior attorney in the office of Attorney General Schmidt, who, of course, was no friend to Dupree. Brancart remained in that office even after Klapper's ruling came out. But once Schmidt decided to run for governor in 2022, Brancart's continued employment became a political issue in the campaign between potential successors. Days after the new attorney general, Kris Kobach, took office, Brancart was no longer employed there. (As of July 2025, Brancart remained listed on the state bar directory as an active attorney, but did not list a work address.)

45

Called to Account

The legal team representing Lamonte and his mother began gathering pages and pages of documents exposing troubling mysteries surrounding several of Golubski's other cases, as they built the civil case against Golubski, some of his fellow officers, and the county.

W. K. Smith, who was Golubski's assigned partner in the Lamonte investigation, was asked by Lamonte's attorneys during his pretrial deposition about one of those mysteries, the 1997 shooting death of a man named Kenny Cheffen outside the Uptown Club on the outskirts of downtown KCK.

Smith's son, Jeffrey, was suspected of firing the fatal shots. Under questioning by Emma Freudenberger, a partner of Barry Scheck's and one of Lamonte's attorneys, Smith testified he had no part in investigating the case and certainly never went to the scene or tried to discourage witnesses from cooperating.

In fact, Smith testified, all he did was accompany his son to court for his trial, to "give him courage and do what was right." The retired detective said he watched as his son denied he had he had committed the shooting. The case ended, Smith testified, in the acquittal of his son.

But Smith gave a series of answers that strain credulity. He did not speak to the assigned detectives nor review their reports; he even testified he had no idea which detectives investigated the case. (Freudenberger showed Smith records listing Golubski, his partner Terry Zeigler, and Clayton Bye as the detectives.) Smith testified he could not recall who the prosecutor was—other than it being a white man with black hair and average height—and could not recall the identity of the judge or if the case was tried before a jury.

Freudenberger then offered an explanation for Smith's memory lapses: There was no court case. Lamonte's team had checked and double-checked with the Wyandotte County court clerk and with the district attorney's office. No case was ever filed. Freudenberger accused Smith of making up the story of the court case because, "you knew you were going to be asked about your role in ensuring that the case was not prosecuted." Smith denied the accusation, but said he had no explanation for why he had conjured a phantom trial.

Though she was shielded by law against the allegations in the lawsuit, Morehead was required to give a deposition under restrictions demanded in advance by the U.S. Attorney's Office. By agreement, Morehead would not be asked anything about her normal practice as a prosecutor, or anything else that might reflect her work as an assistant U.S. attorney.

She testified that the eyewitness identifications of Lamonte were consistent and reliable. She said she never heard allegations from Niko that she wanted to recant her testimony until two years after the trial. "There was no reason I was aware of that questioned the veracity of the prior statements," she said.

Golubski finally testified under oath in a January 2021 deposition and faced a barrage of questions about the allegations that he engaged in horrific and repeated crimes. By then, he had left the Edwardsville police department and briefly worked in security for the major hospital in the region, before leaving that job when the publicity surrounding Lamonte surfaced. (In fact, the Edwardsville police department issued a press release as Lamonte's case was gaining attention, even after he had left the department, stating: "We recognize the serious nature of these allegations, should they be true. Thus, we want to reassure Edwardsville citizens of our unwavering dedication to protecting the rights of all people, and believe all people deserve impartial and effective service from our members.")

The questioning by Freudenberger lasted for hours. More than 550 times, Golubski offered the same answer: "On the advice of my attorney, I invoke my Fifth Amendment Constitutional Rights." He invoked the Fifth Amendment about whether he had paid Black prostitutes. About whether he gave women favorable treatment in return for sex. About how many children he had fathered. About whether any of the women lived in public housing. Had he ever raped a minor in his police vehicle? Taken a minor across state lines for sex? Threatened a minor if she were to tell anyone about them engaging in sex? Had he caused informants to falsely identify innocent individuals?

He invoked the Fifth about all questions involving Ruby Mitchell, such as the details of their conversation on the ride to the courthouse; how she came to say "McIntyre" during the interview, given she did not know his last name; on whether he had paid for her to engage in sex with him, before or after Lamonte was arrested.

On and on the questions went. About Niko Quinn and how she came to name Lamonte. Whether he ever had threatened her, or anyone, about removing their children if they did not offer the answers he wanted. About Stacey Quinn, and whether she had told him that Neil Edgar Jr., also known as Monster, was the murderer. And about why Golubski reported that he could not find Stacey, rather than getting a statement from her.

Freudenberger asked about his handling of the crime scene, and about why he had not sought the driver of the getaway car. She asked about Golubski's past encounter with Rosie McIntyre, and whether Golubski had told her, when she came as directed to the police station, that he would do nothing to harm her boyfriend "if she let you eat her pussy." The attorney went on: "Those were your words, right? You used them all the time?"

Golubski's answer never wavered. He said nothing other than invoking his right to stay silent. At one point, Freudenberger asked him to read for the record what it said on the piece of paper he had with him throughout the deposition. Golubski read the note on the paper out loud:

> "On the advice of my attorney, I am invoking my Fifth Amendment Constitutional right."

Golubski may have been keeping quiet, but residents of KCK were making plenty of noise. In the wake of George Floyd's murder and the protests that followed, the minority community, long resigned to injustice, was stirred to action. Barry Scheck, the well-connected founder of the Innocence Project in New York City who was part of

Lamonte's team, had been part of a discussion group on criminal justice reform launched by Team Roc, the social justice arm of the entertainment organization created by Jay-Z. Scheck considered the abuses in KCK the worst civil rights violations in the country, and brought the situation to the attention of Roc Nation CEO Desiree Perez, whom he knew would be sympathetic to the abuses of so many vulnerable members of the KCK minority community. Before long, Perez heard a presentation from Cheryl, Lindsay, and Tricia Bushnell of the Midwest Innocence Project and was sold. She agreed Team Roc would donate $1 million to help mount rallies, fund advertisements, and increase the pressure to demand greater accountability.

The Unified Government was in the midst of hiring a new permanent police chief to fill the position vacated by Zeigler almost two years earlier. By the spring of 2021, the city's administrators announced that the search was down to four finalists, and each was interviewed by what the city officials billed as a "Blue Ribbon Committee" of business and civic leaders. One of the members was attorney Denise Tomasic, whose husband was the nephew of the longtime district attorney.

Activists expressed frustration that community concerns had been ignored in past hirings of chiefs, who commonly came from within the ranks. And only once in the city's history had a person of color been put in charge: Boston Daniels, who had worked in jobs as varied as ditch digger, Pullman porter, and gas station attendant before joining the force and working his way up, finally, to chief in 1970.

Daniels had resigned less than a year after his historic appointment. Because of his prominence as a Black chief at that moment in time, his resignation made national news. He explained that soon after he became chief a new mayor took office. And once that happened, Daniels said, "I found I was not the chief of police. My power had been taken from me." For the next fifty years, the KCK police had white leaders. Until, after George Floyd and the protests that followed, the city went to fill the vacant chief's position in the midst of the mayoral race.

Doug Bach, the Unified Government administrator, announced that the city had chosen its new chief from outside the department: Karl Oakman, the deputy chief of the department in Kansas City, Missouri. Oakman, the second Black man in history to head the department, had grown up in housing projects in KCK and said he was determined to strengthen relations across the city, in every community.

Alvey said he was seeking reelection to see through several reforms, including improved police-community relations. A five-candidate primary narrowed the field to two finalists, Alvey and Tyrone Garner, a Black man who retired as deputy chief of the KCKPD after a long career on the force.*

The police scandal was front and center during the campaign. Weeks before the election, Team Roc sued to pry open records that would help expose how poorly KCKPD had done at policing misconduct by officers. The lawsuit sought reports and complaints against the department's internal affairs investigators, against officers with a history of abuse, as well as copies of department policies. It was the kind of internal record-keeping that Al Jennerich, the FBI agent, and Julie Robinson, then a young federal prosecutor, had fought to get decades earlier.

"For decades, the KCKPD has failed to provide accountability for officer misconduct," the lawsuit stated. "And, thanks to the blue veil of silence and apparent failure to investigate serious allegations, little of it has come to light."

---

* Another of the original five had been Chris Steineger, a former state senator who was a cousin to the former mayor, Joe Steineger. It was a generational rematch: Four decades earlier, Chris's father Jack Steineger, the leader of the state senate, had nearly been upset for reelection by Lloyd Alvey Jr., David's older brother.

After the primary, Alvey said he opposed an outside investigation of the police department. He noted the KBI had said, in the midst of the protests following George Floyd's murder, that it had turned over its information to the FBI. "Whatever comes out of that," Alvey said, "we're going to take a look." But, he added, "I don't believe we need an independent investigation of the police department."

In contrast, Garner said there had been so many allegations of "nefarious activities" by members of his former department that he was ready to go to Washington and ask for help: "We need the full resources of the federal government to come in here and look at what is really going on with the Kansas City, Kansas, Police Department and take it wherever it goes." He added, "That's the only way the people in Wyandotte County are at least going to have a pathway to rebuilding trust in law enforcement."

Less than a month before the election, CNN broke the news that a federal grand jury was hearing evidence of federal civil rights violations committed by Golubski.* Alvey and Garner each tried to tar each other over the Golubski scandal. Alvey contended Garner knew or at least should have known, as a high ranking official in the department, of the corruption within the department. Garner called the attack a "shameful" effort to tie him to the "egregious" misconduct and noted he had not been promoted to management of the force until 2015—more than four years after Golubski had retired.

Garner contended that Alvey knew, but kept quiet, about the federal probe into Golubski. Alvey responded that the unified government's legal counsel advised officials not to discuss the matter.

---

* Stephen McAllister confirmed that once he became U.S. attorney, years earlier, he was so troubled by the allegations against Golubski that he traveled to Washington to strategize with officials in the Department of Justice about pursuing the case against Golubski. But that apparently went nowhere until the Biden administration took office.

As *The Kansas City Star* columnist Melinda Henneberger put it, Golubski "is effectively on the ballot." Days later, Wyandotte County voters elected Garner to be the first Black mayor of KCK.

It was indeed historic. The county had its first Black mayor, its first Black district attorney, and the second Black police chief. Bach stepped down as the administrator of the Unified KCK/Wyandotte government within weeks of Garner taking office. The commissioners unanimously appointed Cheryl Harrison-Lee to replace him, making her the first woman and first Black person to hold the position.*

By all indications, a new day was coming.

---

* Bach did not leave without a bang: As the *Star* soon put it, WYCO LEADER CASHED IN BEFORE LEAVING. His separation agreement, it turned out, afforded him a "payout worth at least $813,000," including "an astonishing $427,364 in accrued leave." An extraordinary amount, the newspaper noted, for "taxpayers already burdened by the county's high property taxes and low household incomes."

46
Fundamental Change

More than 100 people, mostly Wyandotte County residents as well as several criminal defense attorneys who practiced in the region, gathered in a lounge of the Kansas City Kansas Community College in January 2022. The issue was how to overhaul a system that left indigent defendants represented by poorly paid attorneys, many of whom were appointed to cases despite their lack of experience or skill by the judges who would then preside over those same trials.

It is an issue that vexes authorities across the United States, with more than five million felony cases resolved in state courts annually. Most defendants cannot afford private lawyers. In 1963, the Supreme Court ruled in *Gideon v. Wainwright* that every defendant charged with a felony is constitutionally guaranteed a lawyer, whether the case goes to trial or not.

The system of providing indigents with defense lawyers has plagued the criminal justice system ever since. After all, *who pays for it, and how do you keep costs down?* The public has little appetite to spend taxpayer dollars to help accused criminals win in court.

Most urban communities have enacted a system where some form of public defenders work on salaries. The best of those systems offers defendants the ability to be represented by staff attorneys who receive training, supervision, and access to specialized experts.

But those systems do not always work as designed. In many communities the public defenders end up with unmanageable caseloads and become part of assembly-line justice. Too often, they negotiate pleas to resolve cases without fully investigating or uncovering problems in the prosecution case that might establish innocence.

Across the border in Missouri, defendants were forced to spend months in prison while on waiting lists for a public defender, until a federal judge ruled the delays were unconstitutional and forced the state to provide supplemental funding. In California, where each county bore responsibility for funding its own public defender, the Placer County board once fired its public defender and put out bids for the contract—not because the public defender was ineffective, but to save money. The county then replaced well-regarded but overwhelmed defenders with a competing firm that submitted the lowest bid.

At the time of the 2022 public hearing, Wyandotte County was among jurisdictions that rely on their judges to appoint attorneys on a case-by-case basis. Many defendants in those communities are left with attorneys who have too little experience, inadequate training, and no supervision. In too many of those jurisdictions, the attorneys who live on such appointments know better than to file too many motions or to take extraordinary steps in lining up investigators and experts that might make them disfavored by the judges who appoint them.

It is not so much that judges *want* to ensure that criminal defendants are poorly represented. After all, a system built on the adversarial process depends on two zealous but fair advocates. A woeful defense can lead to a wrongful conviction, just as a woeful prosecutor can lead to a wrongful acquittal. But providing vigorous defenses costs money. On top of that, judges often value attorneys who will not cause disruptions, who will not slow things down through unnecessary motions and arguments and investigations.

Every extra court day, every extra hearing, costs money and takes up time. Judges, many of them elected officials who come out of the prosecutors' office, know that most defendants are guilty. The system simply *can't* spend endlessly on futile defenses that bog down the system.

By 2021, other large Kansas communities and several smaller ones had a public defender system, with staff attorneys, to handle a significant portion of the cases. But Wyandotte County resisted such change. Kansas has long kept the rate meager for court appointed lawyers; for years state officials made a priority of frugality. The hourly fee remained below $70 as recently as 2017. A special legislative act finally raised the hourly rate to $100 in 2020. By 2025, the hourly rate was set at $120 per hour; but legislative cuts in 2025 raised new issues about funding attorneys for indigent defendants.

The system of private appointments also provided the county's judges with power over the defense bar. The system discouraged appointed attorneys from being too argumentative or belligerent if they wanted more appointments. And so, over the years, defendants like Lamonte were given attorneys like Gary Long or Mark Sachse, whom they could expect not to throw too many resources into things.

Soon after his reelection to a second term, Dupree decided to take on that system and fight for a public defender's office to be set up in Wyandotte County for at least a significant portion of indigent defendants.

He undertook a study to show how poorly the system served the accused. Wyandotte County indigent defendants were locked in the county jail an average of fifteen days before their attorneys were even appointed. They were jailed, on average, 128 days—more than four months—and in that time their attorneys, on average, visited fewer than two times. Many of the detained suspects were eligible for diversion and did not need to be locked up at all: two defendants in Dupree's sample who were eligible for diversion rather than incarceration spent more than 100 days waiting in jail.

Dupree also found a pay-to-play system—many attorneys who had contributed to the election campaigns of the judges who appointed them.

Disturbing as Dupree's findings were, they were not surprising. In community after community across the country, judges tend to appoint their friends, former business cronies, and campaign contributors. But what *was* unexpected was that Dupree was even doing the study and launching an effort that would lead to better representation for defendants prosecuted by his office.

One appointed attorney in Dupree's study jumped out: *Gary W. Long II*, Lamonte's trial attorney. Long had been disbarred by the Kansas Supreme Court in 1998, following a long record of neglect and mishandling of cases. But seventeen years later, the Kansas Supreme Court permitted Long to regain his license once he retook and passed the state bar examination. At that moment, the motion that led to Lamonte's exoneration had not yet been filed, so there was not yet any public attention to his inadequate representation.

After he regained his license, Long went back to taking court appointments. Seven months after he regained his license, state records show, Long contributed $100 to the campaign of one candidate for Wyandotte County district court judge—Renee Henry, the prosecutor of Barron Bowling.

Dupree included Long in his list of court-appointed attorneys who were contributing to judges who make those appointments.

When asked why, as a prosecutor, he was taking on the system of court appointments, Dupree noted that both Lamonte McIntyre and Pete Coones, the two exonerations during his first term, were represented by attorneys appointed by the court. "To get a public defender's office would bring about a whole lot more justice for Black, Brown, and broke folks who are incarcerated right now because they have lawyers who care more about their bread and butter and not ticking their friend on the bench off," he answered.

Dupree created a PowerPoint presentation of his study and began showing it to the county's judges and to the members of the state Board of Indigents' Defense Services, which oversees both the public defenders and the funding for the appointed lawyers. The county's judges did not favor abandoning the system that let them control the appointments. Neither did members of the Wyandotte County Bar Association, whose president at that moment, incredibly, was Gary Long.

On the other hand, members of the state board were open to the idea. It worked well in more than a dozen judicial districts across the state, including Topeka, Wichita, Johnson County, and several regional offices in more rural locations. The offices were generally staffed with a senior lawyer in charge, and less experienced lawyers who are trained and then supervised in a way private attorneys generally are not. Wyandotte was the outlier, an urban county without a public defender's office.

A small crowd gathered in January 2022 at the Kansas City Kansas Community College for a public hearing scheduled by the state board to discuss the proposal for a public defender office. It proposed a hybrid system: A Wyandotte County public defender office would handle a portion of the cases of indigents, and private attorneys would take the rest. Three board members and agency staff listened as thirty-seven speakers offered their views.

Supporters included relatives of defendants who had been poorly represented, officials of the local NAACP, and local activists. Federal Public Defender Melody Brannon noted some "deeply embedded systemic issues" in Wyandotte County and said a public defender's office could attack such issues as police misconduct and prosecutorial abuses in a way that private attorneys could not. "The Sixth Amendment should not be for sale to the lowest bidder," she said.

As Dupree spoke about the need for change, citing the results of his study, one member of the private defense bar interrupted: "Don't tell us how to do our job." Members of the Wyandotte County defense bar described how much time they devoted to representing each defendant, whether privately retained or appointed. They told about clients who came to them saying they "did not want a public defender." One even suggested that Dupree was trying to get a public defender established because he wanted lesser adversaries so his office could win more convictions.

Lamonte's case was raised repeatedly. Speakers said it showed the system needed change. Defense lawyers contended that his defense was not what caused his wrongful conviction. But then Lindsay Runnels, Cheryl's associate, who had been a part of the team representing both Lamonte and Pete, took to the microphone. It was true, she said, that both Lamonte and Pete had been the victims of government misconduct that caused their wrongful convictions. But, she said, there was no check on that system from the court-appointed attorneys, who failed to properly investigate or raise issues at trial. "You can't stand up to a system that you ask for payment," she said, "whether it's conscious or unconscious."

The board met six days later in Topeka and unanimously voted to create a public defender's office that would serve as a hybrid system: the office would hire a staff of salaried attorneys, but some cases—the overflow and those involving multiple defendants—would go to private attorneys.

The Wyandotte County public defender's office opened in late 2024, with a staff of ten attorneys, but that hardly solved the problem of providing adequate representation to indigent defendants in Kansas. Heather Cessna, the director of the agency that oversees providing indigent defense, quit abruptly in June 2025, following passage of the state budget that cut funding for indigent representation statewide even after she had warned legislators of a crisis if they did not *increase* her funding. Attorneys were being asked to handle more cases than they could effectively handle, and would soon be ethically forced to decline new cases. While the problems were most stark in rural counties, Cessna warned the crisis was statewide. It was "not a question of if it will happen," Cessna said. "It is a question of when and where. And I can tell you we are on the verge of that every single day in every jurisdiction."

As for Gary Long? It was not long before he was in trouble again with the disciplinary board. This time, three different clients filed complaints. Two claimed he had failed to diligently pursue their cases or respond when they asked about their status.

In June 2022, the Kansas Supreme Court noted Long's disciplinary history. He had suffered personal losses and depression, the court noted, and "the record suggests respondent is a good person and a knowledgeable attorney." Still, the court noted, in seventeen years of active practice, "his clients and judges before whom he appeared filed at least ten complaints."

The Kansas Supreme Court indefinitely suspended Long from the practice of law. A year later, the disciplinary board received even more complaints about Long. In October 2023, Long voluntarily surrendered his license and, the following month, became the rare attorney to be twice disbarred by the Kansas Supreme Court.

If the Kansas disciplinary board was slow and cautious about disciplining Long, it was even more hesitant with prosecutors. The board had long relied on a special committee of prosecutors to probe those allegations, believing they could best recognize misconduct by their colleagues. But Melody Brannon, the federal public defender, said the prosecutors on that committee treated the allegations as "There but for the grace of God, it could be me."*

No member of the Wyandotte County District Attorney's Office or the federal U.S. attorney in Kansas had ever been publicly disciplined, but Federal Public Defender Brannon was determined to change that. Brannon filed complaints against Terra Morehead and others in the U.S. attorney's KCK office that went nowhere for years. She urged the state disciplinary board administrator to sanction those who listened in on recorded conversations. She wrote again about mischaracterizations by Morehead and three other prosecutors when they unsuccessfully appealed Judge Robinson's contempt finding. In their appeal the four stated falsely that the evidence showed they had not listened to privileged calls.

* State officials did not agree with Brannon's criticism, but stopped the practice of limiting the review committee to prosecutors.

Brannon also wrote the board following Judge Robinson's ruling that Morehead committed misconduct by threatening a defense witness in the case of Gregory Orozco. But nothing ever seemed to happen.

After Joe Biden was elected, with Terra Morehead still in the office, Brannon wrote in desperation to the inspector general of the Department of Justice. Her letter began:

> A criminal justice system can only earn the public's deference and assistance through its own moral credibility. This vital credibility is wholly absent from the United States Attorney's Office for the District of Kansas. This absence is attributable in large part to the persistent and pernicious misconduct of a single Assistant United States Attorney: Terra Morehead. But it is also attributable to the Kansas USAO's long-time protection of Morehead and general tolerance of abusive prosecutorial practices.

Her letter went on, "How does she still have a law license? Our office fields this question about Terra Morehead on a regular basis." Brannon contended that Morehead had "abused her power for decades" and "repeatedly directed her abuse towards the people of Wyandotte County, one of the poorest and most vulnerable communities in Kansas . . . The Kansas USAO has lost its way, its credibility and its legitimacy. In the meantime, our clients continue to lose their freedom because of unethical and unconstitutional practices."

"The system is broken," Brannon said in an interview, as her complaints went nowhere for month after month.

47

Tying the Loop

The quest for justice for Lamonte had a ripple effect and brought signs of hope to Wyandotte County. The old guard had been replaced, and Black residents had taken over the top offices. A new system was launched that at least reduced the old cronyism in the appointment of attorneys for indigents. Golubski and many of those with whom he worked were gone from law enforcement.

Jay-Z's social justice organization, Team Roc, had helped arrange for $1 million to be poured into investigations, headed by the Midwest Innocence Project, to investigate other cases of wrongful convictions caused by Golubski and his colleagues. Lamonte had been awarded $1.5 million in compensation for his wrongful conviction, and had helped bring a new law that ensured compensation for others. Terra Morehead had been reassigned within the office to remove her from playing any role in prosecuting those accused of crimes, and disciplinary complaints had been filed, even if they hadn't gone anywhere. And the civil lawsuit brought by Lamonte and his mother, Rosie McIntyre, was headed for a jury.

U.S. District Judge Kathryn Vratil refused efforts by Golubski, the other officers, and the KCK/Wyandotte County Unified Government to have the case dismissed on the grounds that Lamonte lacked proof that Golubski fabricated evidence. Vratil ruled that there was enough evidence of Golubski coercing witnesses that a jury could fairly conclude that he had falsely developed the case against the teenager.

The other officers contended they were not responsible and that Golubski acted on his own. The judge said that would be up to the jury to determine.

Nor did the judge excuse before trial the Unified Government, leaving the government liable if the police department had failed to properly train and supervise Golubski and, especially, if they knew of his improper conduct and did nothing to stop it.

The McIntyres' legal team was exposing a more dramatic and widespread picture of police abuse than ever before seen. One woman, Ophelia Williams, told a chilling account of what happened after Golubski and a group of police showed up early one morning with a warrant and took her two sons into custody in 1999 on murder charges. As Williams testified at a 2022 deposition, Golubski stood alone with her in her living room as the other officers fanned out to conduct a search. She asked him what was going on, but "he was too busy looking at me, staring at me, telling me how nice I looked and that I had nice legs."

According to her account, Golubski returned a few days later and they sat on the couch. As she began talking about her sons, he inched closer. "I really didn't know what he was going to do until he put his hand on my leg and I slapped it off. And then he said he can really help me out, help my sons out." He told her that he knew the district attorney and they drank together at a bar. "And then he put his hand back. But that time he pushed the hands all the way up under my skirt."

Williams asked him what he was trying to do, as she stood up. But then "he stood up. And next thing I know he pushed me on the couch and unzipped his pants," and then proceeded to rape her. He then wiped himself off with paper towels as he left, telling her he would see her again.

Golubski returned several times in the following months, raping her and forcing her to perform oral sex on him, Williams contended.

Asked if she called the police after Golubski left, Williams responded, "No. He was the police. What was I going to say; this policeman just raped me?" He had frightened her into submission—as he had so many others. "He said he can have somebody do something to me and they would never find me." (Of course, there was the added worry about her sons; both were convicted of murder and given harsh sentences; in 2024, Melinda Henneberger of *The Kansas City Star* questioned in a column how the case could *not* have gotten a review by Dupree's office, given Golubski's role in the investigation and the fact that the jurist who imposed a fifty-year sentence on one of the two fourteen-year-old twins was Judge Burdette.)

On two occasions when Golubski showed up, he said he was in a hurry. His partner was waiting in the car outside.

Golubski had made victims of marginalized girls and women, those he felt had no standing, and perhaps not the will, to resist him or fight back. They were not people who were going to be believed if they made complaints about him. They had been beaten down repeatedly in life, and he easily dealt them more pain.

A woman, identified in court records only as "S. K.," gave her own alarming description of abuse by Golubski that began when she was thirteen years old. As she described it during her deposition,

S. K. was a middle school student when Golubski first contacted her in 1997 and said he needed to see her to ask about some undefined incident that he thought she was connected to.

They met in his car in a Walmart parking lot, and Golubski never asked her about anything. He put his hand on her leg, then slid his hand up her skirt and sexually assaulted her, warning if she complained she could forget about seeing her grandmother or brother again. "I was, like I said, lost, confused, had no understanding whatsoever, none. Don't know how I was targeted, don't know how he got my number, don't know why he chose me, but I knew that I was in something that I probably couldn't get myself out of alone."

On repeated occasions over the next four years, S. K. testified, Golubski called her and set up meetings that she was not to disclose to anyone. Each time, he drove them to a secluded area where he demanded that she satisfy his sexual cravings either in the backseat of his car or, occasionally, outdoors. S. K. complied, she testified, "because I didn't want to die." While Golubski was raping her, she testified, "I just closed my eyes and prayed."

S. K. came from a broken home, had previously been in a foster home, and was living with an aunt she trusted. At one point, S. K. confided to her aunt what was happening and her aunt drove her to the police station. S. K. was too afraid to go inside, so her aunt went in alone, and came back ten or fifteen minutes later angry with her niece for lying. The aunt was told that Golubski was a respected officer, S. K. testified, and had been on duty at the times S. K. contended they met.

She knew he was on duty—and that it did not matter at all.

The next time S. K. saw Golubski, he was furious. He knew her aunt had come to the station. He drove to a cemetery and told her to pick out the place she wished to be buried. He struck her and made her walk home afterward.

S. K. spoke of locations that Golubski took her and offered explicit details on their encounters—including one near the Missouri River, where Golubski would take her and joke about her disappearing there. "So the river was always a traumatic experience for me because I felt like I would—I could be in that water and no one would ever know or find me." The river was "torture." When Golubski took her to secluded places, she pulled out hair and left it behind, and bit her tongue and wiped blood, so that if she died, there would be evidence to identify her.

When she was fifteen or sixteen, she passed out in the bathroom at school and was taken to the hospital. There, when she gained consciousness, she learned she had miscarried. "I screwed up," she kept telling herself. "He's going to kill me." When she told Golubski about it, he called her a liar, said she had set him up, and that the pregnancy did not involve him. If she talked about him to anyone in connection with the fetus, Golubski would find out and he was "going to leave my grandma's brain laying on the table," S. K. testified that Golubski told her.

Golubski instructed her to stay low in the backseat when she was in his car, and not to look at anything. Nevertheless, S. K. often peeked. She saw a variety of drugs, including crack cocaine, marijuana, and pills in Golubski's car, and sometimes watched him conduct drug transactions with uniformed police and others. She described one incident when Golubski became upset with an apparent drug dealer who told Golubski he "didn't have it all, but he'll have the rest later." Golubski angrily responded the man could expect "no more free passes."

The mounting evidence made the idea of putting Golubski and the police department on trial especially precarious for the county government. It reported in a financial prospectus that the financial burden the case might impose on the county could have a material negative effect on its finances. Soon thereafter, Judge Vratil ordered settlement talks and directed Mayor Garner to personally attend. If the case went before a jury, the judge warned, it could lead to a "huge" verdict that could bankrupt the financially strapped county.

The two sides met and reached an agreement: The county would pay Lamonte and his mother $12.5 million to end the case. It was shocking and exhilarating for Lamonte. But that night, before the deal had even been reduced to writing and announced publicly, Lamonte had second thoughts. Despite the enormous payment for the small county, the police and Golubski were not required to admit wrongdoing. Lamonte did not feel good about the outcome. *They needed to admit that they did wrong*, Lamonte felt. Not getting the admission felt like a defeat, a failure to ever force Golubski and all those who supervised him to admit the wrongs that had been committed on Lamonte and, for that matter, the women and the entire community victimized by him.

Lamonte called Cheryl and told her that he wanted to back away. It was, Cheryl told him, too late. The deal was struck. It was announced the next day.

Just as Lamonte feared, when the case went before the unified KCK/Wyandotte County board for approval, the commissioners would not acknowledge what Lamonte most wanted to hear. As Commissioner Gayle Townsend put it, her vote was reluctant and based on a financial consideration, not an admission: "This would not mean the Unified Government is admitting to any wrongdoing. It brings final resolution," Townsend said. "It's an expensive choice."

Lamonte's lawyers issued a statement saying Lamonte hoped to put this painful chapter behind him and move forward with his life.

By this point Lamonte, Corisha, and her children had moved to the Phoenix area, less than a half hour from where his younger brother, Reggie, had already settled. His mother Rosie and his other siblings moved to Arizona as well; it was to be a new start for them all.

Lamonte bought a modern home, built in 2016, in a gated community of the North Gateway neighborhood. Lamonte and Corisha preferred the warmer climate, and he had no interest in staying in Wyandotte County. As Mike Bussell had warned him, KCK was not a welcoming place for him.

Lamonte and Reggie began buying real estate, arranging for renovations and flipping the houses. Lamonte also was regularly returning to Wyandotte County, where he remained involved in the barber school and barber shop, as well as in the Miracle of Innocence organization he had set up with Darryl Burton.

The lawsuit revealed that Lamonte suffered significant PTSD from the horrors of the Kansas prison system and from twenty-three years of being told what he could and could not do. He now strived to take command of his life. He sometimes flashed anger, and he tried a variety of ways to find peace.

The five-bedroom Phoenix house in which he lived with Corisha and her children was filled with both Christian and meditative adornments. Lamonte had lost faith over time in the idea of God; he simply did not share the idea of organized religion the way his mother did. But he believed in a spirit within everyone. He welcomed meditation in his quest for peace; he found satisfaction just sitting in the backyard. Corisha, on the other hand, held more overt faith in religion, and grace preceded all meals.

The two struggled. Lamonte did not think Corisha fully understood that he had never had an opportunity to learn how to be a husband and father. It was one of the many ways life had been stolen from him. They argued often and Lamonte finally moved to his mother's house in the town of Goodyear, Arizona.

His marriage had begun to feel like one more trap. Rosie was near death from COVID and would spend months hospitalized and on a breathing machine before she miraculously recovered.

⁂

The fact that Roger Golubski was a free man who never had been called to account nagged at Lamonte. Cheryl and Barry Scheck and Team Roc, among others, had done their best to push for the federal authorities to step in, but there was no sign that anything actually was ever going to happen.

Then the unthinkable happened. Cheryl called Lamonte in Phoenix early one September morning in 2022, weeks after the settlement of the lawsuit. She had extraordinary news: Shortly before 7:00 A.M., FBI agents showed up outside Golubski's house and yelled: "The occupants of 706 come out with your hands up." Golubski emerged, wearing a T-shirt and blue athletic shorts.

Roger Golubski was put under arrest.

A federal grand jury had voted to indict Golubski on six counts of federal civil rights violations. The former officer was accused of abusing the authority of his badge as he sexually assaulted two women on repeated occasions between 1998 and 2002. The two women were Ophelia Williams and S. K., both of whom had testified in depositions before Lamonte's lawsuit was settled.

The first issue after Golubski's arrest was whether he should be held in custody until trial. The government filed a graphic twenty-five-page document listing allegations that Golubski had similarly abused seven other vulnerable women during his years on the force. The motion was parallel to the evidence that Cheryl and her team had amassed on Lamonte's behalf, painting Golubski as an officer who relentlessly abused vulnerable women and threatened them with harm and even death if they went to authorities. The government said Golubski was a danger to the community and would be a threat to those women if set free.

At the bond hearing before U.S. Magistrate Rachel E. Schwartz, Lamonte sat in the front row while Golubski wore an orange jumpsuit, a striking reversal of fortune. Magistrate Schwartz called the allegations "quite shocking," and said that, if true, Golubski had engaged in "reprehensible conduct."

But she said the government had failed to establish that Golubski, by then sixty-seven years old and suffering from renal failure and Type 1 diabetes, remained a threat to the community. She ordered him confined to his house until trial, permitted to leave only for medical treatment or other specific appointments approved by the probation officer.

The ruling distressed Lamonte and others in the courtroom, including Ophelia Williams and Niko Quinn, who did not believe Golubski deserved to be free, even under house arrest and wearing an ankle bracelet. Lamonte rushed out of crowded courtroom as soon as Schwartz announced her decision.

Lamonte had been locked up on the day Doniel Quinn and Donald Ewing were murdered and was only released twenty-three years later. The man responsible for the theft of twenty-three years of his life was getting out immediately. It made no sense at all. "You're looking at the justice system at work," he told a reporter outside. "It's not equal."

The accusation that Golubski committed sexual assaults years earlier quickly came under attack by his lawyers. They contended that women came forward with stories as a result of the publicity surrounding Lamonte's case and the large settlement he received. There was no evidence, Golubski's attorney Christopher Joseph wrote in court filings, that the women had ever alleged the misconduct until after Lamonte's case was the subject of "rumors, rallies, and news headlines." Those who alleged abuse by Golubski were in it for the money.

In truth, of course, Jim McCloskey had started unearthing stories about Golubski's abuses years before Lamonte's case became public; even Golubski's ex-wife and Cheryl and the team of lawyers uncovered many other alleged victims.

Two months after Golubski was charged with civil rights violations for the sexual assaults, another startling legal development occurred. The U.S. attorney's office announced a second, even more shocking grand jury indictment of Golubski. He was accused of taking money to offer protection for three men who were trafficking young women, girls even, and keeping them locked in an apartment where, the indictment alleged, they were forced into sexual servitude. Golubski was accused of raping on occasion one of the young women who was being trafficked. The three men were none other than Cecil Brooks and two of his associates.

Federal authorities were tying a loop that Jim McCloskey and Cheryl Pilate had long tried to tie themselves: Roger Golubski was indicted on charges he took money to protect criminal activity by Cecil Brooks and his gang. It was Cecil Brooks's own cousin and business protegé, of course, who was said to have ordered the murder of Doniel Quinn, the murder that caused Golubski to arrest Lamonte McIntyre.

48
The Defendant Fails to Appear

In frigid weather, days after Golubski was charged the second time, Team Roc held a rally outside the Wyandotte County courthouse. The sign in the background demanded: #JUSTICE4KCK. END KCKPD CORRUPTION. At a table, organizers handed out signs that said, HOLD ROGER GOLUBSKI ACCOUNTABLE.

More than 200 people turned out, along with television cameras and print reporters. Ophelia Williams, one of the women Golubski was accused of raping, called for additional federal intervention to accomplish justice. Tricia Rojo Bushnell, the director of the Midwest Innocence Project, called Lamonte's exoneration "just the first step."

Then Lamonte himself spoke, saying he was there "on behalf of all you victims and all the victims' families, everybody who didn't get justice, who feel like you didn't get justice." Pointing to himself, he told the crowd, "This is what it looks like."

As he walked past, Mayor Garner was stopped by reporters and asked his thoughts. He called "misguided" the notion by anyone "that you would have three Black males that would sit on their hands in regard to allegations that allegedly affected the African American community." Those three, of course, were himself, the police chief, and the district attorney.

Hours later, District Attorney Dupree laid out his thoughts on how to achieve justice without federal intervention. He turned to the board of commissioners of the KCK/Wyandotte County unified government, a board that had once been so resistant to his requests, with a plan to accomplish the meaningful review the community was demanding. The old prosecution files were a mess, handwritten entries in folders that, in many cases, had deteriorated. The only way to accomplish the review of files in such disarray would be to hire a firm to digitize all the old paper files, making it possible to conduct searches across multiple files involving cases Golubski may have touched.

"The world is watching Wyandotte County," Mayor Garner said in response to Dupree's presentation. He and the other commissioners then voted to spend $1.7 million on the digitalization project, an enormous sum for the financially strapped county. The district attorney and the police would work together on the in-depth review, and the DOJ was not even needed.

The idea that local officials, whatever their color, would root out corruption, did not sit well with activists in the community.

Digitizing files was all well and good. But what was needed, they insisted, was something deeper, the kind of pattern-or-practice investigation launched in cities as widespread as Ferguson (Missouri), Baltimore, New Orleans, Cleveland, and Chicago. Such investigations identified what in the culture or policies of troubled departments had caused systemic misconduct; such reviews were followed by a plan, enforced either by consent or by judicial order, to address the issues. Pattern-or-practice investigations had been a valuable tool during the administration of Barack Obama; were curtailed once Donald J. Trump became president and installed Jeff Sessions as attorney general; but then, once Joe Biden took office, had again been resurrected.

The idea of outside officials examining the department's problems, then mandating changes that could be extremely costly did not always sit well with local officials. And while Candidate Garner had insisted that he supported such a probe, now there was a different tune from Mayor Garner, who said he would defer to local law enforcement officials, and Chief Oakman and District Attorney Dupree did not favor federal involvement. The officers who ran the department in Golubski's day were long gone, Oakman noted. It was a new day, and he was prepared to ensure the police acted professionally without any need for the DOJ to get involved.

Days turned into weeks turned into months turned into years, and community skepticism that the injustices would be corrected grew. In four years since Pete Coones's exoneration, the Community Integrity Unit (CIU), as it was rebranded, had made no visible progress.

First came the unwanted havoc that followed after the discovery that a member of the team had tape-recorded his colleagues making vile, racist comments to each other about a host of disadvantaged groups: Black people, gays, disabled, transgender, unemployed and, on top of it all, those who make claims of wrongful convictions.

Dupree fired the employees, but *The Kansas City Star* editorial board put the blame "squarely on Dupree," writing that the incident showed that "Those inside the system either have a conflict of interest or are just not interested." Dupree responded in print that he was engaged in transformational work, changing the culture of an office in which prosecutors passed a "hangman's noose award" as a festive gesture whenever a case ended in a hung jury. Dupree had stopped the practice and added training as well as enhanced attention to cultural issues during the process of hiring new employees.

New attorneys and investigators came and went from the CIU without any more exonerations. Some of that seemed the result of the difficulty staffing the unit with skilled, experienced attorneys who would be willing to live in Wyandotte County, as the local law required. Some of it appeared as legitimate legal disputes over whether the facts failed to establish actual innocence. As nothing happened, month after month, the distrust only deepened between Cheryl Pilate, Lindsay Runnels, and the Innocent Project on one side, and Dupree on the other, hampering the quest for justice in which both sides genuinely believed. By mid-2025, though, there was a new attorney hired to take charge of CIU, offering hope that the unit would tend to the unfinished business of examining the harm done in the past.

More than a year after Golubski was first indicted, a coalition of activists, from the local organization MORE2 to the ACLU of Kansas, signed a lengthy letter to Attorney General Merrick Garland pleading again for federal intervention; leaving the matter to local officials would never be satisfactory. The local police department "has been infected with corruption, crime, and a complete lack of regard for the liberties and rights of the people for whom the department has sworn to serve and protect," the letter stated.

The coalition cited the disappointing track record of CIU, launched by Dupree with so much fanfare but so short on results. And the project to digitize the prosecutors' files, into which the county had invested

$1.7 million, was no panacea; having the old files in electronic form was of course needed but could not solve the problem of finding and proving other cases of wrongful convictions. The coalition wrote to Garland: "We do not know who else is in prison that should not be, and without DOJ intervention we likely never will."

After all, in a system as flawed as Lamonte's case exposed Wyandotte County to be, with a corrupt cop at the center of it, how could there *not* be other cases of suspects wrongly arrested and convicted of crimes they did not commit?

But which ones?

Dozens of cases fell under suspicion because Golubski was the assigned detective. There were questions about other cases in which his role was not obvious.

One month after Roger Golubski was released on house arrest, an out-of-county judge presided over a hearing on the claim by Brian Betts and Celester McKinney that they were wrongly convicted of murder in 1997. The key to the conviction was the testimony of their uncle, who said that he heard the shots and the two young men had admitted their guilt to him.

The uncle had long since recanted and said he falsely accused his nephews out of fear he was going to be himself charged. Over the years their claim of innocence went nowhere, at least until the notoriety around Golubski surfaced. The victim happened to be the nephew of Roger Golubski's ex-wife, Ethel Abbott.

Though Golubski was not named in any reports on the case, Betts and McKinney contended the detective had pressured their uncle to implicate them in the killing. The issue at the hearing boiled down to whether to believe the uncle's account that a detective whom he could only recall as a "big white guy" had threatened him unless he falsely implicated the two men. Golubski took the stand—his first time doing so since Lamonte's exoneration—and insisted he had not been involved in the case. In any event, he said, he had no relationship with the victim, his nephew by marriage.

Asked if he ever pressured witnesses to testify, Golubski said, "Never."

Two months after the hearing, the judge rejected a new trial. While it would be "very easy" to use "this new cloud of doubt cast about Mr. Golubski" to try to throw out convictions, he ruled, the uncle's testimony was not credible.

It was not the answer the community sought; the group MORE2 issued a statement: "It is just the latest in a long history of failures from the Wyandotte County criminal legal system to provide justice for people of color." The statement added: "It should scandalize all of us that innocent people, like Brian and Celester, remain imprisoned while Roger Golubski remains in his own home."

But proving innocence, as Lamonte's case showed, takes time and considerable effort. And time had its own costs.

Early in 2023, John Calvin died in prison of cancer. He insisted he was innocent of a robbery and murder charge that had been investigated by Golubski and for which he had spent two decades in prison. The clock was ticking on other cases of prisoners who claimed they had been framed by Golubski.

Nor were the only victims of injustice at the hands of Golubski those like Lamonte who were wrongly convicted. Former U.S. Attorney

McAllister said that he believed there were "many" more women who had been victimized by Golubski and raised concerns beyond the one officer. "It's hard to imagine he did this for thirty years and no other officers in the department ever knew anything about it."

There were, as well, questions about Golubski's connection to several unsolved murders of women whose bodies were found over time in the area around what once had been Quindaro. As Lamonte's lawyers wrote in one motion in the lawsuit against Golubski and the department, "The murders of these women, who were killed in exceptionally violent ways and who were left with their genitals or breasts exposed, prompted little attention in the KCKPD, despite the fact that the women were well acquainted with certain police officers and, in particular, were well acquainted with Roger Golubski because they had been coerced for sex or information or both."

Golubski's criminal case was assigned to U.S. District Judge Toby Crouse in the Topeka federal courthouse, sixty-one miles west on the tollway from KCK. Crouse had been appointed by Attorney General Derek Schmidt to serve as state solicitor general in 2018, and in that role, joined in briefs on cases from other states that sought to restrict abortion, immigration, and gun safety laws and to support state efforts that added greater scrutiny to voters' eligibility. He further burnished his conservative credentials in 2019 by joining the Federalist Society. He also had brought an appeal to the U.S. Supreme Court on behalf of Kansas, challenging a ruling by the state Supreme Court that limited the ability of police to conduct traffic stops on the highway.

In April 2020, the Supreme Court overturned the Kansas decision, and within weeks Donald J. Trump appointed Crouse to a vacancy on the federal district court. He was confirmed by a 50–43 vote of the Senate. The liberal Alliance for Justice had opposed him, stating, "His record of aggressive advocacy for partisan and right-wing causes suggests he will be unable to act as an independent, fair-minded jurist."

Crouse set a plodding pace for both the case accusing Golubski of civil rights violations for sexually assaulting two women, and the one charging Golubski, Cecil Brooks, and two associates in connection with sex trafficking of minors. Journalists, activists, lawyers, and alleged victims of Golubski drove from Kansas City to Topeka for a series of hearings that stretched out for two years. Crouse often held a baseball in his palm as a stress ball as he listened to a series of arguments by Golubski's attorney urging the judge to dismiss the cases.

The government laid out its case in pretrial filings: Cecil and his two associates had a series of apartments in a complex that Cecil owned, and girls between the ages of thirteen and seventeen, many just released from foster care, were held at the apartment and forced to provide sexual services. The money went to the defendants. Golubski, according to the government, took money from Cecil to offer protection and, when he felt like it, forced himself upon the women, even while in uniform and carrying his gun.

The government listed a series of other teenage girls and young women who were prepared to testify to their own treatment at the hands of the detective. One of the many chilling tales is a woman not identified by name in court papers. Back when she was twenty-one or twenty-two, Golubski saw the woman walking in a park and told her that she was not allowed to be there at that hour. The detective offered to drive her home, but instead, drove her to a small field where he demanded oral sex. When the woman refused, according to the government account, Golubski pushed her into the back seat of his car where he held her throat and raped her.

When the woman cried loudly and screamed, "Why are you doing this?" Golubski had a simple answer:

Because I can.

The pace was so slow that Biden's appointee as U.S. attorney for Kansas, Kate Brubacher, began taking a seat in the back row when those occasional hearings inched forward, a subtle means of demonstrating the importance of the case.

In July 2024, Judge Crouse set a trial date for the civil rights charges accusing Golubski of sexually assaulting two women: It would begin December 2, 2024. Because Golubski was in poor health and required dialysis treatment twice a week, Crouse set a trial for three days each week over a period of six weeks up through the holidays. As for the trailing case, involving sex trafficking, Crouse gave the defense extensive delays to gather and review records, and a pretrial hearing was set for early 2026. A date for the actual trial was not yet scheduled by late 2025.

The delays perplexed Lamonte, who pondered how it could take years to bring Golubski to trial, who remained on house arrest in the meantime. Lamonte, after all, was locked up within hours of his arrest and convicted within six months.

The reason seemed obvious to him. Golubski was getting White Justice. He got Black Justice.

December 2, 2024, finally arrived. Reporters started showing up when the Topeka federal courthouse opened at 8:00 A.M., having been alerted that seating would be limited. Lamonte, who had business to attend to that day, was unable to attend. Cheryl was there to observe, though she had no actual role in the case.

At 8:45, the prosecutors and defense lawyers appeared, but Golubski had not yet shown up. A busload of KCK residents arrived for a rally in front of the courthouse.

At 9:00, when Judge Crouse entered and took the bench, the defendant still had not arrived. Something seemed off.

Potential jurors were gathered in another room, awaiting rounds of questioning.

Defense attorney Joseph told the judge that his client had been "despondent over the media coverage." Three minutes later, a representative from the U.S. Marshal reported that Golubski's electronic monitor showed he was still at his house in Kansas City. At the request of prosecutor Tara Allison, a trial attorney in the civil rights division of the Department of Justice, an arrest warrant was issued, and the judge postponed jury selection until 1:00 P.M. Reporters in the courthouse were without computers or cellphones, but a television reporter came inside to report his colleague had been dispatched to Golubski's home in Edwardsville and found it surrounded by crime scene tape.

Cheryl, who was sitting in the hallway and, as a lawyer, was permitted to have her phone inside, said *The Kansas City Star* was quoting sources saying Golubski was dead.

At 10:30 A.M., Judge Crouse took the bench to be told what, by that point, seemed obvious. The United States was dropping the case on "suspicion of death," Allison said.

Authorities said Golubski had died of a gunshot to the head on his back porch. The coroner ruled it a suicide. It would later turn out Golubski had said he would "eat his gun" rather than being locked up, and left a note behind for his son advising funeral arrangements.

The sudden, shocking end satisfied no one. Cheryl told reporters she had many questions about how Golubski was permitted to be out of custody and to be in possession of a gun in violation of the conditions of his release. Who had he talked to, and who visited him, she wondered. For his part, Golubski's attorney said the apparent suicide should not be taken as an admission of guilt, a position nobody in the audience took seriously.

Lamonte said the ending of Golubski's life did not bring any satisfaction to him or others who had wished for justice for so long. His heart went out, he said, to all those victims "who never got a chance to speak their truth." He said he regretted again having taken the settlement in the civil case, which he called "the best opportunity to hold that man to account."

But he had one more message that he repeated to reporters who called and even on social media: "If anybody thinks one person was responsible for all of that damage, this is not over. Roger Golubski did not damage so many people's lives on his own."

Afterword

Half Full or Half Empty?

It is hard to imagine all the upheaval that occurred in the years since Cheryl Pilate filed the motion saying that authorities had arrested and prosecuted a seventeen-year-old youth for a murder he did not commit. And yet many of the leaders who have fought for change, Cheryl included, remain skeptical that any lasting change has occurred.

Surely, the long history of injustice and neglect for the large, impoverished community of KCK offered reason enough for their doubts. Events have tended to dampen enthusiasm even further.

After the long and hard-won battle to free Lamonte, there has been a lack of success in identifying and correcting other injustices. Dupree had not given up reviewing claims of the innocence of defendants, almost all of them Black men, who had languished in prison. But as he said on the witness stand at the hearing on the claims of Betts and McKinney, not every case that raised concerns merited relief.

There were so many obstacles: Was the evidence of innocence so clearly established that jury verdicts should be disturbed? Were the defendants trying to relitigate issues that already had been considered and rejected? And were some defendants exaggerating whether Golubski even played a role in their cases, treating the name of the disgraced detective as a magical "get out of jail free" card or, even, a potential ticket to millions of dollars?

As the months wore on, skeptics became convinced that Dupree's words were hollow. The mutual distrust between the prosecutor and defense lawyers who both spoke of attacking injustice created an impediment to that goal. The impediment became especially concerning once Donald Trump, who opposed the very idea of Justice Department investigations into police misconduct, returned to office in 2025. Despite what Cheryl had been feeding federal officials, Golubski had, of course, not been indicted until Trump was out of office. With his return to office, the future of the civil rights division to do such work became less certain. Continued progress would be left to state and local officials, making it even more urgent for those who welcomed reforms to work cooperatively.

And yet, for all the setbacks, all the delays, there were undeniable signs that the community was no longer mired in the routine injustice of the past.

The state disciplinary board finally in 2024 scheduled a long-awaited hearing on the conduct of Terra Morehead, conduct that Federal Public Defender Brannon had first complained about six years earlier. Weeks before that hearing was to take place, it was canceled. Terra Morehead had surrendered her law license. On April 26, 2024, the state Supreme Court accepted her resignation and disbarred her.

In early March 2025, the board finally held a hearing against two federal prosecutors implicated in the taping scandal, former Special Assistant U.S. Attorney Erin Slinker Tomasic, and Kim Flannigan. It was nine years since the two first called defense attorney Jackie Rokusek into their office and inadvertently revealed that prosecutors had access to recordings of defense lawyers and their clients. By the time the disciplinary panel finally held the hearing Flannigan was retired and Tomasic had long before moved back to Kentucky.

Gorman, who had succeeded Nick Tomasic and for years was the face of Wyandotte County criminal justice, experienced his own comeuppance. Following his electoral defeat to Mark Dupree, Gorman left the Wyandotte County District Attorney's Office after thirty-five years and went to work as the director of the special investigations unit of the Kansas Department of Revenue. But he was fired after less than a year there, following a *Topeka Capital-Journal* report of allegations that he tormented state workers with grossly inappropriate comments.

As for Lamonte, he shuttled back and forth between Arizona, where his mother and family lived, and KCK, where his barbershop academy, barber shop, and Miracle of Innocence demanded attention. He appeared in classrooms, talking about justice. Lamonte and Corisha continued to have rocky times and good times together; but then in 2025 Corisha cut off contact, sold the house in Phoenix, and moved away. It left an empty place for Lamonte. He began spending more time back in Wyandotte County, and even reconnected, after decades apart, with his father.

Lamonte's case, and all that followed, revealed the challenge in overhauling a criminal justice system that has been operating with egregious flaws for decades. But it is equally true that the justice system in Wyandotte County is a far different place than it had been before Jim McCloskey and Cheryl Pilate began digging into the case of Lamonte McIntyre.

Lamonte himself noted that many in the community have lost all trust that anything good has even come of all the uproar. They see a system where a teenager like him could be convicted within six months of a double murder on Hutchings Street and Roger Golubski, years after he had terrorized a neighborhood, could still be sitting in his home, convicted of nothing. They see defendants, mostly Black men, spend their lives locked up, and a system resistant to change.

But that did not mean nothing had changed. In truth, the arc was bending a little bit. Toward justice. Even in Kansas City, Kansas.

Coda

After reading Lamonte McIntyre's story, one can only hope that the next chapters for him are filled with the peace and fulfillment he was denied for all those years. But the story of Kansas City, Kansas, is far from over. What happened to Lamonte vividly exposed the many ways the criminal justice system can and does fail. The perfect storm of a dirty cop, an unethical prosecutor, deplorable court-appointed defense, *and* a judge who had an affair with the prosecutor? A novelist would have a hard time imagining such a confluence of events converging on one innocent individual. Lamonte's case offered more than a stranger-than-fiction narrative; it offered a chance to examine systemic flaws that pervade courthouses across the country. So throughout my reporting on the case and the longstanding government corruption that bred the unjust system, I undertook reporting, including conversations with more than a dozen national experts in criminal justice, on how to prevent more cases like Lamonte's.*

---

* Heartfelt thanks here to those experts who graciously lent their thoughts to this: Rob Warden, David Rudovsky, Jamila Hodge, Sean O'Brien, Steve Bright, Lara Bazelon, Bryan Stephenson, Madeleine deLone, Larry Marshall, Rebecca Brown, David Carroll, Sam Gross, and Jules Epstein.

A caveat here: Some of those I chatted with contended that my questioning of how to fix the criminal justice system to prevent further cases like Lamonte's was the wrong question. Experts such as Bryan Stevenson and Jamila Hodge cite extensive evidence that the criminal justice system works exactly the way it was designed to work. During the post–Civil War era, many states adopted laws such as "loitering" that specifically were designed to criminalize normal behavior by Black people, enabling them to be sentenced to years of indentured servitude—in effect, continuing slavery. Harsh punishments and lynchings, Stevenson has noted, were designed to perpetuate a racial hierarchy. Nor is that merely a footnote of history, as Stevenson wrote: "Late in the 20th century, amid protests over civil rights and inequality, a new politics of fear and anger would emerge. Nixon's war on drugs, mandatory minimum sentences, three-strikes laws, children tried as adults, 'broken windows' policing—these policies were not as expressly racialized as the Black Codes, but their implementation has been essentially the same. It is black and brown people who are disproportionately targeted, stopped, suspected, incarcerated, and shot by the police." It is in that more recent era, of course, that many young men like Lamonte McIntyre were swept up. As important as it is to acknowledge that foundational issue, for the purposes of this examination, we need not go further down that path.

Through much of the period of my reporting, the signs were hopeful that change was in the air. Following the horrible high-profile tragedies in communities across the country—from Michael Brown to Eric Garner to Freddy Gray to George Floyd to Breonna Taylor and so many others—citizens became increasingly aware that the criminal justice system needed reform. The election of Joe Biden, and his Justice Department under Merrick Garland, brought back pattern-or-practice investigations and even federal prosecutions of officers who had committed civil rights violations, including Roger Golubski.

But suddenly, in late 2024, that optimism was upended by the election, a second time, of President Trump; his early steps to "unleash" local police has dampened the optimism that reforms are inevitable. After the Senate failed to pass the George Floyd Justice in Policing Act, Joe Biden signed an executive order to implement several of the reforms that would have discouraged police misconduct. As soon as he took office, however, Trump revoked the order and appointed a new director of the civil rights division. In the administration's first 100 days, more than half of the 380 staff attorneys had resigned as the mission changed from protecting the civil rights of vulnerable citizens to attacking programs that ensured diverse and inclusive practices. No longer would the civil rights division spend time investigating police abuse; instead, it would investigate Chicago's hiring practices, as one example, simply because the mayor bragged in a speech of increasing the diverse hiring in his administration.

On top of that, Elon Musk, who gained outsized influence as he poured millions into helping Trump win his election, was telling advisors it was time to stop the progressive prosecutor movement that had played a key role in the exoneration of Lamonte McIntyre and so many others wrongfully convicted across the country.

Rather than signaling that the door is closed on reform, the national upheaval makes it more imperative for state and local officials to enact steps that minimize the risk of injustice.

Shocking, to me, was the initial reaction of many of the experts I consulted: Lamonte's case, they said, was not as different as I perceived. Many of the cases of wrongful conviction across the country involved bad cops, unethical prosecutors, and defense attorneys who fail to properly defend their clients. The most striking thing, many offered, was a judge who actually was caught for having slept with the prosecutor.

Truth be told, that detail did not strike me as one of great significance, however much it raised eyebrows. While the fact the judge and prosecutor had been romantically involved was dramatic, in reality, too many judges in too many jurisdictions are too close to the prosecution. In jurisdictions small and large across the country, those who are elevated to the bench—either by election or appointment—are often current or former prosecutors. They have dedicated their lives to seeing that criminals are fairly prosecuted in the interests of public safety, and trust their former colleagues to act honorably. In many cities, individual prosecutors are often assigned to the same courtroom day after day, while different defense attorneys come and go; that familiarity also may lead to bias by judges toward the prosecutors assigned their rooms, whether they sleep together or not.*

What did strike me about the case, from the start, was that it touched on every piece of the system. While I certainly had seen my share of cases involving a bad cop, an overzealous prosecutor, poor defense work by a publicly funded attorney, and certainly, judges who tipped the scales, to Lamonte's misfortune he experienced all of the above, emphatically. As a result, *State v. McIntyre* afforded an examination of systemic problems needing attention from those in search of a just system.

That examination starts with the police, the ones responsible across the country for keeping public safety by solving crimes and making arrests that flip the switch on the criminal justice machinery. Arresting

* In some large cities with public defenders, the defense attorney also may be assigned to the same room; elsewhere, especially in places that rely on appointed attorneys, the prosecutor is a far more stable presence.

the right suspect is commonly easy; police come upon a scene where an altercation has just taken place, hear from a complaining witness, or even observe a crime as it occurs. But solving crimes that occurred outside police presence, with no complaining witness—and dead bodies of course voice no complaint—requires detective work, piecing together evidence to identify the culprit. And it is here that the wrongful convictions are rooted.

There are a variety of things that can and do go wrong in the police investigative stage: Wrongful eyewitness identifications, false confessions, and unreliable forensic tests are three critical, and recurring, issues.*

Just as in Lamonte's case, wrongful identifications by witnesses are incredibly persuasive—juries do not readily discount the word of well-intentioned bystanders who say, with authority, "That's the man"—yet such testimony is too often wrong. The situations are stressful, and the crimes often happen in seconds.**

The problem of wrongful identifications is magnified, of course, when police have the suspect in their mind and then subtly guide a witness into identifying the person they already decided is responsible for the crime. They may create photo lineups that highlight their suspect—including photographs of others who are the wrong height, the wrong weight, the wrong complexion. An officer may, even subconsciously, give hints of which suspect the witness should choose. And

---

* The National Registry of Exonerations, the brainchild of Sam Gross and Rob Warden and driven by the research of Maurice Possley, maintains data on every exoneration across the country, and amply proves how commonly such problems occur.

** First year law students and psychology students both have often been made unsuspecting participants as unannounced intruders enter their classroom, commit a brief disruption, and then vanish. Individual students' accounts of what they just observed, and their descriptions of the intruder, are often dreadfully inaccurate.

once an identification is made, an officer may say things that make the witness more confident of their choice, making them offer an in-court identification with great authority.

Some jurisdictions have adopted safeguards to lessen the risks during the identification process, adopting "double blind" techniques so that the tests are prepared and administered to witnesses by officers who themselves do not know the identity of the person suspected by police. Additionally, research has shown wrongful identifications are less likely if the eyewitnesses are shown photographs one after another, in sequence, rather than all on one page; in sequential reviews, eyewitnesses focus more on comparing the photographs to what they saw, rather than comparing the suspects to each other. But not all jurisdictions require such safeguards, and witnesses like Ruby Mitchell may be influenced to make wrongful identifications even if photographs are shown in sequence. Many jurisdictions, but not Kansas, permit defense attorneys to call expert witnesses to explain to juries the inherent potential error, especially in identification cases made by witnesses of another race from the suspect.

There are other precautions that can be built into the system to guard against wrongful identifications and to guard against other types of problems in police practices that may lead to wrongful convictions. Tape recording of witnesses, especially suspects themselves, protects against officers feeding information to witnesses in their questioning, or badgering suspects to confess regardless of their protestations of innocence. Special safeguards are especially important in instances of minors taken into custody. And increasingly enlightened jurisdictions develop other steps to guard against erroneous convictions that stem from flawed investigations.

Lamonte's case shows, of course, that the systemic flaws go way beyond the police work. Ours is an adversary system, dependent upon two able advocates fairly presenting their cases. That, at least, is the ideal.

In reality, the system is too often far from perfect. On one side are prosecutors, who have the coexisting ethical obligations both to zealous advocacy on behalf of the state but also to ensure fairness and justice. Across the country, state prosecutors are generally elected county by county, and then hire a team of assistants to go into court. Elected prosecutors commonly see the key to retaining their jobs as locking up the bad guys, and certainly to avoid losing high-profile cases that might let dangerous suspects back on the street. Elections for local district attorney may be won or lost on the incumbents' conviction rates; and a lower rate is not what wins the prize. Assistant prosecutors tend to win promotions by securing convictions; internal awards are seldom handed out to assistants who "lose" the big case, no matter how much they may have been guided by ethical rules. Prosecutors in some offices end up in internal competitions to see who can notch the most wins; in the worst examples, prosecutorial offices become what former First Assistant U.S. Attorney Mike Warner described happened to the KCK office of the U.S. Attorney—a rogue office out to win at all costs.

Some tactics employed by overly zealous prosecutors are smarmy, but within the rules. Police turn their evidence over to prosecutors, who have a duty under the U.S. Supreme Court ruling in *Brady v. Maryland* to provide the defense with any evidence that may help the defense case. But in some cases prosecutors may drag their feet on how quickly they turn over evidence that they know a defense attorney may exploit, and first try to win an early plea agreement while the defense remains unaware of the potentially exculpatory evidence. Or prosecutors may discount the potential benefit to the defense, as Morehead did in minimizing the importance of the flash drive of photographs that the police seized from the vehicle driven by drug suspect Gregory Orozco. Aggressive prosecutors may, as Warner described Morehead doing, punish defendants by fighting their bail requests, or seeking enhanced punishments, if defendants dare to exert their right to seek a trial by jury.* In weak cases, as happened in the prosecution of Pete Coones, prosecutors may use evidence that they know is dubious, such as jailhouse informants.

Other tactics, such as the scandal of prosecutors who listened to privileged conversations between defendants and their attorneys for tactical advantage, fall clearly outside the ethical boundaries. Failing to ever turn over exculpatory evidence is clearly improper, an issue that has led to thousands of convictions in recent decades nationwide to be overturned after such evidence belatedly surfaces.** One solution adopted in many jurisdictions is to permit open discovery of the prosecution evidence, allowing for nondisclosure of protected witnesses and other, narrow exceptions.

Prosecutors similarly cross the line when they threaten prosecution witnesses into testifying or threaten potential defense witnesses out of testifying, the type of conduct of which Morehead was accused. And if justice is a goal, prosecutors should be restricted from calling unreliable jailhouse informants, especially those who say they heard confessions from multiple prisoners, absent some strong indicia that their statements should be believed; even then, defendants should be permitted to call experts to advise juries on the unreliability of such testimony.

---

* In a system that would break down if all defendants wanted jury trials, defendants typically are induced to plead guilty to a reduced charge, or at least be assured a lighter sentence if only they dispense with the idea of a trial. Defense attorneys have taken to calling the flip side—the harsh outcome for those who dare to invoke their Constitutional right to be tried by a jury—"the trial penalty."

** There obviously is no way to know in how many files evidence still lies, never shown to the defense, that would undercut the finding of guilt.

❧

The fantasy world of a criminal case, with two skilled adversaries zealously but fairly representing their side, requires honest and adept advocates on both sides. Surely, a forceful, experienced, talented defense attorney can significantly protect clients from wrongful prosecutions. And it is here that the system often fails defendants who lack the resources. Money often creates a two-tiered justice system, offering a just outcome for those who have the financial means but not for those without.

Doing defense work, especially in the most serious cases, requires time, attention, and money. It requires taking the time to visit the jail to interview accused clients both to hear their account of what happened as well as to build rapport with the defendants and their families. It requires being willing to spend time to do the investigative work that can identify potential flaws in the police work: Studying the crime scene to determine if witnesses like Ruby Mitchell could even see clearly the identity of a shooter from her porch; knocking on doors and scouring crime scenes to try to uncover evidence that may challenge the prosecution theory. It requires tracking down prosecution witnesses and potential defense witnesses, and if necessary, making sure they show up at trial. It requires reviewing the reports—hiring experts as needed to undertake the reviews—of coroners and pathologists and forensic analysts.

And of course it requires the willingness to contest the prosecution case, even going to court if necessary, and to present a vigorous and skilled defense.

All of which requires both expertise and money, two critical resources. Imagine if Gary Long had left the jury wondering how a transcript showed Ruby Mitchell saying, "Lamonte McIntyre" to the police, when she did not know Lamonte McIntyre at all. Imagine if Long had gone to her porch and had a crime scene analysis that cast doubt on whether she could have made out the face of the shooter. Imagine if Long had seen in the police reports that Josephine Quinn was outside, and said Stacey Quinn knew who the shooter was, and then worked to determine why the record did not reflect that the police ever even talked to Stacey. Imagine . . .

But who pays for defense attorneys to have the time and ability to undertake that kind of work? The U.S. Supreme Court said in *Gideon v. Wainwright* that even indigent defendants have the right to be represented. But how does the state even establish an effective system to provide that kind of defense?

Many urban communities have long had a public defender system—a full-time staff of attorneys to take on the cases of those too poor to afford private lawyers, and in some jurisdictions, like Kansas, public defender offices are being set up not just in Wyandotte County but in many smaller counties as well. But even more commonly, indigent defendants are represented by private lawyers appointed to their cases.

David Carroll, founder and director of the Sixth Amendment Center, which pushes to ensure systems provide adequate representation to indigent defendants everywhere, notes neither system is automatically superior; both can work, and both can fail miserably.

At their best, private attorneys who are appointed to cases have significant experience and independence. Many highly skilled private attorneys with extensive experience will take an occasional appointment, especially in high-profile cases, at a fraction of what they otherwise would charge, as a way of giving back to the legal community. But that is not the common reality. In many communities, attorneys with less-than-stellar records will take on several court appointments at once, making up for the low fees by handling a larger volume of cases than can be competently handled at once. Often attorneys taking those appointments cut corners. They fail to turn over every stone. They may fail to hire investigators and experts—perhaps unaware they should petition the courts for outside support, unaware how to do so, or simply accommodating the institutional pressure that discourages such dedication to their clients. Too often, they fail to expend enough time and effort to zealously represent a client.

Making matters worse, the attorneys in a vast number of communities, including Wyandotte County historically, are appointed to the cases by trial judges they appear before and to whose election campaigns they have supported financially. Judges may, inevitably, give out appointments for reasons other than seeking zealous advocacy on behalf of those unable to afford the staggering costs of competent defense.

Indeed, judges in jurisdictions across the country are under pressure to get the cases to completion, to keep the conveyor belt of criminal cases moving. Having defense attorneys who slow down that process by zealous advocacy does not necessarily suit the needs of judges. And, certainly, being the judge who presided over the case in which a dangerous defendant is set free—and the negative publicity that may result—is hardly in any judge's interests.

It is perhaps not surprising that Wyandotte County's judges opposed the measure to establish a public defender's office in the county; having the appointment power both offers judges a way to reward certain attorneys with appointments, and to keep attorneys who are too obstructionist from their courtrooms.

Public defender offices at their best have built-in advantages, able to provide attorneys with supervision, training, and staff investigators, social workers, and access to experts, the kind of resources that offer the means to pretrial investigation and review that can uncover the evidence to establish innocence. Attorneys within the same office are able to keep track of any police officers whose testimony seems incredible, of jailhouse informants who are called to testify, and can identify patterns of misconduct in ways solo practitioners are less able to accomplish. Some offices, such as, especially, the Public Defender Service for the District of Columbia, stand out as models of effective public defenders. But not all public defenders are such well-oiled machines. Some pay paltry wages and end up staffed by very inexperienced lawyers. In big cities, some defendants find a new face representing them at court appearance after court appearance. The goal is simple for the attorney showing up for one single court date: Keep the conveyor belt moving.

The funding for public defender offices comes from the taxpayers, of course—commonly, but not universally, through money provided by the state legislature. As elected officials look to cut their budgets, providing a robust defense budget is not a priority, and the caseload of the defense attorneys can grow to impossible levels. Just look at what happened in Missouri in 2018, where the system was underfunded for so long that attorneys were each juggling more than 200 active cases at once—a number far beyond what the American Bar Association considers tenable. The state finally gave an emergency appropriation after the state public defender office began refusing to take any new cases because it was impossible for its attorneys to provide the kind of representation that the Constitution demands. In California, where the public defender is funded at the local level, Placer County commissioners several years ago refused to renew the contract of its well-regarded public defender, and instead put the work out for bids, then appointed a firm whose work had drawn criticism but that submitted the lowest bid.

There has not been, after all, a longstanding lobbying effort to ensure that more money is spent to help acquit suspects charged with crimes.*

* Nor is one likely in the future.

Across the country, overworked attorneys in offices that are not properly funded end up pushing their clients into plea-bargained resolutions and then move on to the next case—and in repeated examples, fail in the process to do the needed investigation to develop a defense.

In Kansas, the agency responsible for providing indigent defense across the state has, in recent years under a new director, taken significant steps to improve the quality of the lawyering it funds, establishing mandated training programs for both appointed private lawyers and public defenders. It is the drive to improve services that motivated the push for a Wyandotte County public defender office that the agency opened in 2024. Winning support from legislative leaders becomes less difficult when the public trough is drained of millions because of the cost of cases like Lamonte's. And yet, the legislature in 2025 cut the budget despite being warned of the consequences by the state agency director, who promptly quit.

The reliance on public funding creates another issue in some jurisdictions: Defense attorneys are discouraged from making too much of a fuss on behalf of their clients; public defender offices become, instead, institutions working so closely with their counterparts in the judiciary and the local prosecutor that they are not effective checks on the system. In some jurisdictions the public defender is a county employee, and the head of the office is appointed by the local judges or by the county board. In contrast, the best public defender offices serve as strong independent voices on behalf of their clients; the Defender Association of Philadelphia, which has a tradition of attorneys fighting for their clients, receives public funding but, like the Public Defender Service in Washington, DC, is a private foundation, run by a board of trustees.

Years ago, the Philadelphia public defenders represented defendants in everything except homicide charges. In those cases, all the county's judges, whether assigned to criminal courtrooms or those who had nothing to do with criminal cases, took turns one by one, appointing defense attorneys in the most serious of cases. Often, the appointments went to friends, friends of friends, cronies, and those who had contributed money to the judges' political campaign.*

The result was that indigent suspects charged with less serious crimes often received far better representation than those charged with the most serious crimes.

No matter how successful a public defender's office may be, some defendants, and especially their families, often err by thinking they need to scrape together money to hire a "real lawyer." Skepticism of public defenders in general has led to many unjust verdicts, families scrape together money to hire the private lawyer who charges a modest sum and, in return, provides too modest representation.

Judges, of course, play a critical role in whether the system is fair and just. It is the job of the judge, in the first instance, to ensure that plea bargains are fairly entered into, and that the facts support an admission of guilt. For those cases that go to trial, it is up to judges to decide what evidence is admissible and what is not; to ensure that both sides advocate forcefully but without crossing the line into unethical behavior in the quest to emerge victorious.

---

* After several judges were removed from the bench as a result of a well-publicized scandal, some of those returned to private practice and received homicide case appointments from their former colleagues. "What Price Justice," Philadelphia Inquirer, Sept. 14, 1992; once the Defender Association began getting Philadelphia appointments, one study found the defendants in those cases were getting better representation than those being represented by appointed attorneys in private practice. Anderson, James M., and Heaton, Paul, "How Much Differences Does A Lawyer Make," Rand working paper, Dec. 2011.

In the ideal world, judges are divorced from public or political influence and are given independence to make the unpopular decisions that justice demands.

In reality, judges are human, have the same internal predispositions and are subject to the same societal pressures as any of us. Too often, cases can be won or lost simply because a judge with biases steered the case in the direction that one side or other sought, most commonly favoring the prosecution. Which lays bare the basic question: How do we ensure that we have the best people on the bench?

In most states, judges are chosen through popular elections. Voters have the view that this is how democracy is supposed to work: to give them a voice in the process. In reality, choosing judges by elections has proven to be fraught with instances of judges who had no business becoming judges. For one thing, most voters cast their ballots knowing very little about the candidates whom they choose. In big cities, voters are left to choose between a string of completely unfamiliar names at the bottom of the ballot. That leaves voters often making decisions based on the perceived gender and ethnicity of the candidate.

Judicial candidates in many jurisdictions join the bench after prevailing in partisan races, giving party leaders, not necessarily dedicated to judicial excellence, the power to put their thumbs on the scale, creating and distributing sample ballots that carry strong influence. Along with political parties, special interest groups can mount campaigns that tilt elections; police unions have played a role in influencing voters based not on any sense of justice but on their support for harsh treatment of defendants.

In Cook County, Illinois, judicial candidates run for specific open seats, and the candidates who have historically been most successful are those with names that sound Irish. Phillip Spiwak, for example, once lost a contest for judge in suburban Will County; Spiwak changed his name and his residence, running and winning a seat in Cook County in 2018 under his new name, Shannon O'Malley. He won even though he refused to submit his qualifications for review by the various bar associations that try to offer voters a sense of which candidates are most qualified.* In Philadelphia, where the judges run collectively for open seats, a deciding factor is where on the ballot the candidate is listed, a decision made by randomly pulling balls out of a coffee can. If there are fourteen candidates for seven open seats, being placed at the bottom of the list represents a tremendous obstacle. On the other hand, a candidate named Scott DiClaudio sought a seat on the Philadelphia trial court in 2015. He had repeatedly been reprimanded by the state for his performance as a defense attorney, but he also won the first position on the ballot, and voters awarded him a seat on the bench. The luck of the draw.

In communities small enough for neighbors to know the candidates, that knowledge for most people has little to do with their abilities and dedication to fair play inside a courtroom.

Once elected, judges stand for reelection after a number of years in most communities; often, those ballots are retention races, with voters being asked to approve or disapprove of a judge continuing to serve. In Cook County, Illinois, judges are removed if fewer than six of every ten voters cast "yes" votes. A tiny number of judges are ever ousted in retention races, absent some high-profile case or cases that led to community rejection. Not surprisingly, many trial court judges are satisfied to stay out of the public eye. Publicity tends to focus on instances where things go wrong; and no judge wants a

---

* Changing one's name for election purposes became so common that the Illinois legislature passed a law, requiring any candidate be identified by whatever name the candidate had gone by before the final months preceding an election.

Willie Horton case, one where a defendant is released to the streets and commits a violent crime.*

While electing judges is a flawed system fraught with unfortunate choices, the alternative—appointing judges—has its own inherent problems. Politics, and political influence, certainly are not absent from appointment systems. The appointing authority—be it the governor or some lower body—may be inclined to choose contributors, or the lawyers who are favored by contributors. They may be tempted to favor ideologues over fair-minded judicial candidates, much the way presidential appointments to the federal bench have been subject to criticism in recent years. In the best systems, bipartisan commissions with legal expertise review candidates and recommend a few of the most qualified candidates from which the appointing authority must choose, or at least offer evaluations of potential candidates and eliminate from consideration candidates whose shortcomings leave them rated not qualified. Such a rating system is often not mandated, and the experience of federal nominations is instructive: For decades, the American Bar Association had a diverse bipartisan panel that reviewed potential candidates for the federal bench and reported its findings to the administration; the incumbent presidents of both parties eschewed lawyers who were not deemed qualified. But in 2000 President George W. Bush ended that practice, when the White House counsel notified

* The case of the infamous William R. Horton played a major role in the 1988 presidential election contest between George H. W. Bush and Michael Dukakis. Horton, a convicted murderer in Massachusetts, had been given a weekend furlough in 1986 from which he did not return; instead, he pistol-whipped, stabbed, and tied up a man before raping his fiancée and stealing the man's car. Dukakis, the Massachusetts governor, had supported the furlough program. So when he ran for president two years later, the campaign manager for his opponent, Bush, was said to comment, "By the time we're finished, they're going to wonder whether Willie Horton is Dukakis's running mate."

the ABA president, "Although the President welcomes the ABA's suggestions concerning judicial nominees, the administration will not notify the ABA of the identity of a nominee before the nomination is submitted to the Senate and announced to the public."

The psychology of taking part in criminal cases one after another, day after day, week after week, in which the police and prosecution have created solid evidence of guilt, plays an important role as well. It is easy to become inured to the fallacy that everyone is guilty, the routine so entrenched that the possibility of innocence seems infinitesimal. Rotating judges and prosecutors through the system is one way at least to guard against that danger.

But such tweaks are only legal Band-Aids, of a sort, to patch over the problems that deny justice. The system urgently needs deeper reforms that can help ensure fairness and minimize the chance of tragic miscarriages of justice. A true solution demands ending the longstanding culture that aspires to remove from the streets in the name of public safety anyone who might appear dangerous. It is a culture that has long pervaded the public mind, impacting how police, prosecutors, and judges went about their jobs. The work too often becomes locking up those suspected of crimes, generally young men of color or impoverished backgrounds. It is a culture that barely recognizes the possibility of innocence of those brought to trial.

Politicians have long ranted about rampant crime across America, finding fear a powerful election tool, and newspapers and television stations highlight every violent crime. It is what political scientist Rebecca Goldstein calls "the politics of crime." Legislative bodies spent the 1980s creating laws to lock up more people for longer periods, overcrowding the hellholes like Lansing and Hutchinson where rehabilitation was extraordinarily remote from the experience of prisoners. The system was never fair: Those who were black or brown-skinned tended to fare worse, as did anyone without money. Crack cocaine, the drug readily available in poorer communities, earned harsh sentences; cocaine powder, the drug of choice in more upscale communities, did not.

Defendants whose only crime was their skin color pleaded guilty to crimes to avoid the harsh punishment they likely faced if they went to trial. By the late 1980s a few crusading organizations, like Centurion Ministries, sprouted up, and a handful of journalists across the country took seriously the need to identify flaws in the system, not merely offer breathless coverage of the local trial of the week. But the general public lived largely in fear of crime, and that fear bred injustice. Jurors, while well intentioned, could not help but be influenced in favor of the testimony of police officers who, after all, were working to keep them all safe, no matter how many family members and friends insistently testified that the accused was with them and certainly could not have committed the crime.

And then came DNA, which suddenly simplified the process for proving conclusively a defendant's guilt as well as innocence. In 1992 Peter Neufeld and Barry Scheck cofounded the Innocence Project at Cardozo School of Law in Manhattan, an organization that fights vigorously using DNA to establish wrongful convictions of imprisoned defendants. A few years later Larry Marshall and Rob Warden founded the Center on Wrongful Convictions at Northwestern University School of Law,* and that project accepted cases, as did Centurion Ministries, with or without DNA evidence. In the intervening years, law schools across the country launched clinics at which students could

---

* Since renamed Northwestern Pritzker School of Law.

become involved reviewing convictions, and a nationwide Innocence Network was formed.

Among the many obstacles to their efforts to establish innocence is the resistance of police and prosecutors to reconsider a suspect's guilt, especially if a jury has affirmed its conclusion. While it is the job of defense attorneys to force the state to prove guilt beyond a reasonable doubt—and ensure even guilty defendants hold the state to the standard that the system demands—only the most unethical prosecutors fight to convict defendants whom they believe innocent. As a result prosecutors take on cases confident from the start of a client's guilt, a certainty that becomes more deeply rooted as the case develops. The result is that in the worst cases, prosecutors become completely blind to the goal of justice, and refuse to acknowledge evidence that refutes their own beliefs.

Take, for example, the position of Anita Alvarez, the former Cook County state's attorney, who fought to uphold the rape and murder convictions of defendants known as the "Dixmoor Five." The five were boys—three were fourteen and two were seventeen—convicted in connection with the rape and murder of a fourteen-year-old victim found near a running trail, shot in the head. Tests established she had been raped. Police interrogations of the youths yielded confessions from three, confessions that contained significantly contradictory details. The semen of none of the five matched the evidence collected from the victim; nevertheless, they were all convicted. The Center on Wrongful Conviction took on the case together with the Innocence Project, and in 2011 the five were exonerated when the DNA was belatedly matched to a man who lived in the victim's neighborhood and had a past conviction for sex crimes. Following the exoneration, Alvarez explained on *60 Minutes* why she refused to acknowledge the five were innocent of murder, stating it was "possible that this convicted rapist wandered past an open field and had sex with a fourteen-year-old girl who was dead."*

After he was elected in 2007, Dallas County District Attorney Craig Watkins established the nation's first Conviction Integrity Unit, providing a unit that could critically examine claims of innocence by defendants the office had fought to convict.**

Thirty-five wrongly convicted prisoners were exonerated during Watkins's eight years in office.***

Before long the idea of conviction integrity units spread, as did a variety of other policies launched by prosecutors who recognized the counterproductive result of locking up so many young men for so long, especially over convictions for nonviolent crimes. Dan Satterberg first took office as the Seattle prosecutor following traditional policies, but gradually moved to become one of the early progressive prosecutors. The shooting of Michael Brown in Ferguson, Missouri, in 2014, and the death in police custody of Freddie Gray a year later, helped launch the Black Lives Matter movement and brought added pressure for criminal justice reform. Soon more prosecutors were winning office on progressive platforms, prosecutors such as the Brooklyn district attorney Ken Thompson, who was succeeded by Eric Gonzalez after Thompson died prematurely; Larry Krasner in Philadelphia; and Mark Dupree in Wyandotte County. The new wave of prosecutors added or

* Alvarez would later contend that the news segment had deliberately distorted her views, and her explanation was intended to convey that truth was not knowable, not that she necessarily believed it was a case of necrophilia.

** Six years earlier, the Texas legislature passed a law permitting convicted defendants the right to apply for DNA testing; the Dallas prosecutors, like prosecutors throughout the state, routinely opposed those petitions until Watkins took office and created the unit to provide independent reviews.

*** Watkins was the first Black district attorney in Texas; many of the progressive prosecutors who have followed him have been Black or female.

bolstered conviction integrity units to undertake independent reviews of past convictions where guilt was in doubt. It was following Lamonte's conviction, of course, that Mark Dupree established the first conviction integrity unit in Kansas.

Many Americans followed the murder of George Floyd along with the horrific list of other police abuses that included the shooting death of Breonna Taylor and gained appreciation for the need for systemic reforms. But the era of progressive prosecutors has brought a significant pushback from many police officers and those who advocate traditional "law and order" systems. In many cases, progressive prosecutors have faced the threat of losing office because of self-inflicted wounds, following either individual decisions that brought public criticism, or policy decisions that transformed prosecutorial actions so much that voters concluded public safety was at risk. Kim Foxx in Chicago never really recovered public trust after she took a phone call to discuss personally intervening on behalf of a Hollywood actor, Jussie Smollett. Chesa Boudin was the victim of a voter recall in San Francisco, after the progressive policies of his office were tied by opponents to increased crime and a sense of decreased public safety; in Los Angeles, opponents mounted a similar campaign to recall district attorney George Gascón, a former police chief and later district attorney of San Francisco, who then won election as Los Angeles district attorney in 2020. The recall organizers explained their reason:

> George Gascón's pro-criminal agenda has turned Los Angeles into a NIGHTMARE. Criminals feel emboldened, residents unsafe, and victims abandoned.*

* Gascón survived the recall petitions; but then was defeated at the polls when he sought reelection in 2024.

But because progressive policies in fact have broad popular support, especially in urban communities, political scientist Goldstein notes most prosecutors withstand such efforts.* In fact, more than fifty progressive prosecutors have been elected in the past decade,** and enjoy broad popularity especially in more liberal and more urban communities across the country.***

Goldstein contends the more concerning threat to prosecutors comes from what she has labeled *toplash*—backlash against reform efforts from governors, attorneys general, and state legislatures seeking to prevent the more progressive policies from taking root, no matter how much the public favored the progressive candidates at the ballot box.

Elected on a reform platform in 2016, Kim Gardner resigned before completing her second term as St. Louis circuit attorney following a series of controversies that caused attacks from the state attorney general and Republican lawmakers. Republicans were incensed when she indicted then-Governor Eric Greitens and things got worse from there. When Gardner's office filed a motion in court to overturn the murder conviction of a man whom her office discovered had been framed by perjured testimony, the attorney general's office intervened, insisting her office lacked legal authority to even ask a judge to reconsider past convictions. Following Gardner's reelection, she faced an effort by the attorney general to remove her from office, contending she had negligently failed to

* In Los Angeles, the effort to unseat Gascón by recall struggled to win signatures to make it onto the ballot; but, months later, Gascón was defeated in his bid for reelection.

** Goldstein notes that defining who is and who is not a progressive prosecutor is itself open to debate, but generally includes prosecutors supportive of measures to reduce harsh sentencing and pretrial detention and to hold police accountable for misconduct.

*** Upon Trump's election, Elon Musk was reportedly urging an attack on progressive prosecutors, raising the possibility that local elections for district attorney would be deluged with money designed to sway voters' perceptions.

prosecute violent crime. She finally resigned from office as state legislators were prepared to enact a bill that would have stripped from Gardner's office the authority to prosecute violent crimes, transferring that power to the governor, who would appoint a special prosecutor.

Other progressive prosecutors have been similarly obstructed by state officials. In Florida, Governor Ron DeSantis suspended the elected district attorney who signed a letter vowing not to prosecute patients seeking abortions or doctors providing them, and then suspended the Orlando prosecutor, accusing her of lenience toward violent criminals. In Pennsylvania, the Republican-controlled House of Representatives voted to impeach the Philadelphia district attorney, Larry Krasner.* As Georgia legislators considered a bill to give themselves oversight of county prosecutors, Fulton County District Attorney Fani Willis pushed back, noting that the state only sought to assume oversight once progressive prosecutors, including those who are Black and those who are women, gained power.

These and similar efforts in other states to thwart progressive prosecutors are what Goldstein labels "toplash," which she suggests is a serious threat to both criminal justice reform and to democracy, by undercutting local officials whom voters chose to support. And as Republicans prey on the politics of crime for political advantage, she notes, the success of reforming the system hangs in the balance. As she stated, "The future of criminal justice reform in the United States turns in part on whether the current generation of progressive prosecutors will succeed or fail in their reform efforts. A significant part of that story is the prospect that governors and state legislators will undermine the efforts of progressive prosecutors or remove them from office."

---

* The impeachment bid failed after Krasner filed a lawsuit, and the state Senate never took up the measure.

❧

When one talks to experts about bringing meaningful reform to the system, many point to the same basic issue: As long as prosecutors, police, judges, and defense attorneys face few if any potential consequences when they act in ways that deny justice, there is little incentive to change. A study by the National Registry of Exonerations found official misconduct by either prosecutors or police contributed to more than half of the cases of wrongful convictions. So finding ways to cut down on misconduct is an obvious way to cut down on more cases like Lamonte's.

Police officers often escape internal discipline for misconduct; just disciplining or firing officers who abuse their badge is difficult. Complaints against officers are generally shielded from the public, and most complaints end without discipline, found to be either "unfounded" or "not sustained" after investigations. Internal disciplinary processes are woefully weak across the country. Police commonly protect each other, failing to speak out about misconduct by colleagues, the legendary "blue line." Police unions across the country have negotiated protections beyond those afforded other public officials, often including a provision that permits officers to appeal suspensions and firings to outside arbitrators, taking the final decision out of the hands of police chiefs.

Prosecutors are widely reluctant to bring criminal charges against officers who engage in misconduct. For one thing, prosecutors and police work together to accomplish public safety, and trust between the two institutions follows. Prosecutors rely on the police to build cases; in the political climate after Minneapolis policeman Derrick Chauvin was prosecuted for the murder of George Floyd, many urban police became cautious about making arrests and pointed their finger at their local prosecutor. Prosecutors who nevertheless seek to hold errant police accountable find it difficult to build sufficient evidence to convince juries to convict a police officer.

As a result, an officer like Golubski, accused of criminal conduct over several years, can be promoted and rewarded rather than disciplined or criminally charged.

Officers also enjoy qualified immunity from civil lawsuits by citizens they harm unless the victims can prove the officer violated a clearly established Constitutional right; even then, the municipalities, not the errant officer's own pocket, are almost sure to be the source to pay the award. The leading empirical study, by Professor Joanna C. Schwartz of UCLA, found cities, counties, and the state reimbursed officers who crossed the line and had lost their qualified immunity 99 percent of the time, even those instances where officers' conduct was so egregious that punitive damages were awarded.

Prosecutors enjoy even greater protections. The National Registry of Exonerations reported that the withholding of exculpatory evidence is the most common form of misconduct, and prosecutors are most often responsible, despite the requirements of *Brady v. Maryland*. In many cases, the hidden evidence that led to a wrongful exoneration is discovered only years later, when new attorneys take over post-conviction proceedings and ask for files that turn out to hold evidence long hidden away. Prosecutors cannot be sued for even intentional acts they take in their role as prosecutor; they only lose that immunity if they go beyond their roles and engage in the investigative phase, such as participating in interrogations of suspects. So when Barry Scheck and Cheryl Pilate and their team filed a lawsuit on behalf of Lamonte and his mother, Terra Morehead could not be included as a defendant despite evidence that she pushed a witness, Niko Quinn, to identify Lamonte as the shooter even though Niko insisted that he was the wrong man.

The case of Ken Anderson stands out. Anderson had been the district attorney in Williamson County, Texas, when he prosecuted an innocent man, Michael Morton, for murder in 1987. Morton was convicted and remained imprisoned until after the Innocence Project took on the case and lawyers filed a request in 2005 for crime scene evidence that could be used to test for DNA. The lawyers found that Anderson had withheld evidence that proved Morton's innocence; after Morton was acquitted the Innocence Project filed a petition urging an investigation into the prosecutor's misconduct. Anderson, who had become a district court judge in the intervening years, ultimately was stripped of his law license and spent five days in the Williamson County Jail once he pleaded guilty to contempt of court over the evidence he had withheld of Morton's innocence.*

What makes Anderson's case stand out, of course, is how rare it is for any prosecutor to face any accountability for committing misconduct, even deliberately withholding evidence that would prove innocence. A study by the National Registry of Exonerations found only four percent of the time did prosecutors face discipline in cases in which their actions caused a wrongful conviction, and only a handful were anything more than a reprimand. Anderson is the only prosecutor known to be put behind bars for his actions.

No doubt, state disciplinary boards are hesitant to impose discipline. In Kansas, after all, a review of almost twenty-five years of cases conducted for this book showed no public discipline for actions by a

* Texas has since enacted the Michael Morton Act, requiring open discovery that is intended to cut down on violations of *Brady*. But even such legislation requires the good faith of prosecutors. One assistant prosecutor, Eric Hillman, filed a lawsuit contending he was wrongly fired from the Nueces County District Attorney's Office for refusing to withhold a piece of exculpatory evidence that the law requires be turned over. The Texas Supreme Court rejected his lawsuit, saying there is no legal protection from termination in such circumstances.

prosecutor. More recently, the Kansas Supreme Court disbarred Jacqie Spradling in 2022 for what the court found "a serious pattern of grossly unethical conduct" in prosecuting a woman for the murder of her husband. Spradling had "repeatedly made arguments to the jury that lacked any evidentiary support," the Kansas Supreme Court found, and then during the disciplinary process made "false statements" to investigators and "lied" to the Supreme Court as she defended her conduct.

All well and good, but the court action came ten years after Spradling's misconduct during the murder trial. Kansas public defender Melody Brannon contends the reluctance to promptly hold prosecutors to account for misconduct impedes justice. Brannon had, of course, filed one complaint after another, dating back to 2016, seeking the disciplinary panel to review the conduct of Terra Morehead; when Morehead finally surrendered her license in 2024 and was disbarred, the disciplinary hearing had still not even held a hearing on the complaints. As Lamonte himself pondered, "How many other defendants have been harmed by her? And yet nothing was done for years."

Discipline of incompetent defense attorneys is also a slow process, and the public record shows overwhelmingly that even meritorious complaints seldom lead to significant discipline. Gary Long and Mark Sachse, to name two, were permitted to continue practicing for years after complaints first were filed citing their failure to properly represent their clients.

And, certainly, judges seldom are held to account for their conduct on the bench. A study of the Illinois process for disciplining judges, to cite one example, found fewer than one in 100 complaints end in public discipline, and the most common punishment was a public reprimand—a slap on the wrist. The state had only two investigators to handle complaints against judges throughout the state. Sadly, Illinois was not an outlier in its lax approach to judicial misconduct.

Rebecca Brown spent years as the policy director of the Innocence Project, studying steps to take to make the system more just. "The system is terrible at holding people accountable," said Brown. "The first step in making the system fail less often is to demand that bad actors suffer consequences for their actions."

That shouldn't be so difficult, should it?

Acknowledgments

There are so many people to thank for their help and support, I know I am leaving out many to whom I am indebted. I apologize in advance.

But I'll start with my family, who read and offered suggestions to so many drafts. To the people who actually made the book happen: Michael Carlisle and Mike Mungiello at Inkwell Management, Jessica Case at Pegasus Books, and Mike Sokolove and Drew Wheeler, who offered invaluable editing, along with Nicole Maher for her work on the publicity. To a person who believed in the book, Lisa Lukas. To Buzz Bissinger, who offered critical advice.

Jim McCloskey opened his files to me, and Cheryl Pilate and her sidekick Lindsay Runnels generously offered so much help. So many people opened their doors and were willing to talk to me. Peggy Lowe of KCUR, who produced the important podcast on Roger Golubski called *Overlooked*, and Anne Lacey at the Kansas City, Kansas Public Library earn special shout outs.

Along the way I've had an incredibly lucky career, but there are so many people to thank for that as well: from John Reque to Don Ferrell to Gene Roberts and Gene Foreman to George Judson to Peggy Engel to, last but not least, Rob Warden. And, especially, to Howard Simon. To those who mentored my legal education, from David Rudovsky, who always steered me right, to Ben Lerner and Lou Natali to Bob Reinstein and Jules Epstein. To Mark Bookman, who also read an early draft. To Neil Cohen, who has always provided a guardrail.

And to my incredible community of friends and colleagues—so many friends—who always have my back.

But most of all, to Lamonte and his mother Rosie, for trusting in me to tell their story.

Notes

PART I: FAILED JUSTICE

Chapter 1: A Double Murder in Broad Daylight

The description of the crime scene on Hutchings Street and the details of the police response come from Kansas City, Kansas, police department reports, including transcripts and notes recorded by officers of statements of witnesses at the scene and evidence and autopsy reports.

The source for the news events of the day come from *The Kansas City Star* and *New York Times* pages from that date. President Bill Clinton's quote is on page A-23 of the *Times*'s national edition, and DOJ Civil Rights Division assistant attorney general Deval Patrick's quote is from A-8 of the *Star*.

When Det. Smith testified under oath about the case in a Feb. 25, 2021, deposition, he said he could not recall actually being assigned to the case or taking a statement from Niko or Josephine Quinn. (Deposition transcript p. 94. Smith's deposition, like others referred to, was taken in conjunction with *McIntyre v. United Govt. of Wyandotte County*, Case 2:18-CV-02545, Kansas District U.S. District Court.)

Details about Ruby Mitchell being brought to the station house are recorded in police notes as well as in Ruby Mitchell's affidavit, taken June 13, 2011, and in notes taken by Jim McCloskey in an April 7, 2010, interview with McCloskey, Mitchell, and Cheryl Pilate. The interview is incorporated into a memo that McCloskey prepared May 12, 2010.

Details about Golubski, including his interest in becoming a priest, were provided by the former detective when he was deposed on Nov. 19, 2020; p. 59.

Chapter 2: Empty Opportunities

Lamonte's description of that day comes from a series of interviews, from the court record, including his formal deposition, June 16, 2021, as well as from interviews with his family members and their testimony Sept. 29, 1994, as defense witnesses in the case *State of Kansas v. Lamonte McIntyre*, 94 CR 1213, Wyandotte County District Court.

The family background information is based both on interviews with him and with his mother, Rosie McIntyre, and, especially, his grandmother, Maxine Crowder.

The history of Kansas City, Kansas, is drawn from sources within the Kansas Room of the Kansas City, Kansas, Public Library. A key source is a series of articles and books by Loren Taylor, historian at the county historical society, especially "The Historic Communities of Wyandotte County."

The Kansas City Star on Nov. 15, 2024, republished photographs from unknown photographers of the Hannibal Bridge as it was being constructed. The accompanying article, by Monte Davis, notes nearly 40,000 residents turned out on July 3, 1869, to celebrate its completion.

The account of the way Eastern Europeans were lured and then mistreated comes from Loren Taylor, "A Historic Overview of Wyandotte County and Its Historic Sites," special sesquicentennial edition.

The rise of the meatpacking industry, and the quote regarding the appearance of "every unsavory vice" come from Taylor in *The Historic Communities of Wyandotte County*, 2005.

The poster that circulated in Kentucky, All Colored People THAT WANT TO GO TO KANSAS! was in the personal collection of Chester Owens, a civil rights activist and historian who became the first Black member of Kansas City, Kansas, City Council in 1983.

The quote about the "unholy scenes" awaiting the Exodusters is taken from Susan D. Greenbaum, *The Afro-American Community in Kansas City, Kansas*, City of Kansas City, Kansas, 1982. Greenbaum's research also detailed the growth of the Black community in the ensuing decades.

The World War II–era brochure of the Chamber of Commerce is in the collection of the Kansas Room, Kansas City, Kansas, Public Library. The history of the GM Fairfax plant, from the war years through the time the new plant opened in 1985, is found in John R. Fuchs, *The History of the Fairfax Plant of GM*, also housed in the Kansas Room.

In addition to the family history provided by the family, Lamonte gave a personal tour of the KCK area, and his recollections of various neighborhoods.

The description of the problems of Wyandotte County in the 1990s comes from a KCUR report from Eleanor Klibanoff on March 6, 2015: "How KCK and Wyandotte County Unified During Troubled Times."

Statistical information on Wyandotte County and its poverty relative to other counties comes from the 29th edition of the Kansas Statistical Abstract for 1993–4, produced by the Institute for Public Policy and Business Research, University of Kansas.

The move of former mayor Richard Walsh was captured in the July 6, 1993, edition of *The Kansas City Star*, by reporter Steve Nicely, "As they leave, a county suffers," p. 1 of the Johnson County edition.

Details of the pizza case come from police reports, supplemented by interviews with Lamonte and attorney Michael Redmond.

Chapter 3: The Wrong Lamonte

The history of the IdentiKit sources includes the promotional detail by Kensington Publishing Corporation on Hugh McDonald's book, *Appointment in Dallas*, and from Look and Learn History Picture Archive. See also *Deseret News* Sept. 17, 1990, Kit Helps Put Suspects' Mugs on File, author Brooke Adams.

The inadequacies of stranger eyewitness identification have been well established, and the leading research includes the work of Dr. Gary Wells at Iowa State University and the impact of misinformation on memory by Dr. Elizabeth Loftus at the University of California-Irvine. Jules Epstein, a professor of criminal law at Temple University, noted in interviews the specific impact sketches and composites can have in creating mistaken identification testimony.

The quote on eyewitness identification comes *U.S. v. Wade*, 388 U.S. 218 (1967), majority opinion by Justice Brennan. At issue was the right to counsel at police lineups. A law review note by Samantha Kay Krasker, "Combatting Suggestiveness in Lineups; Can Legislation Be the Answer?," in *Journal of Legislation*, Notre Dame Law School, 2023, vol. 49, issue 1, pp. 205–232, concludes model legislation has failed to reduce suggestiveness in lineups.

The details of the interview and identification by Ruby Mitchell are captured in the police reports, part of the court record, including a typed transcript of her interview in which she made the identification. Her later explanations are recorded in interview notes taken more than seventeen years later by Jim McCloskey and her subsequent affidavit.

Chapter 4: Why, God?

The details of Lt. Barber's interaction with Maxine Crowder are included in the police reports. The exchange at Fifi's Restaurant is documented in the police reports, in trial testimony, and in interviews with Lamonte and his mother Rosie McIntyre.

The interrogation is based on the officer's reports and testimony, and Lamonte's own recollection of being accused of murder, both in interviews and in a journal that he kept while locked up.

The response to Rosie McIntyre being told the police "don't do that kind of test" comes from her recounting of the incident.

Lamonte's recollection of being locked up comes from his journal and interviews.

Chapter 5: Return to Quindaro

Golubski's return to Quindaro following Lamonte's arrest is captured in his reports and, later, court testimony.

The history of the early settlement of Wyandotte County, tracing back through the Wendat tribe and the forced migration first to Ohio, and then Kansas, is captured in many journals and books kept in the Kansas Room of the Kansas City, Kansas, Public Library. Loren Taylor, a Wyandotte County historian, authored a number of books on their history. Another valuable source is the Kansas Historical Society.

The Trail of Tears' impact on the northern tribes, including the Wyandottes, is fully recounted by Mary Stockwell in *The Other Trail of Tears; The Removal of the Ohio Indians*, Westholme Publishing, 2016.

A history of the Kansas-Nebraska Act, leading to Bleeding Kansas, is recounted by Debra McArthur, *Essential Civil War Curriculum, The Kansas Nebraska Act of 1854: Setting Spark to Timber*, May 2013.

The story of Abelard Guthrie, and his quest of Nancy Quindaro Brown, is widely told, sometimes as romantically, as Bob Friskel's account "Early KCK History: Great Love Story Recounted," *Kansas City Kansan*, Feb. 12, 1967. A deeper account is offered in "A Brief History of the Wyandot Nation of Kansas," by Darren Dane English, a talk given at the Reardon Center, Kansas City, Kansas, March 9, 1995, in honor of the restoration of the Quindaro Townsite Ruins.

Additional information came from the Quindaro Underground Railroad Museum, located in the basement of the Vernon School, which had its roots as the Colored School of Quindaro in 1858. The current building was erected in 1936 and served Black school-aged children until *Brown v. Board of Education*. The school ultimately closed in 1971, and more recently became the site of the museum. Its curator, Luther Smith, died in June 2025, leaving the future of the museum uncertain.

Kansas Secretary of State corporate records list Time Out Inc. in 2006 as the name of the gas station, and Cecil Brooks and Kelly Brooks as the incorporators.

Details of the charging decision on Lamonte are found in police reports.

Chapter 6: The City Is Wide Open

The prison journal kept by Lamonte, along with many interviews, provides much of the source of this chapter.

The state of KCK is noted in a *Star* article from April 5, 1995 (Rick Alm: 'Lone Wolf' to Take City into Uncharted Territory): "Throughout the metropolitan area, Kansas City, Kan., is seen by many as a poverty and crime-ridden backwater, led by the politically corrupt and manipulated by the wealthy few."

The charges in the indictment of Mayor Steineger and his aides are detailed in Reform Platform Helped Steineger Win Office, *The Kansas City Star*, May 20, 1994, p. A-12.

Star columnist Rick Alm on May 26, 1974, wrote on p. 1 of the Wyandotte County section headlined Steineger Should Resign, that included the quote of it "just taking a little longer than most" of the city's mayors to be under attack for malfeasance or incompetence. As Steineger was going on trial, the headline: Steineger Trial Seen as a Blow to KCK Image, appearing on p. 1, Sept. 6, 1994.

Retired FBI agent Al Jennerich provided details about himself and his experiences in Kansas City, Kansas, in interviews. The corruption of Chicago's legal system during his time there is well documented in such resources as *Greylord: Justice, Chicago-Style*, by James Tuohy and Rob Warden.

William Rose received significant support from women voters that helped him defeat the 1905 reelection bid of KCK Mayor Thomas B. Gilbert. *The Kansas City Star* reported afterward, "it is certain that the failure of the police department to close the joints last Sunday, when hundreds of thirsty men" traveled from Kansas City, Missouri, "to get drinks, had much to do with it" (Rose's Plurality was 877, p. 7, April 5, 1905). Rose then was forced from office after an ouster suit was filed against him for his failure to enforce the state's prohibition laws; Rose contended that doing so would cost the city significant tax money without doing anything to reduce liquor consumption. (*Kansas City Journal*, Jan. 14, 1906, p. 11: Mayor Rose Will Testify: Subpoena in Ouster Suit Served on Kansas City, Kas, Executive.)

The ouster petition against Mayor W. W. Gordon was filed by the attorney general on Sept. 3, 1926, accompanied by many affidavits proclaiming, as the *Kansas City Times* headline noted the next day, that the city was wide open.

The Kansas City Times of June 20, 1963, carried the news of the KCK police complaining of corruption that they had been directed to ignore, including the allegation "the town is wide open." (Police Probe by KBI, pp. 1, 8.)

U.S. attorney Robert J. Roth appeared as the guest speaker at the Kansas City, Kansas, Rotary Club and warned of the concentration of organized crime, including the infiltration of the police and local government. *The Kansas City Times* Oct. 25, 1972, p. 5: Organized Crime Influence into Suburbs, Official Says. (The next day *The Kansas City Star* dutifully reported that Police Chief John J. Donnelly responded that "only a few cases that possibly could have been connected with organized crime have occurred in years in Kansas City, Kansas." The chief said the department cooperated with the organized crime strike force.)

"Vice on the Kaw," a four-part series in which two *The Kansas City Star* reporters investigated "massage parlors, gambling, private clubs, and the city's police department," in Kansas City, Kansas. The series began Jan. 4, 1973, on p. 1.

Dailey was among those indicted in November 1973; the indictment brought significant attention in the press, and late that month the mayor, Richard Walsh, said during a radio appearance that "I have complete confidence in Capt. Tom Dailey. . . . To my knowledge he is a very fine police officer, he's a fine gentleman and a family man . . ." (Walsh Supports Daily, *The Kansas City Star*, Nov. 27, 1973). The case went to trial in April, 1974 amid extensive coverage (e.g., Payoffs Made, Former Policeman Says, *Kansas City Times*, April 2, 1974, p. 5) and, after a mistrial, a second trial occurred in May 1974 (Witness Claims Payments to Protect Prostitution, *The Kansas City Star*, May 29, 1974, p. 4). Soon afterward, Dailey was acquitted and awarded back pay for the time of his suspension while the charges were pending: Dailey Voted Back Pay, *The Kansas City Star*, June 27, 1974, p. 4. Further details of the case are recounted in the decision of the U.S. Court of Appeals upholding the conviction of Dailey's codefendant, *U.S. v. Russo*, 527 F.2d 1051, 10th Circuit 1976.

FBI Agent Jennerich transferred from Chicago to the Kansas district in 1986, and upon arrival began investigating illegal chop shops before turning his attention a year or so later to KCK police department corruption (taken from interviews with him).

Kansas voters finally approved liquor by the drink in November 1986, effective the following year. Only West Virginia and Utah were left as states that continued to prohibit such sales, even in restaurants. Upon the voters' approval District Judge Herb Rohleder, who headed the liquor commission that would regulate the sales, commented, "Maybe we can get into the 21st Century before it's too late" (*The Kansas City Star*, Nov. 5, 1986, p. 14-B).

Background on Judge Robinson comes from the court website (https://ksd.uscourts.gov/content/senior-judge-julie-robinson), from the Senate Judiciary Committee hearing record of her testimony at a confirmation hearing Nov. 7, 1991, p. 525, https://www.govinfo.gov/content/pkg/CHRG-107shrg82503/html/CHRG-107shrg82503.htm, and from interviews.

Quinn's conviction was covered in the *Kansas City Times*, Jan. 18, 1988, p. 1: Wyandotte County Sheriff's Son Convicted in Gambling Operations. Cantalupo recounted his role in alerting authorities, and in his assessment of the "redneck mafia," in *Body Mike*, by Cantalupo and Thomas C. Renner, St. Martin's Paperbacks edition, pp. 357–365. See also: FBI Informant Claims Wyandotte County Was Crime Haven, *The Kansas City Star*, Jan. 28, 1990.

Chapter 7: "Historically Corrupt"

The main sources for the details in this chapter, of the challenges facing Judge Julie Robinson and Al Jennerich as they sought to address the corruption in the KCK police department, were a series of detailed interviews conducted of the two of them, separately, in preparation for this book. They recalled that time as a period of crack cocaine destroying lives in the economically blighted portions of the city, and as a result the police corruption directly impacted the lives of vulnerable citizens.

Bernie Smith's indictment by the grand jury received press attention (KCK Officer Accused of Taking Cash for Tipping Off Drug Dealer, *The Kansas City Star*, June 16, 1989, p. 20), as did his seven-day trial, and acquittal (KCK Police Detective Didn't Accept Bribe from Dealer, Jury Says, *The Kansas City Star*, Sept. 28, 1989, p. 1). Smith's defense had been that the money he took from Velasquez in prison was for Smith to deliver as child support. Afterward, Velasquez received a reduced sentence in return for having cooperated with the government (Informant's Sentence Reduced to 70 Months, *The Kansas City Star*, June 14, 1989, p. 4). Many years later, Smith would end up again in police trouble, and provided an affidavit admitting to his longstanding drug use and criminal conduct.

Additionally, the internal memos of extensive corruption within the KCK department, written by FBI agents, were among the documents obtained first by

KCUR reporters Peggy Lowe and Steve Vockrodt, and were featured in their Nov. 9, 2021, report, "FBI has investigated KCK police for decades, but prosecutions were rare." Lowe went on to produce a podcast series on Golubski and KCK police, "Overlooked." The documents later were posted online.

The search committee's willingness to forgive Chief Dailey's criminal brush was reported by *The Kansas City Star*, KCK MAJOR TO BE CHIEF OF DEPARTMENT, April 4, 1989, pp. 1, 5.

The longtime district attorney, Nick Tomasic, did not respond to requests for interviews in the reporting of this book. But Jennerich and Robinson emphasized Tomasic had tried, behind the scenes, to cooperate with them and pass along information. Tomasic was said to be barely speaking to the chief, Jennerich noted.

U.S.A. v. Marshall et al. was filed in U.S. District Court, Kansas division, 2:93-cr-20048, on March 6, 1993. The following day *The Kansas City Star* reported, KCK OFFICER, SIX OTHERS NAMED IN INDICTMENT, p. C-1. The six were charged with conspiracy to distribute crack cocaine that they transported from Los Angeles. The case went to trial months later, and early in the trial appeared the *Star* headline: POLICE ACCUSED OF AIDING CRIME. The six were all convicted April 9, 1993. The headline the next day in the *Star*, p. B-1: KCK OFFICER FOUND GUILTY IN DRUG TRIAL. The conviction was upheld on appeal, *U.S. v. Williamson*, 53 F 3d 1500 (10th Circuit, 1993). Both DEA agent Sparks's realization of an internal leak and FBI agent Jennerich's comment that Dryden was "in and out of the chief's office at will," come from *The Kansas City Star* of Sept. 26, 1993, pp. B-1, B-3, TESTIMONY CITES POLICE CORRUPTION.

Rathbun ran a strong but unsuccessful race as a Democratic congressional candidate in the face of the strong Republican wave in Kansas in 1996.

Judge Robinson provided the description of her final months in the U.S. attorney's office in an interview for this book.

Jennerich's learning of Golubski's abuses, and the failure to pursue them after Judge Robinson was first appointed to the bench, is included in a deposition that Jennerich provided years later to Lamonte's attorneys; and both the former FBI agent and Judge Robinson elaborated on this point during their interviews.

Chapter 8: Being Black in KCK

The 1879 law segregating Kansas elementary schools, the law challenged by the parents of Oliver Brown, was codified in the Laws of Kansas, 1879, chap 81, sec. 1. Then in 1905, following the incident in KCK, the law was made to cover the local high school: Laws of Kansas, 1905, ch. 414, sec. 1. This history is recounted, too, on the website of the Kansas City Kansas public schools. https://www.kckschools.org/about/district-history/segregation-part-1.

I learned of the history of Sumner High School, and how originally it was named Manual Training, from visiting the Quindaro Underground Railroad Museum, located in the old Vernon School, which is a story in itself. The Vernon

School had originally opened in 1858 (in a different building) as the Colored School of Quindaro, creating a program to educate children of freed slaves. The school later was renamed for William Tecumseh Vernon. After *Brown v. Board of Education of Topeka* was decided and the interstate was built through the neighborhood, Vernon School was closed in 1971. https://vernoncenterkck.org/about/.

The impact of the Depression-era housing programs on racial prosperity, including the varying reports by the assessors, was reported in the report H.E.A.T. (Health, Equity, Action, Transformation) by David Norris and Mikyung Baek of the Kirwan Institute for the Study of Race and Ethnicity, Ohio State University, ch. 5, "History Matters."

In the federal lawsuit, the government argued that the county officials had "systematically discriminated against Negroes on account of their race in the operation of the Wyandotte County jail." *U.S. v. Wyandotte*, civil action 3163, filed June 5, 1970, U.S. District Court, Kansas district, p. 5. The government also argued that in addition to the segregation of the cells by race, the jail conditions amounted to cruel and unusual punishment by a variety of substandard conditions, from inadequate training of guards to the lack of any exercise or recreational equipment to brutality.

The records of the investigation of Donald Wilkins's death in police custody, including the discipline that Chief Dailey imposed, were part of an FBI file on the case. The assigned officers were listed in names turned over in civil discovery in the *McIntyre* civil lawsuit. Other potential police abuse cases were uncovered in the KCUR report, cited above, Nov. 9, 2021, "FBI has investigated KCK police for decades, but prosecutions were rare."

The U.S. attorney's focus shifting from the police corruption was discussed both by Judge Robinson and FBI agent Jennerich in their interviews.

Chapter 9: "That's the Man"

The juvenile crime forum was reported in *The Kansas City Star*, June 16, 1994, A Forum on Teens, Violent Crime, p. 1.

The bizarre experiment sending juveniles to experience adult prison, cited in the footnote, is reported in Teens Experience Life in Prison for a Day, *The Kansas City Star*, Oct. 8, 1995, p. 3.

The description of the D4 pod, and his fight with Corey, were detailed in interviews with Lamonte and included in his journal.

The system of appointing lawyers to represent indigents is fraught with problems, in Wyandotte County like anywhere. Heather Cessna, who resigned in 2025 as director of state Board of Indigents' Defense Services in Kansas, provided the historic background of appointments, as well as the longstanding struggling to properly fund attorneys in court-appointed cases in Wyandotte County.

Judge Podrebarac appointed Gary Long to be Lamonte's attorney on May 25, 1994. (After Lamonte was ordered held for trial in adult court, Long was appointed to continue as Lamonte's attorney by the trial judge, J. Dexter

Burdette, on July 6, 1994. The background on Podrebarac was developed from articles in *The Kansas City Star* and *Kansas City Times* articles from his various runs for office, including Nov. 8, 1973, following Podrebarac's election as a county commissioner, and his election upsetting an incumbent judge in the August 1978 primary. It was during that campaign that Podrebarac said his "lifelong ambition" had been to become a judge. Extensive details of the judge's life were included in an obituary that appeared in *The Kansas City Star* on June 15, 1995.

"Illinois Supreme Court History: Juvenile Courts," is found on the Illinois Court webpage, https://www.illinoiscourts.gov/News/388/Illinois-Supreme-Court-History-Juvenile-Courts/news-detail/. See also ch. 5, "The Juvenile Justice System," in *Juvenile Courts, Juvenile Justice*, National Research Council and Institute of Medicine, p. 157. That report also notes, p. 1, that many states began taking a harsher approach to juvenile justice in the 1970s and 1980s, even as incidents of juvenile crime were decreasing.

The juvenile transfer law in Kansas is codified as section 38-1636.

Long's background is based on assorted sources including a personal interview: newspaper accounts of his run for office in 1988; information Long provided on his former website and in his LinkedIn account; his deposition, taken years later in *McIntyre v. Wyandotte County*. After graduating Washburn University Law School, Long opened his law practice in 1988 and, at age twenty-four, ran unsuccessfully in the Democratic primary for the county commission.

Long's early legal troubles, dating back to the year he passed the bar, are revealed in two cases: *In re Long*, 255 Kan 792 (Kan 1994), and *In re: Long* 265 Kan 2 (1998).

The transcript of the June 28, 1994, hearing for Lamonte, included in the court records, begins with the court identifying the lawyers and the members of the audience in the courtroom.

Kansas law establishing a district attorney's office in the larger state counties took effect in 1972, is L. 1972, ch. 71, sec. 1, 1973; ch. 146, sect. 1; April 18.

Information about Tomasic comes from the ATTORNEY ASSISTANTS TO SERVE IN HOUSE, *The Kansas City Star*, Aug. 22, 1972, p. 2; TOMASIC POWERFUL BY LAW, LEVERAGE, *The Kansas City Star*, May 29, 1995, p. 1; remarks by U.S. Rep. Dennis Moore, D-Kansas, in the *Congressional Record*, Jan. 20, 2005, TRIBUTE TO RETIRING WYANDOTTE COUNTY, KANSAS, DISTRICT ATTORNEY NICK TOMASIC, and from AFTER 100 YEARS, OLD WORLD CHURCH CLUB IN KK WAS BOWLING AND A BAR HAS A NEW ALLURE, *The Kansas City Star*, Oct. 28, 2022, p. 1.

Tomasic did not respond to interview requests. Descriptions of him quietly helping Jennerich and Robinson, but within limits, come from interviews with Jennerich and Robinson.

The size of the office is reflected in the chart accompanying, POOR PAY KEEPS REVOLVING DOOR IN D.A.'s OFFICE, *The Kansas City Star*, Aug. 9, 1990, pp. 1–2.

The description of the preliminary hearing comes from the hearing transcript.

Chapter 10: Becoming Muggz

The federal lawsuit on jail conditions was reported in WYANDOTTE TOLD TO ERECT A NEW JAIL, *The Kansas City Times*, March 31, 1987.

The 1970 lawsuit on jail discrimination, KC 3163, U.S. Dist. Court, Kansas, the FBI reports reveal "several instances of prisoner beating and sodomy" which would not have occurred with adequate staffing and training. The government wrote to the court, "In candor, we must advise the Court that, except for racial assignments, the Wyandotte Jail is comparable to those of many other jurisdictions. Overcrowding, idleness, and inmate brutality are salient features of many American penal institutions, and among them the local jails which handle most misdemeanants and serve as the doorway to adult institutions for felons are the most inadequate in every way."

Two decades later, after reporters asked police officials about a complaint, signed by twenty detained men, the police major in charge of the jail toured the facility, called it a "pigsty" and said the conditions were "below a level of common decency." Maj. Harold Brown told reporters that he had not been informed of inmates' complaints and that he could not recall the last time he had visited the facility he oversaw, though the reporters noted it was in the same building as his office. KCK JAIL IS CALLED A 'PIGSTY' *The Kansas City Star*, Sept. 27, 1991, p. C-1.

NEW WYANDOTTE COUNTY JAIL IS NO DUNGEON, *The Kansas City Star*, March 8, 1990, p. C-1.

Lamonte's description of encounters with other inmates come from his prison journal and from interviews.

Background information on Judge Burdette, dating back to his appointment as a judge and first election, is found in MORONEY USES SENTIMENTAL APPROACH, *The Kansas City Star*, July 31, 1988, p. B-1. The article notes Tomasic cited Burdette as "among the most successful prosecutors in county history." On Burdette's background, and retirement: News release on Kansas Courts website upon his retirement: https://kscourts.gov/Newsroom/News-Releases/News/2018-News-Releases/September-2018/Wyandotte-County-district-judge-to-retire-after-30#:~:text=Since%201993%2C%20he%20has%20presided,worked%20in%20Topeka%20at%20St.

Rathbun's "first step" quote is in EX-OFFICIAL IN KCK IS CONVICTED, *The Kansas City Star*, July 23, 1994, p. C-1. His quote that it was only the "top priority" was in "Federal inquiry will continue," *The Kansas City Star*, Aug. 3, 1994, p. C-4. The details of the legal defense fund are included in STEINEGER ARRAIGNED; AIDES START LEGAL FUND, in *The Kansas City Star*, June 3, 1994, p. C-1.

In contrast to the attention Steineger received, Lamonte's case earned three paragraphs in MURDER CHARGES FILED, *The Kansas City Star*, Apr. 19, 1994, p. 14.

The details of the July 6, 1994, arraignment, including Judge Burdette's bail and the reappointment of Gary Long, are contained in court records from the criminal case.

Long's 1988 candidacy, in the same campaign as Judge Burdette, is reported in CANDIDATES RUSH TO FILE FOR KANSAS SEATS, *The Kansas City Star*, June 10, 1988, p. 4A.

In re: Long, 255 Kan 792 (1994).

Long described in an affidavit that he had little experience in murder cases. Affidavit taken April 24, 2015, exhibit in Lamonte's post-conviction case.

Steineger acquittal: *The Kansas City Star*, Sept. 17, 1994, p. 1. The wild party that ensued, ending in Judge Moroney's scuffle, was reported: WYANDOTTE COUNTY JUDGE ADMITS FRACAS, GUN INCIDENT AT BAR, *The Kansas City Star*, Sept. 23, 1994, C-1.

Chapter 11: "I Don't Believe This"

Maxine Crowder's delivery of one white shirt, tan pants, and a brown tie to the jail is recorded on a Wyandotte County inmate property receipt. The U.S. Supreme Court ruled in 1976 that forcing a detained defendant to wear prison garb into the courtroom can so prejudice a jury that it violates the defendant's constitutional rights. *Estelle v. Williams*, 425 U.S. 501 (1976).

The Kansan newspaper, Oct 1994, is housed in the Kansas City, Kansas, Public Library.

Lamonte's account of first day of trial is from his journal and interviews, and the details of the hearing come from the trial transcript.

Morehead's background comes from the deposition she provided in connection with Lamonte's civil lawsuit on April 27, 2021, p. 64, and from her voir dire on day one of Lamonte's trial, when she introduced herself to the jury.

The U.S. Supreme Court in *United States v. Wade*, 388 U.S. 218, 228 (1967), as cited above, warned of the vagaries of mistaken identification. The Exoneration Registry, which tracks the causes of exonerations, reports that more than 1,100 cases since 1989 involve mistaken identification. The Arizona State University Sandra Day O'Connor School of Law project, "Reforming Criminal Justice," Professor Gary Wells of Iowa State University, a leading expert on mistaken identification, offers an extensive study of the failures of many jurisdictions to take steps to protect against such error. "Eyewitness Identification," p. 239.

Lamonte's courtroom outburst is recorded in trial transcript, and was vivid in the minds of Lamonte and Rosie.

Chapter 12: "I'm Innocent. That's It."

Burdette's comments as he denied the motion are part of the court record.

Rosie McIntyre described feelings of desperation and determination as she set out to do whatever she could to overturn the verdict; but recalled with anger the false information she was fed by the man whom, she felt, told her a fictitious story in the hopes it might benefit him. Carolyn Adams would recall in the affidavit she provided, made public in the post-conviction proceedings, how strongly Rosie believed in her son's innocence. In that affidavit and accompanying exhibits, Adams also laid out her reinvestigation, which began with taking a statement from the man making the fraudulent claim. Attorney Long, post-conviction, filed a prompt motion for a new trial, basing it on the new not-credible witness. Judge Burdette rejected that claim and set sentencing for January.

The court record reflects what transpired at the sentencing hearing, where the new attorney, Cornwell, acknowledged it was not the time to be raising new motions; Lamonte's prison journal adds what Lamonte was thinking.

The week after Doniel Sublett Quinn and Donald Ewing were murdered, the Kansas State Legislature passed a law permitting the death penalty to be imposed in certain circumstances, including the act of murdering of two or more people (K.S.A. 21-3439). Because the murders on Hutchings Street occurred before that law took effect, the death penalty was not an option; Judge Burdette was required to impose life imprisonment for each murder, and his only decision was whether to make the sentences concurrent or consecutive.

PART 2: TRAPPED INSIDE

Part 2 is largely based on extensive interviews with Lamonte, his mother Rosie, and Corisha Josenberger, with excerpts from Lamonte's journal, poetry, and correspondence that were discovered in the files of Jim McCloskey of Centurion Ministries. The additional sources are listed below.

Chapter 13: Fresh Meat on the Block

The history of Hutchinson Correctional Facility is provided on the state corrections web page, https://www.doc.ks.gov/facilities/hcf/history. The history of the Elmira Reformatory is found at https://www.correctionhistory.org/html/chronicl/docs2day/elmira.html.

Lafayette Gayden confirmed the story of his first encounter with Lamonte in a telephone interview.

Lamonte's record was also confirmed through his prison disciplinary record.

The Kansas Supreme Court case is reported in *State v. McIntyre*, (259 Kan. 488), argued by Lindsey Erickson and Terra Morehead. The Kansas state bar directory shows Lindsey Erickson was admitted to the bar on Sept. 30, 1994, the day after the jury found Lamonte guilty of murder.

Chapter 14: Curb Your Anger

The hearing before Burdette was heard April 4, 1996, case 94 CR 1213, *State v. McIntyre.* Gary Long also testified at the hearing, stating that he in fact had gone to Hutchings Street and tried but was never able to track down and talk to Stacey Quinn.

Chapter 15: On Their Own

Lamonte's correspondence to Centurion, even before the organization agreed to take on the case, was preserved by the organization.

State records show Lamonte was moved to Lansing on Oct. 30, 1996. The original building, where Lamonte was housed, was "decommissioned," as they called it, in 2020.

State v. McIntyre, State Supreme Court, 1997. No. 76, 519.

The Kansas Supreme Court in 2002 upheld Clemons's conviction at a non-jury bench trial for a 1999 murder, *State v. Clemons*, (45 P 3d. 982). Clemons represented himself at trial and later filed a post-conviction habeas petition contending he had been forced to waive his right to a jury. The Kansas Court of Appeals refused to consider the issue, ruling Clemons had missed the time limit for filing (*Clemons v. State*, 2008; no. 96130).

"Cry Justice Journal," Number 13, New Life Evangelistic Center, New Bloomfield, Mo., 1997.

The noise violation, which Lamonte recorded in his journal, is listed on state corrections disciplinary records as having been imposed Nov. 4, 1996—five days after Lamonte was transferred to Lansing.

Chapter 16: Another Door Closed

S. 736, Public Law 104-132 1996, the Anti-terrorism and Effective Death Penalty Act of 1996, limited convicted defendants' time to file federal habeas claims.

Lamonte's pro se habeas petition, that is, the petition on his own behalf, was filed on July 6, 1997, as Wyandotte County District Court case 97C02329.

Gideon's habeas petition was styled *Gideon v. Wainwright*, 372 U.S. 335 (1963). *New York Times* columnist Anthony Lewis wrote *Gideon's Trumpet* (1989, Vintage), based on the case and its significance.

The U.S. Supreme Court set the standard for determining the effectiveness of attorney representation in *Strickland v. Washington*, 466 U.S. 668 (1984). The Marshall Project examined courts' willingness to overlook the impact of attorneys' drunkenness on effective representation: Ken Armstrong, "What can you do with a drunken lawyer," Dec. 10, 2014. The issue of sleeping defense counsel is examined by Robyn Hagan Cain in FindLaw.com, "Attorney's Nap During Trial Doesn't Mean Counsel Was Ineffective," https://www.findlaw.com/legalblogs/sixth-circuit/attorneys-cross-exam-nap-doesnt-mean-counsel-was-ineffective-1/. More broadly, the issue of attorney ineffectiveness is examined by Professor Stephen Bright, an expert in the field, in a speech whose title crystallizes the issue: "Is Mediocrity the Best We Can Do?," a lecture he delivered at the University of Tennessee Law School reported in *Tennessee Journal of Law and Policy*, vol. 10, issue 1, article 8, Fall 2014.

The accusation of theft of radios, which Lamonte detailed in his journal, is recorded in Lamonte's disciplinary record as Aug. 24, 1997. He was transferred back to Hutchinson on Nov. 19, 1997.

Burdette's order appointing Sachse was dated July 28, 1997, but filed in the court record Aug. 4.

Sachse represented Steineger's chief of staff Peter Adams. K.C.K. MAYOR AND HIS AIDE ACQUITTED, *The Kansas City Star*, Sept. 17, 1994, pp. 1, 22. Sachse's mishandling of cases.

Lamonte complains of never hearing from Sachse, who confirmed in a 2014 affidavit that that was just the way things were done in Wyandotte County in those days.

Josephine's affidavit of Oct. 17, 1997, the date of the postponed hearing, is part of the documents that Cheryl Pilate and Jim McCloskey gathered more than a decade later. In September 2014, Sachse signed his own affidavit confirming that when he met Josephine in the courthouse and she told him what had happened at trial, he immediately wrote it down for her to sign, and then had it notarized in the courthouse that day.

Rosie recounted attending the October date with Josephine but then being left in the dark about a new date. Lamonte was left in the dark as well. He filed a motion, signed by a notary at the prison on January 26, 1998, and filed as part of the record on Feb. 10, stating that he was "disirious [*sic*] of attending the hearing on his motion for new trial" and that he believed he needed to be brought to the Wyandotte County district court so that he could meet with Sachse prior to the hearing. Unbeknownst to Lamonte, Judge Burdette had held the hearing without Lamonte's apparent knowledge and rejected Lamonte's claim for a new trial ten days before Lamonte ever prepared his motion.

Lamonte then prepared another motion Feb. 2, 1998—a week after his first motion—saying that the "level of communication" was inadequate between his attorney and him; Sachse, the motion states, "has failed to interview and investigate defendant witnesses and claims." The new motion sought to replace Sachse as his appointed attorney. And in a separate motion, Lamonte asked for the case (which already had been decided) be delayed. Both of those new motions were received and filed into the court record on Feb. 17, 1998, the court file shows.

That day, Burdette wrote to Sachse saying that the judge "will not entertain motions filed by defendants when they have an attorney to represent them," and that motions "should originate with the attorney."

On March 9, two days after the Wyandotte district court clerk filed a request from Lamonte for the court records in the case, Judge Burdette wrote to Sachse and Morehead that he was scheduling a hearing to consider Lamonte's request for a new attorney—the hearing that Lamonte asked to attend. On April 9, 1998, the record shows, Judge Burdette met with Sachse and Morehead, and Lamonte was not present. Since all of Lamonte's issues had been ruled upon, Burdette ordered, the case was moot.

Chapter 17: Not the Finest

The Kansas Supreme Court issued its decision of disbarment on March 6, 1998. It was based on the string of complaints against Long that were considered by the disciplinary panel Oct. 15, 1997. Following that hearing, even before the court issued its ruling, Long voluntarily surrendered his license in a letter to the court dated Jan. 27, 1998.

The parallels in time to Lamonte's petition for a new trial—which focused on Long's representation—are striking. Josephine Quinn came to court and prepared her affidavit on Oct. 17, 1997—two days after the disciplinary hearings on repeated complaints regarding Long's performance in *other* cases. Judge Burdette held the delayed hearing on whether Long adequately represented Lamonte on Jan. 16, 1998, and ruled against Lamonte.

As in most states, the Kansas Disciplinary Board operates under the Kansas Supreme Court. https://kscourts.gov/Attorneys/Office-of-Disciplinary-Administration/Board-for-Discipline-of-Attorneys. The discipline is imposed by the state Supreme Court after investigation and review by the board: https://kscourts.gov/Rules-Orders/Rules/Rule-225.

Disciplinary action is based on violation of the Kansas Rules of Professional Conduct, Supreme Court Rules 200–240. Like most jurisdictions, Kansas adopted its own code by adapting the ABA Model Rules of Professional Conduct. https://www.americanbar.org/groups/professional_responsibility/publications/model_rules_of_professional_conduct/alpha_list_state_adopting_model_rules/.

The number of licensed lawyers residing in Kansas in recent years was taken from the ABA data collected annually. E.g., the 2024 report https://www.americanbar.org/news/profile-legal-profession/demographics/.

To study those disciplined each year, the first step was to ask the Kansas disciplinary counsel for information on how many disciplinary cases the board handles each year, similar to the way Pennsylvania and many other states report cases.

Kansas does not provide an annual report of attorney disciplines, detailing the number of complaints and their outcome; much as do other states, e.g., Pennsylvania.

https://www.padisciplinaryboard.org/about/reports. The state Disciplinary Board responded in January 2022 that the office does not produce an annual report, but referred me to the fact that I could look up every published opinion on the state Supreme Court page listing all decisions, https://kscourts.gov/Attorneys/Published-Attorney-Discipline-Cases. Through that effort a spreadsheet was created of every identifiable case over the fifteen years, 525 cases of public discipline.

Matthew Works was the attorney whose discipline included limiting his practice to criminal, not civil, cases. *In re: Matthew B. Works*, Kansas Supreme Court, 87967, 2002.

In re: Hawver, Kansas Supreme Court, 300 Kan. 1023, (2014).

In re: Long, Kansas Supreme Court 13564, (1998). The case background details the disciplinary board hearing was held Oct. 15, 1997. The Kansas disciplinary cases for 1998 reveal Long to be among the nine attorneys disbarred that year.

Sachse's unfortunate legal record is detailed in the series of Kansas Supreme Court disciplinary orders. The first was the two-year suspension, based on complaints from seven different clients. The court opinion, *In re Sachse*, 269 Kan. 810, (2000), details Sachse's actions in the cases of the family Sachse represented after a car accident, "The Prater Complaint," and the failure to file the appellate brief on behalf of murder defendant Code Last. "The Laster Complaint."

The Supreme Court lifted the probation noting Sachse complied with its conditions, *In re Sachse*, 84,675 (2003). But then, in August 2005, Sachse faced another disciplinary hearing based on two more complaints, leading to a one-year suspension. *In re: Sachse*, 281 Kan. 1197 (2006). The following year, after the disciplinary board filed a new complaint based on seventeen separate complaints, Sachse voluntarily surrendered his license. In late September 2007 the Supreme Court formally disbarred Sachse (Kansas Supreme Court Bar Docket 12,956 [2007]).

Chapter 18: Dead in the Water

Like several chapters in this section, the information relies heavily on Lamonte's journal and a subsequent series of interviews during which he confirmed and elaborated on what he had written years earlier.

His "use of stimulants" violation, Dec. 11, 1998, is recorded in his Department of Corrections record.

Lamonte was moved back to Lansing on Feb. 2, 2000, according to his Department of Corrections record.

A copy of his "To whom it may concern" letter was saved by Centurion Ministries in its file; Centurion then saved its extensive correspondence with Lamonte over the next several years.

The details of the up-and-down relationship of Lamonte and Corisha were recorded in his journal, and the subject of interviews with both Lamonte and Corisha, together and separately.

Rosie's letter to Centurion—that the mother of one of the murder victims was offering to help, and knew Lamonte was innocent—proved just as significant as Rosie had hoped.

Chapter 19: No One Gets to Skate Through Life

The Centurion files contained the correspondence between Lamonte and Jock McFarlane. Lamonte recorded in his journal his feelings associated with the interest Jock was showing as well as the frustration. Jock also shared his recollections in an interview.

PART THREE: UNCOVERING INNOCENCE

This part relies heavily on memos Jim McCloskey wrote, meticulously describing, step-by-step, every interview on each trip; on documents that Lamonte, his mother and, especially, his lawyer Cheryl Pilate provided; on the affidavits and other documents Cheryl made part of the court record; and, especially, the generosity of figures who agreed to interviews. In several cases, especially during my own early visits to Wyandotte County, Cheryl introduced me to residents who may have been reluctant to talk without her intervention; on several of those early interviews, Cheryl accompanied me and observed.

Chapter 20: Winning the Lottery

The background story of Centurion comes from interviews both with Jim and with Kate Germond; from the organization website and from the information in Jim's autobiographic memoir, *When Truth Is All You Have*, Jim McCloskey with Philp Lerman, Doubleday, 2020. Centurion's background comes from Jim, from Kate Germond, from a visit to the office, and from information on the Centurion website and news accounts. McCloskey's family history also comes from that book, and supplemental research into news accounts of Uncle Matt McCloskey.

Between February 2003, when Lamonte's letter arrived at Centurion Ministries, and April 2009, the date Jim took on the case, Centurion clients who were freed included Timothy Howard and Gary James, convicted together of a 1976 murder in Columbus, Ohio; James Driskell, convicted of a 1990 murder in Winnipeg, Canada; Walter Lomax, convicted of a 1967 robbery and murder in Baltimore; Johnny Briscoe, convicted of a 1976 murder in St. Louis; Kevin Williams, convicted of a 1985 armed robbery in Kenner, Louisiana; Willie Green, convicted of a 1983 murder in Los Angeles; and Darryl Burton, convicted of the 1984 murder in St. Louis. In addition, David Alexander and Harry Granger, convicted together of a 1976 robbery and murder in New Orleans, and Marcus Washington, convicted of a 1975 murder and arson in Queens, New York, were freed by the parole boards, not the courts, after being presented with evidence of their innocence developed by Centurion Ministries.

The Ellen Reasonover decision was handed down by U.S. Dist. Ct. Chief Judge Jean Hamilton, *Reasonover v. Washington*, 60 F. Supp. 2d 937 (E.D. Mo. 1999). Cheryl talked about the impact in interviews with me and, earlier, many places, including KMBC on Aug. 1, 2016. https://www.kmbc.com/article/defense-attorney-describes-case-that-changed-her-outlook/3695626.

Cheryl described her background in interviews with herself and with her husband, Gordon Atcheson; her work history is recounted in numerous articles and various documents adorning the walls of her law office.

The opinion of U.S. Circuit Judge Bye for the three-judge panel remains shocking. As the court turned away Burton's case without a hearing, Bye wrote for the panel, "One cannot read the record in this case without developing a nagging suspicion that the wrong man may have been convicted of capital murder and armed criminal action in a Missouri courtroom. Burton was convicted on the strength of two eyewitness accounts. Since his trial and imprisonment, new evidence has come to light that shakes the limbs of the prosecution's case. One eyewitness has recanted and admitted perjury. The other eyewitness's veracity has been questioned by a compatriot who avers it was physically impossible for him to have seen the crime. A layperson would have little trouble concluding Burton should be permitted to present his evidence of innocence in *some* forum. Unfortunately, Burton's claims and evidence run headlong into the thicket of impediments erected by courts and by Congress. Burton's legal claims permit him no relief, even as the facts suggest he may well be innocent. Mindful of our obligation to apply the law, but with no small degree of reluctance, we deny Burton a writ" 295 F.3d 839 (8th Cir. 2002).

Six years later Cole County Circuit Judge Richard Callahan ordered Burton's conviction overturned. *Burton v. Dormire*, No. 06AC–CC00312 (Mo. Cir. Ct. Aug. 18, 2008).

Darryl Burton, Cheryl, and Jim all provided details of the fight to accomplish justice for Darryl. Cheryl and Jim both recounted their lunch in Jefferson City with investigator Dan Clark.

Jim and Centurion Ministries volunteer Jock McFarlane both recounted in interviews the reasons Lamonte's case stood out; several of those reasons are cited in the report Jim prepared, which were preserved in his files.

Chapter 21: Peeling the Onion

Jim's visits to Kansas City are recounted through his meticulous memos, written after each visit, as well as repeated and extensive interviews.

The agreement was later filed as a court exhibit in *Morgan-Pilate LLC v. Centurion Ministries*, 4-16-CV-01304 (Western District Mo. U.S. District Court, 2016); Exhibit C filed Dec. 22, 2016.

Cheryl's firm and Scheck's firm jointly filed the civil lawsuit on behalf of Fritz, 6:00-cv-00194, *Fritz et al. v. Ada OK*, filed April 14, 2000, Eastern District OK U.S. District Court.

The population of Johnson County went from 62,763 in 1950 to 143,792 in 1960, to 220,073 in 1970. The boom was in sharp contrast to neighboring Wyandotte County. *Population in Kansas by County, 1860–1970*, University of Kansas, https://ksdata.ku.edu.

At a special election April 1, 1997, voters passed the merger by a 60–40 margin at a special election. KCK-County Merger Passes, *The Kansas City Star*, April 2, 1997, p. 1. Voters hoped the consolidated board would cut duplication, and therefore cut taxes, and end the longstanding corruption. At a second special election, voters chose candidates to replace the two separate sets of elected officials with one county commission, headed by the mayor of the combined government. New Board Candidates Face Voters, *The Kansas City Star*, July 8, 1997.

The lawsuit is styled *Bowling v. McCue et al.*, 04-2320, U.S. Dist. Ct. Kansas District, 2006.

Robinson's order on the summary judgment motion is dated March 17, 2009. Jim's memos record that he arrived in KCK for the first of five investigative trips in 2009, and three more in 2010.

Chapter 22: A Detective's Obsession

Jim's routines are evident spending time with him, from his hotel rooms to his lunches to his walks.

When I first arrived in KCK in 2017, the details of Rosie's story were told to me first by Cheryl and then by Rosie herself. But I was warned from the start to be guarded with that information; Lamonte, who was still in prison, had not been told of the abuse his mother described. He learned of his mother's experience with Golubski as the hearing date neared, before it would be revealed in court.

Many of the notes of Jim's interviews document that he made repeated visits to the same person, slowly gathering more detail. The repeated trips to Ruby Mitchell are highlighted to show the effort involved.

Miles's habeas case, ex parte Miles, was filed in the Texas Court of Criminal Appeals, AP 76488, and filed Feb. 12, 2012.

The Savannah Three cases, as they came to be known, were consolidated and decided by the Georgia Supreme Court in *Jones v. Medlin*, 302 Ga. 555, 2017.

The Bowling case is documented through the court record *Bowling v. USA, et al.*, Kansas District U.S. Court, 2:04-cv-02320, and through interviews with Max Seifert and Cheryl Pilate.

Chapter 23: The Shunning of Max Seifert

Max Seifert's background is drawn from his deposition testimony and from a series of interviews with him.

Seifert wrote in his application for a search warrant on Feb. 2, 1999, that he had reliable information that Smith was smoking crack and was passing forged checks, and was selling police gas masks, bulletproof vests, and other police equipment from his apartment. In his 2012 affidavit, Smith wrote that a superior in the department who was "waiting to close" on a real estate transaction with Smith called to alert him that Detective Seifert had obtained a search warrant. The superior warned Smith, according to Smith's recollection, that the police were "going to do a search warrant and kick the door here; they're using it as a way to get in" to Smith's apartment.

Sheriff Leroy Smith was defeated for reelection by retired KCK police division commander Donald Ash. Election Results, *The Kansas City Star*, April 8, 2009, p. 11. The race had noted Ash's repeated criticism of the incumbent. Sheriff's Race Is a Source for Drama, *The Kansas City Star*, April 4, 2009, p. B-4.

The details of Bowling's lawsuit are drawn from the court record *Bowling v. USA, et al.*, Kansas District U.S. Court, 2:04-cv-02320, including the transcript of testimony in depositions and at the nineteen-day trial by Seifert and other officers. Max Seifert's version of events was credited by Judge Robinson in her forty-eight-page memorandum and order handed down Sept. 17, 2010.

Chapter 24: "It Doesn't Satisfy My Heart"

Jim McCloskey's interviews with Doniel Quinn's mother Saundra, and his subsequent visits to Saundra's ex-husband John Quinn and to John's sister Freda Quinn are detailed in his memos.

The tape recording that Saundra made of interviewing John Quinn—in which the name "Cecil Brooks" came up—was found in McCloskey's files on the case.

Chapter 25: A Monster Enters

Neil Edgar Jr.'s propensity for violence, as described by Niko, matched descriptions Jim McCloskey would soon hear from Cecil Brooks and Joe Robinson as well as various other witnesses. By the time Jim heard these accounts, Edgar Jr. entered a guilty plea to second-degree murder for shooting Anthony Conley to death in August 2000 in Missouri (Jackson County, Missouri Circuit Court Case CR00-04587). Years later, Edgar Jr. would be deposed and deny any role in the double murder on Hutchings Street.

As I began researching Lamonte's case even while he was still locked up, Cheryl generously took me on my early visits and introduced me to Kansas City residents, so I could retrace interviews accomplished years earlier by Jim and Cheryl and investigator Dan Clark; undoubtedly some of those witnesses may have been otherwise unwilling to talk to a stranger. At times during those initial interviews witnesses would reveal things that caught Cheryl by surprise. One instance occurred when Gloria Labat described not only that she heard Niko Quinn recant outside the courtroom during Lamonte's 1994 trial, but that Gloria went inside the courtroom to report what she had heard to the prosecutor.

Neil Edgar Sr. was confined to prison for the murder of an adopted son. See You Must Love Discipline, Edgar Children Were Taught, *The Kansas City Star*, Sept. 27, 2003, p. B-1; Kansas Man Loses Appeal for New Trial in Death of 9-Year-Old Son, *The Kansas City Star*, May 16, 2014, https://www.kansascity.com/news/local/article306224.html.

Lamonte confirmed in interviews the content of what Jim reported in his memos about Lamonte's prison encounters with Edgar Sr. Almost eight years after the prison encounters occurred, as she sought Lamonte's freedom, Cheryl would share with the district attorney's office the content of Jim McCloskey's memos regarding Lamonte's conversations with Edgar Sr.

Chapter 26: "This Case Cannot Die"

Many of those who began talking to Jim and Dan and Cheryl about Golubski's abuses would later provide detailed sworn affidavits, which became part of the court record in Lamonte's case. Among them was that of Ethel Abbott, Golubski's ex-wife.

Days after Jerome Gorman won election, *The Kansas City Star* noted that Tomasic's successor had served in the district attorney's office for more than twenty years and, as the chief trial attorney, had reportedly tried more than 200 jury trials and more than forty murder cases. New DA an Old Hand in County, *The Kansas City Star*, Nov. 10, 2004, Neighborhood News Section p. 1.

Bowling's lawsuit was tried without a jury before Judge Robinson, beginning March 1, 2010, and testimony stretched out over nineteen days ending on April 8.

Golubski described his 2010 retirement, with full pension and a reserve commission.

Jim McCloskey considers his interview with Joe Robinson, who is a brother to Cecil Brooks, critical.

The July 23, 2009, press release on Brooks's sentence, issued by the U.S. Attorney's Office in Kansas, singled out, among others, Assistant U.S. Attorney Terra Morehead for her work on the case.

Demographics were taken from census data.

Golubski's quotes are taken from McCloskey's memo detailing the encounter.

Lamonte's quotes come from the journal he kept.

Chapter 27: "Everybody Knows Muggz Did Not Do This"

Jim McCloskey's letter to Brooks, and the accompanying letter from Michael Redmon, were in Jim's files, as was Cecil Brooks's handwritten reply.

The *CSS Arkansas*, an imposing sight at 110 feet long, was brought from Memphis to a shipyard in Yazoo City originally intended to repair steamboats. Two hundred men worked around the clock. The vessel had to be rushed by early July 1862 into the battle of Vicksburg, its protective armor not fully complete. It was said to have inflicted considerable damage to Union ships before it was destroyed, just twenty-four days after it left Yazoo City. The makeshift yard built or fortified several other vessels; but none of the others were completed before the yard was burned in 1863 as Union troops approached. (Shipyard details taken from https://visityazoo.org/civil-war-comes-to-yazoo and from "Confederate Shipyards" by Gary McQuarrie and Neil P. Chatelain in *Civil War Navy* magazine, https://civilwarnavy.com.)

The Yazoo City penitentiary, a high-security facility, was redesignated to lower security in 2020. The Bureau of Prisons website as of July 2025 lists the Yazoo City complex as one medium- and two low-security facilities, housing together more than 4,500 prisoners.

The details of the meeting between Jim McCloskey and Cecil Brooks come from Jim's memo after the meeting; his thank-you note was included in Jim's files.

Corisha provided the details of trying to rebuild her life while Lamonte was in prison; they both discussed their unsteady relationship, together and separately. Lamonte's mother Rosie, who did not trust Corisha and thought she was out to take advantage of her son, also provided her separate perspective.

Maxine Crowder provided details in a series of interviews before her 2020 death.

Chapter 28: Collecting Affidavits

The affidavits became part of the post-conviction case. Saundra Newsome signed hers on Feb. 14, 2011.

Joe Robinson's affidavit is dated Feb. 9, 2011.

Copies of the correspondence documented Jim McCloskey's efforts to arrange another meeting with Cecil Brooks, and the obstacles were contained in Jim's files.

The additional affidavits signed by the end of 2011, and the dates: Ruby Mitchell, June 13; Gloria Labat, June 13; Michael Redmon, March 4; Gregory Hill (Rosie's old boyfriend), Sept. 28; Greg Lauber (troubled juror) Nov. 11; and Freda Quinn, Oct. 21. Additionally a man named Frank Freeman, who knew Lamonte and Neil Edgar Jr., confirmed, among other details, Monster's violence as he "started hanging with" Aaron Robinson and Cecil Brooks in an affidavit dated Sept. 1, 2011. Rashida Martin, a cousin of Lamonte's, said in an Aug. 30, 2011, affidavit her recollection of being with Lamonte on the day of the murders; Martin said no one ever interviewed her or talked to her about being a witness. And a woman named Kendra Dean-Martin, who was described as being a former drug dealer who had a romantic relationship with Monster. In a Feb. 10, 2011, affidavit, Martin described an incident in which Detective Roger Golubski purchased crack cocaine that he promptly took with a woman into a bedroom. The affidavit states Martin was told "Golubski spends big money and will come back again for a similar arrangement."

The prophetic fortune cookie story was recorded by Jim in a memo; both Cheryl and Jim recalled the incident.

Chapter 29: No Place For Honest Cops

Sonny Callahan is listed in the program from Doniel Sublett Quinn's funeral. Jim McCloskey recorded what Callahan told him in his memos, and many years later, Callahan would be interviewed about Golubski by *The Kansas City Star* columnist Melinda Henneberger about a friend of his who said Golubski had repeatedly raped and threatened to have her killed: Former KCK Cop: Friend Told Him Years Ago Golubski Raped Her. 'I Believed Her 100 Percent.'

The case *Max Seifert v. Unified Government of Wyandotte County and Kansas City, Kansas and the Wyandotte County Sheriff's Department* was filed in Kansas U.S. District Court Aug. 9. 2011. Case number 11-CV-2327. Seifert submitted a twenty-five-page declaration on Feb. 4, 2013, that was filed in the civil case *McIntyre et al. v. Unified Government of Kansas City Kansas*, Kansas U.S. Dist. Ct., filed Oct. 11, 2018 (referred in these notes as "*McIntyre civil case*"). Max also was generous in accommodating a series of interviews for this book.

Ricky Armstrong was the chief of the KCK police department at the time he was deposed on Sept. 12, 2012. After his retirement, Armstrong would later become president and chief executive officer of the Kansas City Crime Commission.

Former chief Ronald Miller was deposed Sept. 14, 2012. Miller became chief in Topeka after he retired, and then, in 2015, was named the U.S. marshal for the Kansas District.

Michael York was a major in the KCK police department at the time he was deposed Sept. 11, 2012. Miller would go on to be assistant chief and, when Ron Zeigler retired, served as acting chief.

Tim Hausback was a member of the KCK police department from 1972 through 1989, when he retired for medical reasons after suffering a serious back injury during a police pursuit. Hausback's story was detailed in his declaration, signed April 21, 2022, and filed in the *McIntyre* civil case, cited above, and in a detailed interview at Hausback's home in southwestern Missouri.

Doug Parisi sued the county, *Parisi v. Unified Govt. of Wyandotte County Kansas and Kansas City, Kansas, City Kansas Police Department et al.*, laying out the details of being intensively investigated by internal affairs *after* he had uncovered misconduct by the commander of internal affairs. Parisi also claimed in the lawsuit that Chief Zeigler failed to properly consider Parisi's formal grievance over his firing. The suit was dismissed because Parisi had failed to go through the required legal steps on a timely basis. The facts about which Parisi complained were never addressed.

Chapter 30: Righting Wrongs

This chapter is based on interviews with Lamonte and Corisha, with Jim McCloskey, and with McCloskey's notes and Lamonte's journal.

Chapter 31: A "Good Trick"

As states found it difficult to obtain the components for lethal injections, Missouri struggled to find a solution. Twenty-one prisoners facing lethal injection turned together to the courts, including Herbert Smulls and Russell Bucklew. "Twenty-one Mo. death row inmates sue over lethal drug," St. Louis Public Radio, June 28, 2012. By July of 2013, the Missouri attorney general was threatening to bring back the gas chamber if the courts did not promptly approve Missouri's new method of lethal injection. "Missouri Death Row Legal Battle Could Bring Back Gas Chamber," ABC News, July 8, 2013. https://abcnews.go.com/US/missouri-death-row-legal-battle-bring-back-gas/story?id=19606733#.UeN-vo2TgV0.

Cheryl's efforts to stay Herbert Smulls's executions went through the U.S. Eighth Circuit, *Smulls v. Lombardi.* Case 14-1193, Eighth Circuit U.S. Court of Appeals.

Cheryl's efforts to stay the execution of Russell Bucklew also went through the Eighth Circuit, *Bucklew v. Lombardi,*14-2163, Eighth Circuit U.S. Court of Appeals.

Cheryl Pilate filed a lawsuit on behalf of Bucklew on May 9, 2014. *Bucklew v. Lombardi*, 14-8000 Wester District Missouri U.S. District Court. Judge Phillips's decision is document 17 on the case docket. The case was appealed May 19, 2014, Case 14-2163 Eighth U.S. Circuit Court of Appeals; the panel issued its stay, the full Circuit lifted the stay, and Justice Samuel Alito then imposed a stay on behalf of the U.S. Supreme Court, all on May 20, the day before the scheduled execution (13-10161).

By the end of September 2014, Cheryl and Jim had collected twenty-three affidavits.

Natasha Hodge signed her affidavit April 10, 2014. *The Kansas City Star* columns were published June 27 and Sept. 1, 2021.

Chapter 32: "A Very Corrupt Place"

The series of exchanges between Jim and Cheryl were contained in Jim's files.

Chapter 33: Winking at Misconduct

The tensions as Jim McCloskey sought to convince Cheryl Pilate to file the brief on Lamonte's behalf before his retirement are reflected in email exchanges that were part of Jim's files. Jim, Kate, Paul, and Cheryl were all concerned about the financial pressures.

The full Eighth Circuit U.S. Court of Appeals panel agreed that Judge Phillips was wrong to dismiss the case without a hearing (*Bucklew v. Lombardi*, March 6, 2015).

Judge Phillips then on remand gave Cheryl a series of deadlines to perfect a complaint on behalf of Russell Bucklew.

Chapter 34: Building the Atom Bomb

The affidavit calling Golubski "a member of the criminal community" is dated July 30, 2015.

Timothy Maskil's affidavit, in which he crossed the "Blue Line," is dated Sept. 23, 2015.

Freddie Gray died in police custody in Baltimore on April 19, 2015. It was the latest in a series: Michael Brown was shot to death by a policeman in Ferguson, Mo., Aug. 9, 2014. Eric Garner died while being held in a chokehold in New York City on July 17, 2014.

The *Post* database begins Jan. 1, 2015—months after Michael Brown was killed—and lasted through 2024, when the *Post* decided to stop collecting any more current incidents. https://www.washingtonpost.com/graphics/investigations/police-shootings-database/.

The Exoneration Registry, founded by Professor Samuel Gross of the University of Michigan and Rob Warden, of the Center for Wrongful Conviction, studies every case of defendants' convictions being overturned as evidence of their innocence became established. By July 2025 the registry (exonerationregistry.org) reported more than 3,700 exonerations since 1989.

Blackstone's ratio, said to date to 1769, forms the basis for the presumption of innocence.

In its 2024 report the Sentencing Project reported more than two million people were locked up in jails and prisons across the United States—up from 360,000 in the early 1970s. The U.S. rate of incarceration is far above that of other Western democracies. https://www.sentencingproject.org/reports/mass-incarceration-trends/. Further, the Vera Institute reports that hundreds of thousands of people are locked in county jails while awaiting trial. Those held were defendants considered potential flight risks; defendants who were considered dangerous to the community if released; and, especially, those too poor to be able to post bail, even if they were not considered dangerous or flight risks. https://www.vera.org/ending-mass-incarceration/criminalization-racial-disparities/bail-reform.

Chapter 35: Time for Change

Mark Dupree's background was developed from a series of in-depth interviews, as well as from background articles published as Dupree was first running for office against Jerry Gorman, such as 'A God Thing': New Wyandotte County DA to Inherit Tough Cases, *The Kansas City Star*, Aug. 2, 2016; Mark Dupree Files to

Run for Wyandotte County District Attorney, a Seat Currently Held by Jerry Gorman, *The Pitch*, Jan. 6, 2016.

Melissa Testrake and Lamonte developed a strong bond. In interviews, both describe Melissa playing an important role as he remained locked up.

The Kansas Supreme Court decision in 2014 loosening in what circumstances prisoners could belatedly challenge convictions on the basis of "manifest injustice" was *Vontress v. State*, Kansas Supreme Court 102904, 2014. It did not sit well with Kansas's Republican officials and became part of a struggle between the executive branch and legislative. See the *New York Times* account Outraged by Kansas Justices' Rulings, Republicans Seek to Reshape Court, April 1, 2016. https://www.nytimes.com/2016/04/02/us/outraged-by-kansas-justices-rulings-gop-seeks-to-reshape-court.html?unlocked_article_code=1.WE8.USMg.pm95r5ENiN1Y&smid=url-share.

Kansas lawmakers passed amendments in 2016 setting tighter restrictions on when cases could be considered outside the time limit in what became Kansas Law 60-1507 (Kansas Office of Revisor of Statutes). The amendments followed the state Supreme Court decision in *State,* that gave more leeway to untimely petitions.

Cheryl filed the motion June 10, 2016, to stay Russell Bucklew's case because it was impossible to represent him adequately without funding (*Bucklew v. Lombardi.* 4-14-acv-08000, Doc. 87).

Chapter 36: Boom

Bussell detailed the reenactment in an affidavit, dated June 27, 2016. In an interview he revisited his work from the time of his original skepticism, and how that opinion changed.

Dan Clark signed an affidavit June 16, 2016, similarly describing the steps of their reconstruction.

Bussell stated in the second affidavit that he was unable to get Kobe to detail what was not "kosher." But four years later, under a subpoena, Kobe was deposed in a civil suit brought by Lamonte, and then, three years later, talked to Melinda Henneberger of *The Kansas City Star.* Kobe contended then that he had reported alleged misconduct to his superiors, to no avail—including when he heard of Golubski having been caught having sex in the detective room. Former KCKPD Captain with Cancer: 'I Met Some Very Violent People with Badges, July 14, 2024.

The seventeen-page affidavit of Randy Eskina is dated June 2, 2016.

The new affidavit from Freda Quinn, dated June 18, 2006, states, "People are simply afraid" to come forward, adding she knew Niko had initially lied because "she had been frightened."

McCloskey's affidavit is signed June 27, 2016.

Melissa Testrake and Mike Bussell, in separate interviews, provided the details of the steps to make one last effort to win Brooks's affidavit, and of the way their visit with Brooks unfolded.

The history of the United States Medical Center for Federal Prisoners, widely known as Fed Med, was drawn from an article by Dr. Michael S. Clarke for *Missouri Medicine*, "'The Fed Med' 90 Years in Springfield Missouri," Nov.-Dec. 2020, pp. 520–522. https://pmc.ncbi.nlm.nih.gov/articles/PMC7721423/.

Cecil Brooks signed his affidavit June 22, 2016, adding four handwritten paragraphs to the original draft first prepared years earlier by Jim McCloskey.

Melissa Testrake and Lindsay Runnels described separately their trip to the courthouse to file the 180-page petition, *McIntyre v. Kansas,* 2016-CV-000508.

Rosie has raised with me during several interviews spanning a number of years her surprise upon seeing how Lamonte had changed while in prison.

Chapter 37: A New Day

Dupree's quote is included in an article from Fox 4 by Shannon O'Brien, "Wyandotte County's newly elected district attorney Mark Dupree lays out vision for upcoming tenure," Aug. 3, 2016.

The Star's RECOMMENDATIONS FOR ISSUES, CANDIDATES, ON LOCAL BALLOTS, *The Kansas City Star,* July 22, 2016, 6A.

Television reports began airing on the eve of the primary: "Questions raised about teen's conviction in 1994 double homicide," KMBC, Aug. 1, 2016. https://www.kmbc.com/article/questions-raised-about-teens-conviction-in-1994-double-homicide/3591934.

Primary election day was Aug. 2, 2016. *The Kansas City Star*'s first reporting on Cheryl's motion was Aug. 3. The article appeared on p. A-4.

The lawsuit was filed in Jackson County Missouri Circuit Court, on Oct. 14, 2016, *Morgan Pilate v. Centurion Ministries,* 1616-CV24972, and removed to Missouri Western District U.S. District Court, 4:16-cv-01304, on Dec. 20, 2016. It was dismissed as settled on April 21, 2017.

Sean O'Brien, the former chief federal public defender for the western district of Missouri, who has significant expertise both in death penalty and wrongful conviction cases, filed a review of the record and concluded Cheryl had done stellar work on behalf of Lamonte. In a follow-up interview, O'Brien said the attorney is in the single best position to determine when enough is enough on behalf of a wrongly convicted client; even when the evidence seems overwhelmingly to establish the likelihood of innocence, he noted, courts often reject the idea of overturning jury verdicts. The last thing an attorney would want, he added, would be to walk away in defeat because there were steps that were left unpursued.

Darryl Burton, Cheryl, and Lamonte all described in interviews how Darryl was recruited by Cheryl to help Lamonte cope with the delays. Darryl spoke of his initial reticence in his own interview.

The church information comes from the church website. It listed 24,000 active members as of July 2025. https://resurrection.church/about/#:~:text=The%20congregation%20has%20more%20than,coming%20soon%20in%20Lee's%20Summit.

Corisha provided the details of her interactions both with Lamonte and her own mother.

Corisha also described seeing Lamonte's picture in the convenience store. LOCKED UP AT 17, LAMONTE MCINTYRE HAS BEEN WRONGLY CONVICTED FOR 22 YEARS, MOTION SAYS, was written by Eric Adler and published in *The Kansas City Star* on Oct. 25, 2016.

PROSECUTORS WILL LOSE JOBS WHEN NEW DA TAKES OVER, *The Kansas City Star*, Nov. 12, 2016, p. A-4.

The decision by Gorman to bring in the state to handle a local prosecution case because his successor would not be experienced enough spoke volumes regarding what the establishment thought of the newly elected district attorney. And yet the state attorney general's office turned out to not be a panacea. After the case was thrown out of court the decision received renewed attention. "Former Kansas attorney general reacts after Schlitterbahn charges are dropped," KCTV-5, Feb. 22, 2019; FAILED KCK WATER SLIDE DEATH PROSECUTION TOOK UNUSUAL PATH TO KANSAS ATTORNEY GENERAL, *The Kansas City Star*, March 10, 2019; "Gorman explains his request for state AG to handle Schlitterbahn case," WyandotteDaily.com/gorman-explains-hiss-request-for-state-ag-to-handle-schlitterbahn-case.

Chapter 38: A Fresh Look

Cheryl and Dupree both describe how quickly she began pushing Dupree even before he had taken office.

The movement to elect progressives as district attorneys represented a significant effort to reform the criminal justice system. To accomplish that reform, so contrary to what traditional policing envisions, required money, and George Soros provided a major source of funds. GEORGE SOROS'S QUIET OVERHAUL OF THE U.S. JUSTICE SYSTEM, *Politico,* Aug. 30, 2016.

Mark Dupree's comments took place during a series of interviews in his office.

The day before Cecil Brooks was to be interviewed by Dupree, Cheryl sent to the district attorney a series of documents on March 1, 2017, to ensure the prosecutors entered the interview well-prepared. The outcome of the district attorney's meeting with Cecil Brooks was entered into the record at Lamonte's post-conviction hearing as a stipulation, worked out to avoid Mark Dupree taking the witness stand at the hearing.

Lamonte and Melissa Testrake described in interviews the fear that washed over Lamonte as he was brought from prison to the Wyandotte County jail complex so that Dupree could interview Lamonte as part of that reconsideration.

Chapter 39: "It's Nice Outside"

Melissa and Lamonte confirmed in separate interviews that the gray suit and purple tie that Lamonte wore in court for the hearing had been borrowed from Melissa's brother.

The description of what occurred that week represents what I observed, together with interviews and a review of the transcript of the hearing.

PART IV: SEEKING JUSTICE

Chapter 40: On His Own

The account in this chapter is built on my own posttrial observations, together with the recollections of Lamonte and Corisha and others present. Cheryl Pilate and Lamonte described the next morning.

Lamonte's trouble in simple tasks, such as opening a bank account, are built on my reporting at the time, talking to Lindsay Runnels and Tricia Bushnell, then of the Midwest Innocence Project.

Mike Bussell described arranging the driving lessons and connection to George Jacobs of the barber academy; Darryl Burton and Lamonte describe the decision to form Miracle of Innocence; and the account of Lamonte and Corisha's remarriage is based on their recollections, together with those of his mother Rosie and Melissa Testrake.

Chapter 41: "Sick and Tired" of Injustice

The story of John Gibbs Jr. comes from the descriptions of descendants, from family history captured in the website "Find A Grave," of John Gibbs Jr. and his daughter, Katie Elmira Gibbs Alvey. Katie married Andrew Leo Alvey, and their sixth and final child was Lloyd G. Alvey.

Lloyd G. Alvey's name appears on various records in the 1960s as an assistant city attorney (e.g., *State v. Bobby Joe Spencer*, Kansas Supreme Court, 1960, No. 41554). Lloyd died in 1978. Harriet West Alvey, who died in 2023, married Lloyd Alvey; Harriet's older sister, Barbara West Burns, married William J. Burns.

It was Burns who broke tradition and ran for a "Republican" seat on the district court, winning election over Milton P. Beach. *The Kansas City Times*, Nov. 7, 1962, election results. See also, FILING FOR JUDGE RACE BREAKS A TRADITION, *The Kansas City Star*, June 20, 1962, p. 3; PONDER JUDGE FILING; RACE FOR WYANDOTTE COURT POST SEEN AS VIOLATION OF AGREEMENT, *The Kansas City Star*, June 25, 1962, p. 1; THE NON-PARTISAN ISSUE, *The Kansas City Star*, July 3, 1962, p. 20; SEEK TO GUARD 2-PARTY PACT, *The Kansas City Star*, Sept. 12, 1962; PLEA IN COURT RACE, *The Kansas City Star*, Oct. 17, 1962.

Then when Burns ran next, Alvey ensured he would not have opposition. SEVEN TO RUN WITHOUT FOES—TWO LAST MINUTE WITHDRAWALS LEAVE BURNS UNOPPOSED—A POLITICAL MANEUVER, *The Kansas City Times*, p. 3.

Lloyd Alvey Jr., David's brother, was a twenty-four-year-old tree-trimmer for the publicly owned utility when he ran in 1980 for the state Senate against Jack Steineger, a four-term incumbent who was the Senate minority leader.

Edmond Alvey was elected as one of the original members of the Kansas City, Kansas, City Council, which was formed in 1983. KCK POLITICAL LEADER ED ALVEY DIES AT 74, *The Kansas City Times*, Dec. 28, 1989, p. C-1.

When Connie Alvey won the primary election in 2008, defeating an incumbent judge, Denise Tomasic commented, "Even if people didn't know she was a talented, smart woman who would make a fine judge, they knew her family."

Elected Judges Say Politics Are Left Behind, *The Kansas City Star*, Oct. 27, 2008, pp. 1, 4. Alvey had previously worked in the district attorney's office both for Nick Tomasic and his successor, Jerry Gorman.

Andrew Alvey, as the president of the Fraternal Order of Police unit representing KCK rank-and-file police, went on record as "absolutely opposed" to civilians being involved in the disciplinary process against police officers accused of misconduct. Civilian Probe of Police Actions Opposed, *The Kansas City Star*, Aug. 4, 1983, p. 1.

On the other side of the family tree, Judge William J. Burns died in 1975; among his survivors were his wife, Barbara, secretary for the KCK Parks and Recreation department for eight years. One son, William J. Burns Jr., became chief deputy of the Wyandotte County Probation Office weeks before his father's death; William went on to serve as Wyandotte county clerk, and as county commissioner before resigning to become district court administrator. His wife Nancy, who worked in the county appraiser's office, ran and won a seat on the county commission in 1992, saying in a statement, "We need a servant of the people, not a king or queen" (*The Kansas City Star*, June 11, 1992, p. 2).

Months before the city/county consolidation occurred, columnist Rick Alm wrote that the merged government "won't mean a thing if the public payroll remains clogged like an old sewer pipe with the same old pols and hundreds of their relatives." (Hiring, I Guess It's All Relative, *The Kansas City Star*, Jan. 11, 1996, p. 1, Wyandotte/Leavenworth edition.) Alm's first example: Robert P. Burns, the brother of William Jr., who was hired as assistant city attorney, chosen among twenty-seven qualified applicants (Ibid, p. 8). Burns has since gone on to be elected as a district court judge and, since 2019, chief of the district (University of Notre Dame Law School alumni note, March 29, 2019).

David Alvey's angry response about the family's success in obtaining county positions was reported by Dave Helling, David Alvey Is Not a Voice for Change in Wyandotte County, *The Kansas City Star*, July 19, 2021, p. A-7.

In reporting on the debate between the mayor and his challenger, reporter Steve Vockrodt reported the focus on economic issues: on spending, on taxes, on development and tax incentives. The issues of public safety involved how much was being spent on a security detail for Holland, and on the fire department budget. It was as if the hearings that ended in Lamonte's exoneration, which occurred just days earlier, never happened. KCK Mayor's Race Pits Incumbent against a Stiff Challenge, *The Kansas City Star*, Nov. 2, 2017, p. A-7.

The description of the Alvey family role at the swearing in was described in *The Kansas City Star*, Jan. 10, 2018, p. A-12.

Lamonte and two other exonerees, Floyd Bledsoe and Richard Jones, appeared before the legislature (AP article in the *Iola Register*, Feb. 15, 2018, p. 2) and the bill was passed (Justice Not Yet Achieved for Wrongly Convicted in Kansas, *The Kansas City Star*, May 5, 2018, A10). But despite the compassionate words of the outgoing governor, Jeff Colyer, things were not that simple: Fight for Compensation Likely Will Drag on for Freed Man, *The Kansas City Star*,

Dec. 24, 2019, p. 1. A week later, columnist Henneberger quoted Mayor David Alvey's continued skepticism: KANSAS WON'T GIVE MCINTYRE WHAT HE'S OWED, *The Kansas City Star*, Dec. 26, 2019, p. A-9. District Attorney Mark Dupree's open letter in support of Lamonte was reported by *The Kansas City Star*, WYANDOTTE DA BLASTS TREATMENT OF WRONGLY CONVICTED KANSAN, Dec. 26, 2019, p. A-6. Still, it took weeks more of pressure before the state agreed to pay Lamonte what he was owed, MAN WRONGFULLY CONVICTED OF KCK MURDERS TO RECEIVE $1.55M, INNOCENCE CERTIFICATE, *The Kansas City Star*, Feb. 24, 2020.

Lamonte's civil suit was filed in the District of Kansas U.S. District Court, *McIntyre et al. v. United Government of Wyandotte County and Kansas City Kansas et al.*, Oct. 11, 2018.

Chapter 42: "Amazing," "Disgusting," and "Nasty," Too

The case of Orozco was styled *U.S. v. Orozco*, 15-20074, U.S. District Court, Kansas.

On the heels of Lamonte's case, Robinson's finding of Morehead's misconduct received media attention. FEDERAL JUDGE ACCUSES PROSECUTOR OF MISCONDUCT, THROWS CASE OUT, *The Kansas City Star*, Dec. 7, 2017, p. A-1.

The link between the 2020 report of the Office of Professional Responsibility and the Orozco case were noted, for example, in the March 23, 2021, report by Katie Moore in *The Kansas City Star*, WITNESS SAYS PROSECUTOR TERRA MOREHEAD COERCED FALSE TESTIMONY, p. A-1. Moore's reports of Morehead's work were particularly in-depth.

The recording scandal was first revealed in connection with *USA v. Lorenzo Black, Karl Carter, et al.*, (18-20032, U.S. District Court, Kansas), a case involving multiple defendants accused of drug charges. Federal prosecutors Erin Slinker Tomasic and Kim Flannigan were initially concerned about the source of a document that was floating around the detention facility in Leavenworth that could reveal information about their continuing investigation into contraband being smuggled into the prison. The investigation was high profile, the subject months earlier of a press conference by the U.S. attorney: KANSAS U.S. ATTORNEY ANNOUNCES CHARGES IN LEAVENWORTH PRISON DRUG SMUGGLING RING, *The Kansas City Star*, April 11, 2016, p. 1.

A federal public defender filed a motion on behalf of the approximately seventy-five defender clients who were held at the Leavenworth facility on Aug. 7, 2016, two days after learning of the recordings taking place. That set off the series of hearings, which stretched out over two years. Some notable dates: Judge Robinson appointed the special master on October 11, 2016. On June 19, 2017, the government filed a "Notice of record clarification and correction," correcting statements that suggested Erin Slinker Tomasic had not listened to privileged conversations. On July 14, 2017, the Department of Justice notified Judge Robinson that Steven D. Clymer was appointed to respond to requests from the special master, and on September 12, 2017, Clymer notified the special master that he in large part "must respectfully decline" the master's requests, stating that the district court "lacks authority to investigate and supervise the internal operations and decisions of the U.S. Attorney's Office."

Federal public defender Brannon filed a motion to hold the U.S. Attorney's Office in contempt on Oct. 25, 2017; and when Judge Robinson and Special Master Cohen pressed on, the DOJ appealed Judge Robinson's effort to hold hearings on the contempt. The Eighth U.S. Circuit Court of Appeals panel rejected the appeal, and the hearings appeared finally set to begin. The new U.S. attorney sought to work out an agreement to resolve the dispute, granting relief to all of those defendants whose conversations with their attorneys had been turned over to the prosecutors. But Deputy Attorney General Rosenstein blocked that proposed settlement, in a letter dated July 18, 2018. And the hearings were finally scheduled over several days; Erin Slinker Tomasic testified on Oct. 2, 2018.

Chapter 43: A Pattern of Misconduct

Judge Robinson's 188-page findings were filed Aug. 13, 2019—more than three years from the time Federal Public Defender Brannon first filed her motion objecting to the recordings.

The civil lawsuit filed by those detained in Leavenworth, *Huff and Rapp v. Core Civic Inc and Securus Technologies*, 2:17-cv-02320, was filed June 1, 2017, and proceeded on a parallel track. The civil case finally ended in a class action settlement on behalf of those detained, filed Jan. 28, 2020.

Jay Giannukos's case was originally filed by the government, charging him with possession of methamphetamine with an intent to distribute, on May 13, 2015. *USA v. Giannukos*, 15-20016-01. His unusual resentencing hearing occurred May 10, 2021.

Chapter 44: The Empire Starts to Crack

Dupree's intention of creating a Conviction Integrity Unit for Wyandotte County, at a cost of $350,000, was reported in In a Bad Week for Policing, Integrity Unit Could Restore Trust, *The Kansas City Star*, May 11, 2018, p. A-10. In July Dupree presented the idea to the Unified Government Board of Commissioners, seeking $300,000.

On the eve of a final vote, police chief Terry Zeigler, along with the sheriff and the heads of the police unions representing officers in both chapters, all jointly signed a letter to Attorney General Schmidt on July 30, 2018, in opposition, which the police department posted on Facebook. Schmidt said the next day, in response to *that*, fifty-four progressive prosecutors from around the country, including the district attorneys from Cook County Illinois; Philadelphia; and Brooklyn, NY, all signed their own letter defending Dupree's plan.

At its meeting the next month the unified government board approved $162,000 in seed money to start the program.

Golubski's old partner, Terry Zeigler, who joined the force in 1990, was chosen as chief over four other finalists. KCK Gets New Police Chief, *The Kansas City Star*, Dec. 3, 2014, p. A-4.

Just as District Attorney Dupree began seeking funding for a conviction integrity unit, he charged veteran KCK police officer Rios with misdemeanor battery for his unwanted touching of a female cadet. "KCK police officer charged with sexual battery," KCUR, May 8, 2018; The *Star*, in its May 11 editorial, linked the two events, noting Dupree was trying to build accountability and winning greater trust in the department. Rios ended up pleading guilty and was given a twelve-month probationary sentence. But one year after she had reported the incident, the cadet filed a lawsuit against the department over the incident and then being fired. Lawsuit Says Cadet Fired after Reporting Sexual Assault, *The Kansas City Star*, May 23, 2019, p. A-12. The lawsuit, filed in U.S. District Court, is *Hardman v. Unified Government and Stephen Rios*, 2:19-cv-02251 (U.S. District Court, Kansas district, May 22, 2019), was reportedly settled for undisclosed terms in October 2020 (docket report of case). Once the lawsuit was filed, community activists demanded Zeigler's firing. The protest march for justice, organized around the cadet's complaint, was reported: Faith Group Protests Alleged Sexual Abuse by KCK Police, Demands Firing of Chief, *The Kansas City Star*, June 6, 2019, kcstar.com.

"Too sweet a deal? KCK Police Chief lives in UG-owned lake house," KSHB Channel 41, Nov. 21, 2018. KCK Police Chief Had "Handshake" Deal to Live in County-Owned House for Little Rent, *The Kansas City Star*, Dec. 09, 2018; "Activists sue KCK over police chief lease deal," KSHB Channel 41, Nov. 9, 2018; Investigation of KCK Police Chief Looks into Alleged Double-Dipping in Lake House Deal, *The Kansas City Star*, March 05, 2019; "It Has Been an Honor": KCK Police Chief Terry Zeigler Announces Plan to Retire, *The Kansas City Star*, July 10, 2019.

Wyandotte County District Attorney Draws Challenger Concerned with How Office Is Run, *The Kansas City Star*, Dec. 4, 2019.

Dupree's plans to expand the CIU into a Community Integrity Unit—also including police abuses, post, were described in Wyandotte County DA Announces Plans for New Unit to Investigate Police Misconduct, *The Kansas City Star*, June 11, 2020, includes his quotes about the need to "change the systems." See also: "Wyandotte County DA launches law enforcement accountability effort," KSHB Channel 41, June 10, 2020; "Funds for DA's police misconduct investigative unit approved in Wyandotte County," July 17, 2020; "Wyandotte County Community Integrity Unit "up and running" as DA announces charges . . ."

The decision by Alvey to leave Dupree off the task force won regional attention, Wyandotte County DA Is Left Out of Law Enforcement Task Force Seeking Objective View, *The Kansas City Star*, June 11, 2020; "Wyandotte County DA says task force snub wasn't racist, but he's still fighting 'good old boy traditions,'" KCUR, June 23, 2020; and national: Reform Prosecutor in Kansas Excluded from 'Objective' Task Force on Policing, *The Intercept*, July 26, 2020.

After Floyd's murder, the local protests in KCK focused on Golubski. State Rep. Cindy Holscher was quoted warning about Golubski at one protest: Filmmaker Warns One Bad Cop Can Wreak Havoc; KCK Should Listen, *The Kansas City Star*, June 29, 2020, p. A-7.

The coalition of twenty-seven lawmakers, demanding an investigation of Golubski, was disclosed the same day the KBI announced that it had concluded that Golubski's crimes needed federal, not state, investigation. KBI ALLEGES FEDERAL CRIMES BY FORMER KCK POLICE DETECTIVE, *The Kansas City Star*, July 3, 2020, pp. A-1, 7.

The two-part *The Kansas City Star* editorial appeared July 23 and July 24, 2020. Dupree's response, "I am taking on the system in Wyandotte County. That's why the system is retaliating," appeared July 24. His guest column, ABOVE ALL ELSE, JUSTICE REQUIRES OUR RESILIENCE, appeared July 30.

Dupree's reelection was reported, DUPREE LIKELY HOLDS ON TO WYANDOTTE COUNTY DISTRICT ATTORNEY SEAT, DEFEATING BRYANT, Aug. 4, 2020.

The case of Olin "Pete" Coones is filed in Wyandotte County District Court, *State of Kansas* v. *Pete Coones*. After he was convicted and lost his direct appeal, Kansas Supreme Court 107180 (2014): "Court upholds murder conviction, vacates Hard 50 sentence," cjonline, Dec. 12, 2014, Coones filed a federal habeas petition, *Coones v. Shelton*, 16-3090 U.S. District Court, Kansas, that was denied October 24, 2016. Brandon Bell filed the post-conviction claim, Wyandotte County District Court case 2019 CV 727, on Sept. 2, 2019. The overturning of his conviction was well-covered ("Kansas City, Kansas, Man Freed from Prison after Murder Conviction Tossed," KCUR; and "Wyandotte County DA dismisses murder charge against Pete Coones," KSHB Channel 41, both Nov. 5, 2020. Also *The Kansas City Star*: JUDGE VACATES MURDER CONVICTION OF KCK MAN WHO SAYS HE WAS FRAMED IN MURDER-SUICIDE.

Soon after his exoneration, Coones died: PETE COONES, EXONERATED IN KANSAS CITY, KANSAS MURDER, DIES AFTER 108 DAYS OF FREEDOM, *The Kansas City Star*, Feb. 22, 2021.

Later came questions about Brancart's future in the new administration: "Kansas judge says prosecutor once suborned perjury to convict an innocent man. What will the next AG do?" cjonline, Oct. 31, 2022; PROSECUTOR FAULTED IN KCK WRONGFUL CONVICTION NO LONGER WORKING FOR KANSAS AG, *The Kansas City Star*, Jan. 27, 2023.

Chapter 45: Called to Account

William K. Smith was deposed twice during the pretrial process in Lamonte's civil suit, *McIntyre et al. v. Wyandotte County et al.* The questioning regarding Cheffen arose in the Feb. 25, 2021, deposition, starting at p. 55.

Terra Morehead was deposed for that lawsuit April 27, 2021.

Golubski gave his deposition in two parts. After invoking his right to remain silent hundreds of times in the first part, Nov. 19, 2020, he still returned for more questions April 20, 2021.

The naming of Boston Daniels received wide notice: NEGRO NAMED NEW CHIEF OF POLICE AT KANSAS CITY, Associated Press article in *The Springfield News-Leader*, June 10, 1970, p. 24. His role became a campaign issue, and the new mayor, Richard Walsh, soon took the administrative responsibilities away from Daniels, causing him to describe his new role as "messenger boy." DONNELLY BEGINS CHIEF'S JOB WITH NO RESERVATIONS, *The Kansas City Star*, May 12, 1971, p. 5; CHIEF DANIELS KNEW HIS BEAT, *The Kansas City Star*, May 15, 1971, p. 16.

The process to Chief Oakman's selection is described here: Kansas City Kansas Announces Four Finalists to Be Next Police Chief, *The Kansas City Star*, April 16, 2021. Oakman's selection: Karl Oakman Named KCK Police Chief, *The Kansas City Star*, May 7, 2021.

The mayoral contest was narrowed to Alvey against Tyrone Garner. Former KCK Deputy Police Chief, Incumbent Alvey, Advance to November Mayoral Election, *The Kansas City Star*, Aug. 3, 2021. The pressure to open records came in the lawsuit, Five Things to Know about Team Roc's Lawsuit against Kansas City Kansas Police, *The Kansas City Star*, Sept. 21, 2021.

Alvey opposed outside monitoring: In Politics, Change Is Hard. In KCK, It's Almost Impossible. Meet Mayor David Alvey, *The Kansas City Star*, July 26, 2021; Garner took a different position: "We need to have outside eyes": Former KCK Cop and Mayoral Candidate Seeks DOJ Probe, *The Kansas City Star*, July 26, 2021.

CNN reported the probe: "Federal grand jury investigating Kansas City cop who allegedly 'exploited and terrorized' Black residents for decades," Oct. 14, 2021. That ignited a debate in the final stages, Accused Former KCK Police Detective Golubski Might as Well Be on the Mayoral Ballot, *The Kansas City Star*, Oct. 26, 2021.

Wyandotte County Leaders Name Cheryl Harrison-Lee as Interim County Administrator, *The Kansas City Star*, Jan. 6, 2022.

Bach went out with a bang: "Top Kansas City, Kansas official to step down next week, Wyandotte County has new leaders in new year," KCUR, Dec. 29, 2021. But then: WyCo Leader Cashed in before Leaving, *The Kansas City Star*, Jan. 24, 2020, p. A-7.

Chapter 46: Fundamental Change

Gideon v. Wainwright, 372 U.S. 335 (1963).

I was at the public hearing in January 2022, where the Kansas Board of Indigents' Defense Services received input from the public; and then, weeks later, when the board approved the creation of the public defender office in Wyandotte County. Many members of the Wyandotte County bar were there to oppose the idea, but they were the clear minority in the room. As *The Kansas City Star* wrote afterward, Lack of Public Defender's Office a Scandal in Itself, Jan. 24, 2022, p. A-7.

The funding for indigent defense is a nationwide issue. In 2021 Melody Brannon, the federal public defender, warned that indigent defense "hasn't really been functioning constitutionally for a long time" (ACLU of Kansas, May 20, 2021). The Missouri crisis came to a head after defendants, left in prison waiting for months to even be assigned a public defender, filed suit. Missouri's Public Defender System Sued over Wait Lists, *The Kansas City Star*, Feb. 28. 2020, p. A-1. In California, where public defenders were hired county-by-county, the system came under attack as Placer County went to replace a longstanding public defender when a competing firm offered a lower bid: Low-Bid Law Offer

Argued, *Sacramento Bee,* June 27, 2005. Meanwhile in Maine, the only state that was lacking a public defender system across the state, an investigation by *The Maine Monitor* and ProPublica concluded that the indigent defenders were receiving services from "private attorneys who face disproportionately high amounts of discipline and an office that doesn't supervise them," quoting from A Low Bar for Public Defense, Jan. 24, 2022.

Federal Public Defender Brannon wrote to the disciplinary board Aug. 15, 2016, when the recordings scandal first was unfolding. She wrote again on Dec. 26, 2017, regarding Judge Robinson's finding of misconduct in the prosecution of Gregory Orozco. On Oct. 30, 2020, after Morehead and three other prosecutors appealed Judge Robinson's ruling, Brannon wrote that their factual claim was "demonstratively false." In his correspondence with the Department of Justice inspector general dated July 9, 2021, Brannon detailed specific instances of questionable conduct by Morehead, adding a list of suggested lawyers and judges that the inspector general could interview.

Chapter 47: Tying the Loop

Judge Vratil rejected the motion for summary judgment: *McIntyre et al. v. Wyandotte County, et al.*, 18-cv-2545 U.S. District Court Kansas, Document 686, filed June 28, 2022.

Deposition of Ophelia Williams was taken Nov. 18, 2020.

The deposition of S. K. was taken December 18, 2020.

The financial threat is detailed: Unified Government Warns Investors of Possible Financial Risk from Upcoming McIntyre Trial, May 24, 2022. The status hearing before Judge Vratil, which I attended, took place May 23, 2022.

At settlement talks on June 29, 2022, the county agreed to the settlement. That night, Lamonte called me, having regrets he had agreed to a settlement that would close off the chance to see those responsible for his wrongful conviction put on trial themselves. Cheryl told Lamonte it was too late to back out, that the agreement was reached; and within hours it was publicly announced. "Unified Government to pay $12.5 million to wrongfully imprisoned Kansas City, Kansas, Man," KCUR, June 30, 2022. The Unified Government board voted to approve the settlement at the next meeting, at which Commissioner Gayle Townsend referred to it as a business decision only. "Wyandotte County Will Pay $12.5M to Lamonte McIntyre, Wrongly Imprisoned for 23 Years, *The Kansas City Star*, July 1, 2022, updated Sept. 15, 2022.

I had many conversations with Lamonte during this period, when he and Corisha were struggling, and also visited them more than once in Phoenix.

Lamonte and Cheryl both called me and provided details of when and how they heard of the arrest of Roger Golubski. The account of his arrest appears in 'Come Out with Your Hands Up,' Neighbor Witnessed FBI Arrest ex-KCK Cop Roger Golubski, *The Kansas City Star*, Sept. 15, 2022. The case was filed as *United States v. Golubski*, 5:22,40055, U.S. District Court, Kansas.

Federal prosecutors sought to keep Golubski locked up pretrial: "Feds argue Roger Golubski is too dangerous to leave jail, detailing assaults of 7 more women," KCUR, Sept. 16, 2022 (5:22-40055, Docket number 10). The hearing (docket number 11) and release conditions (docket number 12) are part of the court record. "Judge releases former Kansas City, Kansas, police detective Roger Golubski to home arrest," KCUR, Sept. 19, 2022.

The second case is *USA v. Brooks et al.*, 5:22-40086 U.S. District Court Kansas.

Chapter 48: The Defendant Fails to Appear

I was in Kansas City that week and attended both the Team Roc–sponsored rally and the Unified Government's Team Roc organized its protest soon afterwards. "Jay-Z's Team Roc Ramps up Fight Against 'Troubling' Police Misconduct in Kansas City," hiphopdx.com/news Nov. 20, 2023. "As federal charges add pressure on KCKPD, Lamonte McIntyre rallies for justice," KCUR, Nov. 17, 2022.

Hours after that rally, the KCKPD/Wyandotte County Commissioners voted to give the district attorney funding to digitalize all of the prosecutors' files, many of which were deteriorating, to enable the office to identify and review Golubski's old cases. "Community members wary of KCKPD plan to review former detective Golubski's cases," KCUR, Nov. 21, 2022. But scanning the handwritten files and making use of the scanned files proved a challenge. At an update, months into the project, Dupree told the county board that 1,397 boxes, out of more than 4,600 boxes, had been scanned. Wyandotte County Has Scanned Thousands of Files to Prepare for Roger Golubski Review, *The Kansas City Star*, Sept. 15, 2023.

The troubles of the CIU were well documented. Wyandotte County District Attorney Fires Two Employees for Violating Code of Conduct, *The Kansas City Star*, May 26, 2021; Racist, Hateful Recordings Show the Wyandotte County DA's 'Integrity' Unit Had None. *The Kansas City Star*, May 30, 2021. Once again, the paper gave Dupree space to respond: The Fight for Integrity: WyCo DA Mark Dupree Talks CIU, Race, and Moving Forward, June 14, 2021.

Mark Kind was hired as CIU head following the turmoil. After Firings, Wyandotte County DA Hires Lawyer to Run Community Integrity Unit, *The Kansas City Star*, July 1, 2022. Soon after, the *Star* reported that the internal turmoil had caused a review of potential innocence cases to be stalled when the staff members were fired. DA Unit Believed Prisoner Was Innocent of KCK Murder, Thought Golubski Tainted Case, *The Kansas City Star*, Sept. 25, 2022. Less than a year later, columnist Melinda Henneberger weighed in as Kind quit: Lawyer Hired to Lead Wyco DA's Integrity Unit Has Already Left, and No Wonder, *The Kansas City Star*, June 11, 2023.

Community Leaders Call for DOJ to Investigate Civil Rights Violations by KCPD, KCKPD, *The Kansas City Star*, Oct. 2, 2023.

Ex KCK Cop Roger Golubski Helped Send One Innocent Man to Prison. Are There Others?, *The Kansas City Star*, Sept. 20, 2022. The cases of *Betts and McKinney v. State of Kansas*, 21CV569 and 19CV647, Wyandotte County

District Court, were the subject of the post-conviction hearing Oct. 24 and Oct. 25, 2022. Among those who testified at the two-day hearing were Mark Dupree, Max Seifert, Mark Sachse, and Roger Golubski. *The Kansas City Star* had boldly called them innocent more than a year earlier: Innocent Men Imprisoned for the Murder of Corrupt KCK Cop Roger Golubski's Nephew, May 31, 2021. But the judge, at the end of the hearing, did not embrace that view. "Judge refuses new trial for Kansas City, Kansas, cousins despite 'cloud of doubt' around Golubski," KCUR, and "Judge declines to overturn convictions of men who claim innocence in 1997 KCK murder," both published Dec. 21, 2022. Within months, the men were paroled. "A Kansas man wins parole 25 years after being allegedly set up by indicted KCKPD detective," KCUR, Feb. 25, 2023.

John Calvin's case caught attention in June 2016, just weeks after Cheryl Pilate first filed the post-conviction motion that would lead to Lamonte McIntyre's freedom, and weeks before the primary between Mark Dupree and Jerome Gorman. "Black man serving life sentence for murder while confessed killer walks free," *Raw Story*, quoting KCTV, June 23, 2016. But Calvin's post-conviction petition was denied, and he died in prison before the case earned a second look. Prisoner Who Maintained Innocence in KCK Murder and Sued over Treatment Dies of Cancer, *The Kansas City Star*, Jan. 26, 2023.

By now attention had gone way beyond whether Golubski had locked up innocent men, but to the abuse he was accused of causing to so many Black women. "Former U.S. Attorney believes there are 'many' more victims of ex-cop Roger Golubski," Sept. 16, 2022. The allegations were spilling out not only in the courthouse but in the news accounts, especially by *The Kansas City Star* and KCUR, where reporter Peggy Lowe produced the podcast series, "Overlooked." The first part of the series carried the headline, "Who is Roger Golubski? Exposing a 'chameleon' who built a career on abusing Black women," Nov. 2, 2022. At the *Star*, articles and columns kept coming: "6 People in Golubski Victim's Life Knew the Truth Then. Why Hasn't FBI Talked to Them?, *The Kansas City Star*, Oct. 22, 2023. Woman Recruited by Roger Golubski at Age 12: 'The System Still Goes On,' *The Kansas City Star*, April 24, 2022. "KCK Cop Victimized 'Countless' Women, Lawyers Say; Kansas Hinders Them from Suing, *The Kansas City Star*, Nov. 2, 2022. And then the questions shifted to a topic that had long been a worry to Cheryl Pilate, the series of unsolved murders of Black women: Murdered KCK Prostitutes All Connected to One Man: Police Detective Roger Golubski, *The Kansas City Star*, March 31, 2021; "Family in KCK cold case says FBI wants to know more about detective who worked case," KCTV, March 19, 2021; "Why haven't Kansas City, Kan., police done more about long list of slain Black women," KCUR, Nov. 1, 2022. Shoddy Investigation into 2021 Death Has Ignored Ties to Ex-Cop Roger Golubski, *The Kansas City Star*, Nov. 3, 2023.

Toby Crouse was confirmed as a federal district court judge on Nov. 17, 2020, by a 50–43 vote. He previously had been the Kansas solicitor general, working in the office of then–Attorney General Derek Schmidt. It was in that role that

Schmidt supported several other attorneys general on issues such as abortion and gun restrictions, earning him the opposition from the Alliance for Justice, which discussed the controversial positions by Crouse in a detailed report. Alliance for Justice, Nomination of Toby Crouse, report.

The case of *Kansas v. Glover* involved the state's appeal of the Supreme Court ruling on limiting the police ability to review traffic stops. The U.S. Supreme Court docket shows the case was argued Nov. 4, 2019, and the decision was handed down April 6, 2020. His nomination was recorded as received by the U.S. Senate on May 21, 2020.

The government pretrial motion detailing the allegation that he raped a young woman he saw alone in a park in 5:22-cr-40055, "Government's motion for an order permitting admission of evidence pursuant to federal rules of evidence 413 and 404(b)," pp. 14–16, Nov. 17, 2023. Golubski's attorney contended in response that the women were lying, making false claims in the hopes of getting financial rewards. "Ex-KCKPD officer Roger Golubski deploys old tactic against abuse allegations: Calling accusers liars," KCUR, Feb. 13, 2024.

Afterword: Half Full or Half Empty?

Terra Morehead was reported to be leaving the U.S. Attorney's Office, where she had been limited to only handling civil cases, in August 2023: TERRA MOREHEAD, KANSAS PROSECUTOR WHO 'RUINED PEOPLE'S LIVES,' FINALLY TO LEAVE OFFICE. *The Kansas City Star*, Aug. 11, 2023. Four months later, Dec. 2023, Federal Public Defender Melody Brannon was informed that the Disciplinary Board had set a hearing on the complaint against Terra Morehead for May 2024 (interview with Melody Brannon). On April 26, 2024, the Kansas Supreme Court disclosed that Morehead had voluntarily surrendered her license to practice law, and that the hearing was therefore canceled. The court accepted Morehead's request and ordered her disbarred. *In re: Morehead*, Kansas Supreme Court, 318 Kan. 709 (2024).

In Feb. 2025, a disciplinary panel of the state Supreme Court conducted hearings on the complaint against Erin Slinker Tomasic and Kim Flannigan for their roles in the recording scandal. By that point both had long since left the U.S. Attorney's Office and neither held an active license to practice law in Kansas. Among those to testify were Judge Robinson. As of August 2025, the outcome of the case had not yet been made public.

The Topeka Capital-Journal broke the news of the harassment complaint against Jerome Gorman: KANSAS TAX ATTORNEY ACCUSED OF SEXUAL HARASSMENT, BIZARRE RANTS, cjonline, Jan. 2, 2018. Days later, FORMER WYANDOTTE COUNTY DA LOSES STATE JOB AFTER SEXUAL HARASSMENT COMPLAINTS, *The Kansas City Star*, Jan. 10, 2018.

INDEX

A

Abbott, Ethel, xv, 158–159, 191, 249, 313
Action Investigations, xv, 70–71
Adams, Carolyn, xv, 70–71, 82
affidavits: of Al Jennerich, 196; of Bernie Smith, 140, 141; of Cecil Brooks, 211–213; collection of, 170–173, 191–193, 196, 199–200, 209–213; of Ethel Abbott, 191; of Freda Quinn, 210; of Gary Long, 191; of Jim McCloskey, 210; of Joe Robinson, 171; of Mark Sachse, 191; of Natasha Hodge, 189–190; of Niko Quinn, 81, 82, 88; of Randy Eskina, 210; of Rosie McIntyre, 184; of Ruby Mitchell, 136, 172; of Saundra Newsome, 170–171; of Stacey Quinn, 81, 88; of Tim Maskil, 177, 200–201
African Americans. *See* Black people
alcohol, prohibition of, 33–34
Alliance for Justice, 316
Allison, Tara, 318
Alvarez, Anita, 131, 342–343
Alvey, David, xv, 241–244, 246, 271–273, 287–288
Alvey, Lloyd G., Sr., 241–243
American Bar Association, 100, 334, 339–340
Anderson, Ken, 349
antislavery advocates, 28, 33
Antiterrorism and Effective Death Penalty Act, 91
appeals: in Bucklew case, 188, 191, 196; in Burton case, 124; direct, 79–80; Lamonte's, 79–80, 85; post-verdict, 91–92, 102–103
Armstrong, Rick, 176–177
Atcheson, Gordon, 123
attorney-client communication, 256–257, 261–265, 330

B

Baby Smooth, 83
Bach, Doug, xv, 270–271, 287, 289
Barber, Dennis O., xv, 21–23
barber school, 239, 305
barber shop, in prison, 110–111
Bell, Brandon, 279
Betts, Brian, 313–314
Biden, Joe, xxi, 265, 298, 311, 317, 324, 325
Black Codes, 324
Black Lives Matter, 259, 343
Black people: criminal justice system and, 3–4, 126, 130, 174–175, 202, 224–225, 324, 341; in Kansas City, 11, 44–47; murders of, 126, 175; northern migration by, 9, 11; in Quindaro, 28–29; in Wyandotte County, 271–272
Blackstone, William, 202
Bledsoe, Floyd, 244, 245
Bleeding Kansas, 28
"blue code," 140–141, 178, 179, 201, 287, 347
Board of Indigents' Defense Services, 294
"The Bottoms," 10
Boudin, Chesa, 344
Bouker, Edward, xvi, 216, 228, 229, 231, 232, 245
Bowling, Barron, xvi, xix, xxi, xxvii, 128–129, 132, 137–138, 141–147, 160, 175–178, 273, 293
Brady v. Maryland, 329, 348
Brancart, Edmond, xvi, 222, 277–281
Brannon, Melody, xvi, 256–259, 295, 297–298, 321, 350
break-ins, in prison, 95–96
bribery, 58, 60; by Mayor Steineger, 42; Mayor Steineger and, 32–33, 59–60; police and, 34–36, 145; Thomas Dailey and, 35–36, 39
Brooks, Cecil, xvi, xxv, 29, 197; affidavit by, 211–213; Doniel Quinn and, 150, 152, 160–161; Dupree interview of, 226, 230; Golubski and, 249, 308; meeting with McCloskey by, 165–167, 171–172; Redmon and, 156, 160–161; sex trafficking and, 308, 316
Brown, Adam, 28
Brown, John, 11, 28, 29
Brown, Michael, 201, 202, 224, 324, 343
Brown, Nancy Quindaro, 28
Brown, Oliver, 44–45
Brown, Rebecca, 351
Brown, Terrance, xvi, 15, 21
Brownback, Sam, 207
Brown v. Board of Education, 44–45, 127

Brubacher, Kate, 317
Bryant, Kristiane, 271–272, 276
Bucklew, Russell, xvi, 187–188, 190–191, 196, 200, 207–208
Burdette, J. Dexter, xvii; affair with Morehead by, 157, 186, 215, 231–232; appeal and, 80; attorney's appointed by, 102; denial of new trial by, 69, 81–82, 88; habeas corpus petition and, 96–98; immunity of, 247; Lamonte case and, 57–59, 62, 64, 67; petition and, 215, 216; on recanting of testimony, 81–82, 86, 151, 153; sentencing by, 71; Williams case and, 301; as witness at hearing, 232
Burns, William J., 242–243
Burns, William J., Jr., 243
Burton, Darryl, xvii, 123–124, 193, 220, 239, 281, 305
Bush, George W., 129, 339–340
Bushnell, Tricia Rojo, xvii, 229, 286, 309
Bussell, Mike, xvii, xxviii, 200, 209, 211–213, 238–239, 305
Bye, Clayton, 283
Bye, Kermit, 124

C

Callahan, Sonny, 174
Calvin, John, 314
Capote, Truman, 87
Caprice, KiAnn, 275
Casteliero, Paul, xvii, 120, 195, 196, 198
Center on Wrongful Conviction, 342
Centurion Ministries, xxii, xxiv, 341; cases won by, 120–124; contacting of, by Lamonte, 85–86, 106; founding of, 121; Kate Germond and, 121–122, 198; McCloskey's retirement from, 195–196; Morgan Pilate law firm and, 126–127, 219–220; review of case by, 106–107, 112–114, 117–118; successes of, 117–118; taking of Lamonte case by, 124–125
Cessna, Heather, 296
Charles S. Sumner High School, 44
Chauvin, Derek, 272, 347
Cheffen, Kenny, 282
Chicago, Illinois, 34, 35
Chicago Police Department, 34
Chisholm Trail, 33
civil lawsuits: by Bowling, 144, 160, 175; against KCK/Wyandotte unified government, 175–176, 248–251, 282–285, 299–304; qualified immunity from, 348; by Rodney King, 3
civil rights division, 318, 321, 325
Civil War, 10, 29
Clark, Dan, xvii, 124, 127, 129–130, 132, 151, 155, 184, 187, 209
Clemons, Marcus "Lil C," 88
Clinton, Bill, xxv, 4, 42, 91
Clymer, Steven, xviii, 258–259, 263
CNN, 288
Cohen, David R., xviii, 258, 264
Colyer, Jeff, 245, 246
Community Integrity Unit (CIU), 272, 311–313
compensation, for wrongful imprisonment, 244–251
confessions: false, 24, 327; to other inmates, 278–279
confidentiality, between attorneys and clients, 256–257, 261–265, 330
Conley, Anthony, 154
conviction integrity units, 267–269, 272, 277–280, 343, 344
convictions: overturning, 94–95; time limits on challenging, 91, 207. *See also* wrongful convictions
Cook County, Illinois, 337–338
Coones, Olin L. "Pete," xviii, 277–280, 281, 294, 311, 330
Coones, Olin "Pete," xvi
CoreCivic, 265
Cornwell, Carl, xviii, 69, 71, 79–80, 85, 88
Corrections Corporation of America (CCA), 255
corruption: in Kansas City, 13, 32–36, 58, 128–129, 173, 252; in police department, 38–43, 128–129, 140–141, 170, 173–182, 188, 196, 200–201, 247, 251, 269–270, 288, 312
county jail, 56–57, 69
court-appointed attorneys, 69, 94, 96, 290–296, 323, 332–333, 335–336. *See also* public defenders
Crabtree, Daniel, 262, 264, 266
crime, 14, 340–341, 344, 346; juvenile, 48, 50
criminal defense attorneys. *See* defense attorneys
criminal justice system: as adversary system, 329; corruption in, 243–244, 251–263, 323; flaws in, 206; injustice in, 201–202, 218; public defenders in, 290–296, 332, 334–336; racism and bias in, 3–4, 45, 126, 130, 174–175, 202, 224–225, 324, 326, 337, 341; reform of,

272–273, 286, 290–298, 324–325, 340–341, 343–344, 346–347; role of judges in, 336–340; subversion of, 127; systemic problems in, 326–351; two-tiered, 331
Crips, 82, 83
Croatian immigrants, 10, 52
Crouse, Toby, 315–316, 317, 318
Crowder, David, xviii, 9, 12, 13, 164
Crowder, Johnny, xviii, 9, 16
Crowder, Maxine, xviii, 9, 12, 13, 21, 22, 57, 61, 107, 169, 230
Crowder, Peggy, xviii, 9, 16
Cry Justice, 89
Culp, Steven, xviii–xix, 7, 138, 142, 143, 144

D

Dailey, Thomas, xix, 46, 47, 60, 148–149; corruption charges against, 35–36, 39–40; obstruction of investigation by, 40, 42
Daniels, Boston, 286
Davidson, Lee J., 207
death penalty, 4
death penalty cases, 187–188, 190–191, 200, 207–208
deaths, at hands of police, 201–202
defendants: false confessions by, 24, 327; juvenile, tried as adults, 50; nonviolent, 217, 224, 343; as "presumed innocent," 206; racism in sentencing of, 341; rights of, 256, 257; right to representation for, 256, 290–293, 332, 335
defense attorneys, 69; court-appointed, 69, 94, 290–296, 332–333, 335–336; disciplinary actions against, 59, 99–103, 296–297, 350; effective representation by, 97–103; flawed system and, 331–336; incompetent, 94–96, 101, 269, 350; investigations by, 331; payments to, 332. *See also* public defenders
defense's case, in Lamonte trial, 65
De Los Santos, Jorge, 120
Department of Justice (DOJ), 310–313, 318, 321
DeSantis, Ron, 346
DiClaudio, Scott, 338
digitalization project, 310, 312–313
direct appeal, 79–80
disbarment: of Long, 102, 297; of Morehead, 321, 350; rarity of, 99–100; of Sachse, 103; of Spradling, 350
disciplinary actions, against lawyers, 59, 99–103, 296–298, 350
district attorneys: election of, 329. *See also specific district attorneys*
district attorney's office, 52–53, 57, 142–143
Dixmoore Five, 342–343
DNA evidence, 131–132, 341–342
Donnelly College, 183
Drain, Lamonte, xix, 20, 21, 93, 112, 113, 134
drug dealing, 14, 29, 36, 39; by Lamonte, 113; in prison, 92–93; by Quinn, 149
drug investigations, 38–43
drug sentencing, 341
drug use, in prison, 90, 104–105
Dryden, Edward, 41, 42
Dukakis, Michael, 339
Dupree, Mark, xvi, xix, xx; background of, 203–205; campaign of, 217–218; criticism of, 274–276; as district attorney, 225, 267–269; election of, 219, 222–223, 255, 343; on federal interventions, 310, 311; interview of Lamonte by, 227; Lamonte case and, 221, 224–226, 228, 230, 232, 245–246, 268–269; mayor's task force and, 273; reelection campaign, 271–275, 277, 292; reforms by, 292–295, 311–312, 344; response of, to critics, 276–277; on wrongful convictions, 280, 320

E

Eastern European immigrants, 10, 11
Edgar, Neil, Jr., xix, 152–155, 160, 165, 171, 226, 285
Edgar, Neil, Sr., 154–155
Edwardsville, Kansas, 145, 162–163
Edwardsville police department, xx, 160, 284
Ellington, Ruby, xxvii, 139, 197
Erickson, Lindsey, xix, 71, 79–82, 85, 88, 215
Eskina, Randy, 210
evidence: admissibility of, 336; at crime scene, 6–7; DNA, 131–132, 341–342; exculpatory, 123, 198, 214, 253–254, 261, 329, 330, 348; physical, 66, 214, 269; turning over of, by prosecutors, 329–330; withholding of, by prosecutors, 123, 198, 253–254, 348, 349
Ewing, Donald, xix, xx, 3, 165; motive for murder of, 126; murder of, 5, 6, 21, 167, 171, 212
exculpatory evidence, 123, 198, 214, 253–254, 261, 329, 330, 348
Exodusters, 11

Exoneration Registry, 202, 279
exonerations, 253, 267, 268–269, 279, 294, 312, 327. *See also* wrongful convictions
eyewitnesses, 7; failures in dealing with, during investigation, 210; fears of retaliation of, 152–153, 210; threats to, 152–153, 253, 254, 285, 330; unreliability of, 30, 66–67, 69, 95. *See also specific witnesses*
eyewitness identification, 65–66; judge instructions about, 67, 80, 93–94, 97; in Lamonte case, 18–21, 26, 30, 54–55, 63–64, 67, 123, 124, 134–136, 210, 283, 328, 331–332; mistaken, 18–20, 66–67, 69, 82, 136, 163, 215, 327–328

F

faith, 84, 85, 110, 112–113, 305
false accusations, 119
false confessions, 24, 327
false identifications, 18–20, 66–67, 69, 82, 136, 163, 215, 327–328
false testimony, 120
Federal Bureau of Investigation (FBI), 274, 288; Kansas City office, 34–35; rift between local police and, 40
Federalist Society, 315
Federal Public Defender, 256–257
Federico, Rich, 262–263
Fifi's Restaurant, 22, 23
Fifth Amendment, 284, 285
Flannigan, Kim, 255–256, 264, 265, 321
Floyd, George, 272, 285, 287, 288, 324, 344, 347
forensic tests, 327
Fourteenth Amendment, 94
Fox, Lawrence J., 231–232
Freudenberger, Emma, 282–285
Fritz, Dennis, 127

G

Gage, Lathrop, 248
gambling, 35, 37, 92
gang violence, 5, 14, 152
Gardner, Kim, 345–346
Garland, Merrick, 312, 324
Garner, Eric, 201, 202, 324
Garner, Tyrone, 128, 287–289, 309–310, 311
Gascón, George, 344, 345
Gayden, Lafayette, 78
George Floyd Justice in Policing Act, 325
Germond, Kate, xix–xx, 86, 121–122, 195, 196, 198
Giannukos, Jay, 266
Gibbs, John, Jr., 241
Gibbs, Katie, 241
Gideon, Clarence Earl, 94
Gideon v. Wainwright, 290, 332
Gipson, Francis, 230
GoFundMe campaigns, 237
Goldstein, Rebecca, 340, 345
Golubski, Roger, xv, xix, xx, xxvii; affidavits against, 193–194; allegations against, 43, 132–133, 135, 157–158, 176–177, 196, 200–201, 273–274, 284, 300, 300–308, 313–314, 315; Black women and, 8, 43, 132, 135, 157–159, 174, 176–177; civil lawsuit against, 248–251, 282–285, 299–304; federal prosecution of, 288–289, 306–309, 315–319; immunity of, 248; investigation by, in Lamonte case, 7–8, 17, 18, 21, 26, 29–31, 171, 210, 231; McCloskey and, 163; misconduct by, 132–133, 157–159, 173–182, 184, 188–194, 197, 200–201, 215, 231, 249–251, 269, 274, 300–304; mistakes made by, 30–31; murders associated with, 315; Niko Quinn and, 125; questioning of Lamonte by, 23–25; reputation of, 8; retirement of, 160; Seifert and, 139, 143–144; sexual assaults by, 43, 132–133, 135, 157–158, 176–177, 196, 200–201, 273–274, 300–308, 315; suicide of, 318–319; testimony by, at preliminary hearing, 55; testimony by, in civil lawsuit, 284–285; victims of, 312–315; Wilkins investigation by, 46; as witness at trial, 63–65
Gonzalez, Eric, 343
Gore, Glenn, 127
Gorman, Jerome, xx; 2016 election and, 203, 205, 217, 219, 222–223, 255; as district attorney, 157, 159–160, 202, 205; firing of, 322; Lamonte case and, 159–162, 169, 186, 192–193, 217–218; Max Seifert and, 145–146
government land, in Kansas, 11
Gray, Freddie, Jr., 201, 202, 224, 324, 343
Great Depression, 45
Great Migration, 11
Green, LeRoy, Jr,, 145
Greitens, Eric, 345
Grissom, Barry, 32
Gross, Sam, 327

guilt: presumption of, 340; proving, 342
Gumbel, Bryant, 121
Guthrie, Abelard, 26–27, 28

H

habeas corpus petitions, 91, 93–98, 206–207
haircuts, 110–111
Harris, Kamala, 204, 205
Harrison-Lee, Cheryl, 289
Hausback, Tim, xx, 178–179
Hawver, Ira, 101
Henneberger, Melinda, 190, 289, 301
Henry, Renee, 143, 144, 293
Hillman, Eric, 349
Historically Black Colleges and Universities, 29
Hodge, Jamila, 324
Hodge, Natasha, 189–190
Holland, Mark, 243–244
Holscher, Cindy, 273–274
Horton, William R., 339
housing discrimination, 45
Huron Confederacy, 27
Hutchings Street, 3–4
Hutchinson Correctional Facility, 75–80, 82–84, 87, 96, 341

I

Identi-Kit, 17–18
immigrants, 10, 11, 33
incompetent representation, 94–95, 101, 269, 350
Indian Removal Act, 27
indigent defendants, public defenders for, 290–296, 332, 334–336
informants, 176–177, 201, 222; jailhouse, 278–280, 330
innocence: Lamonte's claims of, 104, 106; proving, 131–132, 156, 342; proving Lamonte's, 126, 131–137; recognizing possibility of, 340
Innocence Network, 342
Innocence Project, 121, 127, 244, 248, 285–286, 312, 341, 342, 349, 351
Intelligence and Investigations Unit, 95–96
Iroquois Confederacy, 27

J

Jackson County, 268
Jacobs, George, 239
Jay-Z, 286, 299
Jennerich, Alan, xx, 34–36; affidavit by, 196; police corruption investigation by, 38–43, 46, 47, 53, 129, 140, 287
Jim Crow laws, 11
Johnson, Christine, 9
Johnson, Donald, xx, 9
Johnson, Donald, Jr. "D.J.," xxi, 14
Johnson, Montre, 169
Johnson County, Kansas, 14, 127–128
Jones, Richard, 244, 245
Josenberger, Corisha, xxi, 108–109, 168, 183–185, 221, 236, 240, 304–305, 322
Joseph, Christopher, 307–308
judges, 225; appointment of, 339–340; appointment of public defenders by, 290–296, 293, 333, 335–336; biases in, 337; disciplinary actions against, 350; election of, 337–339; immunity of, 247; misconduct by, 350; relationships between prosecutors and, 326; role of, 336–340. *See also specific judges*
jurors, 62, 67, 341
justice system. *See* criminal justice system
juvenile court, 50–52
juvenile crime, 48, 50
juvenile defendants, tried in adult courts, 50
juvenile detention, 25, 32, 56

K

Kansas: Black migration to, 11; prohibition in, 33–34
Kansas Bureau of Investigation (KBI), 271, 274, 288
Kansas City, Kansas: bad reputation of, 32–37; Black migration to, 11; civil rights violations in, 286; community of, 13; corruption in, 13, 32–36, 58, 128–129, 173, 252; crack cocaine epidemic in, 5, 14, 36, 39; crime in, 48; establishment of, 29; gang violence in, 5; history of, 33–37; manufacturing in, 11–12; mayoral race in, 243–244; poverty in, 13–14; problems in, 128; Quindaro neighborhood, 26–31; racism in, 44–47; segregation in, 44–45
Kansas City, Missouri, 268; development of, post-Civil War, 10; meatpacking industry in, 10–11
Kansas City Police Department (KCKPD), 132; corruption in, 38–43, 128–129, 170, 173–182, 196, 200–201, 247, 251, 269–270, 288; Dupree and, 225; investigation of, 287–288, 310–313; Lamonte case reinvestigation and, 226; Max

Seifert and, 139–147, 175–176; misconduct by, 132–134, 178–179, 189–190, 248–249; new police chief for, 286–287; racism and bias in, 45–47, 174–175; response of, at murder scene, 5–8; suing of, by Lamonte, 247–251

The Kansas City Star, 58, 218, 219, 221, 222, 274–276, 289, 301, 311

The Kansas City Times, 35

Kansas Department of Revenue, 322

Kansas-Nebraska Act, 28, 241

Kansas Supreme Court: appeal to, 79–80; disciplinary actions by, 99, 100, 103, 296–297, 350; on eyewitness testimony, 67; on habeas corpus petitions, 206–207; ruling in Long case, 59, 293, 296–297; upholding of Burdette's ruling by, 88

KCK/Wyandotte County Unified Government, 128, 289; board of commissioners of, 310; civil lawsuit against, 175–176, 248–251, 282–285, 299–304; federal intervention in, 310, 312–313; reforms in, 310–311, 321; settlement agreement with, 303–304

Kennedy, John F., 18, 118

King, Rodney, 3, 4, 258

Klapper, Bill, 280

Kobach, Kris, 281

Krasner, Larry, 343, 346

Krstolich, James, xxi, 134, 163; investigation by, 7–8, 17, 19–21; questioning of Lamonte by, 23–25

L

Labat, Gloria, xxi, 153, 172, 230

Lane, Bobby, xxi, 142, 144, 145, 189

Lansing Correctional Facility, 87–90, 95–96, 105–106, 155, 341

Larson, Edward, 80

Lauber, Greg, 172, 218, 235

legal representation. *See* defense attorneys

letter writing, by Lamonte, 106, 109

lineups, 19, 21

Long, Gary, xxi, 215, 292; affidavit by, 191; complaints against, 99, 101–102, 296–297; court appointments by, 59, 293; disciplinary actions against, 59, 99–102, 293, 296–297, 350; lack of defense by, 93–94, 97, 331–332; as president of Bar Association, 294; representation of Lamonte by, 49–52, 54, 59, 64–67, 69, 80, 230

lynchings, 324

M

marijuana, 90, 104

Marinovich, Carol, 243

Marshall, Carl, 39, 41

Marshall, Larry, 341

Marten, J. Thomas, 175

Maskil, Tim, 177, 200–201

McAllister, Stephen, xxi, 258–259, 265, 288, 314–315

McCall's Gas Station, 29

McCloskey, Jim, xvi, xxii, xxiv; affidavit by, 210; background of, 118–121; cases worked on by, 137–138; Centurion Ministries and, 85–86, 106–107, 114, 195–196; Cheryl Pilate and, 219–220; collection of affidavits by, 170–173; meeting with Cecil Brooks, 165–167, 171–172; meeting with Lamonte by, 117–118; questioning of Ruby Mitchell by, 134–137; retirement by, 195–196, 198; taking of Lamonte case by, 125–127; as witness at hearing, 231; witness interviews by, 151–153, 155; work on Lamonte's case by, 129–138, 148–150, 156–173, 184–187, 192–194, 235, 308

McCue, Timothy, 141

McDonald, Hugh C., 17–18

McFarlane, Jock, xxii, 106–107, 112–114, 122, 124, 155

McIntyre, James, xxii, 12, 15, 21, 52, 132, 135, 150

McIntyre, James, III, xxii

McIntyre, Lamonte, xxii; arraignment of, 58–59; arrest of, 22, 24–25; Centurion Ministries and, 106–107, 112–114, 117–118, 124–125, 131–137; childhood of, 13; civil lawsuit by, 248–251, 282–285, 299–304; compensation awarded to, 244–251, 299; Corisha and, 108–109, 168, 183–185, 221, 236, 240, 304–305, 322; in county jail, 56–57; court-appointed attorney for, 49–52, 54, 59, 64–67, 69, 80, 230, 294, 295; drug dealing by, 14; Dupree interview of, 227; education in prison of, 163–164, 183; exoneration of, 268–269; family of, 9; in gang, 14; Golubski prosecution and, 307, 317, 319; hearing for release of, 229–232; identification of, by Ruby Mitchell, 26; journaling by, 78–79, 83, 84 164, 185; in juvenile detention, 25, 26, 32, 48–49; lawyer appointed to, 49–50, 51, 52, 59; life after prison for, 322; meeting with Cecil Brooks, 165–167; meeting with McCloskey by,

117–118; murder charges against, 24–25, 26, 31; overturning of conviction of, 232; plea bargain by, 15–16; police interrogation of, 22–24; preliminary hearing, 50, 52, 54–55; in prison, 75–80, 82–84, 87–88, 89–90, 95–96, 104–111, 155, 167–168, 172, 186, 200, 216, 220–221, 228; prison jobs for, 83, 105–106; reaction to guilty verdict, 67–68; rebuilding of life by, 304–305; release of, 232, 235–238; requests for help by, 106; robbery arrest of, 15; sentencing of, 69–71; in solitary confinement, 104–105; testimony by, at trial, 65; Testrake and, 220–221; theft accusations of, 95–96; trial as adult, 55, 57–58; trial of, 61–68; witness identification of, 18–21, 26, 30–31, 54–55, 62–64, 67, 123, 124, 134–136, 210, 283, 328, 331–332
McIntyre, Reggie, 236, 304–305
McIntyre, Rosie, xv, xviii, xxii, 9, 12–13, 184, 192, 216; affidavit by, 184; attempts to help Lamonte by, 85, 88, 89, 96–97, 125; Centurion Ministries and, 113–114; Corisha and, 240; Golubski and, 133, 285; at hearing, 52; ill health of, 305; investigation by, 70–71; Lamonte's arrest and, 22–25; McCloskey and, 132; mental strain on, 107; at trial, 67–68; as witness at hearing, 232
McKinney, Celester, 313–314
meatpacking industry, 10–11, 29, 33
media coverage, 193, 218–219, 221, 236
Meeks, Cordell, Jr., 203, 217
Meyer, Victoria, 31, 48
Michael Morton Act, 349
Midwest Innocence Project (MIP), xvii, xxvi, 220, 229, 246, 277, 299, 309
Miles, Richard, 137
Miller, Ronald L., xxii–xxiii, 144–145, 176, 177
Miracle of Innocence, xvii, 281, 305, 322
Missouri, 28; death penalty in, 187–188; public defender system in, 334
mistaken identification, 18–20, 66–67, 69, 82, 136, 163, 215, 327–328
Mitchell, Ruby, xxiii, 5, 6; affidavit by, 136, 172; description of shooter by, 63, 136, 154; Golubski and, 284; identification of Lamonte by, 7, 8, 17–21, 26, 30, 54–55, 62–64, 67, 124, 134–136, 210, 328, 331–332; McCloskey and, 134–137; testimony of, 215
Model Rules of Professional Conduct, 100
Monster. *See* Edgar, Neil, Jr.
MORE2, 312, 314
Morehead, Terra, xvi, xxiii; affair with Burdette by, 157, 186, 215, 231–232; at appeal, 80; Bowling trial and, 146; Brooks prosecution by, 161; complaints against, 297–298; disbarment of, 350; disciplinary actions against, 321, 350; eyewitnesses and, 97, 151–152, 191, 230, 283; habeas corpus petition and, 97; immunity of, 247–248; Lamonte case and, 52, 54, 62–67, 70–71, 186, 215, 230, 348; Max Seifert and, 146; misconduct by, 252–263, 265–266, 297–298; Orozco case and, 253–255, 261, 265, 298; reassignment of, 265–266, 299; tactics of, 330; testimony in civil lawsuit by, 283; threats to witnesses by, 253, 254, 298; U.S. attorney's office scandal and, 255–265
Morgan, Melanie, 126–128
Morgan Pilate law firm, 126–127, 219–220
Moroney, Leo, 57
Moroney, Michael, 58, 60
Morton, Michael, 349
motive: lack of, 31, 126; for murders, 66, 114, 150, 152–153, 160, 165, 167, 171, 212, 226
murder reenactment, 209
murder scene: events at, 4–5; police investigation of, 5–8, 29–30
murder weapon, 31
Musk, Elon, 325, 345

N

National Registry of Exonerations, 327, 347, 348, 349
Native Americans, 27–28
Neufeld, Peter, 341
Newsome, Saundra Sublett, xxiii; affidavit by, 170–171; Dupree and, 226; Golubski and, 132; at hearing, 52; on Lamonte's innocence, 114, 125, 148–150, 151; McCloskey interview of, 132, 148, 162, 170; release of Lamonte and, 235; as witness at hearing, 231
nonviolent offenders, 217, 224, 343
northern migration, 9, 11

O

Oakman, Karl, 287, 311
Obama, Barack, xxiii, 311
obstacles, after release, 237
O'Malley, Shannon, 338

organized crime, 35, 37
Organized Crime Strike Force, 39
Orozco, Gregory, 253–255, 261, 265, 298, 330

P

Parisi, Doug, xxiii, 180–182
pattern-or-practice investigations, 310–311
Perez, Desiree, 286
petition, to free Lamonte, 186, 188, 190, 192–194, 196, 207, 209–210, 213–216, 217–218, 225–226
Phillips, Beth, 190, 196, 200, 207, 208
photo arrays, 19–21, 30
physical evidence, 66, 214, 269
Pilate, Cheryl, xvi, xxiii–xxiv; Bowling case and, 128–129, 137–138, 144, 146–147, 175; Bucklew case and, 207–208; Burton case and, 123–124; CIU and, 312; civil suit and, 248; compensation for Lamonte and, 246; death penalty cases of, 187–188, 190–191, 200, 207–208; Golubski prosecution and, 178–179, 318, 319; at hearing for release, 229–232; law firm of, 126–127; payments to, 198, 219–220; Seifert and, 175–176; work on Lamonte's case by, 136–137, 156, 162, 172–173, 186–201, 205–206, 209–216, 219–220, 225–226, 228–232, 348
Placer County, California, 291, 334
plea bargains, 15–16, 335, 336
Podrebarac, Matthew, xxiv, 15, 50–52, 55, 80
police: abuses by, 45–47, 201–202, 204, 272, 344; corruption in, 34–36, 38–43, 128–129, 140–141, 170, 173–182, 188, 196, 200–201, 247, 251, 269–270, 288, 312; detective work by, 327–328; protection of, 347; qualified immunity for, 247–248, 348; role of, in criminal justice system, 326–327. *See also* Kansas City Police Department
police interrogations: of Lamonte, 23–25; lying during, 24; recording of, 24
police investigation: by Golubski, 29–31, 210; mistakes in, 30–31, 126, 170, 210, 269, 327–328; at murder scene, 5–8
police misconduct, 224–225, 287, 295; disciplinary action for, 347–351; investigation into, 53, 272–273, 321; reforms to combat, 325
politics of crime, 340–341, 346
Possley, Maurice, 327
post-verdict appeals, 91–92, 102–103
prison: barber shop in, 110–111; friendships in, 95–96; gangs, 82–83, 87; hospice in, 110; jobs in, 105–106; lack of privacy in, 104; life in, 75–80, 82–84, 87–90, 95–96, 104–111; loneliness in, 84, 108, 109, 185; meals in, 82–83; overcrowding in, 340–341; population, 202; school in, 83–84, 183; transfers between, 108; visitors to, 185
prisoners: aging of, 110; innocent, 120–121, 212
prison guards, 89–90, 92–93, 104
prison sentences, 224
private investigator, 70–71
progressive prosecutors, 325, 343–346
prosecution's case, 62–66
prosecutors, 94, 120; disciplinary actions against, 297–298; eavesdropping by, on attorney-client communication, 256–257, 261–265; elected, 329; flawed system and, 329–330; immunity of, 247–248, 348–350; misconduct by, 266, 321, 348–350; new wave of, 224–225; police and, 224; progressive, 325, 343–346; protections for, 348–350; relationships between judges and, 326; reluctance to charge officers by, 347–348; tactics of, 329–330; threatening of witnesses by, 210, 214, 253, 254, 298, 330; toplash against, 345–346; U.S. attorney's office scandal and, 255–265; use of jailhouse informants by, 278–280, 330; withholding of evidence by, 123, 198, 253–254, 348, 349. *See also specific prosecutors*
prostitution, 35, 189–190
public defenders, 290–296, 332; appointed to McIntyre, 49–52, 59; appointment of, 49–50, 294, 335–336; conflict of interest for, 335; funding of, 291, 294, 334–335; shortages of, 49; skepticism of, 336. *See also* defense attorneys
Public Defender Service, 334-335
public defender's office, 294–296
public defender system, 291–296, 332–334
public safety, 340, 344, 347

Q

Quindaro neighborhood, 26–31
Quinn, Doniel Sublett, xx, xxiv, 3, 125, 174; drug dealing by, 149, 152, 165, 167; motive for murder of, 126, 150, 152–153, 160, 165, 167, 171, 212, 226; murder of, 5, 6, 167, 212
Quinn, Freda, xxiv, 132, 149, 172, 210
Quinn, John, xxiv, 4, 5, 30, 52, 114, 149, 150, 171
Quinn, John, Jr. "Smokey," 37

Quinn, Josephine, xxiv, 3–5, 29–30, 163; as eyewitness, 7, 70; at habeas corpus petition, 97
Quinn, Niko, xxi, xxv, 4–5, 171; affidavit by, 81, 82, 88; as eyewitness, 7, 8, 30, 62; forced testimony of, 153, 163, 210, 215, 230, 348; Golubski and, 285, 307; habeas corpus petition and, 96–97; identification of Lamonte by, 55, 63, 64, 67, 71, 80; interview of, by McCloskey, 151–153; recanting of testimony by, 81, 82, 88–89, 125, 151–153
Quinn, Robert, 4, 5
Quinn, Stacey, xxv, 5, 30, 81, 163, 210; affidavit by, 81, 88; Golubski and, 132, 285

R

racial justice: advocates for, 273–274; protests for, 285–286
racism: in criminal justice system, 3–4, 126, 130, 174–175, 202, 224–225, 324, 341; in Kansas City, 44–47, 269; in police department, 174–175
railroad, 10, 11, 29, 33
Rathbun, Randy, xxv, 42, 58, 60
Reasonover, Ellen, 122–123, 193
Redmon, Michael, xxv, 15, 156–157, 160–161, 168–169, 172
right to representation, 94, 256, 290–293, 332, 335
Rios, Steven, 269–270
Robinson, Aaron, xvi, xxv, 152, 153, 156, 160, 165, 167, 226, 249
Robinson, Joe, xvi, xxv, 160, 171
Robinson, Julie, xviii, xx, xxv–xxvi, 47, 252, 287; Bowling trial and, 128–129, 146–147, 178; Orozco case and, 253–255, 261; police corruption investigation by, 38–43, 53; as U.S. attorney, 36–37, 38, 40, 140, 196; U.S. Attorney scandal and, 257–260, 264–265
Rokusek, Jackie, xxvi, 255–256, 264, 321
Rosenstein, Rod, 258
Runnels, Lindsay, xxvi, 188–189, 213–214, 229, 237–238, 248, 295, 312

S

Sachse, Mark, xxvi, 96–98, 102–103, 191, 215, 292, 350
Satterberg, Dan, 343
Savannah Three, 137
Sawyer, Tom, 109
Scheck, Barry, 127, 248, 282, 285–286, 341, 348
Schlitterbahn Waterpark, 222–223
Schmidt, Derek, xxvi, 207, 222, 223, 245–247, 268, 281, 315
school segregation, 44–45, 127
Schroll, Carl, 277
Schroll, Kathleen, 277, 278, 280
Schwartz, Joanna C., 348
Schwartz, Rachel E., 307
segregation, 9, 44–45, 127
Seifert, Max, xxi, xxvii, 132, 137–147, 160, 175–176, 197
sentencing laws, 110
Sessions, Jeff, 311
settlement agreement, 303–304, 319
sex trafficking charges, 316, 317
sexual abuse: by Golubski, 43, 132–133, 135, 157–158, 176–177, 196, 200–201, 273–274, 300–308, 315; police cadet case of, 269–270
Shorty, 110
Sixth Amendment, 94, 256–257, 264, 295
Sixth Amendment Center, 332
slavery, 11, 28
Smith, Bernard, xxvii, 38, 41, 140–141
Smith, Jeffrey, 282
Smith, W. K., xix, xxvii, 282–283; investigation by, 7–8, 31, 46
smuggling, 92
Smulls, Herbert, xxvii, 187–188
solitary confinement, 78, 104–105
Sparks, Harley, 39, 41
Spiwak, Phillip, 337–338
Spradling, Jacqie, 350
Stallings, Gene, 180
state disciplinary boards, 349–350
State v. McIntyre, 326
Stecklein, A. J., 52–54, 62
Steineger, Chris, 287
Steineger, Jack, 287
Steineger, Joseph, xxvii–xxviii, 287; acquittal of, 60, 61; bribery allegations against, 42, 58; charges against, 32–33, 59–60, 96; meeting with Saundra Sublett Newsome by, 148–149
Stevenson, Brian, 324
Strawberry Hill, 10, 52
Sublett, Doniel. *See* Quinn, Doniel Sublett
suicide, 32, 88; of Golubski, 318–319
suspects: minors, 328; police interrogations of, 24; tape recording of, 328

T

Tatum, Jennifer, 230
Taylor, Breonna, 324, 344
Team Roc, 286, 287, 299, 309
Testrake, Melissa, xxviii, 205–206, 209, 211–214, 220–221, 227, 229, 240
Thomas, Clarence, 259
Thompson, Ken, 343
ThunderCats, 152
Tomasic, Denise, 286
Tomasic, Erin Slinker, xxviii, 255–257, 259–262, 321
Tomasic, Nicholas A., xx, xxviii, 40, 52–54, 57, 143, 159, 203
Townsend, Gayle, 304
Trail of Tears, 27–28
Treadway, Tanya, 262, 264
trial: as adult, 55, 57–58; case for new, 172; of Lamonte, 61–68; motion for new, 81–82, 88; right to, by jury, 330
Trump, Donald J., xxi, 311, 315, 321, 325

U

Underground Railroad, 28
U.S. attorney's office: complaints against, 298; scandal involving, 255–265

V

Velasquez, Hernan, 38
verdict, 67
violence: in county jail, 57; gang, 152; in juvenile detention, 49; police, 45–47, 201–202, 204, 272, 344; in prison, 76, 77, 84, 87
Vratil, Kathryn, 299–300, 303–304

W

waiver hearing, 50
Walker, Nate, 121
Warden, Rob, 327, 341
Ware, Dennis, xxviii, 26, 30, 138, 142, 144
Warner, Kenneth Michael, xxix, 260–261
Warner, Mike, 329
Watkins, Craig, 343
Wendat tribe, 27
White, Byron, 259
Wilkins, Donald, 46
Williams, Ophelia, 300–301, 306, 307, 309
Williamson, Ron, 127
Williamson County, Texas, 349
Willis, Fani, 346
witnesses: for defense, 61, 62, 65; false identifications by, 18–20, 66–67, 69, 82, 136, 163, 215, 327–328; at hearing for release, 230–231; police coercion of, 210, 214, 300, 314; for prosecution, 62–65, 70–71; tape recording of, 328; threatening of, by prosecutors, 210, 214, 253, 298, 330; unreliability of, 66–67, 69, 95, 330. *See also* eyewitnesses; *specific witnesses*
Witt, Janice, 271
World War II, 11–12, 33
wrongful convictions: appeals and, 206; cases of, 202, 208, 220, 325–326, 342–343; compensation for, 244–251, 299; exoneration of, 279; false confessions and, 24; faulty police work and, 327–328; investigation of, 291, 299, 311–312, 313–314, 320–321, 341–342; official misconduct and, 347–351; proving, with DNA evidence, 341; review of, 277–280; review of allegations of, 267–269
wrongful identifications. *See* false identifications
Wyandotte County, Kansas, 11–14, 128, 162, 193, 238, 243, 268; history of, 27–29; prohibition in, 33; public defender system in, 291–296; reforms in, 299. *See also* KCK/Wyandotte County Unified Government
Wyandotte County Bar Association, 294
Wyandotte County Commission, 59
Wyandotte tribe, 27–28

Y

Yeatman, Elizabeth, 121
York, Delia, 273
York, Michael, 176, 177, 273

Z

Zeigler, Terry, xxix, 268–269, 283, 286; as chief of police, 181–182, 246; election of Dupree and, 225; housing deal of, 270–271; Max Seifert and, 143–144; police cadet case and, 269–270; retirement of, 270, 271
zoning codes, 45